D0742089

THE IDEOLOGICAL SCRAMBLE FOR AFRICA

THE IDEOLOGICAL SCRAMBLE FOR AFRICA

HOW THE PURSUIT OF ANTICOLONIAL MODERNITY SHAPED A POSTCOLONIAL ORDER, 1945–1966

FRANK GERITS

CORNELL UNIVERSITY PRESS

Ithaca and London

Copyright © 2023 by Cornell University

All rights reserved. Except for brief quotations in a review, this book, or parts thereof, must not be reproduced in any form without permission in writing from the publisher. For information, address Cornell University Press, Sage House, 512 East State Street, Ithaca, New York 14850. Visit our website at cornellpress.cornell.edu.

First published 2023 by Cornell University Press

Library of Congress Cataloging-in-Publication Data

Names: Gerits, Frank, author.
Title: The ideological scramble for Africa : how the
    pursuit of anticolonial modernity shaped a postcolonial
    order, 1945–1966 / Frank Gerits.
Description: Ithaca [New York] : Cornell University Press,
    2023. | Includes bibliographical references and index.
Identifiers: LCCN 2022019500 (print) | LCCN 2022019501
    (ebook) | ISBN 9781501767913 (hardcover) |
    ISBN 9781501767920 (pdf) | ISBN 9781501767937 (epub)
Subjects: LCSH: Nkrumah, Kwame, 1909–1972—Influence. |
    Nkrumah, Kwame, 1909–1972—Political and social views. |
    Decolonization—Africa—History—20th century. |
    Postcolonialism—Africa—History—20th century. |
    Pan-Africanism—History—20th century. | World
    politics—1945–1989. | Africa—Politics and
    government—1945–1960. | Africa—Politics and
    government—1960–
Classification: LCC DT30 .G47 2023 (print) | LCC DT30
    (ebook) | DDC 960.3/2—dc23/eng/20220901
LC record available at https://lccn.loc.gov/2022019500
LC ebook record available at https://lccn.loc.gov
    /2022019501

For Dorien, Theo, and Mathias

CONTENTS

ACKNOWLEDGMENTS

This book tells the story of the ideological scramble for Africa which emerged after 1945. Unlike the "scramble for Africa" which took place between the 1880s and World War I, whereby European powers had conflicting claims to African territories, the post–World War II scramble was more multifaceted and symbolic. More importantly, the ideological scramble included Africans who were eager to compete with the Americans, the Europeans, and the Soviets for the hearts and minds of Africans. In 1965, Ghana's leader, Kwame Nkrumah, concluded he had been involved in a "new scramble for Africa, under the guise of aid, and with the consent and even the welcome of young, inexperienced States" (Kwame Nkrumah, *Neo-Colonialism, The Last Stage of Imperialism* [London: Panaf Books, 1965], 109).

To piece together the elements of this new scramble I had to visit forty-six archives and ten universities in the United States, Europe, Africa, and Asia. I am grateful to the staff of all the archives and libraries who made collections accessible for research. In the Belgian foreign affairs archives, Didier Amaury, Alain Gerard, and Rafael Storme offered assistance. Staff in the South African National Archives was extremely helpful, and Cornelis Muller provided tips and tricks. In Washington, DC, Laurie Baty and Lisa Sleith housed me. Research in the Czech National Archives could not have been completed without Jan Koura. My research in Ethiopia was made possible by Chedza Molefe and Stephen Mayega, Organisation of African Unity archivists. The cups of coffee with Theodros Yoseph, national archivist in Addis Ababa, were a pleasure. In the Kenya National Archives, I was assisted by Richard Ambani, while Anaïs Angelo, Stephanie Lämmert, and Daniel Spence helped me get in touch with Janet Njoroge and Peterson Kithuka. Lucas Müller accompanied me on a trip to Mombasa. The Portuguese foreign affairs archives staff, Alic Barreiro, Isabel Coelho, and Manuel Múrias, went above and beyond, while Alex Marino became an ally in the hunt for sources. In the National Archives of Zambia, Emma, Winnie, and Mirriam, as well as Jason Mwambazi, skillfully guided me through the collections. In Nigeria, Elodie Apard, Ismaël Mazaaz, and Monsour Muritala were indispensable, and Leslie James and Brian McNeil answered my frantic e-mails about Ibadan. Joseph Ayodokun and Josua Olusegun Bolarinwa, fellows at the Lagos Institute for International Affairs, directed me toward important resources. I am incredibly grateful to Lorenz Lüthi, who shared Canadian documents and read the entire manuscript.

Modern academia, with its focus on output and quick reputation building, does not provide a stimulating environment for scholars like myself who seek to write big books. The pressures of an academic job market shackled by neoliberal ideas impeded my progress. While this book made it to press, one can only guess how many other scholars have been stranded on the sandbanks of austerity. I was fortunate to meet people who were willing to refurbish anonymous bureaucratic structures into creative environments. Idesbald Goddeeris, Dirk Moses, and Federico Romero took me on as a PhD student. At the European University Institute in Florence, Robrecht Declercq, Grigol Gegelia, Alan Granadino González, Giorgio Potì, Volker Prott, and James White were amazing fellow travelers. At the London School of Economics, I met Alessandro Iandolo, who has become a close friend, while Roham Alvandi, Joanna Lewis, Piers Ludlow, Sue Onslow, Natasha Telepneva, Simon Toner, and Odd Arne Westad took the time to discuss ideas. At New York University, Fredrick Cooper, Chris Dietrich, Michael Koncewicz, Timothy Naftali, and Marilyn Young provided feedback. In 2016, I had the privilege of being a member of the international studies group at the University of the Free State in Bloemfontein, where Ian Phimister allowed me to write the book as I envisioned it. Matteo Grilli, Tari Gwena-Masakura, Chris Holdrigde, Kate Law, Mrs. Ilse Le Roux, Giacomo Macola, Clement Masakure, Duncan Money, Admire Mseba, Tinashe Nyamunda, Lazlo Passemiers, and Ana Stevenson were great company. At the University of Amsterdam, Liz Buettner, Robin de Bruin, Artemy Kalinovsky, Daniel Knegt, and Ruud van Dijk were all incredible colleagues. In Utrecht, Laurien Crump, Beatrice de Graaf, Jolle Demmers, Rachel Gillett, Corina Mavrodin, Ozan Ozavci, Paschalis Pechlivanis, and Liesbeth van de Grift were and are big supporters of my work. At Shanghai University, Iris Borowy gave me the opportunity to finish this book as a visiting fellow, while Eirini Anastasiadou, Ved Baruah, and Justine Philip provided feedback. Other academics and friends helped as well: Anouk Brodier, Andrea Chiampan, Kim Christiaens, Andrew Copley, David Engerman, Marie Huber, Gert Huskens, Stella Krepp, Zoe LeBlanc, Christopher Lee, James Meriwether, Jamie Miller, Alanna O'Malley, José Pedro Monteiro, Jason Parker, Nathaniel Powell, Robert Rakove, Jayita Sarkar, Gerardo Serra, Elizabeth Schmidt, Giles Scott-Smith, Chris Vaughan, Robert Waters, and Alden Young. Grants from different foundations made this book possible: the European University Institute; the Fondation Biermans-Lapôtre; the European Association of American Studies; the American Studies Association of Norway; the

John W. Kluge Center at the Library of Congress; the Académie Royale des sciences, des lettres & des beaux-arts de Belgique; the Institut Français d'Afrique du Sud; and the National Research Foundation of South Africa. I am grateful to my editors at Cornell University Press, Michael J. McGandy, Sarah Grossman, and Jacqulyn Teoh, as well as my three anonymous reviewers. Remaining errors are my own. I am lucky to have a group of amazing friends: Wim Paulissen and Brenda Jenné, Stijn Sillen, Wout Vandelaer and Lisa Geerts, Kim Swennen and Hanne Paulisen, Jan Stulens and Ine Baptist, Sophie Savenay, Niko Ieronymakis and Romina Gentier, Jordan Molenaar, and Charlotte Roels.

Prior versions of some of the material in this book appeared in the following works: "Bandung as the Call for a Better Development Project: American, British, French and Gold Coast Perceptions of the Afro-Asian Conference (1955)," *Cold War History* 16, no. 3 (August 2016): 255–72, Taylor & Francis Ltd, http://www.tandfonline.com, reprinted by permission of the publisher; "The Postcolonial Cultural Transaction: Rethinking the Guinea Crisis within the French Cultural Strategy for Africa, 1958–1960," *Cold War History* 19, no. 3 (2019): 493–509, Taylor & Francis Ltd, http://www.tandfonline.com, reprinted by permission of the publisher; "Hungry Minds: the Eisenhower Administration and Cultural Assistance in Sub-Saharan Africa (1953–1961)," *Diplomatic History* 41, no. 3 (June 2017): 594–619, by permission of Oxford University Press; and "'When the Bull Elephants Fight': Nkrumah, the Non-Aligned Movement and Pan-Africanism as an Interventionist Ideology (1957–1966)," *International History Review* 37, no. 5 (October 2015): 951–69, reprinted by permission of Informa UK Limited, trading as Taylor & Francis Group, www.tandfonline.com.

This book is dedicated to Dorien and our sons, Theo and Mathias. They made the past decade worthwhile.

NOTE ON TRANSLITERATION

All translations from other languages than English to English are the author's. Russian names and terms follow the Library of Congress transliteration system.

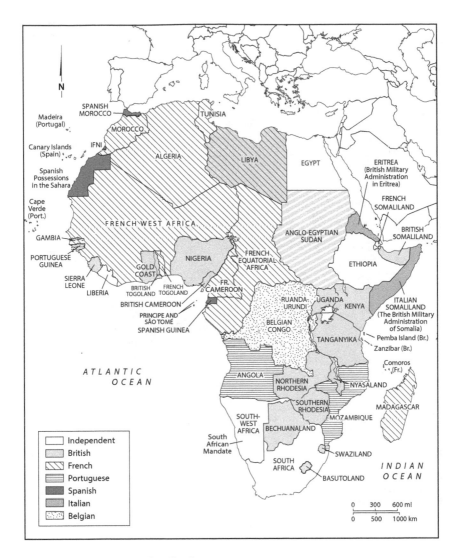

Map 1. Africa in 1945. Map by Bill Nelson.

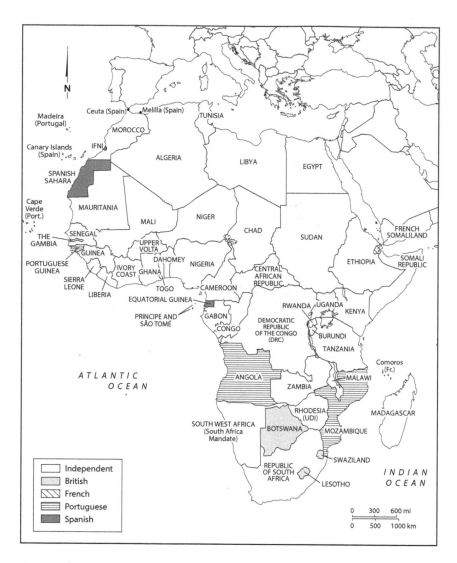

MAP 2. Africa in 1966. Map by Bill Nelson.

Introduction
How African Liberation Shaped the International System

It is March 1961. The blades of two United Nations (UN) helicopters blow dust off Maya-Maya Airport's tarmac in Brazzaville. Rajeshwar Dayal, the head of the United Nations Operation in the Congo (UNOC), exits the first helicopter, while the doors of the second chopper remain closed. Rumor spreads that Antoine Gizenga, successor to Patrice Lumumba, the first prime minister of the Democratic Republic of the Congo, is hiding inside. The arrival of Congo-Brazzaville's foreign minister, Robert Stéphane Tchitchéllé, prompts the head of security to inspect the helicopter to find out who is accompanying Dayal. Earlier that day, Radio Léopoldville announced that Gizenga was placing himself under Dayal's protection.[1] Lumumba had been murdered in January 1961 on the orders of the Katangese leaders, Belgian police inspector Frans Verscheure, and Belgian military police chief Julien Gat, allowing the Belgians, the Americans, and—reportedly—MI6 to all file away their assassination plans.[2] Allen Dulles, head of the Central Intelligence Agency (CIA), supported the elimination reportedly because he had heard US president Dwight D. Eisenhower wish for the Congolese prime minister to "fall into a river full of crocodiles." UN troops had to be kept "in the Congo even if" that decision would be "used by the Soviets as the basis for starting a fight."[3]

While Eisenhower's involvement in Lumumba's assassination remains speculative, what is remarkable is the president's combativeness, since Africa in the 1950s offered little political or military gain, Communist intrusion was a minor

1

threat, and engagement with Africa entailed a tough choice between European partners and anticolonial nationalists. Why, then, was Lumumba suddenly a threat to international stability in the Global North? Conversely, why did leaders in the Global South, who had constructed their political identities on resistance to outside intervention, become ensnared by the Cold War? To answer those questions, one must acknowledge the Congo's strategic importance and mineral riches. However, a principal part of the answer has to consider the ideological scramble for Africa, a struggle for hearts and minds in which African, US, Soviet, and European leaders propagated competing plans for Africa's future. Seemingly inconspicuous machines, such as the transistor radio used by soldiers at Maya-Maya Airport to listen to the news, became indispensable in the spread of Pan-African, capitalist, Communist, and imperial visions of postcolonial order.

Rather than the place where the Soviet and US model competed for supremacy, the continent became the destination for a "crowded safari," as famed British journalist Edward Crankshaw quipped in January 1960. The *Observer* even had to publish a guide to all of the African "isms" to paint a clearer picture of the "ferment of ideas."[4] Pan-Africanism, a liberationist interventionist ideology with universalist aspirations, prompted African nationalists to compete with imperialist, capitalist, and Communist development models. Nationalist leaders tried to attract others who were living outside of their newly established borders to their brand of Pan-Africanism while crafting an anticolonial route to modernity to replace the European version, which was exclusionary and racist. The liberationist case for progress, in contrast, was built on cultural integrity, the notion that successful modernization required an appreciation of African culture. This approach rejected colonial rulers as well as Soviet and US officials who had claimed that the destruction of tradition was indispensable for development.

The liberationist mission to rework colonial modernity, not the anticolonial engagement with the Cold War, shaped the postcolonial global order. The struggle between capitalism and Communism was undeniably intense but was only one of two ideological struggles that marked the twentieth century, with the battle between liberation and imperialism ultimately proving to be more enduring. The liberationist critique of European modernity as inherently racist and unjust emerged in eighteenth-century Saint-Domingue, where a charismatic Black general, Toussaint Louverture, staged a revolt when the Napoleonic state reversed the abolition of slavery. African nationalists in the 1950s were all steeped in this intellectual tradition by way of the French and British West Indies. Ghanaian leader Kwame Nkrumah enlisted the help of Trinidadian journalist Cyril Lionel Robert James and St. Lucia economist Arthur Lewis to replace colonial development with Nkrumah's Pan-African path to modernity, while in Senegal, Léopold Sédar Senghor was joined by Aimé Césaire and Léon-Gontran Damas, poets of French Martinique and French Guiana, to craft a vision of progress in which French and African civilizations were both indispensable.[5]

African nationalists were not a disjointed group who met at conferences, launched a dizzying array of nation-building models, and forged fragile Afro-Asian coalitions to guard against Cold War intrusion and colonial oppression. Rather, their activism was born out of a common ideological ambition to attain anticolonial modernity and make real the promise of the Haitian Revolution. In that respect, liberationists were not that different from other nineteenth-century revolutionaries, such as Marxists who wanted to achieve the aims of the Bolshevik revolution, capitalists who were eager to export the ideas of the American Revolution, or imperialists who sought to spread the Industrial Revolution's benefits.

Ideological deliberations between anticolonial leaders also created a liberationist international system, since Third World nationalists built different types of federative and cooperate structures beyond their own postcolonial state to marshal the economic, cultural, and political capacity required to attain modernity on the Global South's terms. The Cold War was not exported to the Global South. Rather, the East-West division between the US empire of liberty and the Soviet empire of equality was submerged by a North-South conflict in which US and Soviet empires, together with European empires of exploitation, were rebuffed by Pan-Asian, Pan-African, Pan-American, or Pan-Arab federations. The Global South's understanding of diplomacy as a perpetual struggle between liberationists and neocolonialists crashed into the North's tendency to define each political matter in the South as a development problem and hampered policymakers in the Global North, who were forced to constantly come up with new justifications when they meddled with liberationist principles.

These principles—state building with respect for African culture and the creation of a nonracial international hierarchy—had emerged in the eighteenth century, were punctuated by decolonization, and had to be resolved by a modernist transformation. As Robert Komer, member of the US National Security Council (NSC), ruminated in 1964, "sovereignty, legitimacy of legally constituted governments, non-intervention" were "principles vital to" Africa's "long-range independence and prosperity."[6] After 1945, those issues were nowhere more pressing than in Africa. Latin American countries had claimed their independence from Spain and Portugal between 1808 and 1826, as Suriname and French Guiana redefined their relationship with the metropole. In Asia the question of decolonization was settled in the 1940s with the independence of India, Indonesia, and the Philippines, underscored by the French defeat of 1954 in Dien Bien Phu. Great Britain, France, Belgium, and Portugal were forced to turn to Africa to salvage their great power status.[7]

African decolonization turned diplomacy into a confrontation between Communist, capitalist, imperialist, and liberationist ideas, providing historians with a window onto how decolonization affected the Cold War (see figure I.1). The following pages, then, offer a reconfiguring of our understanding of twentieth-century international affairs from East-West to North-South.[8]

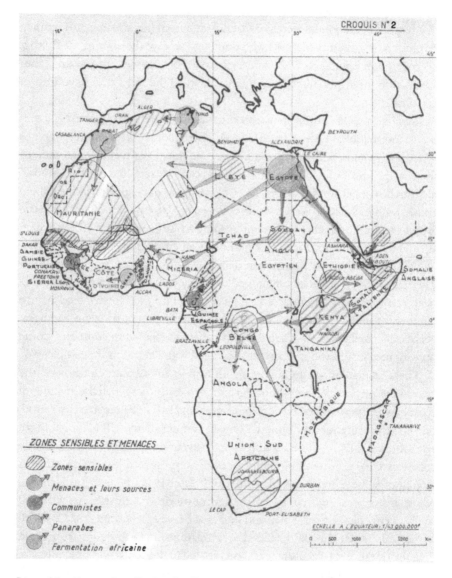

FIGURE I.1. Map produced by French military staff in April 1960, depicting the different threats to the French presence in Africa: Communism, Pan-Arabism, Pan-Africanism, and African nationalism. Image courtesy of AMAE.

The Liberationist Ideology: Anticolonial Modernity

International historians have set aside the powerful globalism of liberation and instead argue that decolonization globalized the Cold War. After the rubble of the World War II was cleared away, Odd Arne Westad famously claimed the United States and the Soviet Union became locked in conflict over the meaning of the Enlightenment's legacy, European modernity. However, from the position of the Global South, that telling of international relations seems imprecise. After all, decolonization not only germinated modernity but also increased modernity's complexity. In revolutionary centers in Accra, Cairo, and Dar es Salaam, an idealized "authentic" image of the past, such as the "African Personality" or *Ujamaa*, was held up as an important corrective. Anticolonial movements did not define themselves in opposition to or in alignment with US or Soviet ideology. Rather, these movements wrestled with interpreting the legacy of the Haitian Revolution and worked to construct anticolonial modernity. For liberationists who wanted a radical break with the colonizer, such as the members of the Casablanca Group spearheaded by Nkrumah, as well as those of the Monrovia Group led by Senghor, who sought a redefinition of their relationship with the metropole, modernization and industrialization were not flawed models but powerful tools for progress that had been wielded by outsiders who had been misguided in their belief that progress required the cultural and psychological destruction of colonial peoples.[9]

From its inception, the very concept of modernity was contested by anticolonial thinkers. A fundamental critique of the European Enlightenment originated in the Haitian Revolution of 1791, when Louverture demanded the universal application of the French revolutionary principles of liberty and equality. That corrective to European modernity was not simply an act of subaltern resistance but also entailed a difficult search for an alternative, a problem exemplified by the fact that this Black revolutionary sought freedom through the same language that had enslaved him.[10] Even though Louverture was leading an insurrection against France, he also wanted to retain the link with the French civilization. After 1945, finding a way out of the psychology and culture of colonial modernity therefore became the core objective of the liberationist modernization project, a search reflected in the contrasting accounts of Louverture's life.

In *Black Jacobins*, C. L. R. James described the eagerness of Haitians to "go abroad" because it provided them with an opportunity to "clear from minds the stigma that anything African was inherently inferior." In 1963, he rewrote his 1938 book because he could no longer see a future governed by anticolonial modernity. His lament that "Toussaint was attempting the impossible" points to

James's disappointment with the results of psychological decolonization. Césaire, in contrast, saw Louverture's death in a French prison cell as a "sacrifice" for Haiti's future. While remaining skeptical about the civilizing mission, Césaire concluded that integration into a French republic on the basis of legal equality was the best guarantee for a type of freedom that included social and economic prosperity. The hunger "for some doctrine" that could lift Africans "from their servile consciousness," in Kenyan leader Jomo Kenyatta's phrase, thus gave rise to two opposing tactics: one stressing Eurafrican hybridization, another prioritizing radical separation from Europe.[11] This fundamental disagreement over colonialism's precise psychological impact, differences over the best way to attain modernity, and the fight over the Enlightenment's legacy animated the debates at the first Pan-African Conference in London in 1900 and remained a problem at successive meetings.

The end of World War II was a watershed moment when this question of colonialism's psychological and cultural influence gained new currency. Disregard for the contribution of colonial troops strengthened anticolonial leaders in their conviction that it was incumbent on them to reverse the psychological and cultural destruction brought about by colonial development. In Northern strategic blueprints, the "African mind" emerged as a security concern, and underdevelopment became a psychological infliction that could be treated through education. Communists and capitalists who wanted to destroy African "tradition" were unappealing allies for African nationalists who believed genuine modernity could be attained only if development was built on precolonial culture. Anticolonial modernity ties in with how many liberationist intellectuals, such as Aimé and Suzanne Césaire, viewed time as a process in which the past is not yet over and the present and future require constant reinterpretation.[12] The Ghanaian "African Personality," Zambian "humanism," and Kenyan "African Socialism" were attempts to give new societies and their foreign policies direction.

In the 1950s and 1960s, policymakers and intellectuals in the North as well as the South thus all spoke the language of psychology and culture when they reflected on decolonization, despite fiercely disagreeing about what aspects were indispensable for progress. "Nation building" required leaders with a stable psychology, according to Lucian Pye at Yale University, while Mau Mau insurgents in Kenya were diagnosed with a psychological disease by British ethnopsychiatrist John Carothers.[13] French and British colonial subjects could transform into "Black Frenchmen" or "Black Englishmen" by adopting the language, leading psychoanalyst Octave Mannoni to claim that the Malagasy could not bear the fact that they were not white.[14] Mannoni's *Psychologie de la colonization* prompted Frantz Fanon, a psychiatrist and key theorist of the Algerian War, to argue the "white man" had robbed nonwhites of their self-worth and instilled psychological disease. Nigerian psychiatrists such as Thomas Adeoye Lambo at Aro Psychiatric Hospital, in contrast, integrated Africans into a universal medical framework that treated them as psychological equals.[15] The symbolic dimension of decolonization was further heightened in the 1950s, since newly independent countries could not "indulge in power politics" but had to rely on "moral and political strength," as Sukarno, the leader of Indonesia, phrased this idea at the Bandung Conference of 1955.[16] The independence wave of 1960 and the Congo Crisis forced the diplomatic corps in North and South to reevaluate their single-minded focus on psychology. A younger generation of freedom fighters felt cultural resistance had not delivered in material terms. In the Global North, socioeconomic approaches to underdevelopment also won out. In 1961, Walt Rostow, John F. Kennedy's key adviser, felt modernization was "psychological," not "narrowly economic," but he acknowledged the "take-off" process could be kindled only through investments that were adapted to the absorptive capacity of developing nations.[17] When Pan-Africanism and anticolonial modernity more broadly lost their appeal in the 1970s, Cold War ideologies found fertile ground among populations and leaders in the Global South who were disappointed by decolonization's results.

Africa's postcolonial state building could therefore never solely be a political or economic undertaking with "Third World solidarity as a form of international class politics."[18] Privileging the struggle for economic justice ignores the long shadow of the Haitian Revolution and the disagreements about the appropriate role of precolonial culture in postcolonial modernity.[19] The story of the African state after empire is the story of cultural assistance: the use of cultural resources, such as education and film, to accelerate development or liberation. These assets were mobilized in Europe to engage in public and cultural diplomacy, "an international actor's attempt to conduct its foreign policy by engaging with foreign publics." Propaganda, the spread of ideas to further one's cause, and public relations (PR), the management of communication between an organization and the public, were both part of cultural assistance as well as public and cultural diplomacy.[20] Despite the propensity to debate the extent to which Afro-Asianism was a symbolic or realist project, for anticolonial diplomats there was no distinction between networks of "intellectuals, artists and writers" and "conventional" diplomacy.[21] To do "nation building," the Global North and the Global South turned to psychology.[22] Eisenhower wanted to help new states, "with their ancient culture," by providing education.[23] Operatives of the United States Information Agency (USIA), a public diplomacy institution created by Eisenhower in 1953, and the British Council, an English language education charity, both viewed their joint English language program less as a symbolic weapon and more as "a neutral skill."[24] The redefinition of information programs as foreign aid often led to misunderstandings when officials met. When the French director of cultural affairs, Roger Seydoux, explained to the director of the British Information Research Department (IRD), Ralph Murray, that he was responsible for cultural and technical assistance, Murray was unsure whether he was the right interlocuter because he deemed "technical assistance" "outside his purview."[25]

Despite this confusion among contemporaries, a comparative analysis of cultural assistance activities is important because it illuminates what US and Soviet power or French, British, Portuguese, Belgian, and African nationalist influence looked like to others. The power of ideas—how operatives believed their operation and the activities of competitors and allies would affect African minds—was a consideration that was embedded in every diplomatic decision about the continent.[26] Operatives adopted and adapted one another's techniques and in effect produced hybrid products of cultural assistance. Misunderstanding over the effect on target audiences of certain types of development deepened the animosity between competitors and accelerated the scramble. The nationalist call for independence was interpreted in the Global North as a symptom of psychological distress, while African leaders thought modernization was a neocolonial trick.

The centrality of psychological decolonization also affected the position of race and anti-racism in a postcolonial order. European modernity had become irreparably damaged by Fascism, exposing the necessity for paradigms that employed different formulas to peel race from the fruit of modernity, such as Senghor's *Négritude* or Nkrumah's Pan-Africanism. Solutions ranged from pan-Black plans, based on the belief that the determinative force of anticolonial struggle was race, to pan-human approaches, which meant that all oppressed peoples should be united in the same fight. Nkrumah harkened back to an idealized pastoral past but relied on modern technology to jump-start development. Césaire believed oppression had more to do with Western colonialism than it did with modernity, while Senghor considered capitalist oppression the principal problem.[27] Nonetheless, there was consensus about the fact that Afro-Asianism and Pan-Africanism could never be merely understood as an issue of skin color. Race was always part of the debate on modernity. Intellectualizing the postwar era as the age of international race relations therefore inaccurately narrows the possible range of international interactions that were possible for African diplomats, most of whom were men. Their vocality should not obscure the crucial role played by Ghanaian market women, who had immense political influence; anticolonial thinkers such as Dorothy Pizer, who took the name Padmore after her marriage; and Suzanne Césaire or Susanna Al-Hassan, who had various ministerial positions in Ghana between 1961 and 1966.[28]

On the ground, Pan-African and Pan-Arab schemes were ranked beside imperialism, Communism, or capitalism and were not understood in solely political or racial terms but viewed as alternative development models. Even for astute dependency theorist Immanuel Wallerstein, this was self-evident. "The strength of the pan-African drive," he wrote in 1961, had to be "attributed precisely to the fact that it is a weapon of the modernizers." If the Pan-African project failed, modernization would also be set back.[29] The interventionist and modernist nature of Third Worldism and Pan-Africanism in particular—obvious to observers in the 1950s and 1960s—has faded into the background of historical understanding.[30] By the 1980s, the Third World had transformed into a place of suffering. Embraced by New Leftist students and contested by dependency theorists, even Nyerere began to use "Third World" and "South" "interchangeably."[31] Yet, in the 1950s, the Third World was not a physical place but an alternative ideological project, an interventionist venture with universalist aspirations that rejected the notion that nonwhites were unfit for self-government.[32] "The Third World today faces Europe like a colossal mass," Fanon wrote, "whose aim should be to try to resolve the problems to which Europe has not been able to find the answers." "An economic program" therefore had to include a new "concept of man."[33] His definition gained currency during the Bandung Conference because it created coherence among those involved with liberation: the poor, nonwhite, and uncommitted peoples.

The belligerence of anticolonial philosophers could not prevent Northern thinkers from claiming the "Third World" as their own. French demographer Alfred Sauvy in 1952 viewed the *tiers état* as a version of the French revolutionary "third estate."[34] US officials believed their development aid programs created the Third World.[35] Andrei Zhdanov the chief ideologue under Iosif Stalin in the Union of Soviet Socialist Republics (USSR), submerged the Third World into his two-camp theory, in which a US-led "imperialist and antidemocratic camp" faced an "anti-imperialist, democratic camp," of which liberation movements and the USSR were a part. Similarly, Mao Zedong espoused his Three Worlds Theory from 1974 onward, locating the People's Republic of China (PRC) in the Third World.[36] Nevertheless, the universalist ambition to remake the world that animated the Third World venture was undercut less by these pressures to become part of a Cold War camp and more by the contradiction of the Third World project itself.[37] Anticolonial leaders were committed to the principle of nonintervention while simultaneously also spawning their own interventionist projects, leading to fights in which they branded one another as neocolonialists.

The liberationist project to decolonize modernity shaped Communist, capitalist, and imperialist designs at every turn. In 1989, one of the Enlightenment's legacies, the struggle between Western capitalist liberty and Eastern Communist

equality, came to an end. The other legacy, the struggle between Northern imperial technocracy and Southern liberationist integrity, continued. As a result,
liberationist history, with slavery as the starting point of a long trajectory of injustice, structures the world we live in today. From refugees to terrorism, it is
colonial injustice and economic inequality that continue to shape our postcolonial times. In my conversations with people in Accra, Pretoria, Addis Ababa,
Nairobi, Dakar, Lusaka, and Ibadan, fundamentally different views of the world
emerge that are rooted in colonialism's wrongs, not the social and political upheavals of the 1970s and 1980s. Historians have avoided a grand narrative of the
Global South and favored "stories of the everyday" because the diplomatic history of "great men" purportedly is already known. Nevertheless, the contours
of the international system that the anticolonial ideological project helped create still need to be examined if we are to appreciate the seismic changes brought
about by decolonization.[38]

The Liberationist World System: Federations of Liberation

The liberationist imagination, which was populated by neocolonialists who
wanted to undercut postindependence progress, made nationalist leaders ambivalent about state-centric nation building and led them to seek protection
within federations. Through continental and regional integration, Africa in particular could be psychologically and economically liberated, while cultural ties
with Europe could be severed or at the very least adjusted, so modernity could
be attained on Africa's terms. The USSR, the empire of equality; the United
States, the empire of liberty; and the European empires of exploitation were
challenged by federations of liberation that sought to prove the potency of their
interventionist ideologies.

Nevertheless, in their study of the Global South's diplomacy, international
historians never abandon the bipolar international system in favor of a multi-
directional analysis of the battle for modernity. The Cold War was not about
Europe or a project to reverse US isolationism, but rather about the export of
US and Soviet concepts of development that fueled a global war of ideas and
created an "international system of states."[39] In that way, the global Cold War
inadvertently is turned into a catchall label for every international event.[40] The
interaction of anticolonial ideologies with the Cold War was a "source" of
"conflict" or an "obstacle to the Cold War's entrance," but that confrontation
did not alter international relations. The Cold War is even seen as multiply-
ing, resulting in "regional" or "pericentric" cold wars.[41] Historians argue that

anticolonial leaders developed "nativist ideologies" in an effort to "close ranks against Cold War politics" or sought to play the Cold War superpowers against each other, which in effect prolonged and deepened civil wars.[42]

This book rejects this characterization of the international system. The Cold War was not unswervingly intertwined with Third World developments. In the 1980s, a supposed high point of Cold War confrontation, neither Leonid Brezhnev nor Mikhail Gorbachev was prepared to risk détente in Europe over their proxy wars in the Horn of Africa. The Cold War in the South was not a "continuation of European colonial interventions" either, since imperial modernization and anticolonial projects broke up what could have been an East-West competition for African hearts and minds.[43] Liberationists who were eager to export their own anticolonial models did not want their countries to be theaters of struggle, forcing the superpowers to constantly deny that they were waging a Cold War battle. Nevertheless, the Pan-African alternative has been cast as a failed project that lives on only as prophetic vision. Fred Cooper explains Senghor's abandonment of federalism in favor of nationalism and authoritarianism as a pragmatic political move.[44] Political theorists and Africanists also limit themselves to "working through" rather than "resolving" the nationalist contractions and point out that it was the Cold War that impeded nationalist leaders' ability to present an alternative to the nation-state.[45] Instead, the pursuit of anticolonial modernity is reduced to an intellectual history of anticolonial thinkers who attempted to unmake the "liberal world order" through their legal or artistic activism.[46]

By correcting geographies and reclaiming utopias, however, historians of the Global South obscure how African visions actually altered imperial and Cold War structures. Interventions, state-led efforts by one country to determine the political direction of another country, were not just Soviet-sponsored or US-led. Newly independent states such as Ghana and Egypt were built on interventionist ideologies and were keen to steer the development process of other countries and build federations.[47] It is therefore productive to think about the Cold War as one mode of knowing, not as a system of states, because it would be difficult to precisely locate more than half of the globe within the Cold War's Eurocentric limits.[48] Conversely, the struggle for liberation created an international system in which Pan-African or Pan-Arab structures were erected to protect against the dominance of the Global North. The split between the Global North and South refers to the split between the decolonial North and South—areas of the world similarly affected by the processes and aftermath of colonization—which is the reason that the USSR and the Australia are deemed to be part of the North.[49] The use of the prefix "Global" has been contested even though usage of the term "Global South" has become common. Already in the 1920s, Antonio Gramsci wrote about how the "Northern bourgeoisie" had "subjugated the South of Italy."[50] In the 1960s, the term was picked up in New Leftist circles by Carl Oglesby, president of the Students for a Democratic Society to claim the "Global South" had to "escape" the "Western empires."[51] Paradoxically, the term gained in popularity by the end of the 1970s, when the Third World ideological project was collapsing and discussions shifted from ideas to global economic structures with the establishment of the New International Economic Order (NIEO).[52]

African Agency in Historical Scholarship

Scholars of Africa's international history have told a different story. Modernization programs have been cast by Cold War historians as a violent feature of the Cold War outside of Europe, forcing postcolonial leaders to choose between capitalism and Communism if they wanted to survive.[53] Africanists as well as global and transnational historians view the Cold War as a force that doomed to failure such alternative political projects as Pan-Africanism, since "Cold War lines" left little "space to imagine new worlds."[54] Instead, the transnational networks where Pan-African and Afro-Asian activism was sustained are studied.[55] Alternatively, intellectual historians and international organization scholars have studied how imagined political futures, international law, and "internationalisms" became a refuge against the destructive power politics of the Cold War. The "Non-Aligned Movement" supposedly created a distance "from the Cold War machinations" that were taking a "terrible toll on the worldly status of internationalism and the UN itself."[56] Conversely, "new imperial historians" have taken the long nineteenth century as their starting point and write about a twentieth century in which the Cold War battle for hearts and minds is glaringly absent.[57] What is mentioned is Cold War militarism, since colonies were incorporated in the post-1945 defense of "the West."[58] These historians have been inspired by a diverse group of political and postcolonial theorists, such as Dipesh Chakrabarty and Partha Chatterjee, who relegate the ideologically divided Europe between 1945 and 1989 to the margins of their analysis, while a nineteenth-century imperial Europe—all but gone by the 1950s—is depicted as the object of their critique.[59]

Despite the efforts of these scholars to analyze actors in the Global South as not merely pawns in the superpower game, their protagonists remain subaltern in character, able only to resist or utilize Cold War or imperial pressures. The Cold War is seen as a static, realist world system that crushed emancipatory political projects. Global Cold War historians in particular cast anticolonial diplomats as people who engaged the rest of the world on Cold War terms without an ideological project of their own.[60] Africanists, new imperial historians, political theorists, and transnational and global historians stress that radical Pan-African and Afro-Asian experimentation persisted in improvised ways or through nonstate activism despite the Cold War's damaging effects. Cooper, for instance, argues that outside powers could provide "sustenance" or "sponsor alternatives," whereas Christopher Clapham concludes that external powers intervened each time African states challenged bipolarity.[61] Similarly, "New Imperial History" has highlighted the immense impact of colonial and anticolonial culture on the metropole, even after the end of formal empire, but colonial actors remain absent from the big diplomatic games.[62] Even scholars on the African continent, during the long 1970s, viewed resistance as Africa's principal form of interaction with the rest of the world. Ali Mazrui argued that Africa wanted to be its own police officer, while Ian Phimister and Terence Ranger debated the precise role that capital accumulation or nationalist resistance played in Central Africa's defiance.[63]

What these approaches obscure is how the Pan-African project competed with and impacted on the Northern blueprints for the continent. Even Matthew Connelly, who made a case for removing the Cold War lens, writes that the Algerian Front de Libération Nationale (FLN) based its strategy on an exploitation of the Cold War tensions to acquire leverage. For Jeffrey Byrne, FLN leaders remained "less the product of ideologies, than of methodologies."[64] Christy Thornton argues that the Mexican diplomats' conviction that they "had a responsibility to carry" their "vision to the world stage" served only as "a justification for some other . . . material or political" interest.[65] Global and transnational historians stop short of giving anticolonial actors an interventionist ideology of their own and instead analyze networks "below and beyond the conventional framings of the Cold War," with effective state-to-state diplomacy the prerogative of Northern actors.[66] Gerard McCann calls on researchers to go beyond the "local resistance" narrative but highlights only "transformative agency within the emerging 'Global South' itself."[67] Historians who have written about the intellectual and legal imaginings of the global have homed in on the capacity of actors in the Global South to remake Northern-dominated international institutions.[68] Nevertheless, the ability to table new postracial international norms and the quest for openings in international organizations to obliterate colonial sovereignty are ultimately seen crashing into Cold War structures, US hegemony, or rigid economic or military structures. The transformative potential of anticolonial ideologies is downplayed.

The methodological solution of theorists such as Gayatri Chakravorty Spivak to "read against the grain" has produced ahistorical narratives about utopian planetary projects.[69] According to Patrick Chabal, Africanist political theory was the study of the impact of globalization on Africa, the causes of which "lie beyond agency."[70] At African universities, the resistance narrative equates post-1945 forms of control with colonial exploitation, putting Africans in a perpetual state of victimhood while European motivations are cast in narrowly economic terms, discounting the nervous improvisation that went into dealing with the fallout of decolonization. Until the early 2000s, African historical essays were valued more as expressions of nostalgia or tragedy than products of academic labor. Nevertheless, African statesmen are still cast as men "of vision and talent," and precolonial history is recovered to claim an African identity, a practice rooted in the Ibadan School of History, dominant from the 1950s to the 1970s.[71]

The agency of actors in the Global South is thus limited to harnessing "the dominant international reality of their age, the Cold War, to maximize potential benefits."[72] African countries are solely seen as targets, even though African nationalists unfolded massive public diplomacy operations to project anticolonial ideologies while demands for African unity, African Socialism, and racial blindness structured the intra-African political debate until 1966, when the continent was swept up in coups. The possibility that African action might actually have altered the Cold War's significance is underestimated.[73] Postcolonial statemen did not only redefine Marxism or capitalism for "their own purposes."[74] Rather, their understanding of nation building and race was exported to the noncolonized world, where it reshaped interpretations of the decolonizing world. African leaders did not face a hostile international system but participated in its constant reimagining and restructuring.

Recovering that process requires an Africa-centered methodology in which African archives, rather than repositories in the metropole, are taken as a starting point. Rather than the amount of African sources, what is important is the sustained reflection on how postcolonial archives alter the findings that stem from depositories in the metropole. Recovering the worldview of African actors in African archives enables the historian to identify conflict or convergence. This emphasis is particularly important since increased access to postcolonial archives has produced a rush for paper reminiscent of the opening up of Soviet archives in 1991, when historians often used new materials to confirm findings they had already drawn from US and European archives.[75] This confirmation bias is strengthened by the nature of much of the postcolonial archive. In the first years after independence, record keeping was chaotic. In 1965, the Office of the President in Kenya ordered "all cabinet minutes and memoranda" to "be destroyed."[76] The National Archives in Nigeria purchased a dehumidifier in July 1960, which, from the evidence of the crumbled documents, is no longer in use today.[77] Furthermore, the postwar archival infrastructure is highly national and reflects the fantasy that "the effects of decolonization could be confined to the realm of high politics." It makes the archives of decolonization difficult to locate and colonial crimes easy to hide.[78] As a result, African documents are haphazard and scattered across the globe, a problem oral history does little to amend, since interviews enable nationalists to shape the record.[79] Critics have questioned whether it is at all possible to ignore the US preponderance in the post-1945 international system, particularly since easily accessible archives in the Global North remain overrepresented in many analyses of the Global South. A systematic Africa-centered approach enables us to test power and discover new sites where it was produced.

An Africa-centered history, in which a multitude of archives and perspectives are brought into dialogue, is therefore inescapably international. Understanding the reasons some international relationships disintegrated and others flourished requires an examination of the history of mutual misunderstanding and clashing interpretations. A multiperspective approach allows for the capture of a reality that lies beyond the sources, recuperating dynamics that would not have been obvious to actors recording their own actions. Critics have pointed out that this multiperspective approach, in which multiple actors and their interconnections are studied, is simply too taxing for one historian to handle.[80] Yet, international historians do not have to be encyclopedists. They rewrite and recontextualize history, in this case, by piecing together the international system that the struggle between liberation and imperialism produced. The twentieth-century international system should therefore be understood as the unintended outcome of a whole host of ideological struggles, rather than the result of a conscious attempt at world making.

When Liberation Altered Decolonization

The study of one federation of liberation, an African union, allows for the revision of long-standing assumptions that underpin our understanding of decolonization and the Global Cold War. Africa is a large and diverse continent, and writing about it as a unit of analysis is inevitably reductive. Nonetheless, Africa was omnipresent in postwar politics: African nationalists in the 1950s and 1960s always referred to themselves as citizens of a country and a continent. This conception of politics was in large part due to the anticolonial activists in Ghana, who set agendas in African international politics, pushing others to think about their political space in continental terms. This book therefore starts in West Africa and shifts to central, southern, and eastern Africa when flag independence pushed those areas into the limelight of the continental and global debate over the meaning of decolonization.

Eight chapters in three parts, each representing a new phase in an internationally shared understanding of modernization, structure the period between 1945 and 1966, when the anticolonial modernization project collapsed. Chapter 1 looks at a postwar elite in the Global North that clung to psychology as a way to sustain prewar development programs, despite a growing unease with racism and the colonial project's ineffectiveness. At the Bandung Conference of 1955, the focus of chapter 2, delegates sought to craft an anticolonial development agenda that not only produced Afro-Asian tensions but also reshaped Northern economic aid doctrines. Ghana's independence in March 1957, analyzed in chapter 3, was a turning point, since Nkrumah, unlike the Bandung delegates, succeeded in charting an alternative path to modernity.

In chapter 4, it becomes clear that British and US policymakers in particular had an increasingly hard time ignoring anticolonial modernization. Negotiations about independence in Belgian Congo, British Central Africa, and French Algeria were profoundly shaped by Ghana's propaganda campaign and reconfigured diplomatic alliances in North and South. The Congo Crisis of 1960, the subject of chapter 5, made clear to diplomats in the Global North and South that psychological modernization had failed. In chapter 6, we see them turn toward socioeconomic modernization but also worry about the psychological effects of industrialization. In South Africa and Rhodesia, an existential struggle to salvage a racialized modernization project became urgent, the topic of chapter 7. By the mid-1960s, the vision of anticolonial modernity collapsed when a younger generation of African nationalists became unhappy with the limited gains of independence. In chapter 8, we see how some leaders turned toward region building to create a New International Economic Order, while others turned to the Cold War superpowers, since they were the only ones deemed capable of delivering progress. Only by the 1970s did Cold War ideologies begin to outcompete liberationist models.

People after World War II had to get used to a world where decisions were made and lives were rebuilt in the shadow of a liberation struggle. Leaders in the North might have felt their decisions were unaffected by how Africans were reworking modernity, building federations, and fighting racial injustice, but solutions to global problems were increasingly affected by the call for liberation. The "Rise of the Rest" has a history that can be examined by analyzing how different actors understood and continuously remade global power structures. The question why people believed that the era in which they lived was constrained by a certain international order, be it "Cold War," "imperial," or "neocolonial," is

therefore more important than measuring the sincerity of political commitments. By approaching "liberation" as a set of concrete responses to the same
challenges that Communism, capitalism, and imperialism sought to tackle, anticolonial ideologies are taken out of the haze of utopianism and positioned as
consecutive parts of twentieth-century diplomacy. The library of international
history should not only be filled with genealogies of different internationalisms
that lost out but also offer books that trace how the liberationist agenda shaped
diplomacy. We should set out to understand not only how the Cold War remade
the world but also how ultimately liberation could become a more powerful
force in international relations.

CHAPTER 1

A Foreign Policy of the Mind, 1945–1954

In 1951, Margaret Trowell of the Makerere Art Institute in Uganda visited Kenyan schools with one of her African pupils, Joseph Nitro, to encourage the European settlers to take an interest in her trainees. Richard Frost, who managed the British Council in East Africa, was excited because the visit would open doors for Nitro, who normally could interact only with uneducated peers. The travelers stayed with Eleanor L. Grosvenor and Major Joceline C. H. Grant, parents of the British writer Elspeth Huxley. The famous article Huxley published, "Two Revolutions That Are Changing Africa," captured the concerns of the guests from Makerere and policymakers in the Global North in the early 1950s: Africans were insufficiently prepared to manage the transition to independence and the leap from "tribalism" to "civilization," even though "tribal" customs had been "swept away by a great tide of Western education." The piece became popular among British, French, Belgian, Portuguese, and US diplomats who had built their Africa strategy on cultural assistance. It is easy to understand why word spread so quickly about these visitors from Uganda, even prompting an invitation to a cocktail party where settlers mused about Nitro being "so cultured," because none of them "had ever met one." Frost, who rolled out education initiatives, felt these settlers were making his life difficult.[1]

We usually think of education in a colonial context as misguided or insincere, with Frost's and Trowell's sense of paternalist duty and the settlers' bigotry as two sides of the same coin. The man whose name has become synonymous with empire, Winston Churchill, embodied that tension. His opposition to India's independence has given him the reputation of a staunch imperialist, whereas his time at the Colonial Office (CO) in the 1920s suggests he was aloof about empire.[2] The French language and republican ideals provided leaders in French Africa and Paris with a common frame of reference, something on which even historians who debunk the myth of a managed transition to independence or a successful "assimilation" agree.[3] Minor imperial players, such as Belgium and Portugal, are evaluated in harsher terms: activities in the cultural realm had to hide exploitation. Portugal's civilizing mission is understood to be an "ideological prop" to shield the empire from international criticism, a strategy emulated by Francisco Franco in Spanish Africa.[4] Belgian politicians such as Prime Minister Paul-Henri Spaak are deemed to be "ignorant" about the Congo. Economic and political interests were the core of diplomatic efforts to seek international recognition.[5] The superpowers, historians agree, were unprepared. Harry S. Truman's public diplomacy toward the Third World "started late" and "lacked coherence," and John F. Kennedy claimed Dwight D. Eisenhower "wanted to avoid Africa as much as possible," a lead many historians since have followed.[6] In the USSR, Iosif Stalin believed nationalist elites were actually part of the bourgeoisie, making him unwilling to pursue a strategy for Africa, whereas the precise role of propaganda and economic aid in Nikita Khrushchev's plans remains unclear. Africa was a "distant front" in the Soviet Cold War struggle.[7]

Such a narrow understanding of cultural assistance as propaganda, enlightened self-interest, merely public posturing, a bid for international legitimacy, or insignificant in diplomatic terms has made it difficult to reconcile the contradictions that emerge from archival boxes that are pulled from dusty shelves in European, US, and African repositories. Particularly vexing is the question why a group of men who had been dragged into a world war over so-called universal values such as democracy, the principles of international organizations, and the tolerability of racism seemed to change their minds once they entered a colonial setting. With the exception of Portugal's intractable position, colonial powers' stance on their dependent peoples—some of whom had invaded the Ethiopian city of Tabora and had fought on the streets of Paris during World War II—is confusing.[8] In the early 1950s, British, French, and Belgian officials invested in cultural programs, proclaiming the benevolence of the civilizing mission as their empires were unraveling and anticolonial activism gained force, requiring historians to explain the gap between ideals and limited results. This question is particularly pressing in the case of the United States, because of its anticolonial origins and preponderant international position. Why did Truman support nationalism and Indonesia's independence in 1949 but refuse to back a provision in the UN charter that would have supported colonial peoples' aspirations for independence? Eisenhower wanted to create stability at all costs, ignored the demands for independence, and supported right-wing dictatorships. At the same time, he tried to uphold the US anticolonial ideal when he wrote to European politicians or spoke during NSC meetings.

In pursuing those questions, explanations for the metropole's decision-making are drawn from events, peoples, and processes within particular national territories, and Cold War impulses have been prioritized. Truman and Eisenhower, at various times, both have been seen as presidents who buckled under domestic opposition and lost battles to increase aid, have been described as leaders who conflated nationalism with Communism, and have been viewed as men who were driven by the need to contain Communism. Debate over Churchill has settled on him being a pragmatist who believed in the civilizing mission but compromised. In the case of France, it remains unclear to what extent the country was able to project cultural power in the 1950s: those who believe the French ability to maintain cultural hegemony was debilitated by the country's swift defeat in World War II and Americanization are criticized by researchers who discern a persistent influence of French ideas. The accusation of Belgian neocolonialism has been questioned by other historians who claim politicians did not care about empire, an enterprise tied in with the church, the king, and corporations. The Congo Free State's cruelty before 1908 has narrowed the definition of Belgian imperialism to exploitation. Brussels's own civilizing mission is understood as a form of publicity, not an ideological project.[9]

Nonetheless, various interpretations fit together when they are seen as part of a scramble for African hearts and minds that was propelled forward by an internationally shared narrative about the 1950s: African decolonization was a problem located in the African psyche.[10] Calls for independence were not ignored by the Truman and Eisenhower administrations because of a Soviet threat; rather, these calls were seen through the lens of psychological modernization. US officials believed they were supporting the case of self-government by psychologically preparing African societies. The Soviet leaders' policy was refracted through Czech interventions in the Global South while the leaders obsessed over notions of backwardness. European empires developed cultural assistance blueprints to alter the underdeveloped mind. Psychology was the main playing field on which policymakers in capitals, officials on the ground, and academics all struggled to come to terms with a new phenomenon: nation building. The term surfaced in the 1950s and became famous because of political scientists who argued that nation building required leaders with a stable psychology and societies that had come to terms with their former rulers.[11] That concern also shaped other aspects of foreign policy, such as economic and military assistance.

However, international uniformity at one level masks the diverse agendas and endless adaptations that marked strategy making. Where the root of underdevelopment was located—in the soul, the mind, or the heart—and how exactly officials believed their operation would create influence were continuous sources of conflict. Pseudoscientific methods were adopted and adapted while competitors and allies were monitored to make sure no country's public diplomats offered information for which colonial populations were not yet prepared. These disputes over the effects of cultural assistance, documented in countless conversations among operatives on the ground, reveal an awareness about the connections between "maturity" and the power of ideas, on the one hand, and the capacity to sustain empire or strengthen the US or Soviet position, on the other. Cultural assistance as a means to prepare, educate, and convince Africans created the illusion of control over a process with an uncertain outcome as liberationist demands for change grew louder.

A Critique of Colonialism

With the myth of European superiority shattered and racism made unpalatable by Fascism, an ideology that had drawn on British and French imperial practices, colonialism as an international organizational principle came into question in 1945. World War II not only strengthened many of the budding liberationist movements that had formed in the 1930s but also made simmering critiques of the colonial system in the Global North more urgent.[12] The origins of these reform movements varied widely but had a common denominator: Africans had to be approached with their supposed innate mental weaknesses in mind or, in the interpretation of anticolonial psychoanalysts, with a solution to repair colonialism's psychological damage.

The French and British postwar engagement with Africa was built on a network of wartime information posts, with Radio Brazzaville continuing the production of news bulletins for a global audience until the 1950s. Paris rethought its use of information only when the French minister of the colonies, Paul Giacobbi, established a commission to study colonial representation in the Constituent Assembly; Madagascar was gripped by a violent nationalist revolt in March 1947; and Dakar became an epicenter of political activism. To diffuse political ambitions, magazines such as *Paris-Match* were offered in the *centres culturels* of Afrique occidentale française (AOF), in the belief that these offerings would meet a more pressing concern of young Africans, social mobility. French culture provided that road to modernity. The experience with *évolué*, colonial subjects who were deemed sufficiently evolved after having followed an assimilation program, led the French Foreign Affairs Ministry to underestimate the political potential of these *centres*, making it possible for the Rassemblement démocratique africain (RDA) to transform them into *maisons des jeunes*, under their own control.[13] A threat to the colonial authority could, in the French estimation, only be imported by people such as the Cameroonian, Ivorian, and Senegalese attendees of the festival of the World Assembly of Youth in Singapore.[14]

The British, in their turn, were confronted with fierce opposition. In February 1948, ex-servicemen of the Gold Coast Regiment, who had fought alongside British troops in Burma, had not been given the jobs and pensions they were promised and began to riot. The Watson Commission, which had been tasked with an investigation, concluded that the "failure of public relations" had caused "the Gold Coast disturbances" and recommended the establishment of an information department.[15] The British believed that their African subjects would accept British judgment as long as decisions were properly explained, a conclusion reached as Harold Innis's argument—that empires existed only because of the telegraph, radio, and railways—became influential. Information departments assisted colonies on the road to self-government with the establishment of radio and press services because they were considered to be "gifts" that created goodwill toward London.[16] When Secretary of Foreign Affairs Anthony Nutting appointed the Drogheda Committee to assess the information effort in 1952, members worried that the United Kingdom would be overwhelmed by aid requests. Likewise, Privy Counsellor John Boyd-Carpenter felt that if UK information offices were built in Nigeria, the Gold Coast, and the British West Indies, it would become difficult to deny other colonies "a similar benefit." The final report recommended shifting the information focus to the colonies.[17]

British and French rule, from the inception, relied on a psychological understanding of underdevelopment. While Victorian neurologists identified the psychological deficiencies of the "primitive man," Belle Epoque republicans called for cultural transformation programs that could teach Africans how to feel French, policies that acquired new meaning after World War II. In 1949 David Stirling founded the Capricorn Africa Society in Southern Rhodesia, with branches in Kenya, Northern Rhodesia, Nyasaland, and Tanganyika. He promoted a future beyond white imperialism and Black nationalism because, as a white liberal, he believed both systems propped up "agitators." Afraid of being swamped by an African majority, colonial administrators and settlers looked toward London, where, since the late 1940s, the Colonial Office had increasingly become populated by psychologists.[18] Their French colleagues operated on similar assumptions. Psychiatrist Henri Collomb and psychoanalyst Marie-Cécile Ortigues, for instance, at the Fann Hospital in Dakar, researched the psychological distress that colonialism had induced. These policies were informed, however, by a different wartime experience. The rhetoric of vague colonial reform espoused by the Popular Front in 1936 helped recast French colonialism as progressive, a notion that was strengthened after a war in which the Vichy regime had trampled on the évolué system that offered the right to obtain French citizenship through education.[19]

Anticolonial activists rebuked psychological modernization and debated the value of the African past as a means to mitigate the damage done to the African psychology. In the French empire, writers such as Léopold Senghor, as well as Aimé Césaire and his student Frantz Fanon, agreed colonialism had robbed nonwhites of their self-worth but disagreed about the remedy. Césaire, like Senghor, was invested in revealing the shared "primitive" origins of European and African cultures. Violence had to be poetic, a "violence poétique," as Césaire argued that the cultivation of a vigorous historical imaginary would result in transformation.[20] His wife, Suzanne Césaire, argued that nature, not culture, provided protection against imperial violence.[21] Fanon, however, believed violent action was the only effective way to cure the psychopathology instilled by empire. He believed the search for a "Negro civilization" in the African past was unhelpful to the "children who labor in the cane fields."[22] In British Africa, in contrast, Nigerian transcultural psychiatrists such as Thomas Lambo and Tolani Asuni, believed integrating African "others" into a universal medical framework was an act of defiance.[23] Nationalists in British Africa also showed an active interest in psychology. While Kenneth Kaunda of Zambia embraced behaviorism, Julius Nyerere in Tanzania studied education at Makarere College and believed genuine emancipation required mental liberation. These competing strategies of violence and culture, integration and a radical break, were termed Africa's "cultural schizophrenia" by Ali Mazrui.[24]

Truman, a man from rural Missouri who became US president on 12 April 1945, advanced a critique of imperialism that targeted colonial development's poor track record. "Old imperialism" had not delivered on its promises because it was motivated by "exploitation for profit." Underdevelopment was not simply the product of tradition but resulted from the "long exploitation for the benefit of foreign countries." When Jawaharlal Nehru of India visited the United States in October 1949, he and Truman agreed that "progress" was possible only if the "obstacle" of colonial rule was eliminated.[25] The president therefore signed the Treaty of Manila in 1946 terminating the Philippines' colonial status, and he supported Indonesia's fight for independence in 1949.[26] The administration also launched Point IV, a technical assistance program spear-headed by White House aide George Elsey and Public Affairs Officer Benjamin Hardy of the State Department; the program sought to replace ineffective colonial development with technological Wilsonianism. Exposure to US technology would help people "find out" that democracy was the key to success.[27] Secretary of State Dean Acheson concurred. Point IV was not a PR stunt but addressed the cause of international instability, namely the "technological revolution," which was overlaid by the "revolutionary ferment of nationalism."[28]

Truman's principled rejection of imperialism on the ground that it was ineffective in developmental terms held implications for the US understanding of nationalism and its relation to Communism. Unlike modernization theorists in the 1960s who sought to encourage "reactive nationalism"—modernization in response to the threat of more advanced foreigners—postwar elites in the 1940s still linked nationalism with World War II and therefore understood nationalism to be a reaction to an economic crisis. History had proved, Secretary of State Dean Acheson proclaimed in February 1952, that the "force of nationalism" was an unstoppable "locomotive" that could either be "constructive" or "destructive." For Acheson, the Schuman Plan, which proposed a European Coal and Steel Community, was an excellent example of the constructive power of nationalism, while the Psychological Strategy Board (PSB) worried about nationalism's destructive power, since Africans desired nationalism's "medicinal powers to remedy all ills."[29] Henry Byroade at the State Department, as well as journalists, talked about how Africans considered nationalism to be magic while writing about Kwame Nkrumah's followers believing that he had left his jail in the shape of a white cat.[30] Nationalists' appetite for resistance delayed technical assistance because it made underdeveloped peoples "particularly concerned with the unhindered development of their own native culture and their own tradition"; but this also helped prevent Communist infiltration.[31] In December 1950, the Bureau of Near Eastern, South Asian and African Affairs therefore concluded that "Communism" had "made no real progress," and Assistant Secretary of State George McGhee admitted in his memoir that the Communist threat was a way to "enlist American interest in Africa."[32] The USSR, while important, did not directly determine the US position on colonialism. Rather, in the US imagination, Communism and imperialism shared undesirable features that were almost indistinguishable.

To tackle the intertwined challenge of nationalism and development, Truman turned to information and training to take away the "fear of the world" that nationalism supposedly instilled. Propaganda that displayed "financial power and technical might," in McGhee's judgment, was only going to "confuse, dismay" and "antagonise the people of Africa" and harm the "political and psychological effectiveness."[33] State Department official Vernon McKay argued "technical assistance projects" had a disruptive effect on African society, making the mitigation of "subconscious resistance and mistrust" a priority.[34] The administration's unofficial Third World expert, ambassador to India Chester Bowles, believed the local posts—the United States Information Services (USIS)—had to get "out of the cocktail rut, and the arrogant social habits" and into the routine of being "humble." Experts had to leave the "airs of superiority" behind and instead provide a detailed explanation of how the United States had achieved its progress. In the process, Point IV's ultimate aim crystallized in the minds of people such as Bowles: underdeveloped societies had to be trained for the "rough and tumble" of democratic individual life, which is the reason that the public affairs officer in India prioritized speaking to students about "the nature of democracy" and "democratic techniques."[35] Acheson agreed that Point IV was meaningful only if it was executed as the junction of the technological revolution and a revolution represented by the "Declaration of Independence and our Bill of Rights." The United States could transmit the "instruments of a better life" that were enshrined in those documents through mass communication, which ultimately would make it possible to develop an appropriate culture that could fulfill aspirations.[36] Technological Wilsonianism allowed Truman to support anticolonial aspirations as he understood them—a call for economic rights— while resisting the detrimental politics of nationalism, which had wrecked Europe. The United States wanted to counter the poverty caused by empire rather than deal with the "economic problems associated with decolonization."[37]

Truman's belief in the power of information as a means to resolve colonialism, which in its "old" form was seen as detrimental to modernization, had its origins in the interwar period. Anthropologists such as Bronislaw Malinowski stressed that development could work only if it was adapted to local cultures.[38] In the 1950s, social psychologists such as Talcott Parsons drew on social psychology and developed techniques to draw men and women into the modern mindset. Parsonian theory had its origins in academic debates of the 1920s and 1930s when European social theory was discussed, a time when classic ethnography began applying psychological insights to analyze the so-called native mind. Consequently, the influential Harvard Department of Social Relations approached modernization as a process that affected entire societies.

Iosif Stalin, who led the Soviet Union until March 1953, was skeptical about the potential for Communist success in Africa despite the establishment of diplomatic relations between Ethiopia and the USSR in April 1943. Like the United States, the USSR cultivated a cultural development strategy. Both Lenin and Stalin had spoken about the need to overcome political, economic, and— above all—"cultural" backwardness among the "nationalities" of central Asia that had been incorporated by the Russian empire. In *Marxism and the National Question*, Stalin defined the nation as a "historically constituted, stable community of people, formed on the basis of a common language, territory, economic life," but also with a common "psychological make-up manifested in a common culture."[39] African territories in the Horn of Africa garnered Soviet attention only because of their geopolitical importance, while Soviet propaganda cast Truman's Point IV as a form of "American colonialism."[40]

Truman's critique forced new and old international players alike to recalibrate their views on empire. In 1949 the Bataka Party in Uganda wrote an open letter to inform Truman that the party's own "progress" had been "retarded by the policies of the Colonial Powers," playing into the White House's understanding of colonial administrators as ineffective. The French ambassador to Washington, Henri Bonnet, purposefully exaggerated the Communist threat in Africa in his conversations with US officials even though his own intelligence services had informed him that there was no imminent danger, an assessment with which UK colleagues agreed. After reading McKay's articles, Bonnet, like his South African colleagues, concluded that US officials were ignorant and unaware of the impact their anticolonial attitude was having. Because Point IV introduced "simplistic anti-colonialist" ideas, the French Foreign Ministry tried to bring the countries that had signed the Brussels Treaty in 1948 together to limit US influence.[41] Smaller colonial powers realized their fate was tied to Truman's stand on empire. Even though António Salazar lacked a propaganda strategy for Africa, he did defend Portuguese colonial claims in order to be able to join the North Atlantic Treaty Organization (NATO).[42] Belgium also opened the doors of the Belgian Government Information Office in New York in 1941 because, in the words of the Belgian minister of the colonies, Pierre Wigny, the United States was "responsible for world politics." When Ambassador Georges Theunis wanted to dismantle the Belgian Information Centre (BIC), Director Jan-Albert Goris was quick to point out that Belgian colonialism required PR to respond to Truman's support for Indonesian independence.[43] Goris believed Point IV and the "colonial idea" were identical, since both provided "material" and "moral" benefits. US anticolonialism was about "sentimentality," not "reason," and Goris worried that speeches on Point IV might incite a revolt. Governor-General of the Congo Pierre Ryckmans, therefore, suggested that Belgium's Congo policy had to be depicted as another type of Point IV.[44]

Like Truman, Belgian politicians emerged from the war with the ambition to transform their "outmoded" imperial project. They wanted to build a moral empire, by reforming the *evolué* system, and create Eurafrica, connecting both continents. The Senate commission that visited the colony in 1947 recommended the formation of a "Union Belgo-Congolaise," and Goris, in a speech

on Belgium's Ten-Year Development Plan in 1950, stressed that Belgian investments were geared toward the "mental processes of the native."[45] The African
subject was approached as the "product of his environment," with "a civilization
of his own," while Belgian colonial propaganda highlighted a wide range of
"tribal customs." The photo story of the visit to Belgium by Mwami of Rwanda
Mutara III centered on his traditional clothing, while a show in 1949 on Radio
Congo Belge delved into the topic of African masks.[46] The often criticized poor
development record of Brussels was thus ideologically motivated. Belgian officials refused to "impose our civilization in its entirety" because the export of
European techniques and science was believed to be ineffective without a transformation of "the soul and the mentality of the blacks." The "political problem"
the Belgians faced in the Congo, Governor-General Léon Pétillon said, sprang
from "ignorance," not "malice."[47]

Cultural assistance therefore became indispensable in the moral empire,
since education transmitted "moral norms" and helped suppress the African
"desire to leave us."[48] In 1952, André Dequae, minister of the colonies and a
Christian Democrat, stressed the importance of the "rayonement moral," while
Pétillon believed the colony's well-being depended not only on "unbreakable
social and economic ties" but also on mental bonds. Ethnography, linguistics,
and psychology were all pressed into the service of reforming the soul. On 10
February 1950, Foreign Affairs Minister Paul van Zeeland requested ambassadors to defend the Belgian colonial record, making it impossible for Marcel-
Henri Jaspar, the ambassador in Buenos Aires, to process the flood of material
coming from Brussels. He faced competition from the Indian and Egyptian Embassies, where every dinner was followed by exhibitions and film viewings that
exalted the progress realized.[49]

The Belgian commitment to preserving local Congolese cultures did not
mitigate colonial excess, as often claimed by scholars and apologists alike, but
instead had to ingrain the notion that the gap between Belgian *colons* and Africans was unbridgeable. Belgian colonialism has been cast as an economic
project Brussels hesitantly took on in 1908 as Leopold II came under fire internationally.[50] A reexamination of the archives reveals that Wigny himself
helped create this myth of pragmatism by asserting that the "Belgian mentality" had never cared about "theoretical schemes." Behind closed doors, however, he lamented the lack of doctrine as well as the limitations he faced in his
efforts to build a moral empire, since he was forced to keep an eye on what
was internationally acceptable when trying to fill the "spiritual vacuum" of
the Congolese.[51] He also admitted that the "Belgian thesis"—considered the
capstone of Belgium's Africa policy by historians—was a way to create a ruse
for other diplomats who were not yet ready to support Brussel's ultimate aim:

the construction of Eurafrica. The Belgian thesis had been developed by Ryck-mans and the secretary-general of the Foreign Affairs Ministry, Fernand Van-langenhove, who argued it was unfair to force colonial powers to inform the UN about their practices while India or Brazil were not asked to do the same, even though their indigenous peoples were also not given democratic repre-sentation.[52] For Wigny and his colleagues, anticolonialism was immoral because it was spearheaded by countries that allowed everyone at every de-velopmental stage to work in government.[53]

The Portuguese did not invest in cultural assistance either. Instead, they opted to vigorously project the idea that the colonies were overseas prov-inces. The *Estado Novo*, a corporatist authoritarian regime established in 1933 by Salazar, with roots in the military dictatorship of 1926, left little room for modernization theories. The ideal of Portugueseness it espoused was so-cially conservative, antimodern, and bucolic. The first state-sponsored settle-ment scheme, the Cela Settlement in Angola, was an expression of that romanticized rurality and welcomed its first settlers only in 1953.[54] In 1945, the same year Amílcar Cabral arrived in Lisbon, Salazar warned "the world which" was "coming" would be "more diverse" with "major social transformation."[55] Two years later, Henrique Galvão, colonial inspector and former chairman of the state broadcaster, wrote a damming report in which he urged Lisbon to take psychological and propaganda measures in order to counteract the exodus of African workers.[56] In response, however, Christianity, not modernity, was relied on to reframe colonialism as a moral enterprise. The Código do trabalho dos in-dígenas nas colónias portuguesas de África, the "Native Labor Code," had already in 1928 forced African males to be in "legal" employment in order to fulfill their "moral obligation to work," while the Catholic church was given a special status in the colonies.[57] In 1945, "Lusotropicalism" was integrated into this justification. Brazilian social scientist Gilberto Freyre devised the concept in 1933 to signal that the Portuguese were uniquely suited to deal with various cultures in Brazil's trop-ical environment. After World War II, Freyre was hosted by colonial governors, gave lectures at colonial research institutes, and was celebrated in the colonial press for his advancement of the idea of a "racial democracy," the notion that the close relationship between slaves and masters had produced a nonracist society.[58]

Morality also formed the core of the Belgian imperial project, which was committed to the humane treatment of colonial subjects, a consequence of Ed-mund Morel's campaign of 1900 against Leopold II. Those promises were held to the light after the war. Reform was driven by missionaries such as Placide Tempels, who published the popular *Bantu Philosophy*, which claimed Africans had their own "world view" and were "equals." Genuine civilizational work could therefore be undertaken only by targeting the soul—*menschenziel*—and going beyond material improvement.[59] Jean Roussel—a missionary of Scheut, a monastic order from Anderlecht, clad in white robes—wrote *The Colonial Duty Doctrine* (*Koloniale Plichtenleer*) in 1952. Worried about the effects material advancement was having on the moral life of Africans and concerned about their susceptibility to "agitators," he argued that effective modernization had to be adjusted to the "psychology of the natives." He also urged colonial officers to cultivate family values, since the "environment of the Congo affects the moral and social life." The root of underdevelopment for officials in Lisbon and Brussels was moral, rather than material or psychological. Jean Herpin, the Belgian ambassador in Mozambique, was irritated by people in the streets of Lourenço Marques who pointed out those similarities when they ran into him.[60]

The internationally shared view of underdevelopment as residing on the level of hearts and minds meant that imperialism was recast as a holistic modernization effort uniquely suited to alleviate not only material but also psychological needs. In practical terms, psychology made it possible to reduce economic investments from the metropole while remaining ostensibly committed to reform.[61] The French and British implemented these ideas in opposite ways. The officials within the Colonial Development and Welfare (CD&W) scheme were convinced that transforming "an attitude of mind" superseded the building of infrastructure. Training courses made texts on "therapeutic" approaches to development, such as James Halliday's *Psychosocial Medicine*, mandatory. In France, the Fonds d'investissements pour le développement économique et social (FIDES) prioritized infrastructure projects, as officials of AOF relied on French culture to diffuse political demands.[62] Likewise, Portugal and Belgium incorporated their moral commitments into the training of colonial officials. Portugal had given missionaries the sole responsibility to "Portuguezise" the *indígnados* via the Missionary Statute of 1941, formalizing an educational system in which Africans had access to rudimentary education, *ensino rudimentar*. The Belgian Colonial School made Roussel's book part of the curriculum in a separate course alongside the course on African psychology. At the opening of the academic year, students were called on to become the Congolese's "political, spiritual and moral guardian." The *Plan décennal*, which was launched in 1949, invested in roads and housing but was primarily "concerned with the expansion of education and the social-medical work."[63]

Preparation for Self-Government

The vulnerability of Point IV and the cultural assistance efforts that accompanied CD&W, FIDES, and the Belgian Ten-Year Plan, as well as Portuguese and Soviet efforts, was their chicken-or-egg quality. Was the spread of modernity going to improve the African psychological condition, or did Africans first have to be mentally prepared before they were able to understand modernity? Stalin got caught up in this catch-22. As historian Alessandro Iandolo writes, for Stalin, real economic development could emerge in a socialist society, a model that could emerge, however, only under the right type of economic conditions.[64] The PSB, tasked with planning US psychological warfare, also questioned technological Wilsonianism in 1953, arguing that tying "our freedom in with our iceboxes" eclipsed the more important message that "freedom imposes duties, as well as grants privileges." Acheson felt Point IV had become a "pie in the sky" concept in need of more "intellectual content." The "Cinderella of the foreign aid family" required more investment in the "right kind of projects" to foster "representative institutions."[65] Doubts about the effectiveness of technical aid, espoused even by Point IV initiator Hardy, reflected a wider trend within the school of psychological modernization theory, which was increasingly turning toward education. Books such as David McClelland's *The Achievement Motive* argued that the need for achievement was like the need for food: one wanted it more the longer one went without.[66] When imperialism was violently attacked, these doubts were thrown into sharp relief, and the Global North came to fully embrace psychology in its engagement with Africa.

Colonial emergencies—an imperial euphemism for anticolonial revolt—forced European, US, and USSR officials to look anew at their cultural assistance blueprints, a policy change that has been eclipsed by the Cold War and the international solidarity surrounding these uprisings.[67] Kenya was a hotbed of insurgency. Naming themselves Mau Mau, a large part of the Kikuyu, a Bantu-speaking people, rose up against the settlers who had seized their land to pay for the debts of the Uganda Railway Company. After World War II, this conflict turned into a battle for independence.[68] When Governor Evelyn Baring declared a state of emergency on 9 October 1952, the Mau Mau mobilized parts of the population through a set of oaths, each expressing a deeper commitment to violent resistance. The problems with the Kikuyu were seen as a failure of the information services, not of policy. At the Colonial Office, Harold Evans was so eager to impress on Charles Carstairs, director of the information service in Kenya, that he had to transform his operation into a genuine information machine that Evans penciled a note while being struck by fever on his flight from Nairobi to Dar es Salaam. From July 1953 onward, Baring was pressured into publicizing the schemes for social betterment to win over insurgents, for instance with a booklet that depicted a helpful multiracial police force.[69]

Similarly, Eisenhower, who moved into the Oval Office in January 1953, questioned the effectiveness of technological Wilsonianism, instead espousing the virtue of civic education. In his memoir, he wrote about how overwhelmed he had been: "In flood force, the spirit of nationalism had grown in all Africa." The determination of the peoples for "self-rule . . . resembled a torrent overrunning everything in its path, including frequently the best interests of those concerned." Although the United States had no direct strategic interests on the African continent, with a "position of leadership in the Free World," the United States—in the words of Eisenhower—did not want to "see chaos run wild among hopeful, expectant peoples and could not afford to see turmoil in an area where the communists would be only too delighted to take an advantage." This imagery of a river that could "burst through barriers and create havoc" was reminiscent of long-standing imagery of uncontrollable hordes. Yet, Eisenhower's choice of words also suggests he was confident about the fact that he could "make constructive use of it."[70]

When he wrote his manuscript, Eisenhower must have reread the notes he made during his conversations with Churchill, the living emblem of the British Empire. A few days before Eisenhower's inauguration, on 6 January 1953, he expressed his views on nationalism's rise over dinner with the British prime minister. The president argued that "dependent peoples" did not automatically look to Europe for guidance but had to be convinced that their only hope of maintaining independence was "through cooperation with the free world." While possibly a slower process, it had the certainty of being "orderly" and "healthy." For the president, colonialism was on the "way out as a relationship among peoples"; the only thing left to do was to focus on eliminating the obstacles that prevented "self-government." In short, a territory could become independent provided it was sufficiently prepared.[71] Initially, Eisenhower urged the imperial powers to impress on dependent peoples that self-rule came with a heavy responsibility. The US presence in Puerto Rico had taught Eisenhower that people would insist on retaining their connections with the mother country once "the native" was told about "the responsibilities and increased costs."[72] Although he also stressed the point to French prime minister Pierre Mendès-France, the president was convinced that Churchill was in a better position to give "a thoughtful speech" on "self-government." When the British prime minister informed Eisenhower about his talks with Soviet leader Georgii Malenkov, Eisenhower responded by asking Churchill to announce an effort by the "Western World to bring educational opportunities to all peoples."[73] The prime minister admitted he was "a laggard" when it came to self-government and "skeptical about suffrage for the Hottentots." Churchill's position disappointed the sixty-two-year-old Eisenhower, who pledged to "never stay around in active position so long that age itself" would make him "a deterrent" to "reasonable action."[74] In 1954, Eisenhower set himself up for disappointment again when he wrote to Mendès-France, whom he found to be "Churchillian in his attitude toward dependent peoples," afraid that his prestige would be reduced if he lost "one iota of . . . influence."[75] In November 1960, in a conversation with Salazar, Eisenhower referred to Churchill, who had "opposed" self-government but quickly realized the "advantages of taking the initiative." Portugal would reach the same conclusion someday, Eisenhower argued, and establish "something like a 'commonwealth relationship.'"[76]

Yet, French and British leaders were not listening, since they were trying to figure out how to effectively deliver on their promise of psychological modernization. To explain why the Kikuyu kept resisting, even after the Colonial Office had sent its PR expert Granville Roberts to create "publicity" for the settlers, the Mau Mau were diagnosed with a mental disorder (see figure 1.1). Anthropologists Max Gluckman and Louis Leakey and former governor of Kenya Philip Mitchell, but most prominently John Carothers, all believed the initiation oath of the Mau Mau was a manifestation of a psychological defect.[77] Paradoxically, the pathological interpretation of resistance also undercut the information effort. Harold Evans began to doubt whether the increase of information was worth his while. A "psychological warfare expert" would be unable to solve all difficulties, since what was needed was someone who could cure the "African mind" and particularly the "Kikuyu mind." Consequently, the British faltered on their commitment to create a UK information service. Only when a survey in 1954 revealed USIA officers were creating problems in Kenya did the Colonial Office decide to step up its information effort.[78] Ultimately, ethnopsychology was a way to rationalize the predicament British officials and settlers found themselves in: the modern imperial enterprise required an information effort, but a defense of colonial decisions implied an acknowledgment of political grievances. In a conversation with Michael Blundell, minister on the war council in Kenya, Churchill displayed this mixture of the pathological and the political. He had been astonished by the change that had come over the "minds" of once "happy, naked and charming people." For him the challenge was not of a military nature, but a question of how to get to the rebels' minds. Yet when Blundell agreed that the killing of "savages" was tragic, Churchill retorted: "Savages? Not savages. They're savages armed with ideas—much more difficult to deal with."[79] In Kenya, the information services were therefore developed through a CD&W grant, which the Colonial Office believed would discourage local politicians from tampering with the truth.[80]

The French believed the Mau Mau uprising strengthened their position in West Africa, because they expected the chaos to spread to their most important competitor, the Gold Coast. Mendès-France, who had come to power in June 1954 after the defeat in Dien Bien Phu and the loss of Indochina, had

FIGURE 1.1. British pamphlet in which the Mau Mau are demonized, warning white settlers to keep an eye on their guns. Image courtesy of BNA.

supported the colonial reforms promised by the Popular Front in the 1930s but kept colonial management practices. The tools Eisenhower relied on to promote self-government were, in the French case, still used to defuse political aspirations. In none of its 157 cultural centers were cultural activities employed to project French ideas. When the people within the political section of French foreign affairs tried to convince the Direction générale des relations culturelles (DGRC) in 1954 to expand into British Africa, arguing that French culture also had a political function, they were ignored. Cultural assistance was a privilege bestowed on Africans hungry for development, not a political instrument aimed at intransigent activists. Wielding it as such would only reward such behavior.[81]

Unlike in Portugal, where Salazar made only cosmetic policy changes, unrest on the continent did cause concern in Belgium. While convinced that the Mau Mau did not have an impact in the Belgian Congo, the Foreign Affairs Ministry admitted there was a risk of "imitation" because air travel and radio had made the world smaller and the spread of lies easier. An educational expansion, in the words of Vanlangenhove, would only make the "native masses" even more receptive to outside "movements."[82] The threat of insurgency helped the Liberal minister for the colonies from April 1954 onward, Auguste Buisseret, to justify his decision to establish an educational system that was not run by missionaries. Hostile ideas were going to be imported if the emerging African middle class, which desired "intellectual freedom," was forced to send its children to Brazzaville and Dakar.[83] The Christian underpinnings of the moral empire made Belgian ministers more attuned to the ideological threat of religion. Islam in particular was considered a "vehicle" for anticolonialism. After a conversation with the charismatic secretary-general of the League of Arab States, Abdul Rahman Hassan Azzam, Ambassador Harold Eeman impressed on Brussels that Islam's "spiritual interests" coincided with Egypt's "political interests."[84]

The White House was pressuring European empires to take seriously their civilizing mission, the duty to remake "primitive" cultures. Eisenhower latched on to postwar commitments to civic education such as the 1946 British development plan for Nigeria, which focused on educating public servants.[85] Nonetheless, he drew a sharp distinction between the "old-fashioned, paternalistic" line taken by the colonial powers and his own plans. When Churchill claimed that newly independent peoples would "recognize the wisdom of our suggestions," the president retorted that "emerging peoples" had to be persuaded to follow their example.[86] Instead of waiting for the colonial powers, Deputy Director Abbott Washburn of USIA was therefore asked in October 1954 to take action on education, especially as reports from the field concluded that Truman's emphasis on "technical advice and training" had been misguided, since "ideas" would not automatically be adopted. Despite little enthusiasm among seasoned officials from USIA and the International Cooperation Administration (ICA), USIA officer Earl Wilson promoted a plan for civic education, and Deputy Director for Education William Russell of the ICA created the "Citizenship Education Project" to teach US democratic concepts. In December 1957, Saxton Bradford of the Bureau of International Cultural Relations sent around the "Bases of Freedom" project to USIS offices in Asia and Africa to encourage the teaching of citizenship in schools and civic organizations.[87] According to Wilson, new nations had to abandon a myopic emphasis on technology and make "men good as men and as citizens."[88] Similarly, Eisenhower's advice to European leaders was part of his "great equation," the combination of spiritual, economic, and military force that guaranteed security.[89] What distinguished Eisenhower from European leaders and Stalin was the US president's willingness to give concrete meaning to the fetishized goal of stable leadership in the wake of looming colonial conflict. The often-asked question whether Eisenhower favored independence is irrelevant: independence was inevitable, in the eyes of the president, but acceptable only if the countries were stable and prepared.[90]

Nevertheless, those sharply different rationales behind cultural assistance were hardly ever clear to Eisenhower, Churchill, Mendès-France, Salazar, and Spaak, men born at the turn of the twentieth century who shared a paternalistic view of African peoples. As a young man, Churchill was a war correspondent during the Mahdist War in Sudan and the Second Anglo-Boer War in South Africa. He believed the virtues of barbarism were "outweighed by the intelligence of the invaders and their superior force of character."[91] Mendès-France, for his part, was a staunch believer in the universality of republican values. As a member of the Popular Front government of Léon Blum in 1936, he had helped design a colonial reform project that sought to liberalize French colonialism while binding the colonies more closely to France.[92] Born in 1889, a little-known university lecturer who entered government in 1928 as finance minister, Salazar addressed Angola's debt crisis and tightened Lisbon's supervision over the colonies. As a Catholic, he believed power originated with God and had to be wielded to achieve the common good, not to reflect the will of the majority.[93] Spaak, despite being an anticlerical socialist, believed colonial peoples had to share the same values as people in the metropole, while World War II had impressed the importance of propaganda on him.[94]

What distinguished Eisenhower from European leaders and even the Soviets, who considered their republics in central Asia to be "backward," was his attachment to the anticolonial origins of the United States.[95] The president preserved a distinction between his plan to provide Africans with education and the debates about racial equality at home. Unlike civil rights activist William Edward Burghardt (W. E. B.) Dubois, Eisenhower did not globalize the "color line" but integrated his foreign policy within the story of US empire. Eisenhower's views had matured during the time he accompanied General Douglas MacArthur between 1935 and 1939 as assistant military adviser in the Philippines, where US teachers had been stationed since 1900.[96] In his diary, Eisenhower describes the locals as children who, due to their "lazy" nature, were difficult to educate. Filipinos, from whom he expected "a minimum of performance from a maximum of promise," were unaccustomed to administrative procedures. His relationship with Manuel Quezon, the Philippine president, remained distant. "Why in the hell do you want a banana country giving you a field-marshalship?" Eisenhower asked MacArthur after he himself had refused this honor.[97] As president, Eisenhower claimed to understand African leaders because of these experiences. In his talks with Nkrumah as well as in NSC meetings, he remarked that the Philippines would have become a dictatorship if the United States had not offered training in democracy.[98]

The Power of Culture

Local officers were forced to improvise as information posts were expanded in the 1940s to aid the war effort. While France kept working through Brazzaville, the British set up offices in Kenya and Nigeria to communicate with the newly established Ministry of Information in London. In Nigeria, the British even tried their hand at writing an African-inspired folktale that alluded to Hitler's reign, *The Owl, Once the Dictator of Beasts and Birds*. Belgium utilized its embassies and only established information offices in London in 1940 and New York in 1941. USIS offices expanded in the colonies of its allies, while the 1948 Communist coup in Czechoslovakia increased the USSR's influence, since Prague's diplomatic dominance in Africa remained intact.[99]

In the absence of a clear directive from Lisbon, governors such as Carlos Alberto Garcia Alves Roçadas in Cape Verde developed ways to communicate government decisions such as the creation of the *Boletim de Propaganda e informação de Cabo Verde*. In its first issue, Roçadas argued that "the knowledge" he already had of the "Cape Verdean psychology" made him optimistic about the long march to progress. Cabral even published in this first issue and demanded political action to address the long droughts.[100] Lisbon relied on mobile movie vans in Angola to show educational films on crime and "moral" behavior.[101]

In the 1950s, local information officers reimagined their work in developmental terms as they adopted and adapted one another's techniques. The confusing and overlapping set of responsibilities within the French and British bureaucracy made it possible for local posts to ignore directives. Even though the Information Policy Department (IPD) within the Foreign Office (FO) emerged as the principal agency, the variety of institutions effectively ended London's stronghold over local colonial administrations that were setting up information departments of their own.[102] Similarly, the Portuguese and Belgian missionaries, as well as Goris in New York, were given a lot of autonomy. At local posts, then, everyday activities, academic insights, and deeply ingrained assumptions about African audiences not only provided officials with a working

theory for their operation but also informed their attitude vis-à-vis other information services. In 1950, for instance, the UK secretary of state for the colonies,
James Griffith, ordered the colonial authorities to cooperate with USIS because
the United States was setting up posts in Algeria, Egypt, Libya, Morocco, Tunisia, Ethiopia, Kenya, the Union of South Africa, Angola, Nigeria, Liberia, the
Gold Coast, and the Belgian Congo. As competition heated up in 1955, UK information offices opened in Accra, the Port of Spain, Trinidad, Kuala Lumpur,
Lagos, and Kingston. Jean Jurgensen at the Africa section of French foreign affairs also encouraged cooperation, but the Information and Documentation
Center of the Belgian Congo was suspicious of USIS activities in 1949.[103]

In West Africa, information services were forced to reevaluate their methods
when Nkrumah was elected as the "leader of government business" in 1951.[104]
USIA officials believed education produced Africans who were interested in the
outside world, including Jim Crow. USIS information about civil rights in Africa
was therefore not primarily aimed at countering Soviet allegations but sought to
repair the damage to the US image that its own education program was causing.[105] Overcoming the "psychotic concern with the whole issue of race-relations
in America" led Fred Hadsel of the State Department in 1955 to offer the Ford
Foundation, the Carnegie Corporation, and the Phelps-Stokes Fund financial
assistance for their African programs because it would prove the United States
was not using aid as a Cold War weapon.[106] As Kennedy's undersecretary of
state, George Ball, later pointed out, it was "the active participation . . . of nongovernmental, voluntary organizations" that made Africans willing to participate.[107] Personal contacts with Nkrumah in particular were valued not only
because USIS was able to draft his speech of February 1954, in which it was announced that Communists could not be employed by the state, but also and
more importantly because he was the archetypical African leader the USIS
sought to promote in other parts of the continent: a US-educated Black man
who wanted a stable transition to self-government.[108] Furthermore, to exploit
the supposed African susceptibility to manipulation that made the preparation
for democracy necessary in the first place, *American Outlook* published a little
comic called *Did You Know*, which always combined two depictions of trivial
facts, for instance about salmon or the length of the Mississippi river, with a
statement on how India with its "free enterprise technique" was outproducing
"Communist China."[109]

In 1949, these techniques led French ambassador to Ghana Marc Renner
to conclude that USIA was providing "luxurious" but "mediocre" propaganda.
While this "manipulation," as he termed it, was no match for French culture,
he worried about USIS's educational activities. In 1950, conflict erupted with

the US consul in Dakar, Perry Jester, when he sought cooperation with linguist Ibrahim Diop behind the backs of the French, a request Diop utilized to play both parties against each other by informing the already irritated French.[110] At the same time, the Gold Coast Department of Social Welfare and Community Development relied on USIS to do its work, much to the disbelief of the French in Paris, who saw the United States becoming a key provider of social mobility, the foundation of French colonial power. Disney films on health such as *Insects as Carriers of Disease* were ordered without any concern for the potential destabilizing effect. Even when USIS advised against showing the films because audiences had been booing, the Gold Coast cinema officer still purchased them because he believed the limited grasp of African target audiences provided a safeguard against undesirable US ideas.[111]

In the Belgian Congo, conflict and cooperation among information offices was also jump-started by a movie. *King Solomon's Mines*, about a hunter who went looking for a missing adventurer in Africa, became popular in Léopoldville. In 1949, J. Van den Haute, director of the Information and Documentation Center of the Belgian Congo, set sail for London where, together with Kenneth Blackburne of the Central Office of Information (COI), he went door-to-door to talk to each of the sections ranging from film to publishing. He was particularly struck by Projection of Britain, the film program for colonial subjects. After his return, Van den Haute began to focus on film and cooperated with the Centre congolais d'action catholique cinématographique. L. Van Bever, head of the Bureau cinématographique et photographique in the Congo, published a report that warned against "modern movies." Instead, indigenous language film had to be relied on to help Africans distinguish between good and bad. Vice Governor-General Léon Pétillon seized on movies as a means to convey family values and keep Africans from drinking beer. On the ground, however, others discerned challenges beyond moral education. Gerard De Boe, head of the production center who had been sent on a mission to study Congolese audiences, believed many of the movies on offer were simply boring.[112]

USIS officers played on developmental clichés to win over the Belgians. USIS emphasized that the African population had to accept "responsible guidance," because even the more evolved Congolese—*évolué*—were slow, lazy, emotional, and unable to fully comprehend democracy. Once USIS had gained the trust of the colonial authority, in 1953, it could focus on African target audiences and cultivate what it considered to be a wasteland "wide open to any serious cultural activity." The British Council offices had been abandoned after the war, while concerts of Radio Congo Belge and overpriced art exhibitions attracted few visitors.[113] USIS, therefore, employed information that was specifically designed to "influence the African away from half-baked attitudes and toward maturity."[114] The French, like the British, were more hesitant, despite their strategic interests, and waited until 1954 to harmonize the activities of the Alliance Française (AF) in Léopoldville, Luluabourg, Matadi, Élisabethville, Usumbura, Stanleyville, and Bukavu, which up until then had mainly serviced the local French community.[115]

In the aftermath of World War II, the psychological tools of empire were reimagined as development instruments. In the Global South, anticolonial thinkers debated the best way to undo the psychological damage colonialism had inflicted. While the heated inter-African political atmosphere of 1960 would come to pit French Africa against Nkrumah's Pan-Africa, intellectual debates about anticolonial modernity after 1945 show a wide range of tactics, ranging from violence to culture, from a radical break with the metropole to constructing a new relationship between colonizers and colonized. The Global North cultivated a shared diagnosis of African psychological weakness. Truman provided technical assistance to fix myopic nationalism, whereas Eisenhower was committed to education, which allowed him to reconcile his long-term aim of global stability and his short-term willingness to be "on the side of the natives."[116] Churchill, Mendès-France, Salazar, and Spaak understood Eisenhower's far-reaching plans and resisted his requests to put their civilizational discourses into practice. At the same time, French cultural diffusion of political claims, British gifts of an information infrastructure, Portuguese colonial intransigence, Belgian efforts at improving morality, US fostering of citizenship, the Soviet hesitance to intervene, and the anticolonial search for modernity on Africa's terms were all efforts spearheaded by people who learned from one another in an attempt to comprehend the postcolonial order on the horizon. The Communist threat or capitalist menace took a back seat to paternalistically inspired concerns about leadership skills in the Global North and worry over the continuing psychological impact of colonial exploitation in the Global South. The Cold War in the South was not a "continuation" of an imperial international system, started by the Europeans, but part of a search for a better modernity initiated by the Haitian revolutionaries.[117] That quest also came to dominate the Bandung Conference.

CHAPTER 2

Offering Hungry Minds a Better Development Project, 1955–1956

Between 18 and 24 April 1955, Indonesian prime minister Ali Sastroamidjojo welcomed African and Asian delegates to the first Afro-Asian Conference in Bandung. At a meeting in Colombo, Ceylon, in March 1954, the leaders of Burma, Ceylon, India, Indonesia, and Pakistan agreed to organize a gathering, and after deliberations in Bogor in December 1954, invitations were sent out.[1] Here was a turning point in postcolonial international relations, an attempt to create some form of common ideology whereby states in the Global South could obtain a place within the international system and exploit the anticolonial momentum. Bandung was a negotiation structured by hard geopolitical interests and was, according to subaltern theorist Dipesh Chakrabarty, based on a "shallow intellectual unity" leading to disagreement about the definition of "anticolonialism."[2] The Indonesians wanted to heighten their prestige; for the Ceylon foreign affairs ministry, a "color line-up against the Europeans" was vital; while the relationship between the Pakistanis and Jawaharlal Nehru was tense due to the issue of Kashmir. Nehru wanted the People's Republic of China to attend because of a communal border.[3] At the same time, the gathering was an event in the Cold War and a means to generate political capital for the anticolonial struggle through symbolic "theatre."(see figure 2.1)[4]

Interpretations of the Afro-Asian agenda and its impact on international relations are therefore bursting with skepticism about Bandung's symbolism.

FIGURE 2.1.   From left to right, Gamal Abdel Nasser of Egypt, Ethiopian delegate Yilma Deressa, Kojo Botsio of the Gold Coast, and Jawaharlal Nehru of India at the Bandung Conference of 1955. Photo courtesy of the UtConn Collection.

Already in 1955, journalists such as Homer Jack and political scientist George McTurnan Kahin, as well as more activist intellectuals such as Carlos Romulo and Richard Wright, were struck by the meeting's "spiritual" and symbolic dimension but at the same time noted the many different national interests. Work that was written in the late 1960s, by writers such as Indian diplomat turned journalist G. H. Jansen, continued to expose what delegates wanted to achieve in geopolitical terms—what distinguished their stance from traditional neutralism and established the idea that non-alignment had originated at the Bandung Conference and was continued at Belgrade in 1961 and at the Cairo Conference of 1964.[5]

This view of Bandung as having little real influence on diplomacy produced a multitude of myths about the conference in the 1970s and 1980s among postcolonial theorists and activists who latched on to Afro-Asia's anti-imperial vocabulary rather than its historical record. By the 1990s, Cold War historians' interest in ideology led them to see Bandung as a challenge to the bipolar order while disagreeing on the precise nature of that challenge. For some, the construction of "an ethno-racial identity" was key in shoring up solidarity, while others considered the "political position" against oppression, not "racial communalities," to be the source of unity. The "attempts by the former

colonial master to get them to choose sides in the Cold War" in itself supposedly also strengthened the Bandung spirit.[6] For students of intellectual and
legal history, the Bandung spirit is considered a breeding ground for a host of
international norms such as "self-determination" and "human rights."[7] As a
result, Bandung's impact on international relations is still seen as limited to
rhetoric, while historians are called on to get behind the smoke screens that
were drawn up by postcolonial statesmen eager to maximize their interests.[8]

The attempt to pin down the core national interest of attendees and the question whether Bandung constituted a normative contribution to global affairs
actually run counter to the nature of diplomacy in the Global South.[9] Focus on
these issues ignores the strategic thinking of delegates who understood that their
seat at international negotiating tables and the implementation of their program
of internationalism, anti-racism, and development could be realized only if they
replaced colonial development with their own modernization program. Conference attendees were less naive than the journalists and academics who wrote
about them. The demolishment of the civilizing mission was a prerequisite to
any real power in international relations, not simply a glue to sustain the Bandung spirit. At the same time, this two-step approach to a postcolonial international order contained colonial echoes, since many Afro-Asian leaders had been
trained in colonial schools and had partly adopted the colonial administrator's
racial hierarchies, which—more than shifting Cold War allegiances—fed the mistrust between African and Asian delegates. In the Global North, the language of
development lulled politicians to sleep, since they believed delegates were asking
for an improved modernization project. Only with the outbreak of the Suez
Crisis did Dwight D. Eisenhower understand anticolonialism's political valance
and realize that he could not rely on Europeans to prepare Africans for independence. Neither the Cold War nor conflicting state interests "suppressed the
Bandung Spirit." Rather, when Bandung's archival scraps are pieced together,
it is the pursuit of anticolonial modernity that stands out.[10]

The Brown Man's Burden

Bandung's delegates wanted to succeed where the imperial powers had failed
and deliver on the promise of modernity, particularly in those parts of Africa
that were still under colonial rule. Afro-Asian participants consciously viewed
themselves as heirs to the nineteenth-century opponents of European modernity, an ideology that—in the words of Ali Sastroamidjojo—through "steam,
electricity and mechanization" had brought imperialism and war.[11] An anticolonial modernization program that took precolonial culture into account had to

replace the colonial enterprise because Europe, in the words of Frantz Fanon, had "not been able to find the answers" to the challenges that plagued its subjects.[12] In 1955, Aimé Césaire also captured the sentiment that drove the anticolonial development agenda when he mocked Europeans because they bragged about their achievements, which amounted to very little.[13] The speeches and discussions in Bandung drew on debates within postcolonial societies where unique development plans were being drawn up. In India, Nehru wanted to set up his country as an example to others. A planning commission launched the Five-Year Development Plan in 1951 after Gandhians, Nehruvian socialists, and business leaders within the Indian National Congress fought over what *swadeshi*, "economic self-sufficiency," meant.[14] In the Gold Coast, the British Ten-Year Economic Plan was replaced by a new £120-million Five-Year Development Plan. Finance Minister Komla Agbeli Gbedemah invited Arthur Lewis, then an economics professor at Manchester University, to come up with a development strategy better suited to the Gold Coast situation. Lewis not only implored leaders to invest in agriculture but also urged "all African people" to "learn to start and to run things for themselves." The government's development progress report of 1955 indicated that the Gold Coast financial situation was unstable.[15]

As a result, Asian leaders, arriving in the pastel-green Chevrolets and Plymouths commandeered by Sukarno, felt compelled to pick up the "Brown Man's Burden," in the phrase of the Indonesian government's *Asian-African Conference Bulletin*. Instead of playing a colonial trick and using the "progressive realization of self-government" as a means to "soften the reality of exploitation," Asia had to pass on aid and expertise to Africa. The prime minister of Ceylon, John Lionel Kotelawala, claimed newly independent states had a "solemn duty" to offer "knowledge and expertise" to prevent a relapse into "other forms of servitude," while Nehru believed it was up to Asia to help Africa, a continent of "infinite tragedy" and "slavery."[16] An analysis presented to the conference distinguished six groups of countries in the Afro-Asian region with different stages of development, a signal that modernization theory was widely accepted.[17] Moreover, the commitment to aid Africa was sustained by the increased popularity of different notions of Asian unity, which created a countermodel to Pan-Africanism. At the Asian Relations Conference in 1947, Solomon Bandaranaike, a minister from Ceylon, proposed an Asian federation as an alternative to the Japanese-dominated Pan-Asian plans of the interwar period. Nehru had already in 1964 envisioned an Asian alternative to the United Nations and considered the League against Imperialism, established in Brussels in 1927, to be an important antecedent to an Asian union.[18] Bandung's final communiqué therefore listed economic development as Afro-Asia's most urgent priority, while countries pledged to provide technical assistance, exchange know-how, and offer experts.

Educated at British public schools, Nehru and Kotelawala as well as African nationalists believed "self-government" could be granted only after preparation. Nehru viewed Africa as a set of successor states to the Raj, to which India would offer guidance while African leaders sent vans with taped speeches on citizenship into the bush.[19] Afro-Orientalist views, which had already been harbored by Mahatma Gandhi, who believed Indians to be on a higher civilizational plain than Africans, were reinforced in the 1950s as newly created postcolonial countries grappled with separatist sentiments on the part of ethnic minorities.[20] In India, the Naga people claimed nationhood, while British East Africa had a sizable Asian population of whom some were descended from indentured laborers.[21] Frictions with African delegates became unavoidable. While the Ethiopians and the Gold Coast observers stuck to their speeches—with Gold Coast delegate Kojo Botsio proclaiming "the continent" was "shaking itself like a giant from sleep" and Tsehafi Teazaz Aklilu Habte-Wold declaring "the system of collective security" had to be extended to "all peoples"—the Liberians complained about being excluded from the committee work on colonialism. In the words of South African journalist Colin Legum, "the African voice" at Bandung "was mainly Arab." Sastroamidjojo feared his "brothers in colonial territories might reproach us" because their interests were being discussed "in their absence."[22] Despite their criticism of imperialism, Bandung attendees thus still wrestled with the colonial discourse of premature independence.

What made anticolonial development different, however, was the conviction that it could be effective and lead to international influence only if technocracy-driven European modernity was delegitimized as immoral, through a battle for ideas. Delegates referred to "moral strength," a form of power available to those who had suffered the humiliations of colonialism. Statesmanship had to be "based upon the highest code of morality," according to Indonesian president Sukarno. "The voice of reason" had to be injected into world affairs through the mobilization of "all the spiritual, all the moral, all the political strength of Asia and Africa." Moral strength, however, was not simply an alternative to power politics but also indispensable for anticolonial diplomacy to work, since the leaders of newly independent countries had experienced firsthand how other imperial ideologies tended to produce colonial violence. Sukarno found an ally in Iraqi prime minister Muhammad Fadhel al-Jamali, who argued that "physical disarmament" had to include "ideological disarmament" and "moral rearmament" to be effective, a nod to the Moral Rearmament Movement, founded in 1938, which had been popular among anticolonial leaders.[23]

The causal relation between technocracy and violence, not ideological preference, also led delegates to home in on the nuclear dimension of the Cold War. The "progress of nuclear science" had led to the Cold War, which proved "mankind" was "morally" unprepared "for the fruits of its own genius." Kotela-wala's characterization of Soviet influence in Eastern Europe as "another form of colonialism," a line secretly suggested to him by the British ambassador to Indonesia, therefore angered other participants who felt the analogy undercut the bigger shared project of moral strength. The East-West struggle was defined as another sprout on the tree of European modernity, on which imperialism had already bloomed and needed to be cut off. Nehru gave the Ceylon delegate the cold shoulder at the Gold Coast party, forcing him to mince words a day later.[24] Like Toussaint Louverture, Africans and Asians felt compelled to respond to technocracy-driven modernity with novel ideologies and a new universal morality. As Indian political scientists Angadipuram Appadorai and conference attendees pointed out, a "so-called realistic appreciation of the world situation," "on the basis of which alignment with a power bloc had been justified," was in fact "not so realistic, as it had only led them to the brink of a world war." "Self-reliance" provided the only "real source of strength."[25]

Besides an enduring critique at the center of anticolonial diplomacy, moral force was also a method to mobilize support through rhetorical appeals, a call to action, and a promise of an increased international stature. Nehru, in particular, operated in each of those dimensions.[26] Nehru considered a meeting where leaders could come to agreements after tiring discussions as an act of defiance in the face of the civilizing mission. In his closing speech he called to mind an Asia that was—"with integrity"—on an equal footing with Europe, no longer populated by "yes-men," a statement that received thunderous applause.[27] The Indian prime minister sought to claim international leadership on the basis of five principles he labeled *Panchsheel*: respect for sovereignty, nonaggression, noninterference, equality and mutual benefit, and peaceful coexistence.[28] In his conversation with Mao Zedong, Nehru indicated as much when he declared "we two countries have a more important purpose in Asia."[29] Strikingly enough, observers in the Global North understood the moral strength approach. R. W. Parkes, counsellor at the British embassy in Djakarta, believed Bandung participants had been swayed by "vital, hopeful" words. He assumed Nehru and his colleagues wanted to be acknowledged as equals, writing how "the East" was "young, eager, drunk with new nationalism and freedom" and "anxious to behave with maturity."[30] Portuguese diplomats discerned an Afro-Asian mystique, something the British embassy in Djakarta also noticed when it was wrongly rumored the Colombo powers had been instrumental for the Dien Bien Phu armistice of 1954. The Belgian ambassador to Indonesia, Willy Stevens, in contrast, believed Bandung mainly served as a distraction from the secession of West New Guinea in 1949.[31]

Even though leaders from the Indian National Congress invited delegations from other countries to study India's technology and education system, the delegates never worked out a systematic approach to assist Africa.[32] The "Brown Man's Burden" became arguably more important as a focal point for policymakers in Washington, Moscow, Paris, London, Brussels, Lisbon, and Accra. In the Gold Coast, where Kwame Nkrumah was rethinking the political valance of Pan-Africanism, Nehru, Gamal Abdel Nasser, and Sukarno became not standard bearers of a new anticolonial international order but competitors in an ideological scramble for Africa. In the French and British imperial imagination, Asian powers were seen as eager to replace Europe. The French ambassador to Djakarta claimed Asia wanted "influence over the affairs of Africa," while the governor of Algeria, Marcel-Edmond Naegelen, talked about the "incompatabilité" between Islam and Asia, assessments Foreign Office official William Allen agreed with as he gleaned from press reports that Asians considered themselves as "champions of the Africans against the white man." The UK representative in Kathmandu wired London that the use of the term "Afro-Asian" was disliked because it made Africans proud.[33] Belgian and Portuguese officials believed the Afro-Asian "seeds of disagreement" gave them a strategic advantage.[34] USSR officials and Czechoslovak diplomats considered Afro-Asian disorganization to be an opportunity to export the Communist model. Even civil rights activist Richard Wright heard the clarion call of development and appealed to the Western-educated elites of Asia and Africa to accept aid and technology, while characterizing Asian and African participants at Bandung as a "gummy mass."[35]

Nonetheless, the accusation that empires had used aid as a pretext for exploitation struck a sensitive chord in the Global North. Before Sukarno had uttered a single word, countries outside of Asia fretted over Bandung's PR implications. After the Bogor meeting of December 1954, British secretary of state for the colonies Alan Lennox-Boyd had wanted to dissuade African territories from participating, even as the Colonial Office warned that African leaders who refused an invitation would be seen as "stooges of the West." Doubts about the most effective strategy lingered until January 1955, when the French informed the Foreign Office that they would bar their colonial elite from going. When, in that same month, the US State Department backtracked on its decision to encourage participation, something Belgium also supported, the British asked Nkrumah to not set sail for Indonesia.[36]

During a State Department meeting, it was clear that no one knew how to respond because Bandung presented, in the words of John Foster Dulles, "interesting problems": the US had to confront Soviet allegations without being accused of exporting the Cold War, a key criticism of the delegates in Indonesia. An Afro-Asian working group led by William Lacy, US ambassador to Korea, recommended that officials stay in touch with allies but information officers not be sent into the field.[37] Much to the irritation of the State Department, the Operations Coordinating Board (OCB)—which had been created by Eisenhower to match high-level policy with public diplomacy operations—disagreed and established a working group to foster "Free World awareness" and put the Soviets on the defensive. Charles Douglas Jackson, Eisenhower's psychological strategy adviser, spearheaded the effort because he believed Bandung would amount to little, making it an ideal venue not only for "earth-wide racial reconciliation" but also for rejecting Soviet allegations about US imperialism. Jackson wanted to announce an economic plan for Asia, express sympathy for the democratic development of Africa and Asia, and avoid the appearance of US interference by making India the dominant power instead of the PRC. Jackson's suggestions made it into a factual booklet that had to avoid the appearance of interference, a consideration that triggered Nelson Rockefeller to abandon his proposal for a presidential speech and Dulles to cancel a press conference.[38]

These debates a few weeks before Bandung capture the duality of the US stance on Afro-Asianism. Officials at the NSC and the State Department considered colonialism and peaceful coexistence to be the two major propaganda challenges of the 1950s and the long-term attitudes of African peoples to be key in unlocking the continent.[39] At the same time, Eisenhower and Vice President Richard Nixon could not bring themselves to see the Bandung participants as legitimate interlocutors. Eisenhower sarcastically signaled that he considered recently independent peoples to be unprepared for the world stage by remarking "facetiously" that the US could best handle the situation by handing out a few thousand dollars to each of the delegates and approving any method "up to but not including assassination of the hostile delegates."[40] Eisenhower did not want to physically eliminate Bandung participants, nor was the potential to win goodwill ignored. On the contrary, the US attitude sprang from the intuition that the only effective approach had to be indirect to avoid the accusation that the US was exporting the Cold War to the Global South. The South African ambassador to Washington, Wentzel du Plessis, agreed, believing that "fighting aggressive communism" would be "seen by the masses merely as a cloak to disguise . . . the perpetuation of Western rule."[41] On 28 February 1955, the US missions abroad were therefore instructed to cooperate with the British; the head of the Philippine delegation, Carlos Romulo, was encouraged to voice pro-US views; and US journalists were asked to report on the conference.[42]

UK minister of state for the colonies Henry Hopkinson agreed. The Afro-Asian meeting was a "bogus affair" but damaging for the British image because of the Bandung organizers' obsession with publicity. The Foreign Office, with State Department approval, therefore supported the conference publicly as it worked to prevent the attendance of leaders of Ghana and the Federation of Rhodesia and Nyasaland. Whitehall approved a behind-the-scenes approach in January 1955, believing that the promotion of justifications for colonial rule would be ineffective. Resolutions unfavorable to British interests, as well as the emergence of an Afro-Asian bloc, had to be prevented, while Communism was to be discredited.[43] Nkrumah exploited those uncertainties by telling Charles Arden-Clarke, the governor of the Gold Coast, that he wanted to send a representative who could provide an antidote to anticolonialism by speaking up for the UK treatment of the Gold Coast.[44]

The Gold Coast leader publicly abided by British demands but secretly tried to acquire influence.[45] Nkrumah tested the waters by allowing Gbedemah to publish an article on a plan to establish diplomatic ties with other countries, a violation of the agreement with the United Kingdom, which had left the governor in charge of external affairs. When the British believed Nkrumah's story—that Gbedemah had acted as a lone ranger—the Gold Coast leader knew he had enough leeway to act independently. In a letter to Nehru that had not been approved by the governor, Nkrumah not only stated that London had barred him from going but also wrote about how much he would appreciate a meeting between Botsio and Nehru. In his approved letter to Sastroamidjojo, however, Nkrumah did not mention meetings. On his return, Michael Francis Dei-Anang informed Arden-Clarke that he had been interested in what was going on behind the scenes but assured the governor's secretary that he had not participated.[46] Eric Kwame Heymann, the editor of the state-sanctioned *Ghana Evening News*, toed the official line when reporting that "the epochal embrace of two continents at Bandung" would "buttress inter-racial solidarity."[47]

The French, for their part, assessed Bandung in light of the loss of Indochina and the possible diplomatic recognition of the Algerian Front de Libération Nationale (FLN). The French colonial tradition of *assimilation* led officials to underestimate the Gold Coast's diplomatic skill, turning Botsio's visit to Nigeria into nothing more than a recreational trip. Since the French were convinced Africans would come to see the Afro-Asian problem as the French did—in terms of the Asian hunger for prestige—they were more concerned with the meeting's supposed attempt to attach Africa to Asia and its effects on overpopulation.[48] A French intelligence officer who had labeled Bandung the beginning of the end for the white race found few kindred spirits at the foreign ministry.[49] The envoy whom Edgar Faure's government had sent to Karachi, New Delhi, Rangoon, Bangkok, and Saigon in mid-March concluded after a conversation with Nehru that much of the anxiety was unfounded and had been fueled by the defeat in Dien Bien Phu. Even the minister of France d'outre-mer, Pierre-Henri Teitgen, who was generally more alarmist about anticolonial activity, was not worried.[50] The fact that the British Foreign Office concluded the opposite, despite being told by the French ambassador that analyzing the African-Asian connection was a waste of time and African participation "made little sense either on geographical or ideological grounds," reveals deep-seated fears harbored by UK officials.[51] The French ambassador to Singapore saw how British embassy personnel struggled to understand an initiative they feared could increase hostility toward the West.[52]

British fears about colonial collapse contrast with the Belgians and Portuguese focus on the balance of power. Belgian ambassadors viewed anticolonialism as merely an expression of realist power politics because Roussel's popular book had concluded Third World elites had "an urge to rule"—"heerszucht"—and lie.[53] Even though the chargé d'affaires in India, Louis de San, expected Bandung to have little to no impact, he still wanted to track preparations because a "new order against the West" would add to the "dynamism" of anticolonial resistance.[54] Willy Stevens, the ambassador to Indonesia, therefore immediately barred the "Ligue internationale des droits de l'homme du Ruanda-Urundi" from going.[55] Portuguese foreign affairs minister Paulo Cunha entertained similarly worries about the impact of Bandung on Goa, which was still held by Portugal and suspended diplomatic relations with India in 1955.[56] Local officials in Goa therefore struggled to contain the anti-Portuguese propaganda pamphlets and public manifestations where "Gandhi caps were prominent." The Portuguese informant in Goa suggested the distribution of pamphlets to show "them they are in the great heart of their Portugal."[57] Eisenhower, struggling to fit Portuguese decolonization into his gradualist approach, asked Nehru to "defer" the issue of Goa but also to "do something."[58]

In the background, Nikita Khrushchev, Viacheslav Molotov, and Georgii Malenkov began to realize there were opportunities for alliances with the Global South, while their colleagues in the German Democratic Republic (GDR) were optimistic about Bandung despite Nehru's proclamation that the division of Germany was "an imminent danger to the peace."[59] Already in 1954, the Belgian ambassador to Moscow understood the fervor with which Indonesian and Indian dancers were welcomed in Stalingrad as a sign of the new wind that was blowing through the USSR.[60] In February 1955, Molotov launched a "special appeal to the uncommitted peoples of Asia and Africa" in his speech to the Supreme Soviet, and in April 1955, Nasser met with Daniil Solod, the Soviet ambassador to Cairo, to close an arms deal.[61] Civil servants from Prague delivered the weapons in September after a secret "Action 105" deal was signed, but were unhappy with the unsavory consequences of the new "unhygienically prepared" diet.[62] The PRC Foreign Ministry, in contrast, remained steadfast in its claim that Indonesia was acting out of strategic self-interest, with Bandung offering an opportunity to "raise its international status, consolidate the existing government and win political capital for the Nationalist Party of Indonesia." The Chinese propaganda strategy took the United States as the "main target of attack," and diplomatic cadres who were "good at socialization and diplomatic knowledge" were sent to Bandung.[63]

When reports from Indonesia arrived, Northern observers breathed a sigh of relief. The so-called inexperience of the Bandung participants had not led to anticolonial anger or a propaganda disaster. Khrushchev was "not impressed" by "Zhou Enlai and Sukarno" and concluded that Nehru was "not a Marxist."[64] The official Soviet press criticized participants for still being influenced by imperialists.[65] In Portugal, Cunha was relieved no specific reference to Goa or Macao had been made, while the ministry of foreign affairs believed African leaders' "position of inferiority" toward Asia benefited Lisbon's position.[66] The Belgian Foreign Affairs Ministry was pleased its colonial project had not been subjected to mud-slinging, while the consul in Lagos reported that Black Africa remained unaffected by events in Indonesia.[67] French civil servants in Africa were informed they had correctly predicted that Africans were not "sufficiently evolved" to comprehend international affairs. In the eyes of Jacques Roux, director of the Ministry of Foreign Affairs' Asia and Oceania section, Bandung mattered less for its anticolonialism than for its geopolitical impact. Zhou Enlai's proposal to negotiate over Formosa had diminished Nehru's position, something Roux was happy about.[68]

Anglo-American officials worried more about Bandung's symbolism but agreed their pre-conference alarmism had been overblown. "Free world principles" had been endorsed and pro-Communist statements avoided, while the State Department predicted the UN would increasingly be utilized in an ideological struggle to force the issue of decolonization.[69] Francis Cumming-Bruce, who advised the Gold Coast governor on external affairs, concluded the delegation had behaved in an exemplary fashion after a conversation with Dei-Anang, who kept his informal contacts hidden. The embassy in Djakarta was happy the delegates from British colonies had proved themselves to be successful products of the British civilizing mission with their "command of English." The Gold Coast party, organized jointly with the British Council in Djakarta, was further cited as evidence. Guests such as Nehru and his daughter had been joined by Kotelawala, Indian diplomat Krishna Menon, Sudanese prime minister Ismail al-Azhari, and Lebanese, Indonesian, Liberian and Ethiopian officials to view a short film on the recent elections to publicize colonialism's benevolence.[70]

When Northern observers sat down to dissect the Afro-Asian speeches in more detail they came to a remarkable conclusion: the Bandung delegates had not rejected colonial guidance but had complaints about the quality of the economic assistance they had received. As a result, foreign aid doctrines were rewritten, something commentators in the 1950s overlooked. When they walked the halls of the Gedung Merdeka, the art deco conference building, Unitarian clergyman and pacifist Homer Jack, historian George Kahin, and diplomats such as Carlos Romulo had been struck by the bold refusal to go along with the Cold War. Their fixation on Afro-Asia's new morality led historians to conclude that the meeting hardly affected the Global North.[71] However, this assessment ignores how, in the Northern imagination, Bandung transformed from an issue of anticolonial resistance into a development problem. Colonial subjects had to be convinced that the imperial powers and the superpowers were still able to provide assistance.

On 30 April, only six days after Bandung's closing session, Léopold Senghor, deputy of Senegal and minister responsible for international cultural matters in Faure's government, informed foreign affairs minister Antoine Pinay about his plan to visit Nigeria, Sierra Leone, and the Gold Coast. Bandung, Senghor claimed, offered an opportunity to revitalize African culture, and with his trip he wanted to examine new ways to combine French and African culture to accelerate African progress.[72] Senghor's combination of French and African culture, codified by *Négritude*, which he had pioneered together with Césaire as a way to reaffirm "Black" values, art, and culture that the French civilizing mission had sought to repress. Through poetry, written in French, Senghor deliberately attempted to counter the claimed universalism of French culture with his own claim to universalism for Black culture.[73] In November and December 1955, Khrushchev and USSR prime minister Nikolai Bulganin traveled India, Burma, and Afghanistan, motivated in part by the success of Zhou's diplomacy. Despite the bourgeois character of many of the leaders Khrushchev met, the lingering potential for anti-imperialist struggle had to be exploited, and more appealing propaganda magazines had to be produced. Khrushchev's denunciation of Stalin ushered in a period of relative openness, allowing for large numbers of Soviet citizens to interact with African elites.[74] Even Khrushchev thus adopted a strategy of improved foreign aid, which mirrored his ambition to create a Communist model capable of increasing living standards.[75] As Vladislav Zubok writes in his classic *A Failed Empire*, "there was a new stake in economic cooperation and trade."[76]

The Soviets' Anglo-American colleagues, in contrast, did not feel the need to study the situation on the ground and implemented policy changes more quickly. Two days before the end of the conference on 22 April, Andrew Berding, officer in the Bureau of Public Affairs of the State Department, sent around a paper that argued that Communism had been successful in identifying itself with nationalism in African because of the European presence. The best way to "use" "nationalistic emotions" and improve postcolonial governmental structures, therefore, was to expand educational programs that foregrounded "democratic techniques." The significance of Afro-Asian aspirations in the realm of diplomacy, however, was harder to pin down. In May 1956, US embassies were instructed to refrain from taking a stance until the seriousness of Afro-Asianism could be established. The British, in their turn, increased funding for the British Council in 1956, at the expense of services with a more pronounced PR objective such as the Central Office of Information (COI). Foreign Affairs Minister Anthony Eden revived a plan from 1954 to propagate the notion of British colonial service, create goodwill, and reduce discontent about the poor quality of aid.[77] The benefits of imperialism had to be promoted in a joint effort with the French, leading British officials to add an "appreciative reference" to their planned UN statement.[78] A Colonial Office pamphlet concluded that both French and British colonialism wanted what was "beneficial and most acceptable to the people." To avoid the impression that the United Kingdom was outperforming France, information offices were instructed to produce newsreels about less laudatory colonial episodes such as the Mau Mau.[79] This led a confused director of information in Nairobi to demand a meeting because he felt the stories he received on Malaya, Cyprus, and French North Africa were creating an impression of colonial chaos.[80]

The Belgians agreed with the assessment of their European colleagues: Bandung's delegates had realized that economic aid from "the West" was "necessary," despite their attempts to forge a "kind of new liberation from the clutches of the West."[81] Yet, the threat level was considered low. Internal divisions had, in the words of ambassador Geoffroy d'Asper, turned the official communiqués into "a Harlequin dress" of "mismatched pieces." Afro-Asian disagreement also put Portuguese officials at ease. Despite nervousness in neighboring Spain about Rabat's claims on the Spanish possessions in the Sahara, no strategic changes were made.[82]

With the exception of Portugal, the Belgians, French, British, Soviets, and Americans thus understood Afro-Asian political aspirations as a call for better developmental aid. This shared understanding of aid in the North led Dulles to contact the British chancellor of the exchequer, Harold Macmillan, who wanted to replace his government's obscure statements about colonialism with a sustained propaganda effort. The British ambassador to Washington, Lord Halifax, had told Dulles's predecessor in August 1941 that a charter on Britain's colonial responsibilities was being drafted.[83] Dulles now returned to that idea by proposing a "Bandung in reverse": a conference where the colonial powers would announce a development plan that could lead to self-determination.[84]

The speeches in Indonesia made Nkrumah ambivalent about Afro-Asian cooperation. Together with George Padmore, Nkrumah wanted to avoid a scenario in which European guidance would be supplanted by Asian and Indian paternalism, and he therefore proposed a "conference to match Bandung on an African scale" where Asians would be observers and Africans would take the lead.[85] At that meeting, the Conference of Independent African States (CIAS) of April 1958, Nkrumah clarified that condescending remarks toward Africa were coming not only from Europe and the United States but also from India and Egypt. The Thames, the Ganges, and the Mississippi, Nkrumah narrated; he laughed and cried out "Africa! Africa! Why? Nile, why don't you go to some place worthwhile? Why don't you stay at home where you belong?"[86] In 1966, while in exile in Conakry, he made this point again: "Internationalism must presuppose Asia for Asians, Africa for Africans." As Nkrumah stressed, "these peoples" had to "see to their own problems," a stance that did not "smack of racism or racialism."[87] Africa's problems would be most effectively solved not with Afro-Asianism but by establishing an African union under Ghanaian leadership. Nkrumah therefore sent a delegation from his own Convention People's Party (CPP), rather than government officials, to Nasser's Cairo Conference in 1957. Homer Jack, who attended the All-African People's Conference (AAPC) in December 1958, found Cold War tensions were only "painted in very pastel tones," while the "ideological battles" between Nkrumah and Nasser and the "tension between the Afro-Asian Solidarity Council and the All-African People's Conference" set the tone.[88] Indian diplomat Subimal Dutt hoped "the emergence of an African personality would not stand in the way of Asian-African cooperation" at the AAPC.[89] Dei-Anang captured the mood when he stated that Nkrumah's politics "after Bandung" could "only be understood in the general context of his African interests."[90] Abbott Washburn more cynically believed Nkrumah was driven by a "lust to strengthen his leadership."[91] The suspicion toward an anticolonial ally seems surprising but is in line with Nkrumah's conviction that "the African was perfectly capable of governing himself." Any type of dependence on others outside of the continent was "part of an imperialistic plan to perpetuate" "economic exploitation."[92] This sentiment made the South Africans anxious and was partly adopted in Ethiopia, where writer Käbbädä Mikael, who became director-general of education in 1956, urged the Ethiopian political elite to embrace the Pan-African cause and no longer imitate Europe.[93]

With the exception of Portugal, Bandung prompted officials in the Global North to renew their commitment to development assistance while weakening the solidarity between the African and Asian components of Third Worldism.

A Question of Aid

This promise to feed hungry minds led to heated debates over the transformative power of economic assistance. Why did a fiscal conservative such as Eisenhower push for aid while at the same time assistance to Africa—less than 2 percent of the total US economic assistance abroad in 1956—remained low?[94] Eisenhower's understanding of Soviet foreign policy, free-market commitment, the fear of encouraging permanent dependence on US aid, and bureaucratic infighting have all been cited as possible explanations.[95] Soviet aid and propaganda to Africa have been characterized as poorly "adapted to local realities," aimed at ideologically transforming societies and used as a way to engage in international trade to obtain raw materials the Soviet economy needed.[96] Likewise, the scholarship on French, British, Belgian, and Portuguese aid has ignored the developmental ambition of public diplomacy, making it difficult to understand how French language teaching, British educational work, Belgian film, or Portuguese basic education were expected to transform colonial societies. French public diplomacy has been characterized as "schizophrenic," while other European cultural efforts in Africa are mentioned only in passing.[97]

All the while, the question whether officials could distinguish nationalism from Communism loomed large.[98] South African ambassador du Plessis, for one, did not believe "the cause of our troubles . . . is communism purely and simply." Rather, the "desire towards self-expression" was more important.[99] For Eisenhower, nationalism—a positive force if leaders were prepared—and Communism were interrelated but ultimately separate challenges. People were "not necessarily thinking in terms of opposing concepts of communistic dictatorship and of human rights."[100] USIS officers were unhappy with this emphasis on the modernizing potential of US ideas and demanded a clear anti-Soviet strategy. USIS Léopoldville used English classes to counter the USSR's anticolonial appeal, while a group of US information officers publicized the resolution against colonialism that had been proposed in Congress to boost the United States' anticolonial credentials.[101] It was therefore the International Cooperation Administration rather than the USIA that took the wheel, giving rise to an enduring conflict between the USIA's PR-minded officials and ICA's technical "how-to-do-it" personnel.[102] The only operatives who credited the Soviet Union with influence in Africa were to be found in the British Foreign Office, which tried to convince the Colonial Office that the "Bandung label" was a way to mask Communism and that Egypt was a "bridge" for Soviet intrusion. Assistant Undersecretary Charles Carstairs of the Colonial Office was annoyed by the Foreign Office's insistence on a "Russian drive" in Black Africa but especially irritated by French talk about Soviet intrusion.[103] In April 1956, French officials raised their concerns with Gladwyn Jebb, the British ambassador to Paris, even though the French threat analysis had revealed that there was no Communist influence in Accra. By feeding the British anxiety, the French sought to contain Nkrumah and Fenner Brockway, chairman of the Movement for Colonial Freedom.[104]

The primacy of the nationalist threat increasingly began to center on one man: Nasser. Senghor, who came from a country with a majority Muslim population, believed a confrontation could "no longer be avoided," since Pan-Arabism and FLN public diplomacy were undermining French prestige.[105] Angola's governor-general banned photographs of Nasser in newspapers because they were put up in homes as a form of anti-Portuguese defiance.[106] The Belgian ambassador to Cairo, Harold Eeman, viewed Nasser as a power-hungry imperialist. This trope of the "anticolonial leader as imperialist" was popular because anti-Arabism dovetailed with the Belgian empire's foundational myth: the story of Arab slave drivers' expulsion from the Congo by Leopold II.[107] The UK Colonial Office's Africa division, like the State Department, admitted that its efforts were directed against Nasser, not Communist infiltration. All the while, other officials in the United States and the USSR viewed Nasser as a possible ally.[108]

To forcefully respond to Nasser's challenge, policymakers wanted to increase the quality of their assistance. Investigations were launched to isolate the factor that made aid programs work. Senghor flew to Ikeja in Nigeria on 11 October 1955, where he was whisked into a car to see the football game between Abidjan and Lagos as journalists wrote about his cosmopolitan figure. Officially, Senghor visited British West Africa to study the educational activities of the CD&W scheme, while his real mission, the export of French language education, was kept secret. Senghor wanted to reinvigorate the link between French and African cultures to jump-start modernization.[109] He believed that "spiritual" and "cultural independence" were necessary preconditions for other forms of independence, but cautioned against conflating the "Bourgeois exploitation" of Africa—which had a European face—with European "civilizational" benefits such as the Latin alphabet.[110] French language education in particular was important since it facilitated the study of science and increased the social mobility of lower classes, who would, like the elites, be able to familiarize themselves with France, which was a "terre d'imagination."[111] Senghor's interpretation of Négritude as a civilizational instrument allowed all members of the French bureaucracy to maintain their own understanding of what French cultural diplomacy was supposed to achieve, from Pinay's emphasis on the economic value of cultural centers to the excitement of the Direction générale des relations culturelles about an enlargement of the information operation.[112] French prestige, science, and the societal model were for Senghor gears in the machine of African modernity, since overcoming ignorance not only entailed learning to read

and count but also required transforming Africans from a "condition of produc-
ers" into a "social function."[113] The DGRC therefore added "technique" to its
name and became the Direction générale des affaires culturelles et techniques
(DGACT).

Eisenhower's doctrine on nationalism and aid was laid out on May 25, 1956,
in a speech at Baylor University. If a stable, prosperous world was to emerge, he
cautioned, other peoples had to become like those in the United States. Strengthening the "Free World" required satisfying "the hunger for knowledge," since
many "cultures," despite being "ancient and rich in human values," lacked the
"needed education."[114] This belief in civic education was rooted in a Wilsonian
brand of internationalism, whereby military or economic intervention could be
effective only if a "community of interests" was established, because the spread
of US values was equated with security.[115] Using civic education to strengthen
postcolonial citizenship distinguished Eisenhower from Truman, who had relied
on technical assistance to project the "benefits of scientific advances."[116] Wilsonianism was also important to John Foster Dulles, who, during a conversation
with du Plessis, sped out of the room to fetch a poster with one of Wilson's
quotes to underscore the importance of gradually ending Apartheid. Du Plessis
saw this as sign of support.[117] Yet, anticolonial voices understood Eisenhower's
message as backing the liberationist cause. The Indonesian ambassador to London, Raden Supomo, also claimed "peoples" were "all too often mentally
starved," "not only physically hungry."[118]

Since US modernity was believed to be nonideological, there were no guarantees that new nations would choose capitalism as their route to modernity.
"Who was going to have title and ownership over these plants which had been
built with US funds?" Secretary of Defense Charles Wilson asked in 1954. "If
the ultimate owner was the state," Wilson believed he would be paving the
road to Communism. When Allen Dulles concluded that the Soviet Union was
attempting to increase its influence in the underdeveloped world, the question of how to provide economic aid without kindling unrest became more
pressing.[119] NSC Policy 162/2 hinted at a solution in 1953 by concluding that
"economic assistance alone" could not be counted on to win over the "uncommitted areas."[120] After 1955, education therefore became Eisenhower's central foreign policy tool, because "whoever brings the African education has the
power to influence him."[121] Clarence Randall—Eisenhower's Africa expert and
chairman of the Commission on Foreign Economic Policy—agreed and opposed the use of aid disbursements because of the lack of control over the
use of funds. Randall identified the construction of educational facilities as the
most urgent need, considered the Gold Coast to be an ideal host country, and
demanded an increase of support for missionary schools.[122]

British and Belgian officials improved the quality of their education programs in response to indications of external ideological influence. Francis Cumming-Bruce, who had been pleased with the Gold Coast delegation's attitude at Bandung, a year later told Anthony Eden that he expected the Gold Coast to slide into chaos after independence if not enough British officers remained, an opinion shared by David E. Apter, the first political scientist who worked on Ghana in 1955. Similarly, in Kenya, unrest was not viewed as making claims, but as "brief flurries of anger after a few drinks of tembo."[123] Long-term educational programs were expanded, and teaching in British Council buildings sought to convince as many Africans as possible to learn English, resulting in increased development and the projection of British values.[124] At the same time, the Colonial Office established a countersubversion committee in Accra, which officially worked to keep Communist publications out but actually sought to counter Nasser to avoid a resurgence of unrest such as the protests of 1954 in the Gold Coast against the cocoa pricing scheme.[125] In Belgium, Jef Van Bilsen published his *Thirty-Year Plan for the Political Emancipation of Belgian Africa* in December 1955. Unlike the *colons* in the Belgian Congo, who were unconcerned after the successful visit by King Baudouin that same year, Van Bilsen lamented the lack of a clear colonial doctrine. Only after a group of Catholic Congolese *évolués* had published their *Manifeste de conscience africaine* and Joseph Kasavubu of the Alliance des Bakongos (ABAKO) had rejected Van Bilsen's plan, in July and August 1956, did the Banque Belge d'Afrique send Paul van Zeeland to investigate. Van Zeeland argued that the cause for the unrest could be found in Belgians straying from their original development task and importing political conflict. The quality of aid therefore had to be improved.[126]

Besides quality, old empires also tried to rely on nonstate actors to heighten the technocratic appearance of their assistance. Smaller empires, driven by cost considerations, actively invested in nongovernmental cooperation. Missionaries had always acted as agents of the Belgian and Portuguese states, but when a cultural palace was constructed in Léopoldville, the work was entrusted to a nonprofit that aimed to stimulate the arts. People such as Pierre Wigny, former minister of the colonies, and William Ugeux, director of the Office de l'information et des relations publiques pour le Congo Belge et le Ruanda-Urundi, created in 1955, were members of the nonprofit's board.[127] Larger empires entrusted nonstate actors with their operations but had more difficulty with handing over control. The interterritorial conference of France d'outre-mer in Fort-Lamy, for instance, ignored Senghor's recommendations as well as the actions of schoolteachers such as Thomas Boateng, a French teacher in the Gold Coast, who had arranged an excursion to Abidjan in cooperation with the Ivory Coast educational services and the consul in Accra.

Instead, press publications and films in Arabic were funded to counter the Egyptian, Soviet, and US output. Similarly, at the conference of Black writers and artists in September 1956, officials of France d'outre-mer paced the floor, worrying about Diop's alleged ties with so-called extremist groups, while DGRC operatives threw a cocktail party.[128] Disputes about how to keep a check on nonstate activities also arose among British officials. Inspired by the Alliance Française's support for French schools, Westminster increased funding for the British Council in 1955. Better training programs for secondary school teachers and headmasters were offered and grants for schools overseas expanded.[129] Yet, UK ambassadors turned to cooperation with the United States to bring down costs. The British Broadcasting Corporation (BBC) wanted to join forces with the Voice of America, while Richard Turnbull, who had dealt with the Mau Mau, called on the US consul to Kenya, Edmund J. Dorsz, to counteract the Swahili broadcasts of Radio Cairo and All India Radio.[130]

Cold War empires, in contrast, embraced nonstate actors as crucial intermediaries between them and the Global South because nonstate actors lessened the Cold War threat perception. In May 1955, the Soviet Union established the Afro-Asian Solidarity Committee, a nonstate initiative that engaged in cultural activities in order to "smooth" over "the official overtones of our propaganda."[131] In October 1956, the US government explored different options to coordinate and fund private organizations while avoiding direct involvement, so as not to raise audiences' suspicion.[132] A conference at Baylor University in December 1956 therefore sought to give substance to Eisenhower's commencement address by stressing attention to basic education as a means to "study this body of principles and . . . teach it to others . . . in Asia and Africa."[133] The cooperation between the State Department and private foundations, through for instance the Institute for International Education, was executed in the spirit of Baylor. The ICA regional director for Africa, Marcus Gordon, aspired to create "productive citizens," while establishing stable institutions was what motivated the Bureau of International Cultural Relations.[134] Eisenhower's reliance on private organizations has been interpreted as a sign of lack of interest in Africa, despite Randall's insistence to keep "pushing for democratic ideals" via teacher and vocational training that could give sub-Saharan Africa "a real chance for free government." It was precisely the "voluntary organizations," Kennedy's undersecretary of state George Ball later argued, that made educational exchange successful. The intricacies of nonstate involvement as well as the debate among officials at USIA and ICA about the relationship between PR and development became contested issues in the foreign aid debate of the 1950s.[135]

On 26 July 1956, when tanks appeared on the banks of the Nile after Nasser's decision to nationalize the Suez Canal, the consensus among Northern public diplomats that the quality of cultural assistance and the hidden hand of the state were paramount crumbled. US officials realized that effective cultural assistance had to be about more than technocratic fine-tuning and had to be clearly distinguishable from the French and British, who had invaded Suez ostensibly to eject Israeli occupiers. What became painfully clear was that "Free World" cooperation in Africa had its limits. Eisenhower's plan to equip Africans with the ideas required to build a stable democracy was incompatible with the British and French use of cultural assistance to reaffirm their position.[136] Eisenhower therefore reaffirmed his commitment to an orderly transition in the most theatrical way possible. In an address before a joint session of Congress on 5 January 1957, he asked Congress to pass a resolution authorizing him to pledge increased economic and military aid. Eisenhower wanted to prevent the Soviets from filling the vacuum the British left behind in the Middle East. At the same time, the so-called Eisenhower doctrine also sought to contain Nasser's Arab nationalism, as Salim Yaqub has convincingly argued. Even though Eisenhower felt "these Arabs" were unable to understand ideas of freedom, he still encouraged Arab unity.[137] John Foster Dulles stowed away his "Bandung in reverse" proposal and instead impressed on other NSC members that they would need to decide whether "the future lies with a policy of reasserting by force colonial control" or whether the United States would "oppose such a course of action."[138]

The USIA impressed on local operatives that they had to stress that the United States resolutely opposed colonialism in order to "implement the Eisenhower doctrine psychologically," since its reception had been mixed. Charles Lucet, the chargé d'affaires of the French embassy in Washington, understood that the doctrine carried the seed of a long-term US development effort in sub-Saharan Africa.[139] Sudanese foreign minister Sayed Muhammad Ahmad Maghoub, in contrast, viewed the doctrine through the Cold War lens and made clear he was "not interested in carrying out either a war or a cold war against any country."[140] South Africa benefited from the Suez Crisis, since trade ships had to pass through the Cape route, but du Plessis feared Afro-Asian politicians such as Sukarno would weaponize the crisis by organizing a second Bandung to show solidarity with Egypt.[141]

More fundamentally, Suez led Eisenhower to develop a three-pronged critique of the progressive aid doctrine. He disagreed with the Economic Cooperation Administration director, Paul Hoffman, who believed the encroachment of Soviet aid could be stopped only if it was matched by a US offer that had no "strings," since allies who could be bought were unreliable.[142] Rather than agreeing with traditionalists such as Treasury Secretary George Humphrey, who saw foreign aid as a short-term security measure, or radical progressives such as Walt Rostow, who seized on aid to improve global living conditions,

Eisenhower suggested a third way. First, the president argued that "neither ed-ucation or mutual aid" in itself sufficed. "Only in their unity" would "we find the strength necessary to do what we need to do." Aid grants could serve as an engine for development only if it had "strings." So-called underdeveloped peoples had to be instilled with a "true desire for individual freedom" to "per-suade them permanently to our way of life." Eisenhower did not believe, as Rostow would later argue, that US values could be grasped solely through the outcome of aid programs. Second, Eisenhower questioned the transformative power of aid. The United States could not simply export the success of its own development, "because the circumstances and conditions that allowed a few men to put a steel plant in a corn field" were "as different from today's condi-tions in most of the Afro-Asian countries as day is from night." He was happy Hubert Humphrey agreed with the president on an issue so close to his heart: aid alone would not result in a transformation of values.[143] Finally, Eisenhower was unsure whether economic assistance could effect political change. He agreed with the progressives that there was value in promoting "economic de-velopment and political progress" even without a Communist threat, but he believed that people had to be educated before they were given assistance.[144] If countries were veering toward Moscow, it was already too late to undertake "programs for their orderly economic development and political progress." When King Mohammed V of Morocco asked the president to support develop-ment in countries on the verge of independence, Eisenhower retorted that the king was "putting the cart before the horse." To be effective, the United States had to provide cultural assistance before governmental structures were in place, a rationale Dulles also raised in discussions about aid to Sudan in 1956.[145]

Eisenhower's aid doctrine was not mere rhetoric. When, on 1 July 1955, the Foreign Operations Administration was replaced by ICA, it reported to Con-gress that Africa needed a different type of assistance. A "Fund for Africa" had to bankroll a special form of aid built on the creation of educational training institutions.[146] French, British, Belgian, and Portuguese empires, in contrast, saw cultural diplomacy only as a lubricant for aid schemes such as the Colombo Plan and the Foundation for Mutual Assistance in Africa South of the Sahara, which was an organ of the Commission for Technical Co-operation in Africa South of the Sahara (CCTA). French and British civil servants met in these commissions to discuss their joint development projects, and pamphlets under-scored the marvels of French and British economic aid.[147] Only for the US presi-dent was cultural assistance the cornerstone of the overall foreign aid strategy.

Bandung Conference participants wanted to expose colonial modernization as false and pave the way for an anticolonial modernization project to acquire international influence, not to sustain the "Bandung spirit." To that end, expertise had to be exported from Asia to Africa, an ambition that paradoxically weakened the anti-imperial solidarity that had been forged in places like Paris, London, and the West Indies during the interwar years. Nkrumah was weary of Afro-Asianism because of the possible impact of Asian paternalism on the Pan-African project.[148] To Northern ears, however, Bandung's ambition to outperform the colonial development project sounded like a cry for improved assistance, which prompted a strategic change. The African "mind" transformed from a security concern into a genuine development target as Northern policymakers raced to be the first to offer Africans education. Cultural assistance schemes would purportedly allow USSR officials to make bourgeois leaders useful for Moscow; lead to the internalization of US values; enable the British to safeguard the transition to self-government; and enable Africans to take advantage of the French, Belgian, and Portuguese culture.

Even though Northern officials did not discern a global landscape altered by the Afro-Asian meeting, this did not mean that their diplomacy was unaffected. Bandung, in conjunction with the Suez Crisis, did force a rethinking of foreign aid strategies in the North. Eisenhower believed education had to be integrated with economic assistance projects to be effective, since the positive outcome of modernization projects would not automatically plant the right ideas in people's minds.[149] Meanwhile, the British, Portuguese, French, and Belgians used informational resources to reassure their colonial subjects of these nations' genuine interest in their subjects' advancement. Nevertheless, anticolonial modernity emerged in full force as a competing model for Northern designs only after the independence of Ghana.

CHAPTER 3

The Pan-African Path to Modernity, 1957–1958

The Bandung delegates had not succeeded in working out a tangible anticolonial development agenda. From 6 March 1957 onward, Kwame Nkrumah picked up the gauntlet and projected a Pan-African modernization scheme beyond the borders of the newly independent Ghana. So great was the interest in the story of Ghana's independence that, with 306 accredited overseas and local correspondents on the scene, there was no room at any inn in Accra, and the BBC was reduced to putting correspondents up in private homes. As Mrs. C. G. Johnson of the West African Cocoa Research Institute served her two sons pancakes for dinner, a man knocked on her door. Standing in the drizzle of Accra's evening rain was a BBC correspondent, who inquired whether he was at the right address. Indeed he was. Mrs. Johnson had agreed to lodge the team, which was there to coordinate the activities of the Ghana Broadcasting Service and prepare a BBC program.[1]

Nkrumah was keen to exploit this PR potential. The press hotel had a radio connection with London and was fitted with a bank, a post office where the new Ghana stamp was sold, a bookstore, and a bar with free drinks, while a fleet of buses drove reporters around. In the midst of all this excitement, the BBC even forgot to broadcast its recording of the independence celebrations. When *The Birth of Ghana* finally aired, listeners heard a story in which the triumph of African nationalism was presented as the product of British imperial policy.[2] Complaints that the featured drumming performances did not represent the country's "true culture" followed.[3] This concern for African culture became the core of Ghana's foreign policy and was even discussed at the last legislative assembly on the eve of independence. The portfolios of defense and external affairs that Nkrumah obtained that night had to help convert Ghana into a "centre for the discussion of African problems." In his independence speech, he declared that "just minutes ago" he had laid out a program to create an "African Personality," a consideration for cultural integrity that was part of the liberationist case for modernity.[4] Whereas imperial development programs had destroyed the "African Personality," Pan-African modernization required cultural integrity to work.

Ironically, Nkrumah—a man who gazed at the world from beneath a pair of constantly frowning eyebrows—was criticized for putting his faith in cultural diplomacy and the spread of ideas. In the 1960s and 1970s. Nkrumah's intellectual capacities were questioned, and he was cast as a "marginal man" who had failed to reach his goal of African unity.[5] Ghanaian bureaucrats who began publishing their memoirs in the 1980s turned Nkrumah into an impatient idealist whose plans were thwarted by corrupt aides.[6] At the end of the Cold War, Nkrumah was characterized as a charismatic leader whose radical Pan-African experiment suffered under the pressures of the Cold War and Western plots.[7] Pan-African activism was sustained only in transnational networks, while Nkrumah turned east.[8] The focus on Nkrumah's failure, alleged hypocrisy, or inability to resist the machinations of the Cold War has eclipsed the actual goals and methods of Ghanaian policymakers who wanted to overturn the psychological and cultural impact of colonialism. By the mid-1960s, participants in a student orientation at the Kwame Nkrumah Ideological Institute (KNII) found themselves writing papers on the need for "mental decolonization," while journalists such as Colin Legum claimed the "emotional impetus" behind Pan-Africanism flowed from the experience of having "mentally" lost the "homeland."[9] Both drew on what had become a recurring theme in Ghana and found expression in Nkrumah's writings, which lamented "colonial students" who were being "seduced" to "surrender" their "personality."[10]

In their efforts to mentally decolonize Africa, Ghanaian foreign policymakers were guided by the Pan-African ideology, which sought to export Nkrumah's modernization scheme of cultural integrity and continental unity through conferences and a network of activists. Ghanaian support for Guinea's independence in October 1958 became a test case for different prescriptions for African modernity and established Accra as a revolutionary center capable of undermining decolonization as planned by the Global North.

The Interventionist Ideology of Pan-Africanism

Nkrumah's belief in the potential of a united Africa to sustain liberation germinated in the 1930s while studying at Lincoln University, where he wrote *Towards Colonial Freedom*, which identified economics as the basis of imperialism. Nkrumah's initial aim, the establishment of a West African union, was reimagined as a continental union under George Padmore's guidance.[11] The meeting with this Trinidadian intellectual occurred in Manchester, where Nkrumah helped organize the Pan-African Congress of 1945. This gathering of political activists, trade unionists, and intellectuals aimed to give substance to Pan-Africanism as a political project. Other anticolonial philosophies had already made their mark by the time the Pan-African Congress was organized. The abolitionist activism of intellectuals such as Alexander Crummell, who still embraced imperialism as a modernizing force, was widely read, while Nigerian nationalist Nnamdi Azikiwe, who met Nkrumah, stressed the importance of economic, political, and mental emancipation in his philosophy, Zikism.[12] Padmore, however, prioritized the political over the economic revolution and stressed that Pan-African ideology provided a counterweight to capitalism and Communism.[13] Richard Wright concurred. He explained Padmore's view as centered on race, arguing "black people" regarded "Russian Communists" and "American, British and French anti-Communists" alike primarily as white men.[14] Nkrumah's star rose to unseen heights, leading to the founding of the Convention People's Party, which with its plea for immediate independence won the elections and turned Nkrumah into the Gold Coast's "leader of government business" in 1951.

Ghanaian independence in March 1957 was a pivotal moment when the political Pan-African project increased its interventionist aspirations, since Nkrumah believed independence would be "meaningless" unless it was "linked up totally" with that of the "continent."[15] Komla Agbeli Gbedemah agreed, declaring during his visit to India in September 1957 that freedom was "indivisible." In the words of the All-African People's Conference Steering Committee, "stable peace" was "impossible in a world that" was "politically half independent and half dependent."[16] If Ghana's anticolonialism stopped at its borders, the country would not be able to remain independent. An increase in Pan-Africanism's interventionism also revived long-standing questions about the limits of intervention: Was Pan-Africanism about race or about a broader struggle that united all dispossessed peoples against oppression? At the International Congress against Colonial Oppression and Imperialism in Brussels in 1927, Black delegates who brought up race were met by representatives who made the case for a broader understanding of Pan-African anticolonialism that included people of non-African descent, with people such as Lamine Senghor, who saw imperialism

stem from capitalism.[17] However, by 1945, what preoccupied Pan-African thinkers such as Padmore was the creation of an autonomous "Pan-African ideology"
better able to "meet the challenge," not the question whether Pan-Africanism
relied for its substance on Wilsonianism and Leninism.[18] Nkrumah did not want
to imitate other "ways of life" but to "adopt or adapt" methods "suitable to our
social environment."[19] After independence, therefore, Arthur Lewis was flown
back into Ghana to devise an economic development strategy in line with Africa's precolonial culture and history, because he did not believe in one single theory of economic growth and attached more weight to the sociological and
historical characteristics of underdeveloped societies. Ghanaian foreign policy
was thus guided by a set of systematically expressed concepts consisting of a political philosophy with anticolonialism and the "African Personality" as its pillars,
a theory of history with the emergence of the slave trade as a turning point, a
vision of the future with African unity and African Socialism on the horizon,
and—finally—an explanation of the international legitimacy of the regime that
relied on non-alignment or positive neutrality and disarmament.

Non-alignment in particular, discussed interchangeably with positive neutrality, provided the basis for Ghanaian diplomacy. Nkrumah shied away from exploiting the Cold War rivalry, because "when the bull elephants fight, the grass is
trampled down." Playing off the USSR and the United States against each other
would not yield benefits but rather result in the destruction of weak nations and
make it more difficult to attain unity. Nonproliferation and peace became crucial
components of Nkrumah's postcolonial order because the survival of independent states depended on it, prompting Nkrumah to offer mediation in places such
as the Middle East in 1958, India in 1962, and Hanoi in 1966.[20] While leaders
such as Julius Nyerere of Tanganyika also expressed their fear of becoming the
proverbial trampled grass, Nkrumah's Monroe Doctrine for Africa made Accra's
stance distinctive. In a speech to Congress in 1958, Nkrumah linked his reading
of Marcus Garvey's "Africa for the Africans" with the US foreign policy doctrine of 1823: "Our attitude . . . is very much that of America looking at the disputes of Europe in the nineteenth century. We do not wish to be involved." Just
as the United States wanted to keep the Europeans out, Ghana believed that "the
peace of the world in general is served, not harmed by keeping one great continent free from the strife."[21] In 1960, the governor in Dakar noted that Nkrumah's
"Monroe Doctrine" had been influential but considered it proof that Africans
were psychologically unfit to play the game of international relations, since
treating "both powers in the same way" was impossible.[22]

Non-alignment in its turn provided a framework for three Pan-African
principles. First among these was anticolonialism. In his college years, Nkrumah
had given a Leninist definition to colonialism, as a system that was driven by

the need for raw materials. Education had only served the spread of European ideas and denied Africans the skills required for nation building. However, by the time Nkrumah watched the fireworks on the eve of independence, he had come to see colonialism in much the same way as liberationist thinkers such as Frantz Fanon did, as a system that oppressed the sense of African self-worth.[23] Nkrumah therefore called on his countrymen on the eve of independence to "change our attitudes, our minds."[24] After independence, neocolonialists remained influential not only in the economic field but also in the political, religious, ideological, and cultural spheres. For Nkrumah, who had been born in Nkroful near the Portuguese slave fort of Santo Antonio de Axim, the slave trade marked the start of this history of continental exploitation. In 1958, he talked about this linear interpretation of history, in which the "slave trade and the rape of Africa" by the Europeans was the starting point, colonialism a new way to enslave Africa, and neocolonialism a more subtle form of exploitation.[25] Similarly, W. E. B. Dubois's wife, Shirley Graham, also identified the kidnapping of Dubois's great-great-grandfather as the birth of the anticolonial struggle.[26]

A non-aligned Africa was further required to allow the "African Personality"—a term coined by American-Liberian educator Edward Wilmot Blyden in 1893—to flourish. The revival of a "common fundamental sentiment" among Africans was vital, since colonialism had not only oppressed local cultures but had also duped generations into believing that the solution for Africa's problems lay outside the continent. Nkrumah's idealized "authentic" image of the African past stressed the importance of autonomy on the international stage where for "too long in our history, Africa has spoken through the voices of others" while accentuating the importance of modernizing on Africa's terms.[27] Non-alignment ultimately had to facilitate continental unification, because neocolonialism's success depended on the existence of small units that relied on the former imperial power or the superpowers for defense and trade. The best way to attain that unity became a bone of contention in the inter-African politics of the 1950s and 1960s. Jomo Kenyatta and Tom Mboya of Kenya, who advocated gradualism, disagreed with Nkrumah's plans, while Nyerere wanted to create an East African Federation (EAF) in defiance of Nkrumah, who claimed regional groupings reduced the appetite for further integration. In September 1958, Kenya, Nyasaland, Tanganyika, Uganda, and Zanzibar even established a Pan-African Freedom Movement of East and Central Africa (PAFMECA) and a freedom fund for East Africa.[28]

Ghana therefore was forced to fight a battle for hearts and minds, aimed at convincing activists in other African territories, while providing fighters in places such as Cameroon, West Papua, Trinidad, and Tobago with a model for progress.[29] African unity was a continental scheme, but Pan-African modernity aspired to remake the colonizing world as a whole. In the words of C. L. R. James, "the modernization necessary in the modern world" could be attained only "in an African way."[30] The federation of liberation became a panacea for the colonial disease wherever it occurred. In 1962, in a letter to all the leaders of the disintegrating West Indian Federation, Nkrumah argued that "a united West Indies" was the only way to deal with "problems created by colonialists."[31] Those ideas—Nkrumah believed—would materialize only if vigorously propagated and cemented in institutions, something Padmore had urged him to do already in July 1956. Padmore was pushing Nkrumah to fashion himself as a revolutionary, leading Nkrumah to exchange favorable references to the Commonwealth for a larger role for Ghana in Africa in his foreign policy speech one year after independence.

Despite the rhetoric, Nkrumah and his aides remained shackled by colonial ideas. His attendance at Achimota—a missionary school where British and African customs were intertwined—fostered an understanding of dependent territories as "backward in education, in agriculture and in industry."[32] Ghana's UN representative, Daniel Chapman, also believed education needed to produce men and women for public service to facilitate the institutional development of the modern self-governing state. Around the same time, Joseph Murumbi, an activist in the Kenya African Union—renamed the Kenya African National Union (KANU) in 1960—and Kenya's foreign affairs minister between 1964 and 1966, argued in a letter to Mboya that the Danish folk schools, with their focus on democracy and competition, had to be introduced in Kenya to provide "political education."[33] Ghana had to step in, train political activists, and provide political information to strengthen future state structures. Nkrumah's embrace of modernization even led him to conceptualize African unification as a process made up of four stages: the attainment of independence, consolidation, the creation of unity and community among the African states, and the economic and social reconstruction of Africa.[34] Consequently, Gold Coast diplomacy before 1957 was pragmatic. Officials attended the course on international relations at the London School of Economics; negotiations with Whitehall in 1954 were aimed at establishing a high commissioner in London, the United States, and Canada; cordial relations with French ambassador Marc Renner were cultivated; and the Ghanaian delegation asked the South Africans, who were struck by the diplomats' friendly demeanor, to set up a post in Accra.[35]

Despite his early restraint, Nkrumah was acutely aware that the age of mass communication had changed the anticolonial struggle. International public opinion was forcing states to act in more ethical ways and exposed colonialism as immoral.[36] In the UN television studio, he reiterated his belief that the founding members of the UN wanted "world public opinion" to "develop on the basis of international morality."[37] Since the professed goal of Ghanaian diplomacy, the spread of the "African Personality," necessitated political education, freedom fighters such as Alphonse Ebassa in Sierra Leone came to rely on publications printed in Accra and believed propaganda to be more "powerful" than "guns."[38] The reliance on "informal diplomacy" with Radio Ghana, the Ghana Trade Union Congress, and the Bureau of African Affairs (BAA) was also the product of necessity, since Nkrumah, like Sukarno at Bandung, had neither a credible military option nor the capacity to demand economic sanctions.[39] The trips of BAA officials therefore often doubled as a cover for intelligence gathering. Until late 1959, decision makers relied on newspapers and letters from friends outside of Ghana. From November 1959 onward, however, a meeting of Ghana's Africa policy organ, the African Affairs Committee, sent out intelligence officers under the guise of cultural, football, or athletic associations.[40] Even though Nkrumah grew to regret his reliance on propaganda in 1966, a decade earlier he, together with other liberationist leaders, had been captivated by communication media as an indispensable tool to acquire moral force. Gamal Abdel Nasser, recalling Wendell Willkie's *One World*, believed "information media" had "reduced the dimensions of the world" and had made the "watertight partitions" around colonial territories porous.[41]

The Bandung Conference had already illuminated that effective anticolonial diplomacy had to include a battle for hearts and minds, because decolonization had generated a veritable glut of blueprints for postcolonial order. The NSC wrote that "the African's mind" had become "a target for the advocacy of Communism, old-fashioned colonialism, xenophobic nationalism, and Egyptian 'Islamic' propaganda, as well as for the proponents of an orderly development . . . closely tied to the West." Ultimately, political orientation would not be determined by the Cold War but by "what the leaders and peoples conceive best serves their own interests, measured primarily in terms of 'independence' and of 'equality' with the white man." "Immature" Africans were "subject to many pressures—Communist, Pan-African, Islamic," Undersecretary of State for Political Affairs Robert Murphy declared.[42] On the other side of the Atlantic, the newly established European Economic Community (EEC) created an Overseas Development Fund. "Free Europe," as former minister of France d'outre-mer Pierre-Henri Teitgen termed it, had to be established as a fifth alternative beside "the American bloc, the Soviet world, the Bandung coalition," and the "Asian-African group."[43]

The wide range of ideological options also made diplomacy within the Global South more convoluted. The rivalry between Nkrumah and Nasser, both offering Zanzibari students scholarships, burst into the open when the Egyptian delegation was not invited to attend Ghana's independence celebration, while Nkrumah's warning about the different forms of colonialism at the All-African People's Conference was considered to be a condemnation of Nasser in the corridors of the meeting. On the other hand, the United Arab Republic (UAR) was allowed to open a cultural center in Accra in November 1958, and a Ghanaian delegate at the Afro-Asian Solidary Conference was photographed pinning a gold star on Nasser's lapel.[44] The Afro-Arab competition was compounded by inter-African conflict. William Tubman wanted to export Liberia's national development program to the rest of the continent in the form of the Fifteen-Year Unification Program. He therefore placed the PR-savvy Joseph S. Coleman, nicknamed "Mister Liberia," in Lagos.[45] At the Conference of Tangier in April 1958, another federation of liberation, the "unity of the Arab Maghreb," was being discussed by representatives of Morocco, Tunisia, and the FLN with the goal of fighting "néo-colonialisme" and the UAR's influence.[46]

The splintering of the liberationist ideology in the course of the 1950s was further exemplified by competing versions of African Socialism. Nkrumah and Léopold Senghor both embraced it to sell their project of social transformation, but they disagreed about the threat posed by neocolonialism as well as the precise relationship between race, economics, and political and cultural rights that had emerged at Bandung.[47] Senghor's spiritual interpretation of African Socialism meant resistance against European economic exploitation and the rejection of what he called "colonialisme africain," Ghana's push for unity. Similarly to W. E. B. Dubois, who considered Black capitalism to be an inadequate response to the challenge of colonialism, Senghor accepted civilization but questioned capitalism. While not wholly uncontested, *Négritude* was building on a shared conviction in Senegalese politics. Even Senghor's rival, Blaise Diagne, defended assimilation while simultaneously criticizing colonial abuses.[48]

For Nkrumah, however, African Socialism was a program for liberation that linked racial justice to economic justice. That link made Ghana more popular than Ethiopia, where an older and more conservative African unification project and a top-down modernization effort were spearheaded by Emperor Haile Selassie. Ethiopianism, a religious-literary movement that had emerged in the nineteenth century and became stronger after the Italian defeat at the Battle of Adowa in 1896, had not been explicitly political until the establishment of the Ethiopian World Federation in 1937 by Melaku Bayen. At the direction of Haile Selassie, Bayen had to mobilize support for Ethiopia during the Italian invasion of 1935 and strengthen the unity between people of African descent. Followers of the Rastafarian movement in Jamaica, who believed in Haile Selassie's divinity and embraced repatriation, had already projected Ethiopia as the promised land, but it was a diaspora the emperor could not tap into politically. Instead,

Ethiopian state propaganda centered on highlighting the long imperial line of succession and the foresight of Emperor Menelik II in beginning the country's modernization at the start of the twentieth century.[49] Rather than ideology, Haile Selassie stressed the material wealth of the continent, which with its "raw materials, military and industrial man-power" had helped win World War II.[50]

Despite the shared emphasis on African history in attaining successful modernization, Nkrumah's vision was more interventionist and socially inspired and therefore caused anxiety among the organizers of the Organisation of African Unity (OAU) conference of 1966, where Nkrumah was expected to make an appearance. A visit could lead the people in Ethiopia to emulate the Saudi population, who had ten years earlier voiced their displeasure with the House of Saud by cheering on the Arab socialist Nasser during his visit. Zambian officials fretted over how a "Nkrumah" crisis would play out, since the emperor and Nkrumah did "not mix."[51]

Accra at the Center of a Revolutionary Network

To convert Ghana's symbolic strength into real influence, Nkrumah and his aides relied on a network strategy. After a web of freedom fighters was spun, political activists would convince the general population and, once in power, fix their gaze on Accra, ultimately leading to African unity. To that end, Accra was converted into a revolutionary mecca, and the Conference of Independent African States (CIAS), 15–23 April 1958, and the All-African People's Conference, 8–13 December 1958, were organized to attract leaders and activists (see figure 3.1).[52] CIAS participants set out to prove that Africans could "manage their own affairs," reversing the logic of Charles de Gaulle's Brazzaville Conference of 1944, which had always irritated Nkrumah because he believed it had been a ploy to thwart "Positive Action," Nkrumah's nonviolent model of resistance.[53] Ghana's increased activism was reflected in the points the organizing committee added to the CIAS agenda, such as "organisation of foreign subversive activities." The Ethiopian minister of commerce, Ato Abebe Reta, captured the shared belief in a symbolic struggle against colonialism when he looked out over the small conference venue with its U-shaped table and declared that it was "the duty" of "the independent nations of Africa to mobilize world conscience and public opinion."[54] In order to defeat neocolonialism in all its guises—ranging from economic penetration and cultural assimilation to ideological domination to psychological infiltration and subversive activities—Nkrumah urged participants to unite.[55] Representatives from the UAR, Ethiopia, and Ghana even visited Rio de Janeiro, where they tried to convince the Brazilian government to

FIGURE 3.1. Ahmed Sékou Touré of Guinea (left) and Kwame Nkrumah of Ghana (right) in the front at the All-African People's Conference in Accra. Patrice Lumumba is seated right behind Touré. 9 December 1958. Phillip Harrington / Alamy Stock Photo.

support the "revolution" in Africa and Asia, arguing that the CIAS was a milestone in the anti-imperial struggle comparable to the Monroe Doctrine. Loyalty to Lisbon, however, thwarted the establishment of an alliance.[56]

Before opening the CIAS, Belgian, Portuguese, and South African officials considered the meeting to be trivial. Belgian foreign trade minister Victor Larock, who had attended the independence celebration in Accra, believed Ghana's independence would not become an example for the Congo and interpreted the CIAS as he did Bandung: a meeting where postcolonial leaders wanted to play a leading role, "un rôle de vedette."[57] US and British officials were confident they could use the meeting for their own purposes. While initially Gold Coast governor Charles Arden-Clarke and US ambassador Wilson Flake wanted to persuade Nkrumah to cancel his plans, by February 1958, both the Colonial Office and the CIA concluded that the CIAS would be effective at containing Nasser's Pan-Arabism.[58] Mohammed Ahmed Omaar, a friend of Nkrumah and Padmore, had reassured the Colonial Office that Nkrumah planned to outcompete both the Communists and the Egyptians. Nevertheless, when the CO tried to force Ghana's interior minister, Ako Adjei, to ensure enough attendees would be critical of Nasser, he refused to comply. Nkrumah was careful not to upset Egypt and Liberia and asked their ambassadors for help.[59] Once the CIAS started, with speeches, discussions, and receptions where Nkrumah and Tubman danced together, the US State Department and Nigeria sent well-wishes while South Africa's prime minister, Johannes Strijdom, demonstratively declined Accra's invitation because France, Belgium, and the United Kingdom had also not been invited, even though they were responsible for "about half of the continent."[60] Only the UK Information Office (UKIO), convinced that the meeting could counterbalance Nasser's influence, set up shop alongside the stands of African independent nations in Accra's Community Centre. Visitors left the conference's crowded publicity display area with an issue of *Commonwealth Today*—read by a Tass correspondent "with true Soviet concentration"—under one arm and a complimentary portrait of Nasser under the other.[61]

After the CIAS ended, officials in the Global North realized they had a propaganda problem on their hands, which was the reason attendance numbers of the upcoming AAPC for political activists needed to be kept low as more expertise in the area of African politics was acquired.[62] Soviet foreign affairs minister Andrei Gromyko regarded African countries as too "backward" for socialism. Nevertheless, the Ministry of Foreign Affairs created a separate Africa Department in July 1958.[63] The Belgian ambassador to the United States, Robert Silvercruys, reported that the hallways of "Bandoeng Africain" had been filled with moderates, but the colonial elite in the Belgian Congo grasped the PR appeal and presented the CIAS in *La Voix du Congolais* as a psychological operation that sought to drive a wedge between Europe and Africa. The Solvay Institute in Brussels therefore created the Centre de documentation et d'études politiques africaines.[64] The British foreign policy bureaucracy also acknowledged the appeal of Nkrumah's propaganda, but disagreed about its exact effects. When the Colonial Office fell back into old paternalistic habits, suggesting that a stern talk with Nkrumah would persuade him to cancel the conference, the Foreign Office did not want to cooperate because it had understood the call for African unity to include the white settlers, whereas the Commonwealth Relations Office claimed a British request to respect settlers would become a propaganda weapon in Padmore's hands.[65] USIS-Ghana published interviews with Chairman Mboya of the AAPC, and African American congressman Charles C. Diggs Jr. organized a press conference in his hotel room, where reporters from the Ghana News Agency, Radio Ghana, and Guinea Press listened to answers that were drafted by USIS.[66] The Canadians in Ottawa worried about the increase of "Nkrumah's prestige" even though the CIAS's "outcome" was "regarded as satisfactory to the West."[67] In Lisbon's estimation, Accra was a "center for anticolonial propaganda" despite the conference's internal divisions. The competition between African and Asian nationalists that had emerged at Bandung was now replaced by a competition between Nasser and African nationalists. Liberia and Ghana, however, in the estimation of the Foreign Affairs Ministry, did not want to sacrifice their interests to Egypt, which formed the UAR with Syria between 1958 and 1961, resulting in a win for Western powers. The consul in Portugal, Antonio de Siqueira Freire, even reported that Padmore believed Portuguese Africa was a difficult target for African nationalist action because the "assimilado" system had effectively destroyed the Black man's soul.[68] Only the French failed to understand the propaganda dimension of the CIAS. Symbolic resolutions were judged to be absurd and seen as an indication of the meeting's failure.[69]

In December 1958, party leaders, trade unionists, and other freedom fighters gathered at the AAPC to "work out a blueprint for the future."[70] The delegates—among whom were two white clergymen and Patrick Duncan of the Cape Town interracial Liberal Party—strove to unite the continent "through propaganda and education."[71] Posters with "Free Jomo Kenyatta" were held up to demand his release; renowned anticolonial activist Michael Scott asked other delegates to protest the South African mandate of South West Africa; Fanon asked Holden Roberto and other Angolan nationalists to recruit eleven fighters to be trained in FLN camps; Mboya declared that the "iron curtain" around Angola had to be destroyed; and the AAPC secretariat sent a delegation to the UN to express solidarity with the Cameroonian anticolonial struggle. Most important, the conference did not profess the benefits of Positive Action, as Nkrumah had intended. Instead, the conference became a platform for one of the most heated debates over the use of violence as opposed to a reliance on propaganda in the liberation struggle. Fanon highlighted how the Algerians had been forced to take up arms in the face of French aggression.[72] Nkrumah, in contrast, was determined to "support every form of non-violent action" and maintained that ideas, not guns, offered the only sure road to victory.[73]

Nevertheless, by 1966, after years of struggle "by other means," Nkrumah seemed to have come around to Fanon's assertion when he voiced his regret about having leaned so heavily on propaganda and his belief that the "African revolutionary struggle" had to be "backed" by "armed struggle."[74] This contradiction has been explained by the idea that Nkrumah's belief in nonviolence soured in the face of the Congo Crisis of 1960. Nonetheless, already at the AAPC Nkrumah refused to respond to Fanon, because both men actually agreed colonialism was ultimately a psychological problem.[75] Fanon, convinced that the psychological chains of colonialism could be broken only through violence, acknowledged that radio was a potent weapon of the French colonizers and Radio Alger an important instrument of resistance.[76] When Fanon became the FLN's ambassador to Ghana, he was acutely aware of how African unification was made more difficult by Louis Armstrong's jazz performances, "American Negro diplomats," scholarships, the Voice of America, and German and Israeli cultural diplomacy.[77] Fanon and Nkrumah diagnosed colonialism in the same way, but in Nkrumah's opinion Fanon's remedy fell short because the transformational mechanism behind violence remained vague. Nkrumah considered *The Wretched of the Earth* to be "a powerful book" but one that lacked a "practical revolutionary philosophy."[78]

What distinguished Nkrumah from Fanon was, therefore, not his principal rejection of violence but rather the belief that violence in itself was not "a cleansing force." According to Nkrumah, freeing Africans from their inferiority complex required the spread of the "African Personality." In his AAPC opening speech, Nkrumah called on delegates not to ignore the ethical and humanistic side of the anticolonial struggle. In the conference resolutions, support for those who were "compelled to retaliate against violence" was combined with an appreciation for others who mobilized world opinion and provided education. At the Positive Action Conference of April 1960, Nkrumah pointed out that "total emancipation" required the conversion of "the passive sympathy of the African masses" into "active participation."[79] For Gandhi's philosophy of nonviolence to work, Nkrumah reasoned, a "strong political organisation" was key.[80] "Positive Action" techniques were therefore taught at the KNII, where courses on political party formation, the organization of elections, party branches, and propaganda vans were on offer.[81] "Strikes, boycotts and non-cooperation" were only "a last resort."[82] The AAPC resolutions laid down the task of creating a network in which freedom fighters would be trained to provide "propaganda and education" to attain African unity.[83]

After Padmore's death on 23 September 1959, the AAPC resolutions were given substance by replacing Padmore's office of adviser to the prime minister on African affairs with the Bureau of African Affairs (BAA). Its creation realized Padmore's dream of a bureau, officially a nongovernmental organization, to support independence movements. Nkrumah named himself as the acting director, and Aloysius K. Barden became the secretary, after Kofi Baako had temporarily filled that position.[84] The BAA almost immediately became the subject of espionage stories. In 1960, Baako fled into the office of the bank manager to evade the suspicious stares of clerks and customers, which he received when he collected a bag filled with dollar bills intended for freedom fighters.[85] Nonetheless, Barden wrote to Nkrumah that the idea of sending out activists had been misunderstood, since BAA officials defined their work in public diplomacy terms.[86] The BAA maintained a research department, protocol division, printing press, library, linguistic secretariat, conference hall, and publications section. Political organizations in colonial Africa were represented by their own personnel in the bureau, who also participated in classes. Other movements, such as the mouvement de libération Nationale in the Belgian Congo, had their materials printed by the BAA presses.[87]

Despite Ghana's ambition to financially support all freedom fighters, Nkrumah understood that handing out dollar bills would not suffice. At the end of 1959, when £20,000 had already been funneled to others on the continent, Nkrumah reiterated that assistance would be given only to organizations that fully subscribed to the idea of African unity.[88] Education, journalism, and increasingly radio were more important than money, because these "Positive Action" techniques would be effective in an era of "national rivalries, ideological competitions and racial antagonisms."[89] For Nkrumah and Padmore, public diplomacy—"every kind of support, short of violence, to the struggle for national independence"—therefore was a "principal plank" of their foreign policy.[90] The resolutions of the AAPC were clear that key to mobilizing a broad cross-section of people was a network strategy, targeting political activists who could in turn convince others to look toward Accra.[91] In Ghana, the BAA turned to political education, revolutionary journalism, and radio to establish its revolutionary network.

Ideological training was the most direct way in which the ties with Accra were established. In September 1958, Padmore decided to emulate the Indian and Egyptian cultural exchange scholarships. The "Young Pioneers," a youth movement, trained youths from Nyasaland and 108 Gambians, of whom 50 returned to their country after completing a youth leadership course.[92] As early as 12 November 1959, Nkrumah announced his plan to convert the Winneba Party College into an institute where selected members of all nationalist movements could be trained to "propagate" the "essence of African unity . . . throughout the continent of Africa."[93] This institute, which became the Kwame Nkrumah Ideological Institute but also the Kwame Nkrumah Youth Training School and the Builder Brigade for unemployed men, was exemplary of the Ghanaian modernization model, which fused African culture and progress. What visitors did not know was that the United States covertly funded the Builder Brigade.[94]

The BAA's dissemination of newspapers also hinged on an educated audience and was meant to create a common understanding among elites about what it meant to be African. As a former journalist of the *Chicago Defender* and the *Pittsburgh Courier*, Padmore relied on newspapers to create an African activist language. In January 1959, he ordered the dispatch of three hundred daily copies of *Evening News* and *Ghanaian Times* to "selected people, news agencies of European countries as well as those of independent and dependent African States."[95] While also read out in public, newspapers were first and foremost meant for an audience that was able to digest academic treatises such as Dorothy Padmore's essay, which posited that the Africans in British Africa had been more successful in safeguarding their Africanism compared with their counterparts in French Africa.[96] The illiterate reader was served through cartoons and postcards that conjured up a rich African past. In July 1958, Padmore asked the Americans to help him improve his mailing list, a move that prompted USIA officials, who understood the power of newspapers, to distribute Padmore's old newspaper the *Pittsburgh Courier*.[97] Nkrumah's commitment to fostering African studies and his invitation to W. E. B. Dubois to manage the *Encyclopedia Africana* project were part of the network strategy that extended a hand to influential leaders.[98]

In 1957, the Ghana External Broadcasting Service and the *Voice of Ghana* were founded, but despite investments in the second Five-Year Development Plan and a visit from Canadian Broadcasting Corporation advisers in March 1958, radio remained part of the network strategy until 1961 when transmitters became stronger.[99] Propaganda was made easily identifiable to draw activists to Accra. In December 1959, Nkrumah asked the broadcast department to begin every news broadcast with a signature call: "This is the Voice of Africa coming to you from Radio Ghana, Accra."[100] Moreover, with its capacity for radio broadcasting, Ghana was able to become a member of the Union of African Radio Broadcasting, which was founded on 23 May 1960.[101] Radio allowed Nkrumah to cement the notion of African unity in yet another institution.

What made Ghana's education, press, and radio network vulnerable was the selection of suitable candidates. Day-to-day life at the African Affairs Centre in Accra, which provided accommodation and meals to the freedom fighters, was rowdy. One student, Evelyn Molabatsi, became so drunk that she verbally abused the center's security guard after almost having been run over by a van. Other women reportedly turned to prostitution, whereas men became caught up in fights, and a Kenyan student had tried to force his way into another student's bedroom at four in the morning.[102] Besides elucidating how difficult it was for Ghanaian men to come to terms with changing gender roles, these episodes also highlight the necessity of carefully considering the political potential of each target group. On 11 November 1960, a special mission left for Sudan, Kenya, and Tanganyika, composed of the BAA director, Barden; BAA board member John Tettegah; and the security officer of the Ministry of Foreign Affairs, W. Wilson. They wanted to understand how the "political consciousness" of different groups could be exploited. No financial assistance should ever be given, Barden wrote, without first having conducted an on-the-spot analysis. Barden's team therefore offered scholarships to Sudanese students because they possessed "the fire kindled by the youth," while women were politically useful because of their wish to "exercise their political rights." Despite the revolutionary rhetoric, the writers of the report paid no attention to the preferences of mass audiences, revealing a Ghanaian strategy built on an elite network of political activists.[103]

In Africa, the network strategy widened the gap between adherents of the violent and nonviolent approach, between radical supporters of immediate African unity and gradualists, and between French Africa and Ghana, with Senegalese politician Cheikh Anta Diop claiming French Africans had been "crushed" at the AAPC because of the absence of translators.[104] In the Global North, Nkrumah's reputation as an influential politician was undercut as concern over hostile public diplomacy grew. The NATO committee on Africa claimed the internal situation, not Communism, determined the continent's international direction and stressed that the committee's existence had to remain secret because newly minted African leaders would brand this venture as neocolonial.[105] Conversely, the Soviet delegation that had attended the AAPC, Iandolo argues, was disappointed with what they perceived to be Nkrumah's pro-Western speeches and his willingness to compromise with the colonial powers. On 18 May 1959, the Communist Party of the Soviet Union (CPSU) supported the creation of the Institute for African Studies to ramp up the Soviet production of knowledge about Africa.[106] The Belgian consul in Lagos argued Nkrumah was far from becoming a dominant force on the continent, and there was little concern about Lumumba's attendance at the AAPC.[107] UK officials still viewed Nkrumah as an ally, while the French considered him to be a small problem, going so far as to argue that he suffered from a mental illness.[108] In the South African press, the AAPC was cast as antiwhite, and Duncan was mocked for his "naivete" since he had claimed the conference envisioned a "place for the white man in Africa."[109] Nkrumah's plea for nonviolence impressed only the US State Department, where AAPC attendees were praised.[110]

From Cultural Assistance to Symbolic Struggle in Guinea

The Pan-African project presented Washington, Moscow, Paris, London, Brussels, and Lisbon with a new challenge, namely nationalist leaders who with the help of an alluring liberationist plan for Africa were able to punch above their weight. When, on 28 September 1958, Sékou Touré of Guinea rejected the new French constitution in a referendum and chose independence, the promise of federations and the symbolic challenge of anticolonialism were thrown into sharp relief. The manner in which anticolonial leaders like Nkrumah and Touré influenced decision making in the Global North in many ways goes to the heart of our discussions about the twilight of empire. By emphasizing the difference with Belgian and Portuguese officials, who were seemingly blindsided by anticolonial demands, and drawing on archives from the metropole, a generation of historians has furthered the notion that French and British plans for imperial reform foresaw the creation of independent states. De Gaulle had enough foresight to realize that African leaders "wanted independence, despite their adhesion to the Community," while Macmillan "presided over a voluntary decolonization" that was not "unorchestrated."[111] Nonetheless, when Guinea chose immediate independence, French civil servants in chaotic fashion packed their suitcases, destroyed infrastructure, and terminated the construction of the Konkouré Dam.[112] The French ambassador, Jean Mauberna, asked teachers who were on holiday not to return.[113]

Ghana and the USSR, but also the British and the Americans, almost instantly rushed to Touré's aid. After reflecting on the "significance of the emergence of the new nation of Ghana" during the independence celebrations in Accra, Richard Nixon concluded that Ghana's success was critical to proving that US "ideas and principles" were applicable elsewhere. Cultural relations would further enable the US to support a brand of "neutralism, which the national independence movements favor," without being accused of importing the Cold War, a recurring concern since Bandung. Dwight Eisenhower agreed and, after Nkrumah's visit to the United States in July 1958, made the point that "the people" of Africa had to be won, since "we can't win it by military activity."[114] Eisenhower recommended "a combination of the broadest and most persistent kind of education" to tame the "spirit of nationalism." "Like men," the administration would have to wipe out the conditions for instability.[115] Assistant Secretary of State for African Affairs Joseph C. Satterthwaite also felt that the United States had to support independence by strengthening the resolve of the new nations "in their own capacities," if a country was "able to undertake its responsibilities."[116] The British secretary of state for the colonies, Alan Lennox-Boyd, believed that any kind of "power vacuum" demanded early intervention. He wanted to provide Nigeria with a radio transmitter as a counterweight to Radio Conakry's hostile broadcasts, even though he did not know whether Touré supported Ghana's brand of Pan-African nationalism or whether he had been seduced by Communist ideas. In 1958, Paris had yet to play the Soviet card, and the French representative in the Anglo-French talks warned that it would be "a serious psychological mistake" if Africans were led to feel that the West was interested in them only for "Cold War reasons."[117]

Nkrumah formed the Ghana-Guinea Union on 22 November 1958, which was enlarged in April 1961 with Mali. Radio Bamako hailed the move as a vital contribution to the "grand struggle of the African peoples."[118] Nkrumah knew the Ghanaian loan of £10 million for Touré would never be repaid, but he wanted to ensure Guinea remained independent to prove the liberating potential of federations.[119] French government officials, who were unable to grasp the influence of African agency in international affairs, were outraged because they believed the British had helped Ghana. The conspiracy allegation angered the Colonial Office because French newspapers stories fed anti-British sentiment as far as the bazaars of Morocco.[120]

To minimize the PR damage, the British informed the French in December 1958 that they were already helping Touré by recruiting English teachers, while radio recordings of the BBC's "English by Radio" course were offered to the minister of education and broadcast a day later on Radio Conakry. While the French representative now suggested that Touré was under Communist control, British officials were adamant about the need for action, "whatever the situation." De Gaulle realized he was rapidly losing influence when the French counterespionage service informed him about the assistance missions that had already visited Guinea. The list included delegations coming from the United States, West and East Germany, and the Afro-Asian Solidarity Secretariat. Guinea had also sent envoys to Ghana, Sierra Leone, Liberia, Togo, Félix Houphouët-Boigny's Ivory Coast, and even the United Kingdom.[121]

French ambassador Louis de Guiringaud explained the lack of interest in French culture by arguing Africans were insufficiently prepared for a culture that came from a "highly civilized" country. The terrain had to be "psychologically prepared" by making the audience familiar with certain aspects of French life, and every cultural manifestation therefore had to be accompanied by an effort to disseminate news about France in an attractive way.[122] In defiance of the official policy in Paris, Guiringaud attended the signing ceremony of the Ghana-Guinea Union. He felt Guinea was not yet lost and wanted to convince Nkrumah of his plan to let French technicians back into Guinea through Ghana.[123] Touré told the French ambassador that he would not sign the Ghana-Guinea agreement if de Gaulle offered an alternative. Additionally, rumors were swirling about the arrival of a Guinean envoy in Paris who had expressed a "desire to stay associated with France" and asked de Gaulle to present the candidacy of Guinea to the UN in November 1958.[124] Guiringaud tried to make the civil servants in Paris see that hostility toward Guinea only gave Ghana propaganda ammunition.[125] Foreign Affairs Minister Maurice Couve de Murville, Michel Debré, and de Gaulle, however, did not understand the PR dimension of the scramble for Guinea and had "been unpleasantly" surprised by the ambassador's move. "Being cordial was one thing," Debré remarked sarcastically, "staying at a reception for two hours" was a different matter.[126] De Gaulle believed the Guineans needed France and would eventually return. The obstinacy of civil servants at France d'outre-mer—who cast the Guineans as "nègres communistes"—further marginalized Guiringaud's position.[127]

The appearance of the US assistance mission in the list of the French secret service is remarkable, since Eisenhower withheld Guinea's official recognition until 1 November 1958, which historians have interpreted as support for France.[128] However, Eisenhower's hesitance stemmed from his belief that it was not in the US interest to reward "premature independence." Rumors about a turn toward the USSR only served to fortify his refusal, because US economic aid would strengthen Moscow if not embedded in a cultural assistance strategy. Eisenhower, the fiscal conservative who pushed for economic aid to the Global South without providing a lot of cash, was therefore pleased that Touré wanted to invest in education.[129] Guinea and the USSR went through a honeymoon period when, in January 1959, the Central Committee authorized a Soviet delegation to visit Guinea to explore the possibility of economic aid, leading to the financing of projects such as a polytechnic school, an airport, and a stadium. In March, Czech weapons followed, and in November, Touré was welcomed by Nikita Khrushchev at the Black Sea. In November 1959, however, the first secretary of the Soviet Embassy, V. I. Ivanisov, toured the country and found that most Guineans had little knowledge of Communism and the USSR.[130]

While de Gaulle's and Touré's conflicting personalities supposedly played a big role in the harsh French retreat, the sources suggest the French already wanted to return in January 1959. They initiated negotiations for a cultural protocol and sent an unofficial envoy, Pasteur Mabille, to investigate what motivated others to go to Guinea, irritating US and UK officials in the process. At the Foreign Office Africa Department, Mabille was assured that the United Kingdom had nothing to do with the Ghana-Guinea union, while John Foster Dulles asked why de Gaulle had granted independence if the general still wanted to intervene.[131] At the Quai d'Orsay, the French remained convinced that the Americans and the British were secretly undermining the French community. Robert Murphy of the State Department told the French ambassador to Washington, Louis Joxe, that Murphy could not understand why the Quai did not allow Joxe to appoint ambassadors if the Soviet threat was imminent, shouting that he was "ready now!"[132] Assistant Secretary of State for Africa James Penfield was also eager to train "civil servants capable of assuming responsibility."[133] On 16 June 1959, Debré instructed his psychological warfare committee to maintain Guinea in the Franc zone and preserve some intellectual influence by building educational infrastructure. By mid-May, after other NATO members could not be convinced of the seriousness of the Soviet threat, a team led by DGACT director Roger Seydoux was sent to Guinea to resume negotiations for an economic and cultural agreement. That decision was driven less by the four thousand remaining French inhabitants than by competitors who had their feet in the door in Conakry, possibly unlocking the rest of French Africa in the process.[134]

Touré hired an African American PR adviser to weaponize the oversupply of aid offers. Ismaël Touré—Sékou Touré's half brother—publicly suggested recognizing the Provisional Government of the Algerian Republic (GPRA) to test how much maneuvering room Paris would give him. When Touré visited the United States in October 1959, he was promised 150 scholarships, the placement of Guinean students, and training for Guinean teachers.[135] Touré tried to use the arms shipments from Czechoslovakia to pressure the British and Eisenhower. In a conversation with Satterthwaite in October 1959, Touré asked for funds to the construct the Konkouré Dam, hinting that the Soviets had already made an offer.[136] In a conversation with the British chargé d'affaires, Wynn Hugh-Jones, in September 1959, Touré denied that Guinea had connections with the Eastern Bloc. He claimed that he accepted an invitation to visit Moscow only under great pressure, asserting that Khrushchev had even sent an aircraft to Conakry. While waving the Soviet-Guinea agreement on cultural cooperation—signed in November 1959—under Hugh-Jones's nose and claiming it also granted financial aid, Touré stated he would not sign it unless he was sure Moscow's aid came with no strings attached. It is therefore unsurprising that de Gaulle's memoires describe Touré as a skillful forger of public opinion.[137]

After 1959, in the face of intense competition, public diplomats behind their desks in Africa were forced to rethink the ways in which they could make their aid attractive. In the words of Deputy Director Leonard James Saccio of the ICA, "How could another Guinea be avoided?"[138] With aid so readily available, UK information officers felt they were dragged into a "ludicrous scramble to give away money."[139] In August 1959, London offered books, water pumps, two child incubators, and twelve portable spraying machines.[140] While settlers in East Africa worried about Ghanaian propaganda, UK officers were unhappy about their US colleagues, who heightened the impact of their aid by driving around "American experts, jeeps and blonde typists."[141]

The USIS posts, however, felt cornered by their competitors, particularly those from the Eastern Bloc. In April 1960, even West German diplomat Hasso von Etzdorf went to Conakry to establish diplomatic relations.[142] Unlike Eisenhower, who prioritized long-term development, the USSR focused on "impact-type projects," which turned "Guinea into a showpiece of apparent development."[143] Khrushchev wanted to create a "window on the new life in Africa" when he appointed the director of the Near East department at the Soviet Foreign Ministry, Daniil Solod, as ambassador in January 1960. As a result, Touré easily obtained more economic aid after his visit to Moscow in September 1960.[144] The US promise of an increased gross national product was "no substitute for a 'showcase.'" Like the Soviets, the ICA would need to start appealing to the "vanity, the hearts or stomachs" of Africans.[145] This inspired the US ambassador to Guinea, John Morrow, to create a mobile medical team, something that was "at once dramatic and easy to implement."[146] Following the example of the British in Ghana, US public diplomats worked to reach a target audience beyond the elite with teams going beyond the "influential few," "into the bush," with film viewings in every village.[147]

Contrary to the US aid schemes, de Gaulle ignored African nationalism in his cultural expansion plan of 1959. While the plan paid more attention to the political "advantages" that came with cultural diplomacy, French cultural assistance to Africa did not transform into a cloak to hide cynical agendas of weapon shipments and business deals, nor were French operatives naive enough to think that aid would simply entice the former African colonies to develop according to a French model, as some writers have claimed.[148] For Paris, assistance was not about creating and selling an image of French grandeur but about striking a deal. The French believed they had something to offer and they expected support in return. Therefore, institutions such as universities, cultural centers, and language schools had to be renovated; French books had to create an appetite for the French language by focusing on scientific, technical, and medical knowledge; and, when possible, educational cooperation had to be made more useful. This service mentality—"véritable politique d'offre de services"—avoided hurting African nationalistic pride and made French culture attractive.[149]

Teachers became the focal point because pedagogical leadership styles were popular among African leaders who believed they had to teach their populations how to become modern citizens. In the new plan for French cultural expansion, there was still no attention devoted to symbolic struggle. De Gaulle's spectacular and radical retreat has received most of the attention, obscuring the fact that French officials of the Direction générale des affaires culturelles et techniques—working behind de Gaulle's back or with his tacit permission—remained in Guinea. The decision of seventy-eight French teachers to stay in 1958 delighted the DGACT, because it meant that in 1960, when France officially recognized Guinea, only twenty-five new teachers needed to be hired, while the inflow of teachers from the Soviet bloc had remained limited.[150] When, in 1960, an increasing number of teachers wanted to leave because they felt threatened by Radio Conakry's anti-French broadcasts, the teachers were asked to stay "to ensure a sustained influence of French culture."[151] After France accorded Guinea diplomatic recognition, the embassy's cultural service was quickly reestablished.[152]

Guiringaud again came into conflict with Paris because he believed French language education could not be separated from African politics, while the Quai held on to the conventional logic behind language education: the spread of the French language and culture would —irrespective of political views—lead to admiration among Africans and should thus be encouraged. However, Guiringaud, the ambassador to Tunis, and the French intelligence service all pointed out that Ghanaians were signing up to learn French so they could spread the "Ghanaian gospel."[153] The Quai's limited understanding of the politics of postcolonial education turned Guinean independence into a genuine battle for hearts and minds, because the field was left open for competitors. In July 1959, one month before the arrival of an ICA exploratory team, the ICA had already sent out African American teacher Marie Gadsden. Christopher Ewart-Biggs, a senior officer at the FO and MI6, wanted to make British rather than US books the standard for English teaching in Guinea. If the Americans convinced a Guinean minister that US books better suited his needs, British officials had to offer more money. Not to be outdone by the United States, J. D. B. Fowells of the British Council traveled to Guinea in January 1960 to make grand promises even though the British had only four teachers available.[154] In 1958, the USIA's English consultant bluntly admitted, as would USIS officials in Conakry two years later, that he saw language education as a way to "reach key groups," and if those people were already sitting in classes organized by the British Council, the USIA would not be able to influence them.[155] At USIS-Conakry, resources were allocated to maximize influence. Students who had already become fluent therefore received more resources. ICA and USIA personnel seeking advice from British expats, particularly in Ghana, were shooed away, and the cooperation that had existed in the early 1950s was replaced by intense competition.[156] All this while, the Belgians and the Portuguese adopted a wait-and-see attitude about Conakry. The Belgian ambassador in Dakar talked about how the leaders in Guinea employed Marxist methods but were not "marxistes doctrinaires."[157] The Portuguese increased their presence in the countryside of Guinea-Bissau, after Cabral had visited Touré following the AAPC, because he considered the newly independent country an ideal training ground.[158]

The Pan-African ambition to construct a modernity based on African culture and unity influenced Ghanaian diplomacy on all levels. On the level of interpretation, Africa's problems were the outcome of neocolonial machinations in the cultural and psychological realm, not the by-product of superpower competition. On the level of foreign policy formulation, Ghana's diplomacy was geared toward exploiting the only advantage it had over its opponents: its African credentials and its "moral strength." On the level of policy execution, violence was viewed as ineffective because it did not address colonialism's underlying problem: the notion that modernity by definition implied the destruction of African self-confidence. Politically active Africans were therefore drawn into a revolutionary network that relied heavily on African leaders, not on a mass audience. This revealed to what extent Nkrumah and his aides remained the victims of mental colonization, the very thing they sought to destroy.

Nevertheless, federations of liberation forced leaders in the Global North to adjust. The first test for the strength of Accra's liberationist route to modernity was Guinea's independence, which became a battle for hearts and minds, with different types of aid on offer. Local officials were forced to improvise in the face of African pressure and began to see one another as competitors in a genuine propaganda struggle. The divisions in the North only became wider when a French atomic bomb was tested in the Sahara.

CHAPTER 4

Redefining Decolonization in the Sahara, 1959–1960

In 1959, France made clear that it wanted to test an atomic bomb in the Algerian Sahara, providing Ghanaian officials with the first opportunity to directly embed their Pan-African commitments to peace and disarmament within North-South and South-South relations. Kwame Nkrumah had already challenged Charles de Gaulle's conception of an Africa under French tutelage in Guinea and now set his sights on the bomb by inviting peace activists to Accra. At the same time, other liberationists began to challenge Ghana's dominance in inter-African politics, with the Afro-Asian Peoples Secretariat in Cairo organizing an Anti–Atomic Bomb Test Day in October 1959.[1] Unlike their European counterparts, African elites saw the bomb not as a Cold War object but as the product of an exploitative international order. In 1967, when the first steps toward the Strategic Arms Limitation Talks (SALT I) were taken, the Zambian ambassador in Moscow, Vernon Mwaanga, summarized the African understanding of the nuclear threat in a message to Lusaka. On a yellow legal pad, he penciled an essay on how military power had aided Africa's enslavement, a pattern the atomic bomb was replicating. SALT I was an effort to "forestall any attempt by non-whites from developing nuclear weapons."[2] The Pan-African interpretation of nuclear imperialism is hard to see because it has been overshadowed by the Cold War, which, as Westad writes, affected everyone because of the threat of nuclear Armageddon it implied.[3]

Nevertheless, the war of words that erupted over the Sahara tests was a stand-in for a more fundamental struggle over the meaning of decolonization for international relations. After all, what did independence mean if empires would still be allowed to use their formerly colonized territories as a testing ground? According to Nkrumah, Paris was engaging in "nuclear blackmail" and "chose the Sahara to demonstrate to African states their political weakness."[4] The problem of African sovereignty was particularly urgent in 1959, a year that was marked not only by atomic fallout on the African continent but also by negotiations between colonial powers and African nationalists in the Belgian Congo and the Central African Federation. With African negotiators and anticolonial propaganda chipping away at the legitimacy of colonial domination, state and nonstate actors in North and South were forced to rethink their positions in the international system. Yet, the impact of African agency remains obscure. How did ideologically driven African nationalists succeed in redrawing the contours of diplomacy in day-to-day diplomatic interactions?

Historians have claimed postcolonial states failed to gain international influence because their high-minded foreign policy doctrines were incompatible with the authoritarianism of domestic politics.[5] Nkrumah's commitment to peace and disarmament, for example, has been viewed as disingenuous.[6] Instead, nonstate actors, such as peace activists and US civil rights leaders, are seen to be circumventing the Cold War as they sustain the original commitment to Pan-Africanism and a just world. Trade unionists crafted a new language of social change to claim their share of power.[7] Decolonization, then, is recalled as a process that was planned by empires but spun to their own advantage by African nationalists, whose original idealism was sustained only by nonstate actors. A reexamination of the archives, however, reveals how old diplomatic alliances within the Global North and Global South fell apart during the course of 1959 not because of Cold War pressures or postcolonial leaders' hunger for power, but because of the commitment of independent African countries to the projection of their ideas. The starting point of this reconfigured postcolonial order lies in Léopoldville.

Negotiating Decolonization in London and Brussels

"The ultimate goal of our actions is, in prosperity and peace, to assist the Congolese people on their path to independence," declared King Baudouin on 13 January 1959. This speech was a response to riots that had accompanied a prohibited political demonstration organized by Kasavubu's ABAKO in Léopoldville. The city had experienced a demographic explosion and a subsequent shortage of public facilities, provided the feeding ground for a crisis. Despite the reference to "indépendance / onafhankelijkheid," the crackling radios of Brussels and Léopoldville had not broadcast a radically new Belgian colonial policy. Rather, the king's speech was a rebuke to the rioting Congolese, who had failed to meet the Belgian civilizational criteria for independence. The "broad intellectual and moral education of the people" was still stressed as a necessary condition for independence. What was new, however, was the king's promise to not "force European solutions onto African peoples" who had their "own character and traditions."[8] Belgian officials were instructed to approach Africans as not only morally underdeveloped but also psychologically different. The king mirrored shifts in Belgian academic research, which was catching up with what other scholars had been arguing in the Global North. In his influential *Psychology of the Black African (Psychologie van de Afrikaanse Zwarte)*, Lovanium University lecturer Paul Verhaegen argued there were psychological differences between Black and white people that had no biological basis and therefore could be adapted through psychological treatment.[9] Independence, therefore, had to be tailored to the psychological particularities of Africans if it was ever to be effective.

An assessment of Africans that relied on psychology rather than morality provided Belgian officials with an explanation for the Léopoldville riots. The Belgian ambassador to London, for instance, believed the "craziness" that accompanied soccer games had been more influential than the All-African People's Conference, despite official reports from Brussels and Lisbon concluding the unrest had been inspired by Accra, not Cairo or Moscow.[10] In March 1959, an investigative commission presided over by Dequae not only debunked the rumor that the colonial authorities had paid for Congolese delegates' attendance at the AAPC but also, and more notably, argued that primitivism prevented Africans from understanding complex reasoning. Only force would be effective.[11] In May 1959, after a trip to the Congo and Ruanda-Urundi, foreign ministry delegates concluded in Fanonian language that the Congolese in the cities, who had a "real thirst for independence and equality with the white man," were suffering from an "inferiority complex" and were constantly trying to seize on mistakes by whites, while Africans in the bush were happy to accept Belgian guidance, something Belgian minister of the colonies Maurits Van Hemelrijck had already noted during his visit in January 1959.[12] This helped explain the placards reading "Vive le Roi Kasavubu," with Baudouin's name crossed out, during van Hemelrijck's second visit in August 1959.[13] The Dutch ambassador to Léopoldville agreed and considered Belgian guidance indispensable in giving the "drunken thirst for independence" direction.[14] By 1959, nationalist agitation, defined by Jan-Albert Goris as the "sentimental" and "imperial attitudes of black ministers of newly independent countries," had become a pressing strategic problem."[15]

In response, the director of the Institut belge d'information et de documentation (Inbel), William Ugeux, and InforCongo developed a new psychological strategy that sought to create an alliance with African nationalist leaders they considered to be appropriate partners. Léopold Senghor was considered an excellent choice and had to be invited by the king, a visit that happened only in 1962.[16] In the moral empire, African politics had always been perceived as an occupation of power-hungry narcissists, but the riots served as a reminder that one needed to guard against nationalist movements that sought to exploit psychological vulnerabilities.

Psychologically vulnerable Africans had taken the place of morally underdeveloped colonial subjects on the Belgian colonial radar, shaping institutional, aid, and military policies. Pierre Wigny, who returned as minister of the colonies in 1958, proposed a Eurafrica based on personal ties with Congolese politicians as an institutional solution. In 1957, Paul-Henri Spaak had already defended Eurafrica because it made it possible to discriminate between people "who had the same ideas as us" and those who "do not love us" but think they can "claim certain rights from us."[17] In light of the European Economic Community's efforts to create a development fund, Gaston Eyskens was asked by his deputy head of cabinet, Harold D'Aspremont Lynden, to consider the creation of a Belgian-Congolese parliament.[18] Policy experts, however, criticized the plan because they felt such an alliance would become an African nationalist propaganda target.[19] Instead, Eyskens approved the creation of "technical assistants" in January 1959 as a way for Belgium to remain involved in aid and to help the Congolese, since he believed the political aspirations of the Congolese did not match their abilities.[20] "Wise and experienced elites were in short supply," King Baudouin claimed.[21] In March 1959, the foreign affairs ministry latched on to the idea and argued that technical assistants—"techniciens belges"—were not supposed to deal with financial aid but had to develop personal relationships.[22] Even Lieutenant General Émile Janssens of the Force Publique devised strategies to control the "mad Congolese." He argued that psychological action allowed for the integration of soldiers within the colonial state's ideological structure by providing the soldiers with "a family," by encouraging personal development through education and the housing of women and children near the military base. The air of calm the troops projected because of their "formation into real men" would—in his estimation—have a favorable psychological effect and discourage riots.[23]

By 20 January 1960—the opening day of the Table Ronde in Brussels, where Belgian officials and Congolese politicians negotiated the transition to independence—Belgian policymakers thus had come to conceive of their interlocutors as wrestling with a psychological problem. Five days before the meeting's opening, the vice president of the Belgian Parliament wrote to Eyskens, who agreed that the "problem of independence" was "a psychological problem," which was the reason "Belgian cooperation" had to be sustained. Belgian rule was justified no longer on moral grounds but on psychological grounds: Africans were mentally unfit for modernity and self-government.[24] The high number of political parties present at the conference was therefore not a vote of confidence on the part of the Belgian government but an attempt to prevent the formation of a united front. All of them, fourteen in total as well as six tribal chieftains, were monitored by the Brussels police and listed in the popular song "Indépendance Cha Cha." Patrice Lumumba was released from prison and flown to Brussels as a representative of the Mouvement national congolais (MNC) to attend the meeting, where he joined the other parties in demanding immediate independence.[25]

In December 1959, Eyskens's political adviser wrote that the "greatest attention" had to be "paid to psychological factors" during the roundtable since these were "of the utmost importance for the African soul."[26] The political roundtable of January 1960 focused on the constitution and the timetable for independence.[27] In his opening speech, Eyskens called on participants to safeguard the geographical integrity of the country.[28] In the course of the preparations for the economic roundtable of April 1960, "maintaining" the Belgian presence explicitly emerged as a top priority.[29] At the same time, there was little interest in funding Congolese development. In March 1960, the Belgian National Bank even insisted on involving "third countries to a large extent in a burden that is clearly too heavy for our country alone."[30] Nevertheless, "individualizing" aid came out on top, since it allowed more control over financial streams.[31]

The economic issues were tackled in April 1960 during a separate roundtable, a scheme the Portuguese considered to be a ploy by Eyskens to maintain military bases in return for financial and technical aid.[32] To safeguard economic ties and limit the financial burden, common institutions that could decide on aid were created. In a letter to Eyskens, influential Christian Democrat politician Frans Van Cauwelaert urged Eyskens to pick up the pace of the decolonization process after the January roundtable while putting Belgian-Congolese cooperation for technical assistance on the table to entice the Congolese into surrendering control.[33] In his opening speech at the economic roundtable, D'Aspremont Lynden expressed the hope that the work that Leopold II had begun would continue and argued that the Congolese and the Belgians had a "community of interests" that needed to be maintained.[34] Sustaining psychological immaturity was essential for the trick to work, as Sylvain Plasschaert, an economics professor and a former colleague of Eyskens, wrote, because it would convince the Congolese of Belgium's good intentions and, at the same time, Africans would quickly realize they were incompetent and needed Belgian help.[35] The rapid granting of independence was thus not an act of goodwill, nor a crude tactic to retain control, but rooted in a pseudoscientific rationale.[36]

The two roundtable conferences of January and May 1960 were not only a negotiation with Congolese politicians but also PR events that had to present Belgium as the ideal postcolonial partner. The real goal of the swift transition to independence, namely continued dependence, had to be masked, which was deemed feasible based on psychological research. A pamphlet on the political future of the Congo reprinted the king's radio speech alongside photos that showcased Africans visiting shops and eating together with white *colons*, emphasizing a "common destiny."[37] Another pamphlet on the Congo "at the brink of independence" reprinted the roundtable agreement.[38] However, when the Solvay Institute of Sociology, which had been conducting ethnographic studies since 1955, began to actually train the Congolese to take part in elections, Wigny voiced his discontent. He claimed politics was being introduced to sow discord and strengthen anticlerical feelings.[39] At the roundtable conferences, Belgian politicians gave in to demands for independence in a matter of months because they believed African subjects were not only morally bankrupt but also psychologically vulnerable.

Brussels's cynical strategy of capitalizing on psychological immaturity by granting independence dumbfounded observers. Lisbon believed the Belgians had stopped understanding Africa because they transferred all responsibilities to the Congolese without hesitation, while disenfranchising "whites."[40] What angered Jorge Jardim, one of António Salazar's closest advisers, was the fact that the Belgians had hesitated for so long to crush the riots in 1959. Joaquim Trindade dos Santos, a military attaché in Washington, was one of the few voices to suggest wholesale reform and the creation of a Portuguese commonwealth after a conversation with his Belgian counterpart.[41] Radio Conakry was also skeptical. The choice to create a Senate in which different regions would be represented was interpreted as an attempt to balkanize the Congo.[42] The British were baffled because they had fiercely advocated the strategy of slow and prepared independence. The chairman of the Rhodesian Selection Trust, Ronald Prain, who played an important role in attempting to reconcile the political aspirations of white settlers and African populations in the Federation of Rhodesia and Nyasaland, considered the Belgian approach to be misguided. "To the simple African mind the connection between the two will be too obvious," he wrote to Federation prime minister Roy Welensky; "all you have to do is riot one weekend and you get independence the following weekend." Consequently, Prain urged Welensky to vote for bills that loosened the ties with Britain. In January 1959, a new constitution was proposed by Governor Robert Armitage. It created a legislative council in which only fourteen of the twenty-nine members would be elected and eight seats were expected to go to Africans. After being met with resistance from Hastings Banda, who after his release from prison had returned via Accra to lead the National African Congress (NAC), rumors of a plot to kill Europeans and Asians began to swell in government circles.[43] The state of emergency that followed, on 3 March 1959, resulted in the death of fifty-one Africans. At an emergency meeting of the AAPC Steering Committee, the "white paper containing allegations of mass massacre plot" was publicly questioned.[44] In May, the Steering Committee even looked for ways to intervene, because it would be a "source of immense hope and courage" to the freedom fighters.[45]

Consequently, as the anti-Rhodesian Central Africa Committee in London pointed out, the federation became "a test case for British policy in Africa."[46] To make its case against a white-dominated federation, Accra exploited the cheap and popular transistor radio. In April 1959, Chad M. Chipunza, African member of the Legislative Assembly of the Federation of Rhodesia and Nyasaland and United People's Party leader, was dragged from his car and assaulted by demonstrators because he had refused to admit in an interview on Radio Ghana that "Africans were treated worse than dogs."[47] The AAPC Steering Committee demanded the removal of troops from Nyasaland as it called on the British people to resist the "discriminatory and repressive Bills" that were going through the Southern Rhodesia Parliament.[48] The settler government in Southern Rhodesia, in response, produced a pamphlet that stressed the developmental work that had been done. A section on "the franchise" was included at the very end and claimed that "Africans" had "always been" "registered as voters."[49] In November 1959, Welensky even lashed out against the United States and the United Kingdom for their lack of support during a luncheon at which the US ambassador was present.[50]

Hostility from Conakry and Accra made the Commonwealth Relations Office (CRO) realize it had made a mistake when it approached radio infrastructure solely as a form of assistance. CRO officials grasped that the transmitters they had helped build could one day be used against them. The Colonial Office's plan to give Nigeria a more powerful transmitter to counter the planned Soviet bloc broadcasting station in Conakry was opposed, while aid grants for African broadcast companies were decreased.[51] During a conversation with Nkrumah in June 1959, Alec Douglas-Home was told that British decisions in Africa were under the close scrutiny of African public opinion. The Commonwealth secretary therefore decided "Afro-Asian propaganda" developments in the Arab world and the manifestations of African nationalism—in Accra but particularly in Nyasaland—required a Colonial Office that was deeply invested in information activities and presented news in the "correct" way.[52]

Rather than improving assistance schemes, as was done after Bandung, UK Information Offices now worked to prevent the liberal story of a guided transition from crumbling under the pressure of Nkrumah's propaganda campaign, which highlighted "racial problems in the Central African Federation and Kenya." In March 1960, Robert Marett of the Information Policy Department would come to label this new approach "the goodwill" strategy, in which a tactical offering of aid had to be combined with "a more or less orthodox type of information job" inside and outside of British Africa.[53] *The Next Ten Years in Africa*, a government report, reflected an acute awareness of the power of African public opinion by warning that reluctance "to concede independence . . . may alienate African opinion."[54] The UK information officers were therefore asked to promote imperial reform as one monolithic enterprise that also involved the French. This strategy also worked through example: "A Commonwealth Economic Plan for Africa might encourage the French to institute a similar scheme."[55] Like Belgium and Portugal, France and the United Kingdom felt pressured to publicly cling to their modernization schemes in the face of African nationalist alternatives.

The Anglo-French defense of a guided decolonization process was difficult, however, because the two imperial powers had diverging ideas about the power of public diplomacy. In 1960, for instance, the Foreign Office had to convince the French not to cease Radio Brazzaville's transmissions, even though they were attacked by Radio Conakry, where Guinean diplomat Karim Bangoura spearheaded an anti-French campaign.[56] Instead of instigating a radio wave offensive, the French Community secretariat increased the number of African pupils in courses on French radio techniques while providing more funding for educational radio. It was Henry Loomis of USIA's Information Broadcasting Service who understood that African audiences had to be enticed to turn their radios on. He combined educational "forum lectures" with popular entertainment such as jazz.[57] The increased awareness of the need to manage the British reputation should not obscure that the assumptions about the psychological state of Africans remained the same. The British High Court judge who investigated Armitage's justification, Patrick Arthur Devlin, dismissed the "murder plot" as a fabrication in his report in July 1959 but repeated that an insufficiently developed information service had been at the root of the unrest. As a solution, John C. Hyde of the UKIO in Uganda proposed the production of a series of films about the federation in which Europeans and Africans cooperated.[58] In October 1959, psychological aptitude tests were still being administered in

Northern Rhodesia to determine whether Africans could be trained for "positions of responsibility."[59]

The Sahara Atomic Bomb and Ghana's Discovery of Public Opinion

Northern assessments about the African psychological capacity for modernization were unsettled by an anticolonial propaganda campaign, which upset policymakers in the North as they tried to negotiate their way out of a complete retreat from the Congo and the Federation. In November 1959, those anxieties came to a head when twenty-two Afro-Asian countries succeeded in having a UN resolution approved that expressed concern over a French atomic bomb test in the Sahara. In the lead-up to the vote, the British considered drafting a watered-down version of the resolution, a plan that was eventually dropped after Harold Macmillan personally intervened because he felt the British could not offend Ghana and Nigeria, the two leading nations behind the campaign against the bomb.[60] Already, at the Conference of Independent African States in April 1958, delegates had condemned the proposal to use the Sahara as an atomic test site.[61] African UN delegates explicitly criticized the French violation of the continent's sovereignty, with Sékou Touré claiming the bomb was about recolonization; but in the end, the UN resolution focused on health.[62] Couve de Murville, for his part, was afraid that the Afro-Asian bloc would only further destabilize the UN with its "unreasonable" demands. Wilson Flake, the US ambassador in Accra, was surprised when Ghana's minister of external affairs, Michael Dei-Anang, reassured him that the Anglo-American vote against the resolution would soon be forgotten.[63]

Dei-Anang's response was an indication Nkrumah wanted to repeat the PR coup that had rattled the Belgians and the British during their negotiations earlier that year. Nkrumah requested the help of other African leaders, such as Modibo Keïta in Mali, to mobilize African opinion, but primarily relied on newspapers.[64] To reach a mass audience, the production of gripping and richly illustrated stories was prioritized. The accusatory discourse focused on the health risks that attended the bomb, rather than the legitimacy of French colonial claims. The *Evening News* appealed to the religious fabric of many African societies by describing the French decision to explode the bomb in apocalyptic terms, while printing a cartoon that depicted the devil guiding de Gaulle to a ballistic missile.[65] Feelings of indignation were also stirred in a more directly religious way, through a prayer published in the *Ghana Times*: "O God of Mother Ghana and All Africa. Thou knowest the peaceful stand, which

Ghana is taking against the French A-bomb test."[66] A discourse on health, pacifism, and religion had to unite a fragile coalition of African nationalists and pacifists beyond the continent. A renowned anticolonial activist, Reverend Michael Scott, who lived in a South African township and was the first representative to speak to the UN on behalf of subjected people, namely the population of South West Africa; Abraham Johannes Muste, a member of the US Fellowship of Reconciliation; and Michael Randle, chair of the Direct Action Committee against Nuclear War were just some of the people who descended on Accra, a city where peace activists, anticolonial freedom fighters, and African Americans found a public forum and a common cause.[67]

Besides the press, the Ghanaian Bureau of African Affairs tried to rouse the public with stories of spontaneous protest, such as the journey of the Sahara Protest Team to the bombing site in January 1960. On Radio Ghana, the trip was presented as a holy war, while the fundraising campaign at a rally in the West End Arena in November 1959 increased the team's exposure. Even though the two teams were stranded in Upper Volta, the mission was still successful: the public profile of the crisis was raised as pamphlets were distributed in French, English, Arabic, and Hausa and spectacular newspaper stories were printed. Komla Agbeli Gbedemah even forced the team to go back to the border after they had been dropped back into Ghana by French soldiers because their confrontations had aroused so much international interest.[68] A rally in Accra was set up by the CCP, the Ghana Trades Union Congress, and the United Ghana Farmers Council to mobilize "world opinion to force France from going ahead with her inhuman activities."[69] Ghana's provocations were effective. Louis de Guiringaud complained about women protesting under his window. When he asked them to leave, they shouted back that a bomb explosion would lead to an embargo of French goods. The Ghanaian government even provided the ambassador with a retired policeman for his personal protection.[70] These women also created organizations such as Ghana's Women's League, Ghana Women's Atom-Test Committee, and the Accra Market Women's Association, all of which were covertly supported by the Ghanaian state. Their open letter rejected the "sugar-coated propaganda" of France and played on maternal instincts: "For us who breast-feed children . . . the Sahara Atom test is most wicked."[71]

By 1959, the imperative of shaping and manipulating public opinion had become central to Ghanaian diplomacy. This is even more evident when contrasted with the African countries that were aware of the PR dimension of the bomb but more concerned about the health risks. Nigerian prime minister Alhaji Abubakar Tafawa Balewa visited London in September 1959 to request British nuclear experts, whom he then posted in Nigerian monitoring stations even though Macmillan reassured Balewa that the Harmattan, a dry dusty Sahara wind, could not carry the fallout in the direction of Nigeria. In February 1960, the Federal Information Service in Lagos even reported on the close cooperation between Nigeria's fallout stations and the UK Atomic Energy Authority, an effective example of the UK goodwill strategy at work.[72] Nigeria's unilateral move and the British guarantees for assistance to Sierra Leone angered Nkrumah, because he felt they weakened the negotiating position of the African bloc.[73]

Ghana's propaganda campaign forced the CRO, the USIA, the French ambassador Guiringaud, and even the German Democratic Republic to publicly take a stance. In October 1960, despite long-standing objections from the French section within the GDR foreign affairs department, the North Africa section decided to put out a disapproving statement through the Komitee der Deutschen Demokratischen Republik für die Solidarität mit den Völkern Afrikas.[74] Guiringaud did not pause to consider the legitimacy of French testing, but he understood that a public response was required in the face of Ghanaian propaganda, because it had led the unintelligent mass audience— "gens simples"—to panic and the educated parts of the public to harbor doubts about French intentions. The ambassador wrote a factual sounding six-page pamphlet based on a speech that Jules Moch, the French representative in the UN disarmament commission, had given during the debate on the Afro-Asian resolution against the bomb. The pamphlet included three diagrams that compared the blast site in the Sahara to those of Nevada and Balkhash to further substantiate the claims about safety. The pamphlet played on the perceived need for prestige of the elite, "les cercles évolués." Someone with a certain level of education, the pamphlet stated, would not want to be guided by the same emotions as the common people. "As an educated and responsible person," the pamphlet went on, "you would not like to be guided by such arguments, only by your judgment."[75] According to the French embassy, the pamphlet was a success. It had been well received among diplomats and at universities and resented by government offices in Accra. Ghana's finance minister, Komla Agbeli Gbedemah, described the pamphlet's content as a blatant lie, and the *Ghana Times* printed a reply, which, according to Guiringaud, merely contained insults. A protest letter from a Belgian professor and former health minister, Arthur Wauters, and a transcript of Gbedemah's speech were handed to the embassy.[76] Guiringaud, like de Gaulle, felt that African leaders had no right to interfere with what they understood to be French affairs. The fact that France, through the Secretariat of the French Community, began offering internships in its energy commission and its atomic facilities—believing this was good PR—further underscores the French inability to think outside of the colonial framework.[77] French officials did not question their right to be in Africa.

The British, who were still struggling to contain the PR fallout from the Nyasaland emergency, attempted to depoliticize the campaign against the bomb and avoided decolonization because they realized that traditional colonialism was on the way out. Instead, the bomb was placed in the context of the Geneva test ban negotiations and the Cold War. The conversation between Macmillan and Balewa, for instance, bordered on the absurd. Although they agreed on a joint Nigeria–United Kingdom commission to measure the nuclear fallout, both men seemed to be living on different planets. As the Nigerian delegation complained about French neocolonialism, Macmillan stoically maintained that the real challenge was nuclear proliferation.[78] In the House of Commons debate, Macmillan evaded the symbolic impact of the bomb. When Labour member of Parliament Fenner Brockway claimed that the Sahara was not only a matter of dangerous fallout but also a problem of African resentment, Macmillan retorted that the technical issues had been studied and further expressed his hope that the Geneva negotiations would be successful. When another MP rose to disagree with Macmillan, stating that the main problem was the affront to African feelings—a view with which British officials in Accra agreed—Macmillan stuck to his position: the Nigerian ministers who had visited London had been concerned about the health risks.[79]

This was a tactical move. Macmillan and UK foreign officers knew they needed to find a PR strategy that balanced the French viewpoint with the need to support Nigeria and Ghana. The Foreign Office believed that its official "public reaction" would become an important element in the future relations with France. Ignoring the hostile reactions in Africa—as France was doing—was not an option, since Ghana's propaganda campaign had fed rumors about a French-British conspiracy to wipe out the African population on the continent. Therefore, UK information officers were ordered to deny any involvement and declare that their own research had found that the fallout did not pose any significant health risk.[80] In a private conversation with de Gaulle, Macmillan voiced his discontent about the French behavior, explaining that it made the British position in Africa impossible.[81]

Conspicuously absent in this war of words was USIA, as a consequence of the Operations Coordinating Board's decision to remain silent. Nevertheless, when Nigerian newspapers began to blame the United States, because the Americans had denied the French access to the "atomic club," USIA director George V. Allen decided that damage control was required. The USIA's response was *Making It Safe to Stop Nuclear Testing*, a pamphlet produced for USIS-Accra that was sent out to all the posts. By describing how the United States had made every effort to share its nuclear technology as well as the USSR's deception of the public, it implied that the United States had been forced into the business of atomic weaponry. The second part of the pamphlet explained that nuclear energy had peaceful uses and that the US test procedure was safe, with only three lives lost since the beginning of the tests in 1945. Still, a few days before the explosion, USIA's guidelines to its posts worldwide maintained that the less said by US officials, the better.[82]

Ghana's propaganda campaign thus forced the USIA and the British to respond in ways that acknowledged African grievances but did not upset de Gaulle, who considered the bomb to be a French affair and African opposition an expression of Ghana-induced mass hysteria. By referring to the Cold War in broad terms, the Anglo-Saxons wanted to remain in the middle of the road. That position became untenable once the bomb was detonated.

Testing Bombs, Testing Alliances

On the afternoon of 13 February 1960, Dr. J. A. T. Dawson of the Atomic Weapons Research Establishment—which manufactured the British warheads—left for Nigeria to join the UK-Nigerian Scientific Committee. During the flight to Lagos, he was called into the cockpit at 4:30 p.m. because the radiation monitor had recorded three milliroentgen while over Kano in Nigeria, an indication that debris from the weapon had traveled in a different direction than had been predicted. After careful study in Lagos, the team concluded that the amount of fallout had been below harmful limits. Dawson then traveled to Ghana to study the data of the Canadians who had quietly set up radiation monitoring equipment at Nkrumah's request.[83] The French military expert who had been sent to Ghana agreed with the positive conclusions drawn by the British expert, which prompted the French government to make the results public.[84]

Once the bomb exploded, the United Kingdom was quick to investigate whether its reassurances about nuclear fallout matched the actual measurements. Even though the UK-Nigerian Scientific Committee concluded that the dust particles that had traveled to Ghana and Nigeria were harmless, Balewa was still angry.[85] Furthermore, when Sierra Leone and Gambia also asked for help in measuring the fallout, Macmillan and CRO officers began to worry about the opportunities this offered Ghana in terms of propaganda.[86] In light of that threat to their public image, the British grew increasingly disaffected with the French. When, at the end of 1960, a new Afro-Asian resolution requested countries to refrain from further testing, the UK delegation in New York was instructed to vote in favor.[87] The bomb and the already erupted

Congo Crisis made the British side with its territories in Africa rather than with France, something the British representatives at the UN kept secret from their French colleagues until just before the vote. The new public diplomacy strategy that the Foreign Office drew up in 1961 stressed that the British record of decolonization had to be clearly distinguished from the French actions.[88] When Colonial Secretary Iain Macleod visited Rhodesia, white settlers already saw the writing on the wall, calling him "sell-out Mac" from their verandas.[89]

In search for a solution to the PR defeats suffered in Guinea and the Algerian Sahara, Guiringaud became an eager student of printed material. He read periodicals such as *Les Nouvelles de Moscou* and *Commonwealth Today*. Particularly impressed by issue 73 of *Commonwealth Today*, which reported on Princess Margaret's visit to the Commonwealth Exhibition, he wanted to start his own publication, which would also have large photographs and articles on de Gaulle's travels abroad.[90] According to the British logic, however, *Commonwealth Today* was not a means to project UK ideas but a guide containing "practical help." In 1953, there had even been a brief discussion about selling the publication rather than handing it out for free.[91] Guiringaud also saw the Ghanaian BAA as a source of inspiration because of its qualitatively superior booklets. In particular, the postcards depicting Africans as being at the foundation of every major intellectual achievement, such as mathematics and philosophy, had caught his eye.[92] Where his predecessor, Marc Renner, had seen the manipulative skills of USIS officers as a weakness, Guiringaud understood that French educational aid would have to be promoted in a spectacular way.

Despite this acute sensitivity to PR, Guiringaud was unable to see the symbolism of the Sahara tests. When he bumped into the British ambassador at a cocktail party, Guiringaud told him that he found the campaign against France unnecessary. "But your bomb is a political affair, is it not?" the British ambassador replied. Guiringaud interpreted this snide remark as evidence of envy about France's entry into the small group of atomic powers. Even when Nkrumah, in a conversation with the ambassador, hinted that his propaganda on nuclear safety was a way to reject French colonialism, Guiringaud still replied that the Sahara was French and that the French access to the nuclear club was not up for discussion, after which he rose from his seat and left.[93] Additionally, the Executive Council of the French Community supported the bomb as a measure to protect French Africa.[94] Senghor expressed his amazement that the 208th explosion provoked such emotion, while the 207 non-French tests had gone unnoticed. The press release of the French embassy on the day of the explosion also downplayed the health risks and stated that the French decision had been made because nuclear weapons had become an inescapable feature of international life.[95] At the same time, the Sahara atomic bomb tests deepened the rift between Senegal and

Mali—which briefly formed the Mali Federation between April 1959 and August 1960—because Premier Modibo Keita of Mali issued a communiqué in which he threatened to organize public protests if the tests were not canceled.[96]

In Senegal, in contrast, the Mali Federation Information Service acted as an extension of the French cultural action rather than mobilizing public support for the federation. In return for help with the spread of French culture in British Gambia in 1959, Mamadou Dia received intelligence about Nkrumah's "actions ideologiques" toward Senegal.[97]

When a second device was detonated on the first of April, even Eisenhower felt forced to react. During a meeting in Washington, DC, on 22 April 1960, he passed on warnings from nine African nations to de Gaulle that nuclear testing in the Sahara was driving them to the Soviet camp.[98] Relations with Haile Selassie had already been frosty because of US support for Somalia, leading to a visit to Moscow by the emperor in June 1959.[99] In Ghana, propaganda became less involved with the peace movement and more aimed at furthering Ghana's Pan-African ambitions. Ghanaian officials lost sight of the possible consequences of their propaganda. Gbedemah, for instance, had been forced to cancel the freeze of all the assets of French firms when other African countries did not follow the Ghanaian example. Ghana's claim within the General Agreement on Tariffs and Trade (GATT) for equal treatment and its application for loans with the International Monetary Fund were weakened by the trade restrictions put in place against France. Nonetheless, the US embassy understood that the sanctions were meant to have a political effect.[100]

More important, in April 1960, international peace activists such as Bill Sutherland became disillusioned with Nkrumah at the Positive Action Conference for Peace and Security in Africa (see figure 4.1). The purpose of the conference was to protest not only the "poisoning of the earth's atmosphere" but also "fake independence" and the escalating situation in Algeria and South Africa. Positive Action was presented not only as a way to "meet the dangers" but also as a way to achieve "complete independence and unity."[101] Jean Allman argues that peace activists were unhappy because Nkrumah was unable to resist the pressures of the Cold War and as a consequence gave them less freedom to experiment. However, Sutherland hardly mentions the Cold War in his memoirs. What he criticizes is Nkrumah's use of the peace movement to advance Ghana's international position.[102] Likewise, when Michael Scott attended the AAPC in 1958, his resolution stressed the importance of facing "the future without genetic damage."[103] Unlike the propaganda campaign before the explosion, however, Nkrumah's speech at the Positive Action Conference presented the nuclear bomb as an attempt to "balkanize" the continent and destroy the "African Personality." Peace activists such as Sutherland were disappointed because original

POSITIVE   ACTION

CONFERENCE

for

PEACE & SECURITY

in

AFRICA

APRIL 7th — 9th, 1960   *ACCRA, GHANA*

COMMUNITY CENTRE

FIGURE 4.1.   The official program of the Positive Action Conference of April 1960. Printed by the Guinea Press Ltd.

disarmament proposals were submerged in the Pan-African agenda. Nkrumah had discovered that the emotions that the bomb raised could be used to mobilize the so-called masses in the service of African unity. International peace activists and Nkrumah went their separate ways not because of the Cold War but because Nkrumah wanted to pursue his own agenda.[104]

USIA described Nkrumah's call for an emergency conference as an attempt to regain his prominent position in the face of other African nationalists questioning Ghana's leadership. Nigeria passed its own motion in its House of Commons condemning France's "disregard of African sensibilities."[105] Lumumba, who attended the Positive Action Conference, congratulated the Belgian government for its willingness to end the injustices of colonialism. Even Nkrumah, in February 1960, expressed his appreciation for the Belgian handling of the Congolese situation, claiming "the Belgian example encouraged the rest of Africa and at the same time constituted a defeat for colonialism."[106] The AAPC Steering Committee struggled with the integration of the viewpoints of all the different actors and limited itself to congratulating the MNC for its success in pressuring the Belgian government.[107] Scholars such as Ludo de Witte have chronicled how the political convictions of the Congo's first prime minister had become more radical and pan-African by 1958. Yet, that evolution was never linear. Lumumba had always been uncomfortable with the color bar, but as an *évolué* who had obtained an *immatriculation*—proving his civilized status— he had absorbed some ideas of the Belgian moral empire. It led him to embrace the Pan-Africanism of a Nkrumah who still had "praise for the British," while wanting to assist the colonizers with figuring out the "Black Soul" (*l'âme noire*).[108] The USIS officers' expectation that Nkrumah would become isolated in his pleas for African unity turned out to be correct.[109] The break between Accra and peace activists and the rift in the early 1960s between an increasingly more radical Nkrumah and more careful African nationalists, such as Lumumba, cast doubt on the claim that Ghana was able to turn the "threat of radiation" into "a platform for equal access to nuclear information," "political and electrical power."[110]

Ghana's enthusiastic adoption of propaganda as a diplomatic weapon to spread its anticolonial modernization model affected old alliances in North and South alike. In the Global North, US and UK officials distanced themselves from Paris, while Belgium's relationship with Lisbon and London soured because of African propaganda campaigns and the swift decolonization of Congo and Ruanda-Urundi. In the Global South, Nkrumah chose to emphasize his message of African unity, which led to a break with the international peace movement. Nonstate actors clashed with newly independent states that wanted to control how their anticolonial modernization project was being sold, a dynamic that also marked the Afro-Asian People's Solidarity Organisation's relationship with Gamal Abdel Nasser.[111] All the while, the attempts of old empires to maintain some form of influence through roundtables and negotiations also made it more difficult for anticolonial activists to outright reject Northern-led decolonization. Lumumba and Nkrumah had to applaud the Belgian decision to fast-track decolonization, while the support of Senghor and others in the French Community for atomic testing forced Nkrumah to concentrate on health risks in his propaganda campaign.

Neither African nationalists nor policymakers in the North were thinking about a Cold War international system in 1959. When the Sahara bombs exploded, the contested meaning of sovereignty was at the core of diplomatic debates. The language of a Cold War arms race helped everyone avoid the real stakes of the debate, namely the future of African self-government. Ghana focused on health risks to sustain its coalition with peace movements outside of Africa. The United Kingdom treated the bomb as an issue of nuclear proliferation to balance its relationship with France, safeguard its own atomic energy interests, and maintain the goodwill of its former colonies. USIA presented the United States as the responsible nuclear nation of the bipolar world. France did not understand African disgruntlement and therefore believed the annoyance of the British and the Americans stemmed from the stronger French position in the Cold War arms race.

By the time the "Year of Africa" swung by, it was not the assertive African nationalist claims but the perceived "primitive" behavior in the streets of Léopoldville that came to dominate decision making in the Global North and South.

CHAPTER 5

The Congo Crisis as the Litmus Test for Psychological Modernization, 1960–1961

By 1960, it had become unclear whether the psychological strategies of the previous decade would work on a continent with self-governing states. On 30 June, King Baudouin still believed in the effectiveness of old ways as he arrived in Léopoldville to attend the independence celebrations. In his speech, Baudouin sung the praises of Leopold II as a "liberator," a term Gaston Eyskens changed to "civilizer," considering it inappropriate. More consequential was his removal of the references to "Eurafrique," because he understood that maintaining Belgian influence required tact. Nevertheless, Patrice Lumumba made an impromptu speech to remind his audience of Belgian exploitation and racism, leading Eyskens to write a speech that celebrated the Belgian civilizational work, which he forced Lumumba to read out during lunch.[1] Only forty-eight hours later, workers went on strike, and riots broke out; Sud-Kasaï province and the mineral-rich province of Katanga, led by Moïse Tshombe, seceded.[2] Belgians left Léopoldville and landed in Brussels, where panic spread to the highest echelons. The minister for the colonies, Raymond Scheyven, contacted magistrates and Archbishop Leo Suenens to obtain an exemption to the legal ban on abortions if pregnancy had been the result of rape in Congo. During a meeting at the office of Justice Minister Laurent Merchiers, where Scheyven and Minister for Public Health Paul Meyers were also present, the rationale behind this decision was explained: "The disruption of the integrity of the family by the birth of a mulatto would be worse than curettage."[3] The Belgian moral empire reared its ugly racist head.[4]

What are scholars to make of this crisis? International historians and Africanists insist on reading this episode as a moment when the Cold War intruded on Kwame Nkrumah's ambition to keep Africa out of the bipolar conflict. The Congo Crisis, like the Sahara atomic bomb tests, initially offered Ghana and the Afro-Asian community the opportunity to play an autonomous role on the international stage—so the story goes. Yet, Cold War constraints and Patrice Lumumba's request for Soviet assistance limited Nkrumah's space to speak from a position of non-alignment, as Nkrumah himself became disappointed and realized that "the space to imagine new worlds" had become a luxury "no one could . . . afford." The competition between the Soviet and the US systems forced anticolonial leaders to abandon their liberationist fight and take the "real" balance of power into account.[5] These stories of Cold War tension leave us wondering what determined decision making about the Congo? How was a climate created in which Lumumba's assassination became imaginable, particularly since other left-leaning leaders, such as Sékou Touré, were allowed to stay in power? Those questions suggest policymakers did not see the Congo as a prize in the East-West competition but rather as a nightmarish outcome of the North-South struggle: an unstable postcolonial state led by a liberationist demagogue.[6]

The Congo as an Educational Wasteland

In 1960, strategists in different capitals of the world tried to determine Africa's global position. For example, Ghanaian diplomats quickly realized that they not only would have to fight neocolonial intrusion but also needed to convince other African leaders of the benefits of Ghana-led modernization. A mission that had set out from Accra in November 1960 urged leaders in Accra to exploit the ethnic tensions in recently independent countries. Ibrahim Abboud's invitation to establish Pan-African trade unions and women's organizations in Sudan was enthusiastically welcomed because it allowed A. K. Barden to limit Gamal Abdel Nasser's Pan-Arab influence by building an infrastructure for the African minority.[7]

Decolonization also strained the US public diplomacy machine. Former assistant secretary of defense for international security affairs Mansfield Sprague was asked to assess whether the changing world was affecting diplomacy.[8] During these Sprague Committee meetings, USIA deputy director Washburn talked about "the trend to a multipolar world" and believed countries that were "not aligned with either side" embraced the US spirit of self-determination. While Washburn operated in the world of symbolic combat and paid more attention to countries such as Ghana that used their prestige as a hard power substitute, the State Department still believed "the world" was "bi-polar" and was "likely to become more so."[9] Nonetheless, when it came to Africa, even the State Department acknowledged that this was not primarily a Cold War problem, while Dwight Eisenhower believed "nationalism was the most powerful force in the world today, and that the pull of independence was stronger than that of Communism."[10] Communist activities were seen as ancillary, at best, to the real problem, which was the "revolution of rising expectations," the idea that unfulfilled, increased expectations create unstable political situations. Communism was a disease that could thrive in the development process, a problem that the United States—in a cynical twist—could create for itself if it did not consciously imprint its values through cultural assistance.[11] Sprague therefore wanted to "preempt" Africa "for the Bloc," something Foster Dulles had also talked about with Eisenhower.[12] Because of independence, it became more important to intertwine the promotion of a favorable US image and leadership training. Inexperienced Africans would not understand the workings of international diplomacy, it was reasoned, which allowed for a distortion of the US image. The cumbersome administrative procedures of aid programs seemed to be particularly unsuited to Africa and could result in so-called negative psychological impressions on African leaders who were deemed to be unfamiliar with bureaucracy.[13] This was Wilsonianism at its most paternalistic: a world run by US standards benefited Africans and Americans alike.

Meanwhile, French diplomats tried to plant the seed of doubt about decolonization's centrality in international affairs by distributing two maps of Africa among their colleagues. One depicted Eastern Bloc penetration through Egypt and Ethiopia; the other displayed Communism together with Pan-African and Pan-Arab arrows coming from Egypt and Ghana. The second map was handed to skeptical British officials with a plea to undertake joint action and hold the line against the African nationalist onslaught. A few days later, Michel Debré gave US Secretary of State Christian Herter the bipolar map of Africa, which Herter found exaggerated. James Frederick Green, the former US consul in Léopoldville, also got hold of the map and understood that the French wanted to deceive him.[14] What Paris failed to understand was that the logic of Cold War containment was not on the minds of US and UK diplomats. Even the NATO committee on Communist penetration in Africa concluded that nationalism was the most pressing issue, particularly because it made the "white man" less confident about his ability to meet the development challenge.[15] What had already become clear in the sands of the Sahara now became more pronounced in the bush of the Congo: psychological modernization had failed. Instead, leaders turned toward socioeconomic modernization: socioeconomic conditions, not African attitudes, became the target of modernization.

In response to the riots and the Katanga secession, the United States quickly voted in favor of a resolution that created the United Nations Operation in the Congo (UNOC), while Britain and France abstained. Afraid it would set a precedent for Rhodesia, Harold Macmillan supported UNOC but not the use of force in Katanga, while Charles de Gaulle opposed the entire operation. Through the anticolonial lens of Lumumba and Nkrumah, the position of the two colonial powers was interpreted as a form of support for Katanga, even though neither the Quai d'Orsay nor Westminster was willing to back the secession, fearing disgruntlement in their remaining colonies, more UN intervention, secessionist claims in the Bas-Congo, and unrest in Congo-Brazzaville.[16] Lumumba, who, together with people like Antoine Gizenga, was committed to maintaining the unitary Congolese state, felt betrayed by his political rivals. He claimed that fellow party member Joseph Iléo, who supported federalism, and Joseph Kasavubu of rival ABAKO, who favored closer ties with Belgium, were "corrupt" "imperial" "puppets." Lumumba's letters to Secretary General Dag Hammarskjöld of the UN are therefore filled with suspicion.[17]

The immense unrest had come as a surprise because many believed that Belgian colonial rule had given the "heart of darkness" a more modern heartbeat.[18] When King Baudouin traveled to Léopoldville for the Dipenda celebrations, he found a clean and modern city that had undergone a dusting with the pesticide DDT to kill the mosquitos. Belgian propaganda centered on the "modern market" and "sports stadium" of Léopoldville, where "the city belles, wearing a plausible imitation of a Paris model" could be seen parading the streets.[19] British Council officials were impressed to find skyscrapers, wide boulevards, and air-conditioned hotels and nightclubs. In 1958, even Nasser admitted to having been impressed by the sights and sounds of Léopoldville.[20] Couve de Murville, for his part, had already in April 1960 predicted that the prosperous Congo would descend into chaos once the "white man" left.[21] In determining why there was so much atrocious violence, de Murville and his colleagues settled on a familiar explanation: the Belgians had insufficiently prepared the Congolese for self-government. Newspaper commentators criticized the Belgian colonial government for creating an uneducated mass while the educational programs of Radio Congo belge, initiated in 1959, were forgotten.[22] In December 1959, US embassy officials panicked when they rediscovered the Van Bilsen Plan of 1955, which estimated that thirty years and fifty thousand secondary school graduates were required to establish government services. What had been a report to justify a continued Belgian presence was read by the Americans as a cry for help.[23] Macmillan accused the Belgians of leaving a "gap that the native Congolese could not fill."[24]

On Independence Day, delegates therefore brought educational assistance plans with them to Léopoldville as former Belgian prime minister Joseph Pholien still recommended that Eyskens seek the advice of the director of an institute in Lulabourg with an expertise in the "Black psyche."[25] Belgium belatedly initiated a crash scholarship and trainee program for students, which by 1962 had to produce two hundred university graduates, and enabled one thousand Congolese to complete training courses of three to six months.[26] Robert Murphy of the US delegation announced that he had three hundred scholarships on offer, as USIA flew in staff and equipment while simultaneously strengthening thirty-three posts in twenty-one African countries. Mazoyer, the French consul in Congo, had been overwhelmed by the stacks of applications on his desk, but following guidelines from Paris he refused to help a Katanga government delegation.[27] For contemporaries, the Congo was not a site of bipolar struggle but an educational wasteland. What was maddening for the public diplomats, who had been hiding under their desks, was that the Congolese seemed to refuse the order that imperial modernity had brought.

The Internationalization of the Congo Education Problem

To fulfill the perceived demand for education, every diplomat realized he had to cooperate. After Raymond Hare of the State Department admitted that he had no clue what to do, Roger Seydoux confessed that France needed help with a request to train two hundred Congolese in French technical schools. The British information officers received an enormous number of applications to study in the United Kingdom from groups such as "Les amitiés congolaises," a motley crew of Congolese journalists and Bulgarian refugees.[28] Ghanaian diplomats and other African freedom fighters were excited, because Congolese independence was the opportunity they had been waiting for. Barden informed freedom fighters in Swaziland that he could not deal with their requests since Congo was "at the moment, more important," since it was in a "strategic position . . . and could be effectively used as a spring-board" for propaganda, a sentiment echoed by the AAPC in Tunis.[29] In line with the network strategy of the Bureau of African Affairs, experts of the Bank of Ghana and Ghanaian doctors, engineers, and civil servants poured into the Congo alongside Ghanaian soldiers. Not only was a secret agreement signed with Lumumba on August 8, 1960, establishing the

Ghana-Congo Union, but Ghanaian chief of staff Henry Templer Alexander also took command of the UNOC troops. Nkrumah even sent special envoys to Brussels to assist and ensure "the transition . . . took place in an atmosphere of goodwill."[30] African nationalists in French West Africa, in contrast, viewed the crisis as an opportunity to send French military advisers into the field, such as Edouard Terzian of the Malian UNOC battalion, to counter "anti-white racism" that Nkrumah's Pan-Africanism supposedly engendered.[31]

At the fifteenth session of the UN General Assembly, which started on 20 September 1960, the problem of African development was internationalized. The General Assembly is remembered for the emergence of the Afro-Asian group, Nikita Khrushchev's Troika proposal, and the debate over UNOC intervention. Nonetheless, what is striking is how many speeches dealt with the need to offer the Congolese education. The UN set up a training and fellowship program to "build up a nucleus of sufficiently trained Congolese personnel to act as government administrators."[32] Khrushchev wanted "to give" the Congolese" not only "material" but also "moral" "assistance."[33] Macmillan declared that administration, health, education, and other services essential to the modern state could be provided more efficiently through larger administrative units such as the UN. His speech was part of the new information strategy that had emerged during the Sahara bomb crisis and presented British colonialism as an undertaking that fostered stable self-government. The UK had already proved willing to relinquish responsibility to colonies that had been prepared for self-government: "Here they are, sitting in this hall . . . who dares to say that this is anything but a story of steady and liberal progress?"[34] The French wanted to internationalize the educational problem by increasing imperial cooperation, since de Gaulle believed chaos in the Congo had resulted from division. Cooperation had to put a check on US ambition and discourage opposition groups in French Africa from calling on the UN to intervene. In his letter to Eisenhower, de Gaulle argued that it made little sense to give more responsibility to the UN, an organization in which "the West," "the birthplace of common sense and freedom," would be outcompeted by the Afro-Asian bloc and the USSR.[35] He therefore supported Portuguese colonial claims.[36] De Murville also believed that "France had an important role to play" in the Congo and was not to be placed under the "international and benevolent tutelage" of the UN.[37] The UN had to be prevented from becoming decolonization's principal manager.

Eisenhower hinted at such a scenario in his speech as he advocated "an all-out United Nations effort" to strengthen African education. The image of a president who only reluctantly participated in the UN General Assembly hardly does justice to the zeal with which Eisenhower called on his fellow delegates to provide the Congolese with "the mental tools to preserve and develop their freedom." Without an international effort at psychological modernization, "loud speakers in the public square" would "exhort people to freedom," leading to disappointment and instability. Eisenhower also pledged to assist the UN in matters of African security, proposed the establishment of a UN fund for the Congo, and wanted to involve the UN in long-term modernization efforts via a program the International Cooperation Administration was developing in October 1960.[38] Before the General Assembly, ICA secretary Alice May had sent out a transcript of Eisenhower's speech and, after he spoke, she distributed among different UN delegates an illustrative draft resolution that covered all the president's Africa proposals.[39] When UN officials complained about feeling excluded, Herter instructed the US delegation to make a contribution of two million dollars to the budget of the United Nations Educational, Scientific and Cultural Organization (UNESCO) for aid to education in Africa. He wanted the announcement to be dramatic and well timed to ensure "maximum strategic and psychological impact."[40] Eisenhower also welcomed African UN delegates to the White House, sent them on a tour across the United States, and demanded the distribution of films in Africa that accurately depicted the United States.[41] Nevertheless, he remained willing to sacrifice the US public image if doing so served the orderly transition to independence. The United States therefore joined France, the United Kingdom, Belgium, Australia, the Dominican Republic, Portugal, Spain, and South Africa in abstaining from the vote on General Assembly Resolution 1514. The anticolonial resolution had been put forward by the twenty-two Afro-Asian countries in December 1960 and constituted a "Declaration on the Granting of Independence to Colonial Peoples and Territories," which carried by a vote of 89–0 in the UN General Assembly.[42]

Nkrumah entered the General Assembly as a vindicated man. The crisis in the heart of Africa justified not only "his continuous outcry" against "the threat of balkanisation in Africa" but also his "daily condemnation of neocolonialism." The Congo Crisis validated the Pan-African worldview and did not collapse the international politics of the Cold War into Africa but instead strengthened Nkrumah's conviction that Africa's problems could be solved only by a joint African front.[43] Touré, who gave Amílcar Cabral a base in Conakry in 1960, agreed. Despite a "new way of life with its own values," which was "being built up," Northern policymakers looked only for "traces of their own" Cold War "ideological antagonism in Africa," Touré claimed.[44] Ousmane Ba of Mali redefined the "uncommitted nations" as being "committed" to "the anti-imperialist cause." Representatives who tried to put Mali "under the Caudine Forks of such and such a bloc" were regarded with suspicion as "imperialist schemers."[45] Tsehafi Taezaz

Aklilu Habte-Wold of Ethiopia argued that "liberation" was an "essential condition for" "peace in the region" and drew parallels between the UN in 1960 and the League of Nations in 1936, when Ethiopia protested the Italian invasion to highlight Haile Selassie's anticolonial credentials.[46]

Even though African delegates in their speeches focused on redefining the international system, with federations of liberation and their own anticolonial routes to modernity, they did agree with their Northern colleagues that education was key in stemming the Congolese bleed. In August 1960, Nkrumah had already turned the Conference of Independent African States in Léopoldville into a meeting where the distribution of aid to the Congo was discussed to keep the problems in the heart of the continent under African control.[47] Yet, on the eve of September 5, 1960, the situation got out of hand when President Kasavubu fired Lumumba, leading the prime minister to also dismiss the president. With parliament disapproving both actions, Congolese politics entered a stalemate, and plans for Lumumba's elimination began to take shape.[48] Unlike their counterparts in the North, African leaders did not see the lack of education and the political problems this created as a design flaw but as an inherent feature of the civilizing mission. Touré talked about an "imperialist philosophy which restricts human development."[49] "It is certainly not the fault of the African peoples," Tsehafi Taezaz Aklilu Habte-Wold exclaimed, "if the governments which oppressed them for centuries have deprived them of the benefits of education and technical progress."[50] In his own speech, Kasavubu thanked UN members for their aid but mainly reaffirmed that he was the only legal representative of the Congolese people, while Lumumba roamed the halls of the UN building to look for support after his own delegate to the UN, Thomas Kanza, had gotten Nasser to agree to "everything" he had "asked."[51]

Portugal and Belgium were the exception and ignored the heart of Africa in their speeches. Pierre Wigny claimed "the Congo was well equipped to cut an impressive figure as an independent state," a point he buried under a long speech on the UN and relations with the Communist world.[52] Likewise, the Portuguese delegate Vasco Vieira Garin talked about the Congo in passing. He focused on Nkrumah's claim that African territory was made Portuguese "by the stroke of a Portuguese pen" to "avoid discussion of their dark deeds."[53]

The fifteenth General Assembly of the UN was not only a historic meeting where the Cold War stakes of the Congo Crisis were raised with each thud of Khrushchev's shoe on his desk, emphasizing his belief that "US imperialism was no longer all-powerful."[54] More important, different aid philosophies for the Congo were put forward that intensified conflict on the ground, where cooperation had already broken down since the landing of UN troops on 15 July.

The Congo as a Problem of African Politics

The prioritization of white lives by Europe and the United States set up a clash with the Congolese government, which, with Ghanaian support, worked to expel the Belgian troops and reunite the country, while the USSR sought to capitalize on the unrest. An ambiguous UN mandate had made cooperation difficult, but it was the disagreement about the final goal of a Congolese development program that perpetuated mutual mistrust. As USIS officers phrased it, the Congo's long "isolation" from the outside world meant that the first country to establish a foothold would have a disproportionally great influence.[55] Nonetheless, the French, the British, and the Americans agreed to continue their cooperation, because they all believed the actions of their interlocuters would eventually also serve them. Only Lisbon openly supported the Katanga regime, out of fear the unrest would spread to Angola.[56]

The British Foreign Office saw the crisis as another opportunity, after the debacle of the second French atomic bomb test, to convince Congolese politicians that the liberal image of British imperialism was fundamentally different from French colonialism.[57] Initially, the Commonwealth Relations Office had only encouraged the Ghanaians to deploy troops, believing Ghanaian success would lessen the irritation among Kenyan nationalists and prevent a "spill-over" of conflict into British territories.[58] One day later, the CRO had already changed course and set up an aid operation, because it realized assistance would be more appealing PR, especially in the contrast with the French intransigence in Algeria. For the Information Research Department, Congo was a "paradise," because anti-Communist material was in high demand. The colonial newspapers of Léopoldville, the *Courrier d'Afrique*, and *Actualités Africaines*, as well as radio broadcasts, relied on information bulletins, while priests and even two lecturers at Lovanium University used Information Research Department pamphlets, such as *The Interpreter*, as teaching material.[59] By improving its public image, the United Kingdom would also benefit financially, thanks to the presence of companies such as Unilever, Shell, Barclays, and a large contingent of British missionaries. Business interests were submerged in a broader set of UK concerns.[60]

France, like Belgium, was interested in winning over Congolese officials to avoid a situation in which the UN would become the sole interlocutor for educational and technical assistance. The Direction générale des affaires culturelles et techniques (DGACT) was convinced that cooperation with other Western countries, outside of UN structures, was still possible. Cooperation became more feasible after October 1960, when the first Congolese students who had been funded through the ICA Third Country Scheme arrived in Paris. ICA funded training in countries outside of the United States in an attempt to get as many as possible ready for government positions. De Murville was convinced he could parachute French experts into key positions in the new Gizenga-led government.[61] What the French understood as a step toward cooperation was in fact a US attempt at putting stable state structures in place. Eisenhower wanted to ensure a steady supply of teachers and educational material through cooperation. To entice the British to collaborate, the State Department stressed that a "Sovietized Congo," so close to the East African colonies, would be disastrous, particularly with the already considerable influence of Cairo. The British Council agreed to cooperate only because it felt that competition would give the entire operation a political complexion in the eyes of the Congolese and further damage the British liberal imperialist reputation.[62] Western cooperation was thus based on a fragile balance of subtle misunderstandings.

Nkrumah, in contrast, was alone in his support for Lumumba. William Tubman publicly voiced his irritation about Ghanaian assistance, while Kasavubu tried to confiscate Ghanaian and Guinean pamphlets that had been hidden in packing cases filled with medical supplies destined for the UN Hospital. With little support from other African leaders, Nkrumah turned to the Congolese population. The mobile cinema van of the Ghana Information Services, which had been unloaded to entertain the troops, was secretly used to promote African unity. Nevertheless, Nkrumah remained unable to secure support for the creation of an African High Command, which he had proposed at the AAPC in 1958.[63] Moreover, under the pressure of the crisis, Nkrumah's relationship with Lumumba quickly soured, despite Ghanaian propaganda claiming the opposite and notwithstanding Lumumba's goal—like Nkrumah's—to "maintain our personality." Ghana's ambassador to Léopoldville, Andrew Djin, informed Nkrumah that the high regard Lumumba once had for the Ghanaian leader was quickly fading away.[64]

Meanwhile, other African leaders were keen to take the lead in the Congo. David Dacko of the Central African Republic held a press conference in which he claimed the UN was "doing colonialism." Abboud and Tubman informed Hammarskjöld that they were contemplating the withdrawal of their troops, since the UN was not fulfilling its obligations. After the secretary of the French Community, Jean Foyer, aired his discontent about UN influence, Prime Minister Mamadou Dia of Senegal in his turn wanted to draw on the disgruntlement Foyer's statement had generated among African leaders. To give the Congo Crisis a "caractère essentiellement africain," Dia tried to set up a conference in which African leaders could come together. Senegalese UN delegate Ousmane Socé Diop called on his African colleagues to look for a solution during a "table ronde." Unlike "certain African members" who were only using "this international stage as an instrument of propaganda and demagoguery"—thinly veiled criticism of Nkrumah—Senghor wanted to apply the "méthode sénégalaise" and negotiate. "No economic assistance plan for the Congo" could be approved, Dia proclaimed in the UN General Assembly in September 1960, until the recipients of that aid had taken part in a "round table meeting of all the Congolese movements."[65]

The Congo Crisis transformed into a problem of African politics, which was increasingly being dominated by military men and authoritarian rulers. Leaders in the Global North had already fretted over this problem before it emerged. In 1958, de Gaulle's closest adviser, Jacques Foccart, began to build a network that connected authoritarian African leaders to Paris.[66] In August 1959, the district administrator of Kindu in the Belgian Congo wrote about the dangers of the "volksmenner" (demagogue) who could undermine colonial authority and became an authoritarian in the case of immediate independence.[67] The Belgian ambassador to Dakar argued political parties were formed "around personalities" who knew "how to impose themselves through personal factors," while claiming voters were naturally drawn to traditional chiefs. A continued colonial presence would be the only way to prevent this turn to authoritarianism, which attracted supposedly morally and psychologically underdeveloped Africans.[68] In a conversation with Murphy in April 1958, Louis Joxe, French ambassador to Washington, claimed that democracies could not "be created overnight" because Africans had a "natural element of susceptibility to authoritarian regimes." Murphy retorted, however that it was US policy to help the "native African races" without being dragged into an East-West struggle.[69] Despite Richard Nixon's misgivings about the African ability to combine democracy and development, the State Department waited until May 1959 to present a policy that aimed to turn the trend toward authoritarianism to the advantage of the United States.[70] During an infamous meeting, State Department officials claimed that little prestige would be lost by identifying with an authoritarian regime if these leaders invested in progress.[71]

While this was often considered the birth of a cynical policy in support of right-wing dictators, Eisenhower and his aides maintained their belief in civic education. Relying on military leaders could be only a short-term solution.[72] Guided by fears that saw the United States transforming into a garrison state because of the Cold War—foreshadowing his speech about the adverse effects of the military-industrial complex in 1961—and embracing the export of the US democratic model, Eisenhower pleaded that young military leaders had to be influenced through military assistance programs. Without training, people who had lived "so long under dictatorships" could not be expected to "run a successful government."[73] Nixon agreed that there was "a vital interest" in helping to develop "governmental institutions which are based on principles of freedom and democracy."[74] In 1959, both men called on Clarence Randall, who advocated "better education for civilians" because he discerned too much readiness to "give up pushing for democratic ideals," as well as General William Draper, who established a presidential commission on US military assistance.[75] Their ideas were picked up by the Sprague Committee, whose members saw the mutual defense agreements as a "unique psychological opportunity" to encourage the armed forces to make "an enlightened and positive contribution" to long-term development.[76] Defense agreements would "create a sympathetic attitude" toward US efforts to help the armed forces along that road to modernity. The training programs, which had been designed to teach the armed forces how to use modern equipment, had "collateral effects" on attitudes such as instilling leadership qualities and US values. Through the Military Assistance Advisory Group, local armed forces could be encouraged to work on economic and social development. Posts on the ground agreed.[77] A plan entitled "The Collateral Effects of Training Foreign Military" materialized in May 1960 and sought to use information programs to create soldiers who could help guide the state toward political stability, economic viability, and eventually democratic institutions.[78] While all NATO members thus concluded that Africans were attracted to "authoritarianism," the members' concrete responses differed markedly.[79] The British, the Belgians, and particularly the French sought to exploit the move to authoritarianism in a straightforward fashion, while Eisenhower was looking for ways to maintain democracy.[80]

Still, the narrative of the demagogue leading an uneducated population had real consequences when it began to center on one man: Patrice Lumumba. During the Congolese election campaign, Lumumba had been branded as a slick politician. In May 1959, Belgian minister for the colonies Maurice Van Hemelrijck, described Lumumba as "a political chameleon" with a strong tendency to tell each audience what it wanted to hear.[81] The Dutch ambassador was also less worried about Lumumba's leftist sympathies than his talent for instigating unrest.[82] Baudouin told the US ambassador only three days before independence that the king was "fully aware of Lumumba's weaknesses" and "the fact that he was not very honest." Nonetheless, the king still considered him to be "the logical man to form the government."[83] By indicting Belgian colonialism on Independence Day, Lumumba therefore unknowingly confirmed these clichés of the African strong man who could attain stability if he adhered to Northern imperial norms but when insufficiently educated turned to demagoguery. Belgian distaste for Lumumba in particular went beyond diplomatic strategy: the Belgian embassy in Brazzaville saw an enemy of the moral empire, a man who was "anti-Christian."[84] Nevertheless, Lumumba became a liability only after having been placed under house arrest on September 14, 1960, and when he escaped to his stronghold Stanleyville in November, even though a month earlier Wigny had already asked Eyskens to resist the urge to openly denounce "sinistre Lumumba."[85] The Portuguese ambassador increasingly grew worried, even though, in August 1960, he claimed that Lumumba's acceptance of foreign aid from various sources was mainly aimed at solving his domestic problems and did not indicate any foreign allegiance.[86] UK ambassador to Léopoldville Ian Scott wanted the UN to halt its protection of the Congolese prime minister to make possible Lumumba's departure, his imprisonment by Mobutu, or a new constitution that would prevent Lumumba from exercising dictatorial powers. Foreign Office officials preferred "killing him."[87]

Eisenhower and State Department operatives were fed numerous reports that played into their preconception of the Congolese as "a restless and militant population in a state of gross ignorance—even by African standards."[88] In May 1960, for instance, in the run-up to the Congolese elections, the US president had been surprised by the flurry of political activity, which he found remarkable since he was unaware that people in the Congo could read. W. Averell Harriman, the president's self-appointed emissary to Kinshasa, predicted an "emotional" Lumumba would continue to cause difficulties because he was a "rabble-rousing speaker" who had shrewdly maneuvered himself through Congolese politics.[89] At USIS-Léopoldville, Fitzhugh Green believed that Lumumba was a "magnetic demagogue" who had clawed his way into the driver's seat of government through "gangsterism."[90] Clare Timberlake, US ambassador in the Congo, felt Lumumba had only created chaos for the two months he was in power.[91] Even the founder of the African Studies Association in the United States, William O. Brown, criticized the "premeditated exploitation by Mr. Lumumba of racial hostilities" as a "device for political mobilization."[92] In September 1960, the antipathy toward Lumumba was so strong that Herter understood Abboud's belligerence during a conversation with Herter as a request to get "rid of" Lumumba.[93] Likewise, when Allen Dulles heard Eisenhower's wish that Lumumba would "fall into a river full of crocodiles," Dulles could interpret this only as a green light for Lumumba's assassination.[94] The Eisenhower administration was thus pushed into acting. The French were an exception. They never publicly accused Lumumba of being a Communist, because they did not want to become involved in the Congo's internal affairs—leading the French embassy personnel to hide every time they saw a Belgian official in the street.[95]

New Plans for Africa

The chaos of Congo-Léopoldville became a self-fulfilling prophecy spurred on by imperial decline. Lumumba's reputation as a demagogue had materialized amid an atmosphere of riots that—far more than his alleged Communist sympathies—eventually sealed his fate. While a Soviet takeover was the worst-case scenario, the CIA station chief in Léopoldville, Larry Devlin, could imagine an immediate and far more pressing danger: Lumumba in power, with chaos as the inevitable result.[96] When the Congolese prime minister was eventually assassinated on the orders of Katanga's leaders and with Belgian support, the chaos that ensued confirmed the diagnoses of Africa's disease of immaturity and highlighted that a new strategy toward Africa was needed.

As soon as news of Lumumba's assassination hit the newsstands in February 1961, Barden left for Léopoldville to meet the new prime minister, Antoine Gizenga, who lost no time in summoning a cabinet meeting to devise a joint strategy. A direct communication line between Nkrumah and Gizenga was established, troops were secretly supported, vital public services were funded, and continuous radio propaganda in Congo by independent African states was made possible.[97] The Pan-African lens led Nkrumah and Barden to believe that Lumumba's assassination had resulted from a lack of inter-African cooperation.[98] The public diplomacy strategy was adjusted accordingly: the public, rather than potential African leaders, trade unionists, or freedom fighters, was now Ghana's main target. Nkrumah had come to realize that unifying the African continent required a clear and coherent ideological message presented in an emotional and appealing way. Newspapers such as the *Spark* and *Voice of Africa* were filled with fake telegrams, cartoons, and rumors to mobilize the population, amounting to a published form of *radio trottoir*.[99]

This new strategy was exemplified by Ghana's utilization of Lumumba's murder (see figure 5.1). The letter Lumumba wrote from prison to his wife, Pauline, was distributed by the BAA as a pamphlet because it embedded the Congolese struggle within the continental fight for liberation: "Long live the Congo, long live Africa."[100] When Ghanaian officials found out that the son of Maurice Mpolo—a party militant and associate of Lumumba who had been executed together with him—had fled to Somalia, they flew him over to Accra, not to train him but to use him as a propaganda prop.[101] In July 1961, *Voice of Africa* published an interview with Denis Prosper Okito, son of the late president of the Congolese senate and the third man murdered alongside Lumumba. In his interview, Okito praised Accra's massive technical assistance operation. He had been "touched by the way a small country like Ghana . . . selflessly devoted itself to the welfare of the Congo" by offering "troops . . . technicians, health per-

FIGURE 5.1. A mourning parade for Patrice Lumumba on 2 February 1961 in Accra, with women who were reportedly raging against Joseph Kasavubu and the United Nations. Keystone Press / Alamy Stock Photo.

sonnel and administrative officers." After 1961, Ghana's technical assistance was not only meant to create a revolutionary network but was explicitly used to project an image of Ghana as the principal guide to anticolonial modernity. "We know that if Ghana's numerous suggestions . . . had been followed," Okito went on, and the Force Publique had not been strengthened by "the foreign imperialists," "a military dictatorship . . . would never have arisen."[102] BAA officials also wrote a letter to Lumumba's wife. Instead of an enumeration of imperialist crimes, they played on readers' emotions and attempted to convey Lumumba's death on a personal level: "'Mummy, Lumumba has been killed,' grieved my little boy and his eyes moistened with tears as he brandished his clenched little fist."[103]

The emotional allure of liberation was not lost on the conspirators in Katanga, who, a day after Lumumba's execution, sprang into action when local miners stumbled on an arm protruding from the soil. The bodies were hacksawed to pieces and dissolved in acid, and other remains were burned. What the flames could not consume, however, was the symbolic value of this African leader. Viewed as a hero by some, a Communist and a demagogue by others, and above all a threat to stability, murdered in the "year of Africa," Congo's first prime minister embodied Africa's anticolonial route to modernity. Even Tshombe—who had played a big role in Lumumba's assassination—understood he had to ask Nkrumah in 1964 to tone down the Ghanaian attacks against him. Convincing African public opinion of his innocence was a matter of political survival.[104] A USIA report concluded the "Lumumba symbol" was omnipresent.[105]

Lumumba's murder has been cast as a moment when Nkrumah realized he had to play the Cold War game while seeking rapprochement with the USSR. Outside of Africa, Nkrumah's preference for an emotional anticolonial discourse was interpreted as a move toward the Eastern Bloc.[106] Nonetheless, documents from the Ghanaian archives show how non-alignment was maintained. On 3 March 1961, an adviser questioned the wisdom of rigorously adhering to non-alignment, since aid had to be obtained from "all sources abroad." He urged Nkrumah to exploit the Cold War. Most outside observers already assumed that there had "been a definite move on Ghana's part to play the East off against the West."[107] Like Nkrumah, the AAPC Steering Committee viewed the calamities on the continent through a Pan-African lens. The crises in Algeria, the Congo, and South Africa and the French atomic bomb tests did not mean the Cold War had arrived on African soil. Rather, these crises were colonialism's death rattle. The real problem was the failure to unite. Political parties, trade union organizations, youth movements, and women's groups therefore had to win the hearts and minds of African populations to achieve African unity.[108]

Ghana's strategic shift to the public was matched by public diplomats in the North, who lost faith in their ability to psychologically develop Africans. With Mobutu's ousting of Soviet diplomats, the Soviet Union's strategy in Ghana, Guinea, and Mali was also thrown in doubt. Nevertheless, Czech diplomats in Mali remained hopeful, reporting they had finally discovered real Marxists in Bamako.[109] For Britain, the Congo was the place where the "goodwill" strategy had come to die. In 1961, the Foreign Office concluded that the promotion of its own achievements would never work if the British could not criticize other colonial powers. The hesitance to compare the United Kingdom's successful decolonization trajectory to the "chaos left by the Belgians" was abandoned, and a major operation "to convince African opinion" that "our policies in Kenya and the Federation are morally right" was set up in support of "the worldwide projection of the UK colonial policy."[110] The public diplomacy competition with the United States and France intensified. When officials from the Foreign Office's Information Research Department traveled to Elisabethville, Usumbura, and Bukavu in 1961, they told the Americans that the IRD's operation was limited to Léopoldville, a blatant lie. Despite Macmillan's attempts to plan decolonization, de Gaulle's insistence in 1958 to jointly decide whether to stay or go, and claims that de Gaulle's African policy profoundly influenced British decisions, it was the Congo Crisis in combination with Nkrumah's Pan-Africanism that drove the British to emphasize the uniquely liberal character of their enterprise and drag France and Belgium down if necessary.[111]

The Congo also changed the mindset of French officials. Ambassador to Ethiopia Jean Sauvagnargues called an emergency meeting on 20 January 1961 to set up an information campaign to convince "less informed" Africans about the French nuclear tests, something that had never crossed the minds of French policymakers before. A massive propaganda campaign in English was set up, a proposal for an African Atomic Energy Agency to survey the peaceful uses of atomic energy was launched, and a heavily publicized seminar in Paris was organized.[112] French officials visited the BBC External Services and concluded the fifteen-minute program beamed to French Africa was insufficient, leading them to cooperate with the BBC French language service.[113] Officials at the French Ministry of Cooperation felt they had to catch up with the British, who had invested massively. The British white paper the French had read struck them as highly relevant to their own situation and led them to more aggressively market French socioeconomic solutions and cultural achievements. "As a nation, Great Britain has a great deal to offer," the French read, yet "we delude ourselves if we think that in a fiercely competitive world these things are self-evident." Every effort had to be made to ensure others understood UK ideas and policies. Word for word, that was the same approach that the French felt they needed in a world where everyone courted the favor of Africans.[114]

Like France, Portugal realized it had to step up its public diplomacy campaign toward Africa in response to the Angolan War of Independence, which erupted in February 1961. Harsh repression forced thousands of northern Angolans to flee to the Republic of Congo, where Cyrille Adoula provided training in an attempt to establish a revolutionary center. Cabral's pamphlet *The Facts about Portugal's African Colonies* caused a stir because he pointed out the flimsiness of the Portuguese "civilization process," which was "carried out" by "an underdeveloped country, with a lower national income than . . . Ghana."[115] Minister of the Overseas Provinces Adriano Moreira therefore advised the settlers to form armed groups but at the same time championed colonial law reform, such as the repeal of the Estatuto do Indigenato, which had denied Portuguese citizenship to indigenous peoples.[116]

Officials in Brussels also began to realize they had a PR problem on their hands, particularly in Katanga, which was being kept afloat by Belgian advisers. An embattled Belgian government had to deny UN reports that confirmed the presence of Belgian mercenaries, while Elisabethville officials restarted Radio Katanga Libre in response to UN representative Michel Tombelaine, who had amplified this charge via the official Katanga radio.[117] The increased importance of PR was nowhere more clear than in the way in which Brussels supported the creation of a Congolese confederation. Jef Van Bilsen had already, in July 1960, tried to convince Tshombe that a confederation between Léopoldville and Katanga would be "the best possible polity," making Lumumba very distrustful of Van Bilsen. Yet, the minister of the Belgian Congo and Ruanda-Urundi, August de Schryver, and Raymond Scheyven, the minister who had to take care of the economic and financial matters of both territories, both felt success could be attained only if Katanga took international public opinion seriously.[118] Katanga's PR firm in Geneva had focused exclusively on attracting foreign investment, cementing its reputation as a puppet of mining corporations.[119] A conference in Tananarive, on the island of Madagascar, in early March 1961 brought together secessionist leaders Tshombe and Albert Kalonji of Sud-Kasaï as well as Prime Minister Joseph Iléo, who was keen to eat away at Gizenga's political base, since he did not participate. With Belgian support, it was agreed that most matters would be handled by the regions, while the central government would primarily be responsible for foreign affairs. Even though Tshombe thanked Eyskens for his support, publicly Eyskens found it unwise to declare this a victory for Belgian diplomacy, since he felt scrutinized by African and Asian countries. So as not to raise suspicion and leave a vacuum for Nasser and the Soviets, he congratulated the Congolese leaders for reaching an agreement "without outside interference." He also helped Adoula open up an information office in Brussels in October 1961.[120]

Belgian worry over Afro-Asian activism led Robert Régnier, Brussels's high representative for Burundi, to exclaim that Prime Minister Louis Rwagasore had to be killed, which happened on 13 October 1961.[121] This anxiety was matched only by a fear of white Rhodesian settlers and Afrikaners, believed to be conspiring to dismantle the Congo. A Katanga delegation showed up in Salisbury seeking support from, among others, the South Africans, who were drawn to the Congo not only because of its mineral riches but also because they had always believed Belgian rule resembled Apartheid.[122] Lúcio Lara, spokesperson for the Movimento Popular de Libertação de Angola (MPLA), saw that connection as an "unholy alliance" in southern Africa, a "white Africa of Salazar," "Verwoerd," "and Welensky," with Tshombe as a partner.[123] In Rhodesia, Katanga's secession had rekindled dreams of white federation, particularly after Welensky declared that conversations with Belgian entrepreneurs had led him to believe in the feasibility of an attachment of Katanga to Rhodesia. In the Rhodesian parliament, he characterized the UN intervention as "illegal." Allowing "the Katanga Government to be overthrown by force of arms" would in his estimation weaken "the moral position" of Western countries in West Berlin.[124]

John F. Kennedy—who became US president in January 1961—created the Congo Steering Committee, which had to strengthen weak state structures and counter insurgency. Believing aid was to be the engine of socioeconomic modernization, he exchanged Eisenhower's educational assistance strategy for aid grants. To ensure the political survival of Cyrille Adoula—an anti-Communist trade unionist turned prime minister—the committee sought to invest in journalism.[125] According to the chairman, Assistant Secretary of State for African Affairs G. Mennen Williams, misinformation had created a "psychological vacuum" that was being filled with rumors.[126] The contingency plan for the Congo therefore stressed that the legitimacy of US-backed Adoula and the defeat of Gizenga, who enjoyed Soviet support, depended on the establishment of a modern public administration.[127] Communication between the government and the public was particularly important, since modernization theorists believed that insurgencies could thrive in so-called primitive societies where governments were weak.[128] A $10,000 grant was to pay for an operator to train personnel, provide radio-teletype equipment to a news agency wire service, and ultimately create a Congo-wide information network.[129] The UN's public image was also to be improved by installing a ticker service to keep a check on the international news that local newspapers and international press agencies received. An inter-African mutual assistance service would provide communications training.[130] While Kennedy's backing of Mobutu has stood out in the historical record, the Steering Committee stressed that a military man's influence would be lost in the vastness of the Congo.[131]

Ultimately, the Congo emergency brought inter-African conflict to the surface and turned Nkrumah into a formidable opponent in the ideological scramble. A direct consequence was the creation of the Casablanca group, which included Nasser, Nkrumah, Touré, and Modibo Keita of Mali. They cemented the Pan-African anticolonial worldview by officially defining neocolonialism as "the survival of the colonial system in spite of formal recognition of political independence in emerging countries."[132] In May 1961, the Monrovia group was established as a response: a political grouping of twenty to twenty-two states, with the Brazzaville group at its core, that defended French African interests. Nkrumah's interference with the affairs of other African countries also irritated USIS officers in Léopoldville, who now made more aggressive plans.[133] Harriman even wanted to get a "group of independent African states" together to offset Nkrumah's ambitions.[134] When Chairman Mark Mwithaga of KANU was arrested carrying a letter in his pocket from Ghana's BAA that promised support, Nkrumah lost his credibility with the British, because Ghanaian subversion was not helping the UK case of a smooth transition. After 1961, Nkrumah's brand of Pan-African modernity was rapidly losing allies.[135]

In Congo-Léopoldville, Northern and Southern visions of a modern independent Africa clashed. Elements of all ideological projects on offer have found their way into historical writing. Business interests,[136] Cold War political concerns,[137] Belgian involvement,[138] and the inexperience of Congolese politicians[139] are not only historical explanations but also all expressions of imperial, Communist, and capitalist development projects obsessed with stability. The anticolonial project was animated by the fear of what might happen to the Congo without a push for African unity, a view echoed in commentary that focuses on the Congo as "a likely trouble spot," as a playground for the great powers, or as a place inextricably linked with human suffering.[140] Understanding why Lumumba was assassinated and why the Congo Crisis was internationalized therefore requires a more profound appreciation of the anxieties about postcolonial order, which became entangled with what might happen if the Soviet Union or the People's Republic of China succeeded where the West had failed and—in the Ghanaian liberationist case—what might happen if the entirety of Africa suffered the same fate as the Congo. Old concerns about "premature independence," which preceded the Cold War, were galvanized by new worries, since psychological modernization had not resulted in a reorientation toward Northern norms and practices. Ghanaian training had also failed to convince the leaders of newly independent countries of the need to follow Accra's modernization model.

The riots in Léopoldville taught the diplomatic corps from Flagstaff House to the White House that their interpretation of Africa's position in the international system, as being in dire need of guidance, had been correct, but the paths chosen—the USSR's urging of genuine socialism, US reliance on civic education, the exclusive spread of French culture in French Africa, the British creation of goodwill, the Belgian moral-psychological approach, Portuguese counterinsurgency, and the ideological training of freedom fighters by Ghana—had been misguided. What liberationists, Communists, capitalists, and imperialists all learned from the Congo Crisis was that the spread of their form of modernity could result in emotions that were difficult to manage. Social and economic structures on the continent therefore became the preferred development targets after 1960.

CHAPTER 6

Managing the Effects of Modernization, 1961–1963

The shift toward socioeconomic modernization in the wake of the Congo Crisis revealed an increased appetite among leaders in North and South to build development programs on industrialization, not education. Yet, this change also raised concerns over the psychological effects of intervention. In June 1961, after lunch, John F. Kennedy invited Nikita Khrushchev for a stroll around the lush gardens of the US embassy in Vienna, where interpreters tried to keep up as the two men debated the merits of their models. Kennedy remarked that the Soviet Union wanted to eliminate free systems, while Khrushchev was under the impression the US "wanted to build a dam" to prevent the development of the "human mind and conscience." Paraphrasing Mao Zedong, Kennedy claimed power was at the "end of the rifle"; Khrushchev retorted that there was "no immunization against ideas!"[1] Terms such as "immunization" and "vaccination" had been commonly used by psychological warfare experts in the 1950s but were now employed by leaders in the North to explain non-alignment, which was considered to be a psychological disturbance in the development process. Diplomats wanted to transform anticolonial nationalism and non-aligned internationalism into something that was more "constructive" and less "emotional," through the modernization of socioeconomic conditions.[2] African nationalists also adopted pathologizing metaphors, understood those investments as a potential threat to authentic African culture, and worried about the consequences of interference.[3] Kwame

Nkrumah believed the continent needed to be sheltered from neocolonial propaganda; Hastings Banda in Malawi was adamant about African uniqueness; El Ferik Ibrahim Abboud of Sudan defined "political ideology" as a type of intrusion because it led to "political indoctrination"; and Haile Selassie talked about "engorgement"—a gradual process that destroyed identity.[4] A non-aligned position therefore had to include active resistance against non-African ideologies and neocolonial intrusion.

Scholars have disregarded these psychological conceptions of non-alignment and instead have set out to uncover what distinguished it from traditional neutralism.[5] The antagonism between a realist and racial understanding of the Non-Aligned Movement (NAM) has endured in part because of JFK's contradictory record, which is complicated by the president's preference for relying on informal advisers.[6] In recent books, the president and his aides emerge as people who were perceptive enough to distinguish Communism from nationalism but who lacked the sensitivity to acknowledge the adverse effects of their modernization program. Social distress was considered to be a technical problem, and they had sympathy for the African nationalist cause.[7] In the Soviet Union, nationalism's revolutionary potential was, historians conclude, exploited by Khrushchev. The scholarship on French, British, Belgian, and Portuguese decolonization has never found a firm footing either. Explanations for the liquidation of the British empire alternate between economic and geopolitical factors, while French research has fostered narratives that drift between positive assessments and accusatory accounts. Belgian postcolonial politics is a story of secret subversion, and the Portuguese end of empire one of surprise for Lisbon.[8]

Yet, the commitment to socioeconomic modernization that defined the first years of independence also comprised the fear of a development process turned sour in the North. Underdeveloped people were believed to be incapable of coping with fast-paced industrialization. Postcolonial citizens might also turn on their new leaders, a fear harbored by African elites. Both South and North therefore sought to transform anticolonial nationalism into something more suited to their own aims.

The Belgrade Conference and Anticolonial Emotion

The assumption that modernization was potentially dangerous and would reach down to the personality led to worry in the Global South. Cultural and psychological resistance had been instrumental in undercutting colonial authority but risked turning destructive after independence. Nationalist leaders now faced popular demands to eradicate poverty and were obsessed with managing the psychological repercussions of economic development. Kenneth Kaunda worried about a "psychological time-bomb," "a reversion to non-constructive patterns of behavior," resulting from the "political frustration" that had accumulated during the anticolonial struggle. Other African intellectuals pointed out that the disappearance of a common enemy had led to an upsurge of tribalism and the turn away from the unfamiliar into the security of tradition. Already in the 1940s, Jawaharlal Nehru worried that "nationalist passions" would "turn against him" after independence.[9] Even Nkrumah had to admit that "decent standards of living" were important. A text that an editor of the *Spark* had written ended up on Nkrumah's desk and signaled the official embrace of a new understanding of the "African Personality," in which human development was viewed as the product of environmental factors.[10] When delegates gathered at the Non-Aligned Conference in Belgrade in September 1961, these concerns trickled down into debates about the best way to politically harness the anticolonial sentiment, leading to the development of two factions.[11] Idealists such as Ibrahim Abboud and Nkrumah continued to stress the need for mental decolonization and wanted to create an "ideal international society." Realists such as Ahmed Ben Bella of the Algerian provisional government, GPRA, prioritized the need for socioeconomic development and saw the NAM as a lever to acquire financial resources (see figure 6.1).[12]

In the Global North, vocal anticolonialism—already on display during the Congo Crisis—came to be seen as a disturbance in the development process. Unlike the Bandung Conference, which the North understood as a call for a better type of development, the Belgrade meeting strengthened the notion that anticolonialism was an emotional response to technical change. Khrushchev had been "annoyed" by Yugoslavia's "non-aligned" position, but was pleased with Nkrumah's approval of the Soviet proposal for a Berlin peace treaty, which confirmed his understanding of African nationalists.[13] Kennedy's Task Force on Africa worried US-led modernization would be washed away by anticolonialism's "revolutionary tides."[14] Mennen Williams claimed that, without a clear modernization project, anticolonial nationalism would result in frustration, encountering "people" who desired "our aid" while lacking the "capacity for expressing gratitude."[15] The Commonwealth Relations Office also encountered an angry Nkrumah who fumed about "fake independence," leading the CRO to exchange the "goodwill" strategy for a straightforward propaganda policy.[16] Lisbon's informants worried about the delegates from the Movimento Popular de Libertação de Angola at Belgrade, but invested a lot of time in determining who the least radical conference participant was, ultimately deciding on Haile Selassie. Not only technocratic optimism but also

FIGURE 6.1. Haile Selassie (right) and Kwame Nkrumah (left) during the Non-Aligned Conference in Belgrade on 9 September 1961. Keystone Press / Alamy Stock Photo.

anxiety about the possible adverse psychological effects of intervention by development workers thus shaped diplomacy after 1960.[17]

This desire to manage "anticolonial emotion" in North and South was fueled by innovations in anthropology and the social sciences that highlighted the need to devise modernization projects with an eye for the local setting in which they were introduced. At the Institut Mirovoi Ekonomiki i Mezhdunarodnykh Otnoshenii (IMEMO; Institute of World Economy and International Relations) in Moscow, development economists tried to figure out how best to implement Marxist concepts in the Global South.[18] In the West, modernization theorists such as Walt Rostow and Max F. Millikan advocated economic aid alongside technical assistance and assumed that cultural differences were only footnotes on the road maps to modernity, while cultural relativist anthropologists such as Bronislaw Malinowski and Audrey Richards at the London School of Economics, Claude Lévi-Strauss at the Collège de France, and Jef Van Bilsen at Ghent University popularized participation observation in so-called primitive societies.[19] Pivotal in this dual view on modernity was Margaret Mead's *Cultural Patterns and Technical Change*.[20] Mead found it necessary to think about the changes that were introduced by technical experts in order to protect the mental health of a world population in transition. Change introduced emotional tension, which had to be addressed, or the individual would remain in "a state of malad-justment or frustration."[21] Richards recommended that development officers be relied on to convince local populations. John Strachey, a British minister who had been involved in the abortive Tanganyika groundnut scheme of the 1940s, warned that mastery of the physical environment would be ineffective if inter-cultural conflict was ignored. French structuralist Lévi-Strauss showed that all cultures shared underlying patterns but stressed that cultural differences were adopted at a young age and could be unlearned.[22] A report from MIT's Center for International Studies (CIS) informed its readers about the unsettling effects of the take-off process and therefore defined economic assistance as "funda-mentally, political and psychological."[23]

Nevertheless, because of the NAM's ambiguity, unease about Belgrade only gradually transformed into diplomatic action. The NATO Council ignored Paul-Henri Spaak's concerns about a third bloc and concluded that "nothing par-ticularly new" had emerged. Couve de Murville and the French embassy in Yugoslavia predicted the establishment of a UN caucus to demand more aid. US and UK diplomats, in contrast, fretted over NAM support for Khrushchev's Ber-lin peace proposal.[24] What dominated the discussions over a White House mes-sage and the design of a British pamphlet, however, was a concern over delegates acquiring an "unjustified sense of importance" as a result of roused anticolonial emotion.[25]

Demonstration in the Global North

The risk of an unchecked emotional response, in the form of anticolonialism and non-alignment, demanded a foreign policy that acknowledged those views. A "strongly-marked vein of sentimentality" led the British Foreign Office to present British aid as a form of support for African unity. Contrary to the case in Belgium, where the notion of "allying" with "Black African" "supranational-ism" had been considered but was quickly laughed off in the nervous winter of 1959, the FO considered this type of alliance to be viable. Nevertheless, in the United Kingdom, uneasiness also abounded. Operatives on the ground be-lieved Pan-Africanism could serve as a dam against Soviet encroachment, but Information Policy Department research in Kenya predicted violence would reemerge under emotional stress, since nationalist self-confidence was fragile and "tribal."[26] Information services were therefore instructed to support Pan-Africanism: French language education had to bring British and French Africa closer together, and the United Kingdom was presented as a "far-sighted coun-try" willing to cooperate with African governments.[27] Conversely, the French

African elite had to be sold on the idea that accepting non-French aid would strengthen inter-African cooperation. In a meeting with his French colleague, the FO official therefore nodded quietly as he evaded French requests to secure better BBC treatment.[28]

In contrast, the newly created French Ministry of Cooperation wanted to steer African societies away from Pan-Africanism, because it was deemed unrealistic.[29] Instead, Charles de Gaulle hurriedly elevated existing bilateral and multilateral agreements to the level of official policy, known as *Coopération*. France provided economic, military, and cultural aid, and in return the Brazzaville group transformed itself into the Union africaine et malgache (UAM) and agreed to vote with France in the UN General Assembly.[30] De Gaulle's televised speech in July 1961 in which he defended this new policy was indicative of the level of improvisation. The cost of empire had made disengagement inevitable, de Gaulle declared, in his calculated political vernacular. But if France could "establish new relations based on friendship and cooperation," "tant mieux!"— all the better![31] De Gaulle's talent for adopting existing ideas even led Jacques Foccart to conclude that the general was not interested in Africa.[32]

Similarly, foreign affairs officials in Brussels could not fathom that anticolonialism was a political project and talked about a "sentiment anti-colonialiste."[33] The ambassador in Dakar found Guinean officials irrational because they warmly welcomed Pierre Mendés-France in August 1960.[34] In May 1961, embassy officials even hatched a plan to ask Haile Selassie to mediate in favor of Belgian soldiers who had been captured, arguing that the Belgian king could confer with the emperor.[35] Prime Minister Théo Lefèvre, assuming anticolonialism was a temporary emotional outburst, cultivated the fantastic notion that African leaders would return to ask for help. With the increased displacement of populations in the north of Angola in 1961, even the Ministério do Ultramar realized it had to address the complex social problems and its "lack of knowledge of the psychology of African societies." The Institute of Education and Social Service in Luanda was established to train social workers and educators.[36]

Unlike his NATO allies, JFK was less confident about these tactical benefits, because he viewed anticolonialism as a product of half-hearted colonial modernization, which had destroyed tradition and disregarded psychological and social disruption. Africa had become a "potentially dangerous place."[37] Renewed modernization was not without risk, since a second moment of rupture could exacerbate existing frustrations. "Modern nationalism," Kennedy wrote "has a twin heritage. In one of its aspects it reflects a positive search for political freedom and self-development, in another it is the residue of disintegration."[38] Modernity was a two-headed creature with the "power to abolish all forms of human poverty and all forms of human life."[39] His call to appreciate nationalism as a force separate from the Cold War has been viewed as a sign of sympathy for the anticolonial cause. What is striking, however, is his assessment of nationalism as not necessarily a positive force, in line with Rostow's suspicion of individuals who were torn between the old and modern way of life.[40] Kennedy authorized counterinsurgency operations not only "to defend against communist rebellions" but, more important, to cushion the blow of development and invest in a "political effort," in line with Mao's dictum, which Kennedy knew by heart: "Guerrillas are like fish. . . . If the temperature of the water is right, the fish will thrive."[41] By controlling the water's temperature, by managing the socioeconomic circumstances, the guerrilla fish would not be able to multiply.[42] The US Information Agency had to monitor the thermostat and develop a strategy for the "immunization of those sectors of foreign society" that were most likely to be the "breeding ground for insurgency." Experts such as Rostow and General Maxwell Taylor considered a government right after independence to be weak, and USIA was called on to build a relationship between governments and their population with weekly newsreels.[43] With the promotion of "social reforms," such as a health care project in the Sudan, USIA director Murrow claimed his staff had become "less publicists for America, more propagandists for progress." This is what Rostow and communications guru Ithiel de Sola Pool labeled the demonstration effect: the exhibition of modernity's advantages would stimulate emulation.[44] Counterinsurgency specialists were "fire fighters" who did not just tackle insurgency after it broke out but worked to prevent it.[45]

Kennedy rejected a conventional battle for African minds and considered public opinion a nuisance.[46] When Richard Nixon returned from Accra in 1957, Kennedy quipped that the people of Africa were interested in a decent living standard, not doctrine. Despite C. D. Jackson's attempt to plant an inkling of the political warfare problem in Kennedy's mind, JFK mocked USIA's traditional information task as the "selling of free enterprise." It is no coincidence that Kennedy is mentioned only in passing in USIA's official history.[47] JFK's dismissal was based on a simple calculation supported by influential social scientists such as Daniel Lerner, who argued that information media enabled peoples in the Global South to imagine a better life but also risked turning the revolution of rising expectations into a revolution of rising frustration if demands for development were not met.[48] All levels of the administration were in agreement on this point. The "New Frontier" people saw anticolonialism as "a state of mind, a psychological hangover from the past." Colonialism "produced habits of opposition not of responsibility."[49] The Policy Planning Staff claimed US development offered the "moral equivalent of anticolonialism" and defined neutralism as only incidentally a reaction to the Cold War.[50] Robert Good, secretary of JFK's Africa Task Force, underscored the importance of dealing with the negative emotion of anticolonialism and believed the prevention of Communist intrusion in Africa was "the minimal objective." Modernization had to continue where anticolonialism stopped and turn frustrated behavior into a rational can-do attitude. This was what Kennedy meant when he spoke about positive neutrality.[51] In contrast to Belgian and Portuguese confusion and de Gaulle's and Macmillan's opportunism, Kennedy's perspective could only see a threat to US-led modernization, a threat punctuated by the mysterious death of Dag Hammarskjöld in September 1961 in a plane crash near the airport of Ndola, Rhodesia.[52]

Khrushchev further explored the "non-capitalist path of development," which had been devised by Modest Rubinshtein of the Institute of Economics in the mid-1950s and was supposed to lead to industrialization via a large state sector. In October 1961, in a letter to the Communist Party of the Soviet Union, Khrushchev referred to countries of the "National Democracy" type, which could most successfully make the transition because they did not reflect "one class interest."[53] At the Institute of Oriental Studies, the primacy of industrialization over cultural or bourgeois predispositions was established in the work of the institute's deputy head, Rostislav Ul'ianovskii. Like his colleagues in the West, he argued that it was changing socioeconomic structures that altered minds. In the Marxist-Leninist vernacular, rapid economic development and industrialization would lead to a growing number of workers acquiring class consciousness, a conclusion with which Boris Ponomarev of the CPSU international department agreed. Categories such as "progressive" were flexible enough to allow potential allies with varied persuasions to be friendly with the USSR.[54] Yet, what Karen Brutents of the CPSU International Department remembered in 1961 was how "ill prepared" they felt.[55]

Washington, like Moscow, struggled to understand the intricacies of the African psyche and culture and turned to London and Paris, where officials offered their know-how. The UK Foreign Office settled on a "pragmatic theory." Whether ancient civilizations had existed or not, Africans wished that there had been such civilizations, leading African peoples to suffer from "touchiness." French analysts were more tolerant of these emotions, claiming the African state of mind was conditioned by economic and social circumstances. Political independence and economic dependence had led them to behave like adolescents desperate to assert their independence, even if it was not in their best interest. The problem was not that modernization had happened too quickly; rather, more was needed. Cultural diplomacy therefore had to contribute to economic development.[56]

After consultations with experts, it was concluded that influencing attitudes required an alteration of the socioeconomic structures. This insight was shared widely. Even in Southern Rhodesia, the African Farmers Union agreed that not "inherent traits of character" but "unfortunate political and economic conditions" determined the fate of "the rural African."[57] There was disagreement over the specific gear that needed to be engaged to get the modernization machine turning. USIA's operation, for instance, was pressed into the service of the demonstration effect, since Rostow claimed traditional societies were governed by "reactive nationalism" and would walk down the development path only when they felt threatened by more advanced foreigners.[58] Strident anticolonialism became beneficial in the long run and English teaching a means to facilitate the emulation of "our machine age productivity."[59] By drawing parallels between the US experience and African realities, USIA sought to demonstrate what modernity looked like without offending African target audiences and to illustrate shared notions of freedom. A comic book called *They Wanted Freedom* combined the ancient history of African kingdoms with US comic books.[60] In the meantime, French officials started to pay attention to the comfort of their filmgoers because they noticed the popularity of spacious theaters in which USIS offered high-quality color film. A "clientèle" had to be formed, which is the reason that the French cultural attaché in Accra deliberately stayed in a second-rate hotel that was frequented by Africans to make contact easier.[61] The British Council concentrated on the distribution of books to improve the British image. When the British Council officer Paul Sinker drove Barbara Ward, an anthropologist specializing in Africa and one of Kennedy's advisers, to the airport, he therefore impressed on her that US assistance was unnecessary. The increase of US books for Africa in 1962 had to communicate what modernity meant.[62]

Immunization in the Global South

Nevertheless, what the United States saw as the demonstration effect, the USSR viewed as the first step toward the Soviet model, and the Europeans saw as a type of PR, was interpreted in African capitals as an attempt at ideological intrusion. In Accra, Nkrumah therefore sought to immunize Africans from foreign ideas since, in his analysis, neocolonial manipulation in the cultural and ideological sphere had led other African leaders to turn away from him.[63] Through "teleguided diplomacy," imperialists, like shady puppeteers, pulled the strings of anti-imperialist states "to make us cut each other's throat."[64] Julius Nyerere felt Nkrumah's assertive Pan-Africanism was ineffective and instead advocated a step-by-step approach to continental unity, while Sékou Touré proclaimed that Africa required cooperation, not "philosophical formulae or doctrinal theories."[65] The representative of the Zambian United National

Independence Party (UNIP), who was staying at the offices of the Bureau of African Affairs, was irritated by Ghana's paternalism toward other African countries.[66] Disagreements about African unification played out in debates about the appropriate role of propaganda. Nkrumah called on ambassadors to "create public opinion" and push Africans into adopting a "militant attitude" against interference, while opening exhibition windows in New York and London.[67] Ghanaian officials doubled down on their strategy of circumventing political leaders and instead directly targeting the African public through gripping stories. Ghana was presented as a modern nation through articles on the development secretariat's projects, such as the Tema Harbour. A teacher experimenting with test tubes had to convey that an intensive study of science was a crucial feature of Ghanaian education. Reports on Haile Selassie's visit cast Ghana as an international leader. Between 1961 and 1964, seventy-six African students from Basutoland, Bechuanaland, South Africa, Kenya, Uganda, and Somalia passed through the Government Secretariat School in Accra, technical schools, teacher training colleges, and universities.[68]

The *Patterns of Progress* booklets Ethiopia produced also sought to establish the country as an epicenter of African modernity, albeit with a much longer tradition than Ghana had. One booklet explained that it was Emperor Menelik II who had already "fully realised the importance of education in Ethiopia for the preservation of the country's independence and the maintenance of progress."[69] What was different about Ghana, however, was that the image of the modern nation had to provide the launching pad for a *radio trottoir* strategy that appealed to a mass audience with emotional propaganda and rumors. Newspapers such as the *Spark* and *Voice of Africa* were filled with cartoons and rumors illustrating the neocolonial plots that ensued in the absence of African unity. The Office of the President produced *The Ghanaians*, a movie that urged African countries to follow the modern Ghana by showing students engaging their lecturer in a building that was still under construction.[70] The director "abused" "sophisticated techniques" because "the devil doesn't have to have all the good tunes."[71] Even the attempt on Nkrumah's life in Kulungugu on 11 August 1962, when the Ghanaian leader was handed a bomb concealed in a bouquet of flowers, was seized on as an opportunity to "strengthen" "Ghana in African Affairs."[72] Nkrumah ordered Aloysius K. Barden to organize a demonstration against neocolonialism in Accra, albeit one that was to appear spontaneous. The director of the Bureau of African Affairs asked every staff member of the bureau to write a slogan while a news item was prepared. He wanted to gather no less than fifty thousand demonstrators by bringing to Accra freedom fighters; Convention People's Party members; ex-servicemen; and Asafo companies, a traditional warrior group. Although he got only a small gathering of children to hold a French flag and signs, the plan with its focus on spontaneity points to a sensitivity for PR that had been absent before 1960. The BAA saw the bomb in Kulungugu as an opportunity to make a call to resist neocolonialism, not as a final nudge for Nkrumah to align with the Soviet Union.[73]

Ghanaian non-alignment was redefined in propaganda terms, a move that fundamentally altered Accra's bilateral affairs, its stance on international organizations, and its relationship with freedom fighters. Kojo Botsio explained that the appearance of non-alignment was as important as adhering to the principle. "The manner and timing of foreign policy statements" was essential. Trade relations, diplomatic alliances, and foreign aid relations could not be entered into lightly; even student scholarships had to be allocated in such a way that they were not only genuinely non-committed but, more important, also "seen to be non-committed."[74] When Leonid Brezhnev, chairman of the Presidium of the Supreme Soviet between 1960 and 1964, visited Ghana in February 1961, visits from Tito, Léopold Senghor, and Mennen Williams, as well as Nkrumah's own visit to the United States in March 1961, were all scheduled in close proximity to showcase Accra's non-alignment.[75] International organizations such as the UN, in Nkrumah's interpretation, had been abused by imperialists to manipulate public opinion during the Congo Crisis. A non-aligned bloc had to "make certain" its "resources and facilities" were "not used to bolster up states who" were "defying world opinion."[76] Non-alignment—in the words of diplomat Kwesi Armah—also greased the wheels of the "machinery" that funded liberation movements, which were increasingly becoming splintered along Cold War lines. Without a clear-cut choice, bureaucratic infighting over which of the many liberation movements to support was avoided.[77]

This theatrical form of non-alignment drew on a peculiar array of sources. To make the neocolonial threat emanating from the United States more palpable, the ghostwriters of *Neo-Colonialism* quoted from *The Invisible Government*, a New Left pamphlet, because it cast the US government as a "grouping of individuals and agencies" dominated by the CIA.[78] Nkrumah was also inspired by de Gaulle's theatrical foreign policy, which defied US power within NATO, and Nkrumah's critique of French colonialism was drowned out by his admiration for de Gaulle's "effective penetration," since Paris, with its assimilation strategy, had achieved what Ghana aspired to do.[79] If de Gaulle and US beatniks challenged US power, Nkrumah could not lag behind. He became a silent ally of de Gaulle in his search for a world that was not dominated by the superpowers, an alliance strengthened by Botsio's visit to France in June 1965.[80]

Principally, however, non-alignment was a means to immunize Ghanaians from foreign propaganda. Michael Dei-Anang ordered an investigation into the press releases of every embassy in Accra after he stumbled on a US research project on psychological methods "used by the Capitalists and Colonialists to win over Ghanaians." The East and the West were barred from using Ghana as a "propaganda forum" after Nkrumah learned that psychological warfare plans were developed in NATO meetings.[81] Nkrumah also tried to personally convince other African leaders of the need to immunize their populations against neocolonialism. In a letter to Nyerere in December 1961, Nkrumah wrote about how successful African economic integration hinged on a "stable political direction," which only a common ideological project could provide.[82] In a letter to Jomo Kenyatta, Nkrumah conveyed that public opinion had to be managed because the press was a "deadly weapon" that remained in the imperialists' arsenal and required an "effective antidote." He offered to send an expert from the Guinea Press, a government-sponsored corporation, to assist local journalists.[83]

Internationally, Ghana's strong anticolonial stance gave it a reputation for being subversive. When Sylvanus Olympio, the president of Togo, was murdered in 1963, the BAA became the key suspect.[84] Kennedy and the Europeans primarily understood African nationalist "immunization" as a product of incomplete modernization, not Cold War tension. It was not Nkrumah's flirtation with the Soviet Union but his assertiveness that caused nervousness, because it could rouse others "to vent their apprehensions and frustrations." USIS officers had tolerated Nkrumah's anti-Americanism, which they interpreted as a response to the "increased propaganda competition" on the continent, but by August 1963, other operatives advised increasing the "African awareness of . . . the communist influence in Ghana" to reduce Nkrumah's appeal.[85] When British diplomats fought over the same question, the CRO concluded that Nkrumah had no desire to throw in his lot with the Communists. Only by 1963 did the British realize that the Ghanaian influence in East Africa came at their own expense, since the BAA funded Ugandan trade unions, circulated forged British telegrams, and supported the opposition in Zanzibar. The French did not fear Nkrumah, believing he suffered from a mental illness that had prompted him to proclaim he was the "messiah."[86]

The Psychological Repercussions of Aid

Ideologically charged disputes about postcolonial intervention led to a reconsideration of the aid strategies in North and South. Central in these debates was an often-overlooked item in the catalog of modernist fears, namely the psychological effect of foreign intervention. Ever since famed demographer Frank Notestein asserted that technology could alter peasant psychology, development theorists had been apprehensive about the ethics of their interference.[87] Fears had already bubbled to the surface in May 1960, at an International Cooperation Administration conference on aid to Africa where speakers stressed the "psychological dangers of over-selling a US government effort" that was financially constrained. The dangerous psychological element of "let down" was addressed by the Kennedy administration, which wanted to modernize socioeconomic conditions to change behavior.[88] In its Senate report of March 1960, for instance, the Massachusetts Institute of Technology's Center for International Studies (CIS) had noted that the most fundamental change required was "psychological," the need to show people the world could change. In a memorandum to the president, Rostow stressed that decisions about investments had to be made with the "absorptive capacity" of developing nations in mind, but at the same time he stressed the importance of "shooting high to maximize the psychological and political effect" of US cash. Rostow believed people were driven by more than rational economic considerations and understood the risk of unfulfilled aspirations.[89] As he wrote to Kennedy in 1961, "we have stirred great hopes in Asia, the Middle East, Africa and Latin America [and] we must back our play or those hopes will fade."[90] The manager of those hopes was the development diplomat, a character introduced by World Bank director Eugene Black. This diplomat was supposed to be an artisan of economic development who illuminated the choices before decision makers in the underdeveloped world. The State Department welcomed the idea because it provided a long-term solution to insurgency and an effective means to overcome psychological resistance against modernization. Development diplomacy's effectiveness depended on communication lines throughout the underdeveloped world, which had to provide the information required to strengthen the modernization process.[91]

The British, French, Belgians, and Soviets, in contrast, were not afraid to publicize their aid efforts, despite Hammarskjöld's resolve to turn the 1960s into a cooperative UN decade of development. After the Guineans turned away from the Soviet Union in December 1961, the CPSU started to doubt its ability to effect change in Africa through economic aid alone.[92] The "Guinean Syndrome" made the Soviets more hesitant to support the "African Socialist" experiment in Mali and led Khrushchev to publicly demand ideological purity. In February 1960, more direct indoctrination at the Lumumba Friendship University was initiated, while Soviet lecturers helped design the curriculum of the Kwame Nkrumah Ideological Institute even though Soviet propaganda appeared not to be particularly successful or well adapted to local circumstances.[93]

In Belgium, the newly minted minister of foreign trade and technical assistance, Maurice Brasseur, developed a "technical assistance policy" based on a report Van Bilsen wrote in which he recommended a policy of *déblocage*, a variation on Rostow's take-off doctrine. Van Bilsen was asked to head the newly created Agency of Development Cooperation but initially refused because he believed the second part of his report, on the need for international cooperation, was ignored while the Belgian aid contributions were played up to improve the country's public image.[94] Stories that had been put out by UN operations officer Sture Linnér, who claimed his troops in Katanga had been fired at from the Belgian consulate-general, had to be countered. After the formation of a new government by Cyrille Adoula in August 1961, Belgians who were part of the *gendarmerie katangaise*—the rank-and-file troops of the secessionist army—were asked to leave.[95]

Unlike Belgian officials, who were accused of propping up their "hatchet man" Moïse Tshombe, de Gaulle aspired to become the preferred interlocutor for the Global South by breaking the bipolar mold and letting the "non-alignés"—among whom de Gaulle counted himself—emerge.[96] The French *action culturelle* had to help alleviate societal needs, in effect expanding Senghor's philosophy, which viewed the French language as a modernizing force uniquely suited to boosting African development.[97] In January 1961, at the meeting of the chiefs of missions, it was decided that assistance projects had to be "visible," since acquiring a "moral advantage" over competitors meant it had to be clear that French aid possessed a distinctive power to develop societies.[98] International Cooperation Administration officials could never understand why Paris sought to enhance "African self-government" but also worked to achieve the "opposite."[99]

Whereas the French approach was still fairly subtle, the British Foreign Office decided on a "wholesale overt propaganda" campaign that sought to "glamorize technical cooperation."[100] By 1961 it was implied that there was a mutual interest between Africa and the non-Communist world, and a so-called enlightened common Western philosophy on aid had to be promoted.[101] The move had been inspired by the Soviets, who were believed to be more successful because they overlaid their efforts with a "forward-looking philosophy."[102] The enormous scale of the Volta River Project was therefore heavily publicized in spite of the US efforts to downplay the project in order to avoid potential disappointment.[103] The British, in their turn, could not fathom that the US preferred to "batten down and weather the storm." Meanwhile, Whitehall's eagerness to cooperate with Washington deepened the conflict with Michel Debré, who felt double-crossed.[104] He claimed the eagerness with which Kennedy's instructions were being followed caused "psychological damage" and a loss of African respect, making French aid the sole guarantee for the full socioeconomic development of the continent, an argument Chadian minster of economic and foreign affairs Gabriel Lisette had already put forward.[105]

All the while, African nationalists were guided by an immunization logic in their acceptance of foreign aid, effectively the reverse of doctrines in the Global North. Nkrumah and Kenyatta believed they could accept foreign aid so long as they guarded against the ideological accompaniments. The *Spark* therefore ran articles that described foreign aid as a form of mutually beneficial trade.[106] Tom Mboya claimed Kenyans were "capable of gauging the ulterior motives" of those who offered assistance.[107] Nyerere also wanted education to liberate body and mind because "colonial education" had "induced attitudes of human inequality."[108] For Nkrumah, the "African Personality" was not threatened as long as Ghana kept investing in ideological education. He instructed the freedom fighters in 1958 not to ignore the "spiritual side of the human personality," because Africans' "material needs" made them vulnerable to subjugation.[109] If technical training was offered without an ideological component, students would become a liability to the new state.

The different rationales that buttressed foreign aid clashed when Kennedy announced the establishment of the Peace Corps, which launched its first operation in Ghana and relied on US youth to execute development projects. On 24 March 1961, Special Council to the President Ted Sorensen met with Peace Corps director Sargent Shriver and decided publicity by USIA had to be limited, not because of 1960s idealism but to prevent "unwarranted expectations," eliciting questions from operatives on the ground who were used to selling the United States.[110] Nevertheless, the Peace Corps still provoked a response because others who were in the business of development reasoned about aid in terms of publicity. The French Ministry of Cooperation created its own Volontaires du Progrès in April 1963, with aid workers arriving in Dakar in September. The British, who wanted to piggyback on the enormous US aid operation, applauded the similarities with their own Voluntary Service Overseas.[111] The Belgian king announced a peace volunteers initiative in October 1962 to improve the Belgian reputation, damaged by the Katanga debacle. To avoid turning the department into a temping agency for unemployed young people, in February 1963, Brasseur sent former minister of Congolese economic and financial matters Raymond Scheyven to New York, where he received help with the setup of a "Peace Corps belge."[112] Eager to increase the share of aid from other countries, US operatives offered training to Belgian planners.[113] In Ghana, the funds were welcomed, but the ideals were shunned. Reporting on the Peace Corps was forbidden, and French "Volunteers for Progress" were mocked.[114]

For Nkrumah, economic aid was a powerful instrument for change that could be accepted if African societies were ideologically molded. While the demonstration strategy compelled the Kennedy administration to continue its efforts at convincing Nkrumah, the Soviets and the Europeans shunned both approaches and concluded that PR was a necessary component if their post-independence aid strategy was to yield political results.

Clashing Modernization Doctrines

As a result, cultural operations became a self-enforcing cycle of misunderstanding, which led to conflict in newspapers, at schools, and at cultural centers. Opinions about the ways in which public diplomacy affected target audiences were so radically different that an attempt to improve relations often ended up causing an aggressive response. As prolific USIA operative John Brown argued, the globalization of popular culture where "people all over the world wear blue jeans" coincided with a renewed appreciation for "chauvinistic forms" of "local culture."[115]

The first moment when Northern and Southern modernization doctrines clashed was the newspaper war, a battle for hearts and minds between Ghana on one side and the United States and United Kingdom on the other. The seeds of war were sown by Ghana's emotional stories about neocolonialism, which Northern observers believed to be a symptom of frustration. The *Voice of Africa* published forged telegrams in which UK officials blatantly admitted to manipulating Africans, and its first issue contained a picture of a French policeman who allegedly made sure people would vote in favor of de Gaulle's Algerian policy. The *Spark* ran sensationalist stories about CIA operations, while Dean Rusk's son was alleged to be stationed in Nigeria. Publications also became more visual with cartoons and large photographs: a strong African man strangling a white colonial officer or an armed African officer leading his men into battle. This blend of rumors, sensationalism, and cartoons, already tested in the Sahara bomb test campaign, now became the BAA's core strategy. What plagued the newspaper was not illiteracy—newspapers were read out loud in public, and leaflets were widely used from Accra to the coffee houses of Mogadishu—but distribution problems.[116] What is more, Barden wanted "as many as possible . . . to buy and read *The Spark*."[117]

In the course of the newspaper war, Ghanaian diplomats radicalized. From 1962 onward, journalists were prohibited from copying foreign newspapers because the wording could contain hidden messages. Instead, the BAA began publishing the *African Chronicler*, a bulletin containing dry and factual information obtained from the foreign press.[118] In 1964, Richard Wright turned this push against foreign news into a coherent theory at the Ghana Institute of Journalism, where revolutionary journalists were trained to discard the BBC style of journalism and incite people to action. Soviet writing was praised because its blend of facts and commentary clearly showed a political orientation, while the literary tendencies of French journalism made it useless. The revolutionary journalist was an instrument of the African revolution and therefore required a solid ideological basis.[119]

For US officials, Nkrumah's shift toward emotional appeals confirmed their diagnoses. Newspapers were a "major outlet" through which Nkrumah "vented frustration and anger."[120] Instead of becoming less involved, as Nkrumah had hoped, the United States felt compelled to intervene. In March 1961, Kennedy personally asked Acting Secretary of Public Affairs Carl Rowan to prepare a press analysis that concluded that there was an "information vacuum" that prevented Africans from fully enjoying the "very essence of freedom." Posts such as USIS-Dakar increased their wire services, while more African journalists were invited to the UN. The British struggled to understand how, simultaneously, the United Kingdom could be branded an imperial power in Ghanaian newspapers while aid was welcomed in radio addresses. When Ghana minister of information Kwaku Boateng apologized by citing journalists' poor grasp of the English language, his British counterpart quipped that their knowledge of offensive English was impeccable. French ambassador Louis de Guiringaud began to worry at the end of 1960 that the Ghanaian press could infect African minds continent-wide and demanded an English language expert so he could respond to allegations.[121]

The notion that Africa was struggling with an "information vacuum" became widely accepted, but only Kennedy sprung into action, because he believed Nkrumah's anticolonialism was derailing the entire US foreign aid strategy.[122] The White House was walking a tightrope, since Congress demanded that aid grants purchase allegiance while African countries demanded sincerity.[123] Ambassador Francis Russell was a fierce opponent of the Volta River Project but recommended its financing, because backing down would instill doubt about US capabilities in the entire Global South.[124] An NSC meeting held on the return of a presidential commission that had requested Nkrumah to soften his harsh tone confirmed that approval of the Volta River Project was the only possible course of action, because a refusal to proceed would be misunderstood across Africa.[125] Consequently, Ghana's journalism became the core of US-Ghanaian relations, leading NSC specialist on Africa William Brubeck to include "information media" and "posture on major international issues" among his eight criteria for evaluating future development projects in Ghana.[126] William Mahoney, the new US ambassador to Ghana in 1962, prioritized the improvement of the US public image.[127] Until Kennedy's assassination, Edgar Kaiser, CEO of the aluminum company that had taken on the Volta River Project, visited Nkrumah every few weeks to plead for moderation. When exiled opposition leader Kofi Busia testified in the US Senate about Ghana in December 1962 and Senator Thomas Dodd began talking about the "first Cuba in Africa," Kaiser visited Nkrumah's office once again.[128] "How can President Kennedy go on with his foreign aid program, how can he risk the whole foreign aid program?" Kaiser asked.[129] More than any Ghanaian flirtation with the Soviet Union, it was this "information vacuum" that shaped US-Ghana relations.

Another conflict was brewing in the area of education when bureaucrats at the helm of US aid inverted Eisenhower's strategy and argued values would be more quickly grasped through programs of common action, not education. In his foreign aid address to Congress on 22 March 1961, Kennedy redefined education as a way to develop human resources.[130] USIA officials were unhappy with this use of education for its own sake, arguing people were being supplied with guns without an effort being made to convince the people against whom the guns should be used.[131] Washburn therefore tried to blend concerns about psychological immaturity with the new aspiration for socioeconomic modernization: "A democratic government does not flourish on empty minds, any more than it does on empty stomachs."[132] His efforts were quashed during a fourteen-minute conversation in the Oval Office, in which funding requests were met with Kennedy's lack of interest.[133] When Adlai E. Stevenson mentioned Eisenhower's General Assembly speech in his own UN address, he gave the president's words new meaning by casting African education not as a means to preserve democratic freedom but as a tool to facilitate industrialization.[134] Kennedy found an ally in Van Bilsen, who had already tried to impress on Lumumba in July 1960 the importance of "ressources humaines." Like Kennedy, Van Bilsen wanted to internationalize aid and create an institution in the Congo that could match experts who were already in the country with projects, a Léopoldville version of the Agency of Development Cooperation he had wanted for Belgium.[135] Van Bilsen, who prioritized training and rejected food aid because it did not address structural underdevelopment, argued that Belgian aid had to be "non-engagé idéologiquement."[136]

Other European empires turned education into PR. Scholarships and radio education had to form an elite abroad that not only possessed a French cultural frame of reference but also, and more important, followed French practices that contributed to economic and social progress. While the British Council paid lip service to the cause of African unity by inviting French-speaking teachers, British cultural officers were eager to compete. Like generals preparing for the spring offensive—with strategic maps to boot—a report on French-speaking West Africa aimed at undercutting the French presence in Africa, since the director of the British Council's Africa department, Elwyn Owen, concluded that the French were successful only because they actively excluded aid from other countries. In the face of this competition, USIS officers on the ground became uncomfortable with Kennedy's technocratic view of education. In April 1963, Assistant Secretary of State for Education and Culture Lucius D. Battle asked Rostow to develop English language teaching not for its own sake but as a tool for projecting US values.[137] The Soviets agreed with Battle and viewed European and US policies as deliberate attempts to lessen the African and Asian appetite to learn Russian, leading the Soviets to increase the number of scholarships.[138]

Likewise, Ghanaian officials no longer shied away from projecting their own Pan-African ideology abroad, in the Positive Action Training Centre of the Kwame Nkrumah Ideological Institute in Winneba.[139] Since most students came from countries that were not necessarily wedded to socialism, the BAA—which had devised a ten-week training program—decided to remove socialism from the curriculum. Instead, Positive Action techniques and courses on political party organizing, with topics such as elections, party branches, and propaganda vans, were foregrounded. The decision to give PR priority over ideological training led to a fight between Barden and Secretary of the National Council for Education Amishadai Larson Adu, who wanted to give the institute an academic direction. Barden, however, wanted people to fully embrace African liberation and Nkrumahism.[140] This confusion led to PR fiascos, such as the group of forty Somalis who were in Accra to receive short-term training, in accountancy, nursing and midwifery, agriculture, and chemistry, but who instead went on a hunger strike because they were unhappy with the living standards. These disaffected students, together with African students who had been sent to universities in the Eastern Bloc, knocked on the door of the US embassy.[141]

Northern and Southern modernization doctrines also clashed in a third arena: the cultural center, the USIS version of which was widely imitated. The British Council, for instance, abandoned the separation between informational diplomacy and cultural assistance and instead created centers with reading rooms, exhibition spaces, and cinemas. The British had also been impressed by the French center in Fort Lamy, which not only contained a museum, an auditorium, and a youth center but also had been designed by Le Corbusier in 1960. Even though the French thus seemed to stick to their high culture strategy, in the face of Ghanaian competition, French teachers of the Alliance Française at the University of Ibadan wanted to copy the centers of USIS and the British Council.[142] Moreover, the cultural centers established through the bilateral cooperation agreements with the newly independent states of former French Africa now had to unequivocally promote France. An inspection report on the newly opened embassies in Central and East Africa concluded that exhibitions, film, and radio were most effective. "Information" became "above all a mental attitude."[143] Ghana could not lag behind. The envoy conference of 1961 decided that "Africa's cultural unity" made the "cultural medium the best means of promoting political unity in Africa." The African Affairs Secretariat began producing appealing pamphlets, troupes of dancers were sent to other African states, an arts festival was organized in Accra, and academic scholarship on African culture was subsidized. The *Voice of Africa* ran articles on Ghana's cultural heritage, and Accra sponsored scholarship reminding historians that the "black races" had cradled civilization. At new Ghanaian cultural centers, tape recorders, films, and pictures about Ghana were used to illustrate the cultural unity of the continent.[144]

In that strategy, USIS officers transformed into enemy troops because of their assumption that modernization would lead to a convergence of societal norms and cultural identities. On 11 January 1963, therefore, the removal of the cultural affairs officer, William B. Davis, was demanded, while Carl C. Nydell, regional medical officer, was arrested on the runway in Accra, where Kofi Baako personally notified him that plans for a coup had been found in his suitcase. When Edgar Kaiser and Chad Calhoun pointed out that these arrests endangered the Volta River Project, Nkrumah backed down. The eviction of cultural officers in Ghana, Guinea, and Mali was resisted because USIS officers feared that without their cultural centers, African leaders would only escalate the tensions of the transition process.[145] Contrary to their mission to build more understanding, the cultural centers thus became a focal point of conflict in Africa.

Diplomats in North and South worked to exploit decolonization, the other international reality of their age besides the Cold War. On a continent that was preoccupied with African culture as an engine of anticolonial modernity, cultural centers, newspapers, and education became battlegrounds and cultural officers the bearers of dangerous ideas, a notion even political opponents like Mobutu and Nkrumah could agree on.[146] In an international environment obsessed with technocratic socioeconomic modernization, however, Nkrumah's emotional propaganda strategy marginalized Pan-Africanism as an irrational project for postcolonial order. Accra's ideological offensive seemed to validate what modernization experts had been arguing: vocal anticolonialism was an emotional response resulting from the stresses that came with development. The Belgrade Conference had forced policymakers in Paris, London, Brussels, Lisbon, Moscow, and Washington to take a long hard look at "anticolonialism," "non-alignment," "neutralism," and "Afro-Asian solidarity." The bold attitude that characterized these diplomatic positions was measured against imperial,

Communist, and capitalist modernity, while non-alignment was listed as a symptom of underdevelopment. As operatives in the Global North geared up to alleviate the postcolonial condition, they met African leaders who viewed vocal anticolonialism as a means to immunize their populations against neocolonial ideas. That cycle of misunderstanding proved to be an impediment to a stable postcolonial order.

CHAPTER 7

The Struggle to Defeat Racial Modernity in South Africa and Rhodesia, 1963–1966

The liberationist promise of anticolonial modernity instigated a crisis in the last holdouts of racial modernity in southern Africa, where a battle for hearts and minds raised questions about the position of race in the international system. On 19 March 1964, W. Averell Harriman departed for London, Accra, Lagos, and Léopoldville onboard a C-121 Constellation aircraft after US president Lyndon B. Johnson tasked Harriman with a mission to investigate the different crises that held the continent in its grip. When he arrived in Accra, Michael Dei-Anang handed Harriman a memorandum in which Kwame Nkrumah urged the US delegate to tackle the problem of the "racialist British colony of Southern Rhodesia," believing it was on the brink of collapse. Portugal, the memorandum read, would also not "maintain her colonial possessions" and the "Apartheid regime of South Africa" could not "continue indefinitely." This prediction that the settler colonial project was gasping its last breath defied Pretoria's interpretation of decolonization. Turmoil in Congo and Algeria were viewed in Pretoria as the outcome of failed "integration" projects. South Africa's prime minister, Hendrik Verwoerd, did not want "safety on the basis of some form of multi-racial political society" and argued that 1960 had proven that South African "moderation" would only lead to more pressure to give up on the creation of "separate nations."[1] This fundamental clash over what "the year of Africa" meant for southern Africa made Nkrumah and other African nationalist leaders fearful of a "civil war" of "a racial nature," since it would also pose a threat to "world peace" and "involve Great Powers from outside the African continent."[2]

The trepidations surrounding race war in the 1960s raise the question of how the protagonists in settler Africa, Verwoerd and Rhodesian prime minister Ian Smith, and their principal challenger and direct neighbor, Kenneth Kaunda of Zambia, understood one another, as well as the hostility they faced from the outside world to their vision of postcolonial order. What decolonization meant for the battle for hearts and minds in southern Africa is difficult to grasp, since both Pretoria and Salisbury had a reputation for keeping their regimes afloat by remaining isolated. Analyses of Apartheid until the 1960s were dominated by the liberal paradigm, which cast Afrikaners as racists obsessed with survival. Marxist scholars in the 1970s, in contrast, argued that racism had been beneficial to the growth of South African capitalism.[3] The Rhodesian Unilateral Declaration of Independence (UDI) has been viewed as motivated by capital accumulation and corporate interests, as well as being the inevitable outcome of a long tradition of resistance.[4] As doubts about the profits of Apartheid and the benefits of Rhodesia's UDI emerged and archives opened up, scholars began to research the Afrikaner nationalist ideology and the settler concepts that underpinned both projects. Discussion of how Apartheid was rebranded as an African nationalist project as well as how Ian Smith justified UDI in international terms have resulted in more complex narratives.[5] The Zambian and Tanzanian ideologies, in contrast, which drew contemporaries in with their philosophical concepts of humanism and Kenyan African Socialism, were given attention from the very beginning. These were understood as world-making projects that ultimately failed or, conversely, as pragmatic instruments aimed at limiting domestic dissent. *Ujamaa*, for instance, has been described as an ideology full of "inconsistencies." Kenyatta's commitment to African Socialism has been seen as a tactical move to bypass political rivals, rather than as an ideological tenet of Kenya's foreign and domestic policy. All the while, Zambian humanism was solely meant to transcend tribal ideologies.[6]

These cynical interpretations, however, ignore how African ideologies were not merely postcolonial, but also postsettler. Settler conceptions of underdevelopment had structured much of society up until independence, and the defeat of racialized visions of modernity could therefore never be solely tactical.[7] Settler societies had twisted concepts such as democracy and modernity beyond recognition, and the existence of settler states in the international system therefore constituted a fundamental threat to the survival of African independent states. In September 1961, for instance, Roy Welensky had claimed that the Katanga secession was a clear case of self-determination comparable to the people of East Berlin demanding their freedom.[8] Behind closed doors, however, he argued that Katanga was "an ideal buffer between ourselves and the wilder forms of Pan-Africanism to the north of us."[9] The settler assault on international norm-making led newly minted African leaders such as Kaunda, Kenyatta and Nyerere to integrate ideas of radical equality and Christian universalism within their visions of postcolonial order: *Ujamaa*, humanism, and African Socialism. As Miles Larmer argues, the United National Independence Party's nationalism was "materialist, redistributive, socialistic in a form influenced by missionary Christianity, anti-'tribal' and unitary."[10]

As a consequence, Zambian and Tanzanian nationalism was not self-consciously anticolonial but was concerned with broader questions of race and social change. Humanism and *Ujamaa* were, as has been argued by David Gordon and Emma Hunter, open to interpretation and therefore harnessed as powerful symbols in the ideological scramble for Africa.[11] The Zambian, Tanzanian, and Kenyan information effort forced white settlers in southern Africa to look for new ways to salvage their racialized vision of modernization, producing a very peculiar battle for hearts and minds. Whereas Nkrumah and Léopold Senghor had cultivated universalist ambitions about decolonization so they could change the world, the value of anticolonial universalism for southern Africa was altogether different. The Frontline States—a loose coalition, including Zambia and Tanganyika, that was created to speed up liberation in southern Africa—reversed that reasoning. They worked to ensure that universal principles and international norms such as democracy and anti-racism, referred to as "non-racialism," were also applied when it came to Africa. "The idea of democracy," as Kaunda argued in 1964, had "a wider" and "more important application . . . in the realm of international affairs."[12]

To expunge racism and safeguard the independence project for southern Africa, a monumental information effort was required. As the Zambia Broadcast Corporation (ZBC) explained, universalist ideals such as "non-racialism, non-tribalism, humanism and Pan-Africanism" were "attitudes of mind," which could not be "implemented through legislation."[13] What was needed was a sustained campaign to transform hearts and minds, since Zambian information officers faced not only settler intransigence in Africa, but also Europeans in the metropole who viewed themselves as moderates in comparison to the settlers, a process Jean-Paul Sartre had described in 1961 as "self-estrangement."[14] Moral considerations, anti-Communism, and strategic resources all shaped the diplomacy surrounding Rhodesia's white-dominated UDI as well as South African Apartheid, but it was the perceived impact of decolonization on the minds of white settlers that informed decision making at every turn. Attitudes about race, underpinned by pseudoscientific research; "racialism," a belief that race determines human traits; and, conversely, the anti-Apartheid stance all came to be seen as psychological defects requiring targeted psychological action.

South Africa's Struggle against an "Emotional Issue" (1963–1965)

After 1960, Pretoria began to repackage Apartheid as a particular type of socioeconomic modernization via targeted propaganda campaigns in the United States and Western Europe. Verwoerd, for instance, drew parallels between Apartheid and the European Economic Community, since under his plan, each territory in South Africa would maintain its own political infrastructure but cooperate economically.[15] It was a succinct way for the National Party (NP) to explain Verwoerd's vision of "good neighborliness," which actually consisted of cramping Africans in territories that were separated from the places where Afrikaners lived.[16] Attention was diverted away from South Africa as a bulwark against Communism, and the South African Information Service worked to "disprove the assumption" that Apartheid's demise was good for the United States, as Ghana's radio signal was being jammed.[17] In December 1963, Minister of Foreign Affairs Eric Louw lamented the so-called double standard, because the UN General Assembly adopted resolutions whereby member states undertook not to provide South Africa with arms while not similarly excluding the African states that had "threatened an attack."[18]

South Africa viewed anti-Apartheid activism as a symptom of psychological distress brought on by the loss of empire. In April 1960, Wentzel C. du Plessis explained that his commitment to public diplomacy sprang from a determination to "diagnose" and address the sudden emotionalism that had come over his fellow white man.[19] "Equal rights," in his view, were not universal, and civilization was a characteristic of white men only.[20] Ideologies such as "die Humanisme" and Communism were, in the Afrikaner worldview, all forms of "egalitarianism"—ideologies that talked about equality—which could only be fully realized by a global government, a "wêreldregering." "Under the pressure of growing liberalism—which was in fact conditioned by the communist ideology," so-called white nations had experienced a change in spirit.[21] The increased appeal of these ideas in the northern parts of the white world were explained, not as a Cold War product, but as an ongoing search among whites to grapple with the loss of influence and territory that decolonization had brought about. Du Plessis understood the criticism of South Africa as a psychological response to the self-doubt of European whites. This understanding of anti-Apartheid activism as an emotional expression of white anguish was shared by others in the South African bureaucracy. The South African information office in Canada, for instance, concluded in September 1965 that Apartheid was an "emotional issue" that could therefore not be addressed via reasoned argument because attempting to do so would only provoke a hostile response.[22] That acute sense of loss in the realm of global prestige, du Plessis argued, had originated during the two world wars. Those feelings flowed from a human urge to seek more freedom and the simultaneous inability to cope with that liberty. Du Plessis's psychological justification for a war of words consciously drew on Jan Christian Smuts's anthropological concept "Holisme," which considered psychological and social factors as intertwined and saw humans and societies join ever-larger wholes, from small local units to nations and commonwealths, culminating in global forms of association such as the League of Nations.[23]

Conversely, policymakers in the North understood Apartheid as the product of white anguish. In the United Kingdom, Apartheid was seen as a "temporary aberration," promoted by anti-British and Nazi-associated Afrikaner nationalists who did not subscribe to the British ideals of multiracialism and threatened the stability of British rule elsewhere.[24] In "The White Redoubt," an influential memorandum published by the State Department in 1962, settlers and Afrikaners emerge primarily as a frightened group among whom the crises in Congo and Algeria had kindled "white fears," in an echo of the Kennedy administration's analysis of frustration.[25] The NSC worried about the creation of "Bantustans" because these territories set aside for the black inhabitants of South Africa were poorly thought out and would unleash forces that "South Africa may not be able to control," leading to an increase of the frustration that came with modernization.[26] LBJ's goal for South Africa was therefore "averting racial conflicts between [the white-ruled] parts of Southern Africa and the rest of the continent," while Mennen Williams in his speeches tried to circumvent "one of the most hotly debated questions" on that continent, namely the "future of Europeans in Africa," by stressing the need for socioeconomic modernization. "Both the Africans and the Europeans," he quipped, had to "get on with the job that must be done."[27] The African Studies Association president, William O. Brown, even dedicated his presidential address in 1960 to the "white man," who was in "crisis" due to the "tendency towards polarization on a racial basis."[28]

African nationalist leaders and anticolonial thinkers, in contrast, viewed Apartheid as a moral problem, and settlers and Afrikaners were viewed as inhumane and psychologically disturbed. Anticolonial thinkers such as Frantz Fanon argued the settler had become "crazed by his absolute power and by the fear of losing it" and had forgotten "he was once a man."[29] Fanon's mentor, Aimé Césaire, also believed that one had to "study how colonization works to decivilize the colonizer."[30] The trope of the disturbed *pied noir* had been popularized in 1942 by Albert Camus's existentialist novel *L'Étranger*, which depicts the life of a man who, void of any feeling, kills an Algerian, but this trope had its antecedents in Joseph Conrad's 1899 novel *Heart of Darkness*, a story in which an ivory trader named Kurtz becomes crazed due to his stay in the Congo Free State.[31] In 1920, W. E. B. Dubois's *Souls of White Folks* adopted a similar conception of white supremacy as a system that reduced Blacks to things and claimed "ownership of the earth."[32]

The psychologized language in which Apartheid and anti-Apartheid were cloaked altered policymaking on both sides of the postcolonial divide. African nationalist leaders began to reevaluate their reliance on the boycott of South African goods, which had been embraced at the All-African People's Conference in 1958 by people such as Tom Mboya. How effective would be an appeal to moral standards of universal justice—a tactic rooted in nineteenth-century humanitarianism—if South African whites were psychologically inept?[33] Pretoria, on the other hand, believed it was incumbent on South Africa to make the Western Bloc aware of its "mental illness" ("geestessiekte"), which had caused the acceptance of the Communist notion that all races were equal. Afrikaners had to step up, since the white world had become split into two Cold War camps, and Ghanaian Pan-Africanism had fanned the anticolonial flame, "uprooting" the white man.[34] In their zeal to embrace their role as moral guide, the South Africans severed themselves from the white world in crisis and made a case for their exceptionalism. Unlike in Kenya and Algeria, the reasoning went, in South Africa, "white communities" constituted a "unique separate and self-contained nation."[35] South Africa's PR campaigns in the 1960s were therefore not primarily meant to convince a target audience in the Global North or South but rather sought to give whites back their sense of "self-worth" by promoting the cultural contributions of whites.

Apartheid also intensified and challenged the socioeconomic management of decolonization that powers outside of Africa had embraced. LBJ and JFK called on the USIA to manage the frustration that emerged from quick-paced decolonization by encouraging "moderate whites."[36] The strategy the US Bureau of African Affairs proposed in January 1964 was a combination of African nationalist support and a campaign to persuade "as many as possible of the white population in South Africa that there is an alternative preferable to the Verwoerd Government policy."[37] Officials such as Mennen Williams quickly pointed out, however, that they could not "merely lecture Africans on the need for restraint. . . . We must convince them that restraint . . . best serves their interests."[38] "Educational assistance" was therefore secretly provided to Black South African students. Harriman also looked for private organizations that could be used as a front.[39] The public affairs officer for South Africa, Argus Tresidder, embraced frustration management and wanted to reshape the public understanding of South Africa as a "meeting place of the races of Africa," to avoid a race war with a "well-organized, armed and radically indoctrinated" resistance. Since "scientific, cultural and education activities" were not yet "contaminated by racialism," these activities provided the most effective tool to create a multiracial situation conducive to effective modernization (see figure 7.1).[40] Even Dwight D. Eisenhower, who was invited to South Africa in 1962, maintained his own notion of a gradual transition: "We were making progress. What more could be asked of a country?" He would not "go out to a country and tell it what it should do to solve its problems."[41]

For Harold Wilson, the moral argument that African nationalists advanced made it more difficult to continue Harold Macmillan's PR approach to Apartheid, which mimicked the US strategy. In his "Wind of Change" speech to the parliament of South Africa, on 3 February 1960 in Cape Town, Macmillan had separated the racial issue from other diplomatic concerns. The South African High Commission in London downplayed the speech's impact as an issue of

FIGURE 7.1.   US Information Agency photo showing Norman Kessel, a student, and Mr. J. M. Rakate, a businessman, reading pamphlets on space at the USIS-Johannesburg Library in September 1960. Photo courtesy of NARA.

disagreement: "To-day we don't agree on everything. We don't agree on the racial problem."[42] Wilson, in contrast, came to power with a public commitment to end arms sales to the Apartheid regime.[43] Nevertheless, the British Council ignored Wilson and believed that refusing to deal with South Africa was a "short-sighted policy." Rather than a "self-imposed boycott," they looked for ways to increase cooperation and expand their involvement in African education.[44] France similarly focused mainly on its language education. Paris had opened its first cultural center in Pretoria in 1956, when funding and staff had become available as posts in Syria, Jordan and Egypt closed in the aftermath of the Suez Crisis.[45]

The Belgians and the Portuguese viewed South African racism as excessive, despite the existence of a color bar in the Belgian Congo and forced labor practices in Angola and Mozambique. In his memoirs, Jef Van Bilsen described a trip to Cape Town in 1946 that felt like "looking into a mirror," as he concluded that "racism, segregation and the colour bar" were also deeply rooted, but less severe, in the minds of whites in the Congo. Nevertheless, in 1964, Paul-Henri Spaak expressed his support for the South African argument that Afrikaners were also African and therefore deserved the right to self-determination.[46] The Portuguese were not worried about racial war but did fear that activism in South Africa could spill over into the Portuguese parts of the continent.[47] At the last meeting of the UN Security Council in November of 1965, the foreign ministers of Liberia, Madagascar, Sierra Leone, and Tunisia requested the Council to discuss Apartheid, but, as the Zambian UN representative noted, Rhodesia's UDI already dominated the debates.[48]

UDI and Racialism as a Psychological Defect (1965–1966)

On 11 November 1965, Ian Smith, newly elected Rhodesian prime minister since April, made a Unilateral Declaration of Independence. This independent Rhodesian state was salvaged from the rubble of the Central African Federation of Northern Rhodesia, Southern Rhodesia, and Nyasaland, which had collapsed in 1963. A decade earlier, the two Rhodesias had been federated with Nyasaland as a compromise between those who demanded independence from Great Britain and the officials at the Colonial Office who were responsibility for Black Africans in Northern Rhodesia and Nyasaland. In the background, the threat of amalgamation into the Union of South Africa kept looming, leading the governor of Southern Rhodesia, Evelyn Baring, to ask London for a solution in 1943. After a review of the federal constitution by the Monckton Commission in 1960, the

Macmillan government recognized the right of federal territories to secede, and a new constitution was approved in 1961. The Congo Crisis of 1960 and the "Wind of Change" speech of 1961 fueled rumors of a possible UDI. Smith mobilized Rhodesian opinion, drawing Rhodesia into the ideological scramble for Africa with a distinct vision of white settler modernity.[49]

The creation by Smith of an *indaba*—a gathering—of Rhodesian African chiefs that demanded independence as well as the publication in April 1965 of a white paper that argued UDI would not damage the economy drew Nkrumah's attention. The Ghanaian leader had already, in July 1963, applied the lessons he had learned from the Sahara atomic bomb tests campaign and the Congo Crisis to pressure the UK government into action against Smith's predecessor, Winston Field. A pamphlet, ostensibly written by Nkrumah, made the case that a deal between white Rhodesians and the British was impossible because racism was "part and parcel of the settler system." The systemic nature of racism made it impossible for an "individual settler" or a "group of settlers, however well intentioned," to end the crisis. The British approach, which consisted of replacing one group of "disloyal" settlers with another, would therefore not work. To address this situation, Ghana felt the "only remaining course" was "military action from outside." An internal memorandum from 1961 highlights that officials in Accra were afraid "imperialists" were arming South Africa and were "establishing nuclear warheads of the most modern design in the Union." Uniting Africa therefore had to prevent being "destroyed by greater military forces."[50]

Before UDI, the Zambians had already rejected plans for African military intervention and instead kicked their propaganda machine into overdrive, particularly after their own independence in October 1964. Like the Ghanaians, officials in Lusaka also believed British officials had to be convinced of the fact that Africans in Rhodesia were capable of self-government. Two months before UDI, Chairman Isaac Mumpansha of the ZBC drew up a communication plan that had to paper over the differences between the warring anticolonial factions in Rhodesia, Robert Mugabe's Zimbabwe African National Union (ZANU) and Joshua Nkomo's Zimbabwe African People's Union (ZAPU), by stressing that the fight for Rhodesian Africans was a fight for "our kith and kin." Intense competition had led ZAPU to request aid from Czechoslovakia in October 1965, while political chaos weakened the African demand for self-government when talking to Whitehall.[51] More important, Mumpansha's communication plan sought to create information material that conveyed that Africans had experience in the fields of administration and civil service. At the same time, Africans in Rhodesia were roused to political action, since they, according to the Zambians, did not seem to realize that independence required "sacrificial acts."[52]

UNIP members had already relied heavily on public diplomacy before Zambia's independence, since chiefs and the local population in Katanga had to be encouraged to forge a "brotherhood between the Congolese and the Zambians." Zambian nationhood was fragile because chiefs in Luapula Province had aligned themselves with the Katangese secessionists while Moïse Tshombe kept highlighting the precolonial unity of the Lunda and Bemba by arguing that "before the Europeans," "Katanga and Rhodesia formed one vast territory." After independence, the small, colonial-type information department was therefore expanded. "The advent of UDI" further increased "the importance of the office" in London and led to a Zambian student being housed in a room at the Ghanaian BAA, from where he had to project Zambian ideas. UNIP furthermore opened up a party office in Elisabethville in January 1963. Meanwhile, the "complexity of the work" increased, with transnational examples being relied on to develop innovative PR techniques.[53] The Zambian ambassador to Washington, Rupiah Bwezani Banda, for instance, learned from the Rhodesians, the South Africans, and the Portuguese, "as unsophisticated as they" were, that it was important to invite journalists.[54] In August 1965, Zambian diplomats initiated a campaign that aspired to "give a clear understanding of the Rhodesian situation to the rest of the African States and the world."[55]

Despite the Zambian investments in information infrastructure, disagreement between African countries about the best way to fight UDI only deepened in the course of the mid-1960s. The Commonwealth Conference of 1964 in Lagos had left Joseph Murumbi disappointed and Ghanaian representatives reeling as they accused Abubakar Tafawa Balewa of being a coward for not supporting immediate independence for Rhodesia.[56] The disagreement between Zambians and other African nationalists was bitter, because policymakers in Lusaka seemed to share the same ideas as their colleagues in Pretoria when it came to modernity. Profoundly shaped by their experiences in the part of the continent dominated by white settlers, both rivals agreed that notions of racial difference, racism, and "civilizational difference" were part and parcel of modernity itself and doubted whether modernity could be expanded to include Africans. The resistance they faced when promoting "humanism" as well as Apartheid was dismissed by Zambians and white Afrikaners alike as an expression of psychological defects brought about by decolonization. The ideological scramble in southern Africa defies the easy dichotomy implied by the "unholy alliance" that viewed the Portuguese, Rhodesians, and South Africans as one impenetrable bloc.[57]

Kaunda sought to reverse the harm done by modernity and based his domestic and foreign policy on a "humanist approach." "Society" had to be kept "man-centred," "no matter how 'modern' and 'advanced' in a Western sense" Zambia would become.[58] Similarly, in Tanzania's Swahiliphone public sphere, a demand for "maendeleo"—meaning progress or development—was always coupled with a desire to not break up social relations.[59] The South African secretary of information between 1961 and 1963, du Plessis, agreed in a cynical and radical fashion: modernity was only meant to benefit "civilized men." He wanted to harden the divide between the "civilized" and "uncivilized" parts of society, to make sure the latter group would remain untouched by modernization. Cecil Rhodes—the British mining magnate and imperial entrepreneur who had "sought to equip" his African neighbors with "intellectual development"— was held up as an ideological example, a founding father of sorts.[60] Consequently, the UN charter on human rights was co-written in 1945 by South African prime minister Smuts, who believed in an unbridgeable evolutionary divide between whites and blacks and as a consequence worked to turn human rights into a white privilege.[61] To avoid race war, Zambian public diplomats were tasked with breaking white settler modernity and instilling the "common man" on the continent with the "government policy of Pan-Africanism."[62]

Zambia's expansive public diplomacy and African tactical disagreements shaped the strategy of non-African diplomats in the period before UDI. The United States condemned plans for UDI, leading Chairman Clifford Dupont of the Rhodesian Front Party to bitterly attack the United States in the Federal Assembly in March 1962 for using Pan-Africanism and the UN as instruments to pursue a policy of "economic colonialism."[63] The State Department policy planning staff "revisited" the "White Redoubt" in March 1965 and concluded that the diplomatic landscape had changed. The "weakness, frustrations and neuroses" of anticolonial leaders was providing "both the Communist World and the 'White Redoubtists' with opportunities." This "twofold polarization," teaming up "blacks" and "communists," on one side, and "whites" and "the West," on the other, was weakening the US position in Africa. Needless energy was being wasted on projects unrelated to modernization. The State Department's Africa section therefore wanted to exploit the economic ties of Zambia and Tanzania with Rhodesia and South Africa to stimulate moderation and jump-start development. The response was once again found in federation, with the creation of a "Zone of Peace," a "regional 'defensive' strategy among the contiguous states." Economic development was promoted as a means for "releasing national energy and reducing the temptation to use the 'liberation struggle' as an escape for domestic problems." Relief for nationalist frustration was offered by building the Tanzania-Zambia Rail Link, which would further "close economic association." Offering the Tanzanian and Zambian leaders an economic alternative in the event of "a rupture with Rhodesia in the likely event of UDI" was considered so important that the Chinese were even allowed to cofinance the railway's construction.[64]

In the United Kingdom, officials fretted over what to do in case of UDI. In line with their earlier multiracial approach, in which the more liberal settlers were enlisted in the service of the British colonial policy, the high commissioner hoped to find a prominent politician to recruit as a loyal partner. The Foreign Office's Rhodesia Department believed its "best hope of reaching the objective would be the emergence of a European successor government ready to negotiate."[65] Nevertheless, when the Foreign Office and Commonwealth Office argued that the British reluctance to use military force meant that only "other means of persuasion," such as "information media," had to be relied on, Britain's high commissioner to Rhodesia, Sir John Baines Johnston, explored what course of action was possible.[66] After a conversation with the Rhodesian high commissioner to London, Evan Campbell, he realized that UK public diplomacy would be impossible. "The idea of an appeal to the European public in Rhodesia over Mr. Smith's head" was "attractive in theory" but "extremely difficult in practice," since it required showing Europeans in Rhodesia they were "reasonable" without alienating the African Commonwealth members.[67] Consequently, Wilson mainly employed information media to dispel the notion that the United Kingdom was going to intervene militarily.[68]

In Brussels and Lisbon, the specter of irredentist claims dominated decision making. In Belgium, there had been concern about the ties between Rhodesia and Katanga ever since intelligence reports in 1961 had shown that Welensky and Tshombe had met in secret.[69] In July 1960 Van Bilsen wanted to dissuade Tshombe from working with Rhodesia by arguing that Katanga would be kept in an inferior position as a producer of raw materials for the industrial centers in the south, if it ever came to a merger.[70] On 5 September 1964, Welensky's successor, Ian Smith, twice visited António Salazar—a man with an aquiline nose— in the Estoril Fort to request support for a UDI. Smith felt the British Commonwealth was increasingly being dominated by African nationalists. The Portuguese leader was interested because Salisbury's offers for assistance in the ongoing Angolan War of independence had always been blocked by London. In his memoirs. Smith notes that Salazar was worried about the evolution in Southern Rhodesia and therefore continued the "policy of evolution in Mozambique and Angola." In short, Portugal—unlike Brussels—publicly distanced itself from UDI but privately encouraged it.[71]

Smith ignored all protest and declared independence. Modeling himself on the US revolutionaries, he paraphrased the first words of the US independence declaration and stressed how in the "course of human affairs history," it "may become necessary for a people to resolve the political affiliations which have connected them with another people." In Brazzaville, Smith was less heroically named "the White Tshombe" because, like Katanga, Rhodesia mounted a major symbolic challenge to the dominant logic of decolonization, which dictated that states with majority African populations could become independent only with the approval of that Black majority.[72] Appalled by the United Kingdom's willingness to grant independence to Northern Rhodesia and Nyasaland, shocked by events in Kenya and Congo, and inspired by Tshombe's white mercenary state of Katanga, Smith felt UDI was a more orderly solution to the "racial problems" the continent faced, unlike "African nationalists" who wanted only to get their way by stirring "up sufficient trouble."[73]

UDI's symbolic challenge to African decolonization forced African leaders to rethink their approach to the Rhodesian problem. They drew inspiration from the different types of anticolonial struggle that had been effective in the past and in that way fueled intra-African disagreement over the right course of action. The Algerians, for example, suggested an internationalization of the struggle, emulating their own fight against France. In their estimation, Wilson had not applied sufficient "psychological pressure and moral persuasion," despite having control over the UN's "consensus machine."[74] Instead, the UK representative at the UN had worked hard to keep UDI off the agenda to "keep our hands as free as possible for negotiations with the Rhodesian Government."[75] United Arab Republic diplomats, in contrast, argued that the only possible course of action was to "put an end to the fascist oppressive regime in Southern Rhodesia" through military intervention, a strategy Kenyan diplomats also supported. They believed the Organisation of African Unity had to be "showy and propagandist" about its military undertakings. Agostinho Neto of the Movimento Popular de Libertação de Angola argued that the armed struggle in Angola, Mozambique, and Guinea-Bissau provided a model for effectively undercutting the "imperialist collusion of Salazar, Ian Smith and Verwoerd."[76] Kaunda and Banda, however, were annoyed by the enthusiasm they encountered at the OAU about a military assault and the severing of ties with the United Kingdom. Kenyatta's "lofty ideas" would only lead to more instability without an "effective implementation," they argued. Military intervention without a credible commitment to action was perilous. "African nations" were mistaken if they believed they could only behave as "ferocious little animals which" could "snarl to frighten away the big beast (presumably without a real fight)."[77] The Algerian approach had already proved ineffective for the Zambians. In March 1966, Vernon J. Mwaanga, ambassador to Moscow, returned empty-handed after officials in Poland, Austria, Yugoslavia, Czechoslovakia, and East Germany refused to commit to a Rhodesian tobacco ban.[78]

Most OAU delegates, particularly those from radical countries such as Guinea, understood Kaunda's objections as the result of neocolonial intrusion. In their estimation, Zambia had become a "British puppet," guided by an imperialist "modus operandi."[79] The *Zambia Mail* therefore found it necessary to stress that "no country can claim to be working harder than Zambia for the early downfall of the Smith regime," while simultaneously having to deny that Kaunda was hesitant about hurting Rhodesia to avoid "irreparable harm" to Zambia.[80] To contain UDI's effects, Zambian diplomats therefore began to redirect their attention to the inter-African arena. In February 1966, the Zambian high commissioner to Ghana, Matiya Ngalande, was sent to Guinea and Mali to explain how their economic survival depended on Rhodesia and why their hesitation about breaking ties with the United Kingdom was not motivated by neocolonialism. It was conveyed to Sékou Touré, who took Matiya Ngalande to Touré's house on the beach, that Guinea's commitment to "fight for the cause of Rhodesia, both morally and physically" was counterproductive. In Mali, Modibo Keita was given a "full picture of the position of Zambia," while Keita assured his Zambian interlocuter that he would not "betray the interest of Africa to foreign powers." To divert attention away from the neocolonial accusations, Ngalande raised the issue of "their neighbours i.e. Senegal, Ivory Coast and Upper Volta of the OCAM group," which were also "not really independent as their policies are teleguided by France."[81] The question of how exactly to tackle UDI and Apartheid thus sowed division among African nationalists. They had all had different experiences in their struggle for independence, which framed their views about postcolonial order. The "settler issue" definitely did not provide "African nationalists" with a "theme on which all" could "agree."[82]

After UDI, the focus of the public diplomacy campaign therefore shifted from the United Kingdom to Rhodesia. The United Kingdom was flooded with hostile propaganda emphasizing that the British had always acted to the detriment of Zambia's interests. More important, the psychological makeup of the settler—a recurring theme in strategic discussions—became a major talking point for anticolonial thinkers and politicians.[83] Diplomats were struggling to understand why their anticolonial strategies were ineffective. In their OAU report on the situation in September 1967, the foreign ministers of Algeria, Senegal, and Zambia maintained that they were still "convinced that the only appropriate solution to this problem" was "the use of force," while Nkrumah maintained that African unity was the only effective answer to UDI.[84] Much as in the Global North during the Congo Crisis, psychology offered African diplomats with an explanation for why the strategies they had employed so successfully during their own independence struggles were not working for white Africa. To regain the upper hand in the African diplomatic arena, Zambian diplomats presented themselves as experts on white settler psychology. A Sudanese envoy "felt that Zambia had a special knowledge of the psychology of racialism" and was therefore uniquely suited to lead the fight against UDI.[85] Mumpansha thought West Africans were not fully aware of the "mentality of white settlers" and needed Lusaka's expertise.[86] Kaunda wanted to prevent Africa from being dragged into a race war, a "racial and ideological explosion," and continued to ask the White House and Harriman for help in preventing it.[87] Psychological knowledge of the white settler became an indispensable weapon in the liberationist struggle against Rhodesia. This knowledge allowed Kaunda, in the words of the Commonwealth Office, to return from a world tour in June 1966 with renewed confidence, as a "pace-setter against all the remaining white regimes in the continent."[88]

Smith felt the pressure of the African public diplomacy campaigns, leading him to complain to Kaunda about ZBC programs that advocated "violence and subversion."[89] Much to LBJ's displeasure and in the face of Ghanaian and Zambian protest, Rhodesia therefore set up an information office in Washington, DC.[90] Like that of Pretoria, Smith's Rhodesia information services strategy hinged on presenting Rhodesia's African competitors as deranged. The public diplomats claimed the image of Rhodesia as "a country of racial violence" was built "upon emotional fantasy."[91] The Smith regime's violent oppression was depicted in a pamphlet on terrorism as "things the Afro-Asian circus (with their Communist allies and masters) would like the rest of the world to believe," while African nationalism was cast as promising "pie in the sky for everybody."[92] Pamphlets downplayed the racial tensions in the federation, and other publications claimed in April 1966 that the ZBC incited Africans in Rhodesia to commit acts of violence.[93] At the same time, Smith claimed to be a legitimate international actor, as he kept repeating that Whitehall had promised that "in the event of the Federation breaking up, independence would automatically follow from Southern Rhodesia."[94]

In a conversation with US secretary of state Dean Rusk, who had been tasked with figuring out the Rhodesian problem, Robert Komer raised his fear that UDI could have implications beyond southern Africa. In his memorandum to LBJ in December 1965, Komer argued that "we ought to duck this mess if we can afford to, leaving it to the British or others." "Rhodesia itself" was not "very important to us," but action on the issue was "critical to all other Africans" because "all their anti-white instincts" had been aroused. Economic sanctions would be ineffective, since "African frustration" was growing about ineffective crisis management by the United Kingdom and the UN. In response, African attention had to be redirected to economic development.[95]

In December 1965, Balewa flew to London to confer with Wilson, who also nervously fretted over an appropriate response. since UDI was quickly becoming a test case for the British approach to the dilemma of race.[96] Wilson assessed UDI in global terms and believed "the results of these policies may be dangerous not only for Rhodesia but for a far greater area of Africa; they may extend even wider and involve the world."[97] James Nicholas Allan at the Foreign Office and Commonwealth Office had already noted in May 1965 how UDI had plunged the British self-understanding of decolonization into a deep crisis. Smith's challenge meant the "British visions of multi-racial societies in East and Southern Africa" had failed, and from now on, countries such as Southern Rhodesia could only become either "a white man's country or a black man's country."[98] As in the United States, socioeconomic modernization became a panacea for the problems of British decolonization and a means to paper over racial differences. Wilson's view that "not war, or communism" but "hunger" was "the most urgent problem" was testament to that new belief that an "escape from such poverty" was "a real possibility."[99]

In 1965 Telegrafnoe agentstvo Sovetskogo Soiuza (TASS), the USSR's propaganda agency, claimed the United Kingdom had refused to intervene to prevent the establishment of a "white racist minority government," proving that the British were acting in accordance with a wider imperialist plan that sought to prevent full liberation by retaining the southern part of the African continent under white domination.[100] The USSR had no diplomatic relations with South Africa, but the Czechoslovak government did maintain the small diplomatic post it had established in 1926 throughout the 1960s, mainly to stimulate trade. At the same time, Czechoslovakia refused to recognize UDI and sought to increase its trade with Zambia, to keep that economy afloat.[101] From October 1966 on, Czechoslovakia also trained Zambian military officers and helped arm and train the UNIP Youth Wing as a civilian militia that could be activated in the event of a foreign invasion.[102]

The ideological scramble in southern Africa diverged from the struggle in other parts of the continent because the South Africans and Rhodesians clung to a program of racial modernity that centered on supposedly unbridgeable civilization differences. African nationalists, in turn, wrestled with the best way to debase the Afrikaner development model and the settler more broadly. Proponents of bold military action in West Africa were gradually overtaken by supporters of a public diplomacy approach in Zambia, because the racism white settlers and Afrikaners expounded came to be seen as a psychological defect. Addressing it required an integrated socioeconomic response, according to Northern diplomats, and a calibrated psychological approach, according to their African colleagues. By the mid-1960s, it had become clear that the increasingly complex nature of liberation required a new strategy. The anticolonial ambition to create an international order in which federations of liberations challenged empires was abandoned. Instead, African nationalists increasingly turned to the Cold War powers and regional units, because both options provided them with the economies of scale required for the enormous need for development.

CHAPTER 8

The Collapse of Anticolonial
Modernization, 1963–1966

By the mid-1960s, African nationalists began to wrestle with the limited material and political gains that anticolonial modernity and federations of liberations had delivered. Liberationists who had pointed to neocolonial interference in the 1950s to explain their failure at creating new economic and political structures were pushed aside by pragmatists who explained persistent underdevelopment as the product of international economics and structural dependency. To meet the demand for better living standards, leaders recast their federations of liberation in regional terms and tried to build a New International Economic Order (NIEO), while others turned to the Cold War superpowers for support. When the Organisation of African Unity meeting took place in Accra in October 1966, the city was swept up in debates about union government, which was rumored to be implemented in the course of the gathering. According to Zambian delegate Henry S. Meebelo, streets were "teeming with posters bearing unity slogans," children were reenacting television dramas on African unity, while State House, where the conference took place, was "built to reassert this Ghanaian continental expansionism" and enchant the delegates into uniting. Diplomats gossiped that Haile Selassie had rushed to offer a multistory office block to the OAU secretariat after learning of Kwame Nkrumah's plans. The Ghanaians, according to Meebelo, became disappointed with the "whole 'ideology' of a Union government" after the decision to hold OAU conferences in Addis Ababa.[1]

Disagreements among African idealists and pragmatists about the most effective way to attain modernity not only played out on the streets of Accra in debates over the merits of federalism and regionalism but had already burst into the open during the Belgrade Conference of 1961 and became sharper in the early 1960s, when economists began to question prevailing development doctrines. By 1964, a new generation of African leaders, who had been subjected to racial modernization schemes in southern Africa, championed iterations of liberation that prioritized material, social, and economic change, not immunization against neocolonial ideas. These leaders believed, in the words of Amílcar Cabral, that "the attitude of each social group towards the liberation struggle" was primarily "dictated by its economic interests," a conscious rebellion against a cultural Pan-Africanism that had not delivered.[2] As Jeffrey Byrne writes in his study of Algeria, for all their celebration of cultural emancipation, the new postcolonial elites staked their legitimacy on an appeal to the material self-interest of their citizens.[3]

By the mid-1960s, independent African countries, superpowers in détente, and empires in decline all struggled to provide large-scale material development. Socioeconomic modernization, championed by African nationalists and modernization theorists alike, required a vast amount of financial resources, leading to an embrace of regional economic entities such as the East African Federation in the short term, as well as the NIEO in the long run. In conversations among historians of the Global South, the mid-1960s come up as a time when the "spirit of limitless possibility" was crushed by "conservative" state-centered forces.[4] Likewise, the scholarship on the Global North has stressed narrowing prospects and harsh power politics. LBJ, for instance, is seen keeping Africa off the agenda because he faced opposition in Congress, while Leonid Brezhnev's rise to power is believed to have led to an increase in military spending in the USSR.[5] The gap between the Commonwealth's "lofty" rhetoric and its actual achievements has mystified scholars, while in Belgium and France the transition to development aid in the 1960s was overshadowed by the Faustian bargain between the metropole and authoritarian leaders, as well as the Portuguese empire's increasingly violent decolonization.[6]

Yet, the impulse to create regional entities does not reflect a conservative-nationalist retrenchment. Instead, it highlights perpetual doubts about the African nation-state's ability to deliver on the material promise of modernity.

Regions as Incubators of Modernity

Once the immediate fight against colonial oppression was over, leaders in the Global North and the Global South began to doubt whether their plans for a decolonized Africa could be realized. The Zambian Information Services admitted that "up to the time of independence," the country's "role was plain—it was to organise our forces" against colonialism. After independence, the harder task of defining a "new role" and a new society emerged.[7] In Kenya, Jaramogi Oginga Odinga—vice president and Jomo Kenyatta's political rival after 1966—remembered how long it took him and his fellow freedom fighters to realize that "the time when accession to independence was progress" was over and more energy needed to be invested in "the political and economic content of independence."[8] In 1960, Odinga had accepted aid from every source, even asking the German Democratic Republic to ship its goods through the Cairo bureau of the Kenya African National Union, while requesting assistance in Prague in July 1962.[9] In 1964, Nkrumah saw "first stage decolonization" come to an end and the "demands for political unity, the liberation of the rest of Africa and economic independence becoming general insistent and vociferous."[10] The CIA viewed West Africa as an area "plagued by chronic instability," which resulted "in further delaying badly needed economic measures."[11] By 1966, LBJ believed "most of the developing world" was in "crisis"; Nikita Khrushchev had already been deposed in November 1962 in part as a result of criticism from politburo member Dmitry Polyansky, who pointed out that Moscow's assistance to African "progressive regimes" had led to "deplorable results."[12]

Nkrumah's interventionist Pan-African project—already under fire for its intrusive methods—was now blasted by a younger generation of African leaders for being a political project built on the assumption that ideological purity could tackle technocratic challenges. While Kenyatta and Léopold Senghor had disliked Accra's Pan-African foreign policy because of Nkrumah's domineering attitude, African nationalists in southern Africa were weary of his foreign policy of cultural authenticity, because it was not coupled with material advancement. Kenneth Kaunda's Humanism did not want to "over-emphasize the importance of preserving our past society at the expense of the material development of the people," while Julius Nyerere's Ujamaa celebrated "African tradition" because in a "traditional African society everybody was a worker."[13]

Born in Butiama and educated at a Catholic school, Nyerere transformed into one of the most prominent intellectuals of African economic development. He located the seed of underdevelopment in inequality, which had to be combated through regional integration on an international level and a return to the socioeconomic conditions of "African communalism" domestically.[14] The "African Personality" had turned "African unity" into "merely an emotion," and since "African nationalism" was "meaningless," "anachronistic" and "dangerous," "regional association" became the only alternative to bring an "immediate strengthening of our economies."[15] Nkrumah's recipe of combining industrialization with cultural and psychological resistance was insufficient. Instead, liberation had to be attained domestically by returning to precolonial social relations and by becoming economically "self-reliant." Nyerere turned to "villagization," a form of socialist agrarianism based on the conviction that the large-scale industrialization of Tanzania was undesirable. Education had to not only instill ideas but, more important, "prepare young people for the work they will be called upon to do in the society."[16]

Internationally, Nyerere was the most vocal member of a group of African leaders who rejected Nkrumah's Pan-African Monroe Doctrine, which had sought to immunize the continent from neocolonial cultural intrusion. As Nkrumah doubted the value of the "African lobby" in the UN General Assembly, believing "pious resolutions" were "no substitute" for an ideological war of words, Zambian and Kenyan delegates promoted utilitarian definitions of non-alignment.[17] For Kaunda, non-alignment was about engagement, not isolation. A focus on "practical co-operation in financial, economic and trade matters" was "a sign of realism" because it provided the Zambians with a "framework in our dealings with the outside world," which made it possible to "praise" and "condemn."[18] Kaunda had already exhibited this type of diplomatic pragmatism when, as a freedom fighter, he accepted support from both Nkrumah and the more conservative Haile Selassie.[19] In Kenya, Assistant Minister for Commerce and Industry Stanley Shapashina Ole Oloitiptip even erased Cold War bipolarity altogether from the Kenyan definition of non-alignment, eliminating the tyranny of choice and the focus on outside intrusion. He considered African Socialism to be the only possible political stance. "The fundamental conflict of our era" was not between Communism and capitalism, but between "totalitarianism and the free way of life" with Communism and Fascism on the totalitarian side and capitalism and socialism on the democratic side.[20]

In 1964, then, these African nationalists helped transform regional and continental units from liberationist horizons into instruments of structural economic change (see figure 8.1). Immanuel Wallerstein, who in 1961 had defined Pan-Africanism as a distinct type of modernity, by 1967 considered the "movements for regional unity" to also include moderate statesmen who "wanted entry into the world community as equals but" no longer sought "to transform the nature of this world community."[21] Unlike Nkrumah, Nyerere acknowledged that there were "varied paths to Socialism" while "different areas" could "advance on the road to unity at different speeds."[22] The efforts to establish an East African Federation (EAF) exemplify how federations lost their liberationist content and became a development tool, prompting Nkrumah to undermine the EAF's creation. On 5 June 1963, Nyerere, Kenyatta, and Milton Obote of Uganda signed a declaration of intent after Nyerere had tried to postpone independence to attain

FIGURE 8.1. Jomo Kenyatta (right), Julius Nyerere (left), and Milton Obote (center) wave at the crowd before entering the hall in Nairobi where the East African Heads of Government Conference was held on 18 April 1964. Cola images / Alamy Stock Photo.

federation first. With Tanzania's independence, hope for a federation was lost, even though a merger between Tanganyika and Zanzibar was achieved.[23] Joseph Murumbi and Tom Mboya had a hard time convincing Obote, who had been pressured by Nkrumah and feared a federation would make Uganda "fade into insignificance."[24]

The EAF had to increase the capacity for economic development and therefore had to exploit the biggest advantage theorists such as the popular Swedish development economist Gunnar Myrdal had identified: economies of scale. The language of "self-reliance" was mobilized in Nyerere's vision of African Socialism.[25] In practice, however, Zanzibar welcomed teachers from the German Democratic Republic in September 1965, and Kaunda was eager to link the technical training facilities with the US Agency for International Development (USAID) because the "new regional emphasis" made it possible to pay for East African integration with US dollars.[26] The EAF was also a stepping-stone toward an improved position in international economic relations. In the words of Odinga, "federation could accelerate the impetus for development" and simultaneously turn "East Africa into a force to be reckoned with."[27] In a speech at a conference of the United Nations Food and Agricultural Organization in Rome in 1964, Nyerere built on those ideas and launched the notion of a "New International Economic Order." Because this "World Economic Development Plan" was "not realistic," federation was a first step to attaining "modern prosperity" from "international trade," which operated "like a two-way suction pump; it sucks more from the developing countries into the developed countries than it puts into."[28] The East African Common Services Organisation, which had been founded in 1961, therefore stressed that any plans for an association with the European Economic Community required a solution so the common external tariff toward third countries could be maintained.[29]

By 1963 Nkrumah and Nyerere thus became locked in an ideological struggle over the meaning of unification. While Nyerere believed federation would help him engage the world on more equal terms, Nkrumah had always held on to federation as a tool to ward off the cultural and psychological intrusion that made development and emancipation impossible. In a letter to Nyerere, Nkrumah wrote that there was still confusion in Europe because the continent had failed to unite politically. Sound economic integration needed a "stable political direction, force and purpose." The existing divisions were easy to transcend, because they were the result of linguistic differences and thus artificial: "We can even make love without the help of any language!" he quipped. The dependence on former colonizers was psychological and could not be resolved by economic cooperation alone.[30] The "demand" for "new factories to produce the essentials of twentieth century life: clothes, shoes, refrigerators, bicycles, automobiles," could only be successful with "a continental plan" and could never be solely "technical." The accountancy details were less important than the "acceptance of continental planning in principle."[31] For Nkrumah, Nyerere's EAF was soulless and therefore doomed to failure.

For Nyerere, Nkrumah's talk of an "African Personality" and "immunization" sounded old-fashioned, painfully out of touch in a world where international influence came to those who could offer a guaranteed, "scientific" route to modern material progress, a route that was increasingly becoming regional in its expression. In *Africa Must Unite*, Nkrumah therefore even tried to put Nyerere's pragmatism on its head by arguing that "the necessary capital" could "only be accumulated by the employment of our resources on a continental extension."[32] Continental unification would be the only way to "carry out the full economic reconstruction essential" for the "fulfilment of the hopes and aspirations of the African revolution."[33]

Disputes about the modernizing potential of a United Africa and an East African Federation caught the Northern imagination and amplified the scholarship of economists who sought to understand the critical role of regions in the development process. LBJ had come to power at a moment when Walt Rostow's modernization theory had begun to show signs of rust and the inefficiency of large-scale modernization programs was beginning to raise questions in the United States and the USSR, while the failure to maintain influence via technical assistance programs prompted old empires to rethink their approach.[34] François Perroux's regional development theory highlighted the importance of "growth poles," and Myrdal's "cumulative causation" claimed underdeveloped regions benefited from growth in developed regions through "spread" effects. Myrdal's ideas, in particular, had a big impact, since he located the cause of underdevelopment in structural inequality and believed underdeveloped countries had a lot to gain by building regional units.[35] In this flurry of theoretical revisionism, Nyerere's bold new development model, *Ujamaa*, emerged as a shining alternative, jump-starting a period of "Tanzaphilia."[36]

Rostow instantly recognized the appeal of ideas such as the EAF and sought to control these new Third World regional units, which he understood to be another expression of psychological distress brought about by technical change. Many of the "post-war troubles," he believed, "centered around men who were radical, ambitious revolutionaries, who carried maps in their heads of how they would like the world to look." Sukarno's map indicated what "the proper expanded racial boundaries of Indonesia should be"; Mao Zedong "distributed hundreds of millions of maps" with a boundary that "laps well over into Russian territory"; Fidel Castro had "a map-like vision of the Andes as a great guerrilla base"; and Nkrumah, on his map, became "the Emperor Jones of Black Africa."[37] LBJ, in particular, believed "the world was not ready for a global solution" to the perceived crisis of decolonization and instead fostered regionalism to redirect the assertive nationalist discourse of Nkrumah and others inward, while NSC staff member Edward Hamilton sought a reorientation from "flamboyance" to "harshly practical problems."[38] In the early 1950s, US modernization theorists considered regions to be remnants of preindustrial societies, fated to be eclipsed by the inexorable march toward the homogeneous nation-state. By 1964, when African nationalists took the helm, the nation-state became a less appealing vehicle for progress, and regions returned as a means to harness the power of nationalism and address nationalism's negative effects.[39]

For the US empire of liberty, regional integration became a means to sustain the nation-state while providing a check on the aggressive or unwelcome tendencies of anticolonial nationalists. For Rostow, regions helped minimize the frustration in the Global South, because the total amount of aid could be increased through cooperation. In his memoir, Johnson wrote that the "answer" to managing a world made up of many different nation-states was "somewhere between a world community and a system based on narrow nationalism."[40] After LBJ became president in November 1963, Rostow wanted to utilize the United States' "limited margin of influence on the course of history" to help create a friendly "multipolar world." The bipolar standoff and decolonization, Rostow believed, had given small nations an artificially strong bargaining position, and the communications revolution, weapons of mass destruction, and modernization had made US power more diffuse.[41] "An alternative to isolationism" as well as "over-involvement" needed to be "built in one part of the world after another" so the United States could "take its fair share" and others could "take more responsibility."[42] Other members of the administration agreed. W. Averell Harriman claimed that the United States, because of its continental expansion, was uniquely able to understand the "deep desire for continental unity," while Secretary of State Dean Rusk, a committed internationalist himself, celebrated regionalism.[43]

After forcing Khrushchev to step down in October 1964, the politburo under Brezhnev's leadership also raised doubts about African nationalism, mainly because of financial constraints. Igor Kolosovskii, deputy head of the Department of African Countries at the Ministry of Foreign Affairs, complained about the stream of aid requests. In light of the failure to keep Guinea and the Congo within the Soviet sphere of influence, the economic aid policy became more selective and pragmatic. Nevertheless, Brezhnev did not completely reject Khrushchev's "non-capitalist" development path. As Alessandro Iandolo contends, IMEMO worked out policies of import substitution through industrialization that echoed dependency theory, according to which resources flow from an underdeveloped periphery to a core of wealthy states. Moreover, the Soviet Union was instrumental in the creation of the United Nations Conference on Trade and Development (UNCTAD), urged on by UNCTAD secretary-general and principal dependency theorist Raúl Prebisch, who was keen to include the Soviets. Khrushchev had already become more cautious in the provision of aid in light of the Congo fiasco. In line with other countries in the mid-1960s, he began to promote a policy that focused on international structural inequality.[44]

Doubts about the effectiveness of colonial modernization led the Commonwealth and the French *Coopération* to be rebranded as technocratic organizations, ideally suited to providing effective development aid. Historians describe the Commonwealth as a "loose voluntary association of states" and as a "disillusionment" in the 1960s, an "international organization" in the 1970s and 1980s, and an "intergovernmental organization" created to ease the loss of empire in the 1990s and 2000s.[45] In the late 1960s, the organization was refurbished as an enterprise that sought to provide education and economic aid on a regional scale. Already, in 1962, Andrew Cohen, UK representative to the UN Trustee Council, had asked Mboya to create a committee of East African advisers who could increase cooperation. "Much of the success of the Colombo Plan," he believed, had "been due to it having started as a Commonwealth co-operative effort."[46] By the mid-1960s, when the Commonwealth secretariat was created, the French began to doubt whether Michel Debré's contention—that French culture was uniquely suited to Africa's socioeconomic needs—still rang true. The close relationships Jacques Foccart had fostered with African leaders also enabled those leaders to complain about the slow pace of progress. David Dacko of the Central African Republic signaled that the French assistance was "poorly adapted to the nature of African countries and its inhabitants."[47] The transformation of the Union africaine et malgache (UAM) into the Union africaine et malgache de coopération économique (UAMCE), which focused solely on economic affairs, was meant to address those concerns. A successor organization, the Organisation commune africaine et malgache (OCAM), which comprised the original twelve UAM members and Togo, developed closer regional economic cooperation and even created an airline, Air Afrique. Nevertheless, African nationalists were not impressed by the regionalization of the French aid policy. Touré understood OCAM to be a French propaganda product, "pour la galerie."[48] Zambian diplomats believed that Senegal, Ivory Coast, and Upper Volta within the OCAM group were "not really independent" as their policies were "teleguided by France."[49] The Zambian High Commission in London claimed the military coup of 1965 by Christophe Soglo in Dahomey was a prime example of how loyalties toward the former colonizer bred instability.[50]

The different rationales behind regional integration, which created a divide between younger and older African leaders as well as bigger and smaller empires, played out in the run-up to the foundational meeting of the OAU in May 1963. At the preparatory conference, Ghanaian diplomats "forcibly" "explained" the "necessity of having one continental government." Kojo Botsio attempted to smuggle the logic of federation into the name of the future organization, pleading for the use of the term "union." However, it was Ethiopia's draft agenda that was accepted by a majority of the delegates, because it centered on the less ambitious "establishment of an organisation of African states" rather than "the creation of a Political Union of African States."[51] Nevertheless, the OAU became an arena of South-South diplomacy where all aspects of liberationist politics were discussed: modernization efforts, public diplomacy, and armed conflict. Even though the institution's effectiveness has been questioned, the prevalence of authoritarianism criticized, and the dream of unity was delayed, ultimately—like the UN—the OAU institutionalized a set of postcolonial international norms. The liberationist notion that the world was structured along colonial and neocolonial lines and the idea that international history was warped by the injustice of slavery and colonialism were cemented in an international organization. Secretary-General Diallo Telli therefore felt that the OAU's "symbolic importance" had to be exploited, and information officers struggled against neocolonialism. In 1965, Abdennour Abrous replaced the prolific Hailu Wolde Giorghis as an information officer.[52]

Once the OAU was established, different actors tried to incorporate the organization into their own vision of postcolonial order. Radical African states tried to keep the organization clear of neocolonial influence. H. E. D Busumtwi-Sam of the Ghana High Commission in Kenya accused the OCAM of wanting to "break the OAU."[53] Touré, in contrast, believed the tumultuous OAU meeting in Cairo in 1964 proved that the African public debate was dynamic and could unfold without outside interference. Belgian and Portuguese officials were relieved to find out intra-African divisions limited the OAU's effectiveness and diminished the United Arab Republic's influence.[54] Only LBJ believed the OAU offered a solution to the problems created by nationalism. In a speech on the OAU's birthday in 1966, LBJ committed the United States to building "regional organizations of developing continents" and linked the OAU with US values by declaring that the OAU charter protected the "inalienable right of all people to control their destiny" with "freedom, equality, justice and dignity" as "essential objectives."[55] Violent conflict could be prevented by ensuring "the accidents of national boundaries" did not necessarily "lead to hostility and conflict or serve as impossible obstacles to progress." More important, through the OAU's "multilateral effort," the unproductive energies of anticolonialism could be redirected toward the "wise" task of development. The OAU would be relied on to manage the three international trends that made US power more diffuse: the OAU could "strengthen the regional economic activities," "increase the number of trained Africans," and "develop effective communications systems."[56] This attempt to create what Bill Moyers called a "Johnson Doctrine" for Africa focused on regionalism and was rooted in views on anticolonial nationalism that had already emerged during the Kennedy administration.[57]

For the State Department, the Simba Rebellion brought into focus that the OAU was "more important in our world relations." On 5 August 1964, Congo-Léopoldville's third-largest city, Stanleyville, fell to the Simbas, a Lumumbist anti-Western rebel group whose political arm was led by Gaston Soumialot and Christophe Gbenye, who considered Moïse Tshombe's return to Congolese politics as prime minister in July to be illegitimate. Tshombe recruited South African and Rhodesian mercenaries to squash the rebellion while the OAU was struggling to define a continental response because the rebels reportedly received support from other African countries. Congolese armed guards, suspicious of foreign interference, escorted UAR and Algerian diplomats and their families to the banks of the Congo River, where they forced them to cross over into Brazzaville.[58] The more radical African leaders in the OAU distrusted Tshombe, leading Michael Dei-Anang to openly support the anti-Tshombe faction.[59] On 11 August 1964, Paul-Henri Spaak and Harriman approached the French, Italian, British, German, Dutch, and Canadian ambassadors to try to come up with a military response, while also pressuring Tshombe into sending out requests for troops from other independent African countries. Through regional cooperation in Europe and Africa, Spaak wanted to get rid of the mercenaries and convince Tshombe to not attack Élisabethville. While secretly negotiating with Gbenye to get him to accept Tshombe's leadership, Spaak played on LBJ's fears of unhinged Africans.[60] He referred to the very man he was secretly talking to as "losing his head completely." Nevertheless, LBJ's advisers, such as Rostow, were irritated more by Europe's inefficient regional cooperation, which had forced LBJ's hand.[61] Harriman, incited by Mobutu Sese Seko, had "heard all over the Congo about massive French assistance." Yet, when Harriman inquired about this with the French ambassador, he "smiled but did not reply." In November 1964, Belgian colonel Frédéric Vandewalle launched operation Ommegang, an offensive against the Simbas, which resulted in Operation Red Dragon, in which Belgian paratroopers were parachuted into Stanleyville with US assistance to free white hostages.[62] Chaos continued, even leading Nkrumah to plead with Belgian prime minister Théo Lefèvre to "do everything" in his "power to make it possible for us in Africa to establish peace in the Congo."[63]

The State Department's Policy Planning Staff concluded that the "airdrop" had negatively affected the US image in the region because it exposed "our undisguised power and sent tremors through the unstable governments of East Africa"—governments that Rusk noted were "in a highly emotional state over imagined dangers from the Congo Air Force and advancing mercenary columns." This had led—in the US analysis—to a split between East African officials and radical Africans who supported the rebels together with the Communists. The State Department was willing to tolerate a "relatively high degree of instability in the Congo as long as" the country did not evolve into "a launching pad for major African intervention or the basis for large-scale Communist exploitation." In April 1965, US ambassadors in East and Central Africa recommended the creation of "Zones of Peace," a "regional 'defensive' strategy" that would promote "economic development" as "a means of releasing national energy" and make it possible for African leaders to establish their "liberationist credentials" without "militant confrontation." African as well as Communist firebrands had to be kept in check through regional cooperation, which limited African nationalists in their ability to play the Communist card.[64] When Tshombe slandered Mobutu as a recipient of Communist assistance and when Tshombe's envoys showed up in Washington, DC, to ask whether the United States could provide even more aid than Foccart was supposedly already giving him, the envoys were met with skepticism.[65]

Regionalizing Aid

The difficulties and financial burdens of large-scale material improvement rekindled debates over the effectiveness of economic aid and the appropriate societal and economic structures required to generate change. Prebisch's UNCTAD report, an analysis of the political economy of Third World development, set the agenda for an upcoming meeting focusing on trade preferences for developing countries. Nyerere, who sought to "anticipate" "market changes which are beyond our control," hailed and actively supported the conference, which opened on 23 March 1964, because of its focus on the preference system for development purposes, which guaranteed preferential treatment for imports from developing countries without an obligation to grant any preferences in return.[66] The adoption of the Cairo Declaration at the Conference on the Problems of Economic Development—held in Cairo in July 1962 and attended by developing countries—had put trade preferences on the agenda. UNCTAD affected thinking in the industrialized North and forced a change in the only remaining systems of regional trade preferences: the Commonwealth and the arrangements between France and its ex-colonies.[67] Nationalist leaders tried to attain the goals that the NIEO had set by creating new regional units and by working through existing regional structures.

Some in the Global North, such as Belgian minister of foreign trade and technical assistance Maurice Brasseur, explicitly used UNCTAD to increase their influence. The *Plan Brasseur* of November 1963 sought to temporarily allow underdeveloped countries to export goods at a lower import rate to increase their industrial output. Rather than a general agreement, Brasseur envisioned a differentiated approach on an item-by-item basis. Developing countries felt this plan would lead to a competition among themselves for the goodwill of industrialized countries and opposed it. Brasseur also clashed with Jef Van Bilsen, who wanted to support UN aid efforts because a small country would be unable to bear the burden of industrialization on its own. The Organisation for Economic Cooperation and Development's plans to create a Development Center where international aid and expertise could be pooled had inspired him to prioritize cooperation. Simmering tensions within the Belgian foreign affairs ministry over the internationalization of aid burst into the open. Despite agreeing with Brasseur on the need for industrialization, Van Bilsen did not want to mix development aid with trade, due to the outlandish influence of corporations in the Belgian colonial enterprise, while Brasseur was more concerned with hard economic interests.[68] The relationship between Brasseur and Van Bilsen was complicated further by the difficult relations between Belgium and the government of Cyrille Adoula after the latter accepted the federal constitution that the U Thant Plan—a plan named after Hammarskjöld's successor—had outlined in 1962. In its wake, Foreign Minister Spaak asked his chief of staff, Robert Rothschild, to set up a new assistance system on the highest level of government, the Office de l'Assistance Technique et de Reconstruction Administrative, which had to get rid of Tshombe's "conseillers prives belges," experts such as René Clemens who were operating in a private capacity.[69] During friendship treaty negotiations in Brussels on 2 August 1963, tensions ran high. André Dequae suddenly left without shaking any hands just as Adoula had agreed to postpone his departure, forcing Spaak to personally intervene. Rather than simply engage in a turf war, Van Bilsen and Brasseur debated globally shared questions about the role of international cooperation in development aid.[70] The federal solution also offered the Portuguese, whom LBJ found "bungling" and "incompetent," a way to retool their empire. The very idea of a white federation with southern Africa kept the Portuguese empire afloat in the face of the colonial wars in Angola and Mozambique, because it provided implicit support from Rhodesia and South Africa.[71]

For French and UK officials, regionalism provided a means to deal with the financial burdens of modernization, but also a guise for the neocolonial features of their Africa diplomacy, which African public diplomacy had highlighted. In France, Jean-Marcel Jeanneney, who led a commission tasked with devising the

Coopération doctrine, was keen to set up a structure that could reject claims of exploitation. Therefore, the commission argued that France ought to give preference to investments that take place in a regional framework" to address the power imbalance that existed between Africa and France.[72] To enjoy the benefits of aid—considered to be so great that it was recommended to even include countries outside of the "Franc zone"—the degree of "integration of the economies" had to be "appropriate" and therefore regional rather than continental.[73] This led de Gaulle to declare to Murumbi that he supported "the move for unity within the African States."[74] Nonetheless, in Nkrumah's reading, the report "aimed to foster economic dependence, even while granting political independence."[75] In 1964, the British cooperative approach was elevated to official policy when Andrew Cohen became the permanent secretary of the Minister of Overseas Development.[76] African Commonwealth members, however, did not buy into the cooperation story and demanded that the BBC instead of the Foreign Office provide the "training of staff for overseas broadcasting organisations."[77] Nkrumah wanted to become a Commonwealth member not because he believed cooperation was possible, but rather because membership gave Ghana an outsize amount of influence, as the "first truly African nation to join."[78]

In the US, LBJ continued JFK's strategy of "frustration management." Already, as a senator, Johnson had wanted to safeguard the "Fifth Freedom, the freedom to learn," by sponsoring a bill that made the use of surplus foreign currencies for university education abroad possible. Education was an indispensable component of a liberal international system with "modern [self-governing] societies," and LBJ therefore supported the creation of educational television for "Less-Developed Countries" in 1965.[79] In a speech to Congress, he echoed Kennedy's rationale when explaining his focus on education: "A high school diploma should not be a ticket to frustration."[80] At the same time, LBJ felt the trend to multipolarity had to be managed by grouping African countries into a joint institutional aid arrangement. He therefore asked the US ambassador to Ethiopia, Ed Korry, to reshape the African USAID programs around regionalism in 1966. The Korry Report's forty-two recommendations were implemented by Assistant Secretary Joseph Palmer, who sought to strengthen "multilateral donor coordination mechanisms." Under Secretary of the Treasury Joe Barr was in favor of US participation in an African Bank fund, which was to strengthen the African Development Bank, created in 1963. The US Information Agency was employed to sell the regionalization of aid, since African countries feared receiving less assistance.[81]

In contrast to the cases of the British and French empires, for the Americans regionalization was not driven by political and financial calculation but by a reevaluation of the effectiveness of economic development in the postcolonial world. Rostow considered regionalization to be an important tool for amassing a sufficient amount of investments suited to the absorptive capacity of developing nations, arguing that all countries were able to contribute to the "resource diet on which new nations develop." Like "vitamins in human diets, the American ingredient may be relatively small in some cases, but it is qualitatively vital."[82] As long as the development diplomat provided clarification, the source of aid was less important. The National Academy of Sciences, for instance, utilized USAID funding for a conference on agricultural research in Congo that brought African, European, and US experts together.[83] Harriman agreed that "full industrialization" could only "be achieved on the basis of African unity."[84] When Tanganyika and Zanzibar formed a union in April 1964, LBJ was pleased, not because it would help stem the spread of Communism but because of the economy of scale that had been created.[85] Nevertheless, USAID officials and Mennen Williams held on to a classical interpretation of aid and resisted regionalization because it entailed giving up US leverage over African regimes and denied Williams the opportunity to make a big symbolic gesture.[86]

Nowhere was the US commitment to aid regionalization clearer than in the Food for Peace program, established under Eisenhower in 1954. In December 1963, Ralph Dungan, White House special assistant to the president in the Kennedy administration and a member of the task force on foreign aid, urged Assistant Secretary for Economic Affairs George Ball to talk about "this AID thing because the President," Dungan believed, had indicated "he would like to see something more drastic done."[87] Out of these discussions a multilateral approach to the "world food problem" emerged, since "the deficit would be of such a magnitude as to be beyond the capacity of the food exporting countries." The US wanted to help the World Food Program of the Food and Agriculture Organization of the United Nations with the identification of appropriate World Bank financing and the creation of a capital assistance operation.[88] On 12 November 1966, LBJ signed into law a revamped Food for Freedom Bill, which provided "freedom grants" on a "multilateral basis" to solve the "food-producing capability of US farmers," which would be unable to "suffice indefinitely in a world that must feed a million new human beings each week."[89]

In the USSR, Leonid Brezhnev and Prime Minister Aleksei Kosygin also questioned the effectiveness of Soviet aid to the Global South. They wanted to limit the financial damage of Khrushchev's "adventurism" in the Global South and wanted to ensure Moscow would not get into regional conflicts. In 1966 Kosygin denied aid requests from Uganda, Guinea, and Algeria and argued trade ties had to be mutually beneficent, something Khrushchev—who believed in the power of noncapitalist industrialization—had been less interested in.[90]

The growing realization that effective aid required cooperative regional structures shaped the way Zhou Enlai's visit to Accra in January 1964 was assessed. At the airport, he was greeted by Kofi Baako and Botsio under the watchful eye of a soldier on top of a Radio Ghana van with a Bren Gun mounted on top of it. As he drove off the tarmac for his sightseeing trip, Zhou Enlai saw only a few scattered crowds as he peered out of the window. His trip, which had to raise enthusiasm for the second Asian-African Conference in Algiers in 1965 and strengthen the PRC's Third World credentials in the aftermath of the Sino-Indian War of 1962, received a mixed response.[91] The British believed "the Chinese bored the Ghanaians" because they were "backward" and had "no aid to offer."[92] The French ambassador to Hong Kong agreed with his predecessor that antiwhite sentiments were the only "cement" of the Sino-African coalition.[93] Smaller imperial powers doubted whether the PRC would be able to parlay the PR goodwill generated by this visit. In the Congo, rebels might by inspired by Mao's *On Guerilla Warfare*, but the Belgians did not believe these tools would actually be used. Lisbon read the Sino-Tanzanian Joint communiqué through the lens of Lusotropicalism and happily noted that the document condemned racism but did not refer to Portugal.[94] The State Department believed "the involvement of Communist China in aid and trade programs in Africa" had "positive aspects," since the PRC would have to struggle with the "realistic pressures of day-to-day world politics" and the continued strain on the economy.[95]

Rather than springing into a Cold War reflex, leaders in the Global North understood that effective economic aid was difficult and necessarily had to be regional, an approach the PRC had not adopted.

The Turn to Cold War Ideologies

Besides regionalism, the collapse of anticolonial modernity also instigated a turn to Cold War development models, a transformation that fundamentally shaped the 1970s and 1980s. The conclusion that structural economic dependence, not neocolonial intrusion of the cultural kind, had caused underdevelopment lessened the ideological threat of the Cold War ideologies. Younger African leaders began to look toward the Cold War superpowers because they were the only actors capable of carrying out the Herculean task of modernization. They had deep pockets and could boast impressive examples of rapid industrialization. Cabral—Nkrumah's junior by fifteen years—had been drawn to Pan-Africanism, had received five thousand Ghana pounds in 1962, and even visited Nkrumah in his place of exile in Conakry, but Cabral believed "the people" were "not fighting for ideas, nor for what is in one man's mind"; rather, they "accept the sacrifices demanded by the struggle in order to gain material advantages."[96] Resistance against Lusotropicalism was important, but the *assimilado* could overcome cultural alienation only through armed struggle and the identification with the *indigna*, the African masses.[97]

Conversely, Nkrumah had been eager for Cabral to comment on a draft of Nkrumah's *Handbook of Revolutionary Warfare* but could never let go of the psychological and cultural dimension of his worldview. He still talked about "Imperialism" having done its "utmost to brainwash Africans into thinking that they need strait-jackets of colonialism."[98] For Cabral, the use of an "upsurge of cultural activity" as a "weapon in the struggle for independence" was a "mistaken idea." The "liberation struggle" was "in its essence" political. There was no need for a "cultural renaissance," as Nkrumah and Senghor, had claimed since only the bourgeoisie had embraced colonial culture. The masses were the real "source of culture," untouched by colonization.[99] To only solution was a "People's War," built on Marxist principles, an acknowledgment of the crucial role of the rural masses in a successful guerrilla campaign, and the elimination of class distinctions.[100] As Patrick Chabal concluded: Cabral "came to view Marxism as a methodology rather than an ideology."[101]

The Portuguese, in their response, increasingly moved toward public diplomacy. In September 1964, the Portuguese Foreign Ministry realized it had to develop a more robust response to the significant public diplomacy threat of the Partido Africano da Independência de Guiné e Cabo Verde (PAIGC), which was eroding Lusotropicalism as the army and white settlers became demoralized. Lisbon's propaganda therefore cast Cabral as a Communist: "Cabral é um comunista puro."[102] Pan-African symbols that were pinned on PAIGC uniforms were deemed to be radical; the PAIGC flag, which contained red, was discredited on the grounds of it being a Communist color; and journalists also had to be shown around, because Cabral kept inviting them.[103] Nevertheless, when military officer António de Spínola arrived in Portuguese Guinea in 1968, he concluded that "nothing had been done to encourage "real socio-economic development" while demanding more political solutions to solve the "Guinea problem."[104] Moreover, the Portuguese had a hard time convincing their allies. In December 1962, the French consul in Bissau wrote that he did not believe the Portugese secret services when they informed him Soviet planes were stationed in Dakar to transport light arms for Cabral. Instead, the consul was impressed by Cabral's command of the French language, which led him to convince Senghor of Cabral's good intensions. The French ambassador in Conakry also believed Cabral to be "distinguished and elegant," particularly since "he speaks our language very well." The French ambassador to

Sofia wrote that the Communist Party in Sofia was actually getting tired of "libérateurs noirs" such as Cabral because they were less committed to the struggle and more at ease at receptions.[105] Even Senghor worried more about rebel movements across his border than Cabral's leftist tendencies. He employed his *méthode sénégalaise* and urged the PAIGC's rival, the Frente de Luta pela Independência Nacional da Guiné (FLING), to negotiate a peaceful settlement. Inspired by the French Community, he proposed a Luso-African Commonwealth, a new regional entity. The Belgians responded to the increasingly violent nature of African politics in a similar fashion and invested more time and effort into public relations. In cooperation with the Adoula government, the Institut belge d'information et de documentation (Inbel), created in 1961 to replace InforCongo, distributed information while the Rwandan government received support from Brussels to attract more tourists, expand external information services, and attract journalists.[106]

Strikingly, the turn to Cold War ideologies did not immediately intensify the violent conflict, as global Cold War historians contend. The superpowers in the 1960s were actually reluctant to escalate warfare on the continent and worried about indiscriminately pouring weapons into newly independent countries during the early stages of fighting because it complicated the management of modernization, an already fraught process tied up with discussions about frustrations and effectiveness.[107] On 25 March 1960, Deputy Director Leonard James Saccio of the International Cooperation Administration fretted over the request he was going to get to support African armed forces, particularly since a "military establishment" would only function as a "symbol of newly won sovereignty." To "keep down the general armament level" and "keep Africa out of the East-West arms race," he wanted to provide "arms for the limited purpose of internal-security" through the UN.[108] In his speech in front of the fifteenth General Assembly in September 1960, Eisenhower had already expressed the hope that "the African states" would "establish a new regional machinery in order to avert an arms race in this area."[109] In 1966, that goal acquired new importance, but the rationale transformed with NSC member Edward Hamilton arguing that it was problematic to "waste scarce resources on arms" because it hindered the modernization process.[110] In September 1966, he therefore proposed a program, "Safe Conduct for Development in Africa," which would not only quietly explore whether the Soviets could be brought on board but also would deny economic aid to those "who refuse to join and continue to waste scarce resources on arms."[111] During a coincidental conversation on the beach, the Soviet ambassador in Somalia downplayed the threat that emanated from the USSR's arm sales to the Somalians, arguing that because of the "backwardness of people," these were being used only during "parades." US Ambassador Thurston Raymond LeRoy, however, felt the "resources" spent on these arms purchases were wasted because they were needed for social and economic development.[112] The downplaying of the Soviet arm shipments to Somalia was part of a broader strategy. In a letter to Haile Selassie, the Soviets tried to calm the emperor, stating the delivery had consisted of "quite modest and moderate supplies" to a "young independent state which practically has no regular army" and was "no menace whatsoever."[113] Moreover, the Soviets relied on Nkrumah to distribute those weapons below the radar. On 14 September 1964, in a conversation with Georgii Rodionov, Soviet ambassador to Ghana, Nkrumah confirmed that he had agreed to channel Soviet arms to Agostinho Neto's MPLA. Afraid Nasser would use Somalia as a springboard to increase his influence, Nkrumah meddled.[114]

Besides the superpowers, Nyerere also gave a speech in Mogadishu in which he called on African leaders to stop the influx of weapons because it was fueling an arms race.[115] East Africa was in the grip of the Shifta War between 1963 and 1967. The ambition of some in the Northern Frontier District of Kenya to join Somalia led to border conflicts. On 10 March 1966, a Jeep was stopped at a police post in Garissa, where the passengers declared they were fleeing the persecution they faced as non-Somali citizens.[116] Acknowledging there was "no purely military solution to this problem," the Kenyan Ministry of Defence in January 1966 wanted to invest in "straight propaganda" as well as "psychological warfare" aimed at demoralizing the opposition.[117] The Voice of Kenya opened a service in the North Eastern Province and was tasked with countering the propaganda of Radio Mogadishu."[118] Particularly innovative was the regional cooperation with Ethiopia in the development of a three-pronged strategy. There was a so-called factual approach, which forged a failed state narrative about Somalia. Propaganda broadcasts "regularly" emphasized the dangers of "outside forces" being drawn into the conflict, while a narrative of good "neighborly" relations was projected.[119] By 1966, even violent conflict was addressed on a regional basis.

By 1966, the year of the anti-Nkrumah coup in Ghana, liberationism had effectively altered the globe, an evolution that most strikingly had taken place in the minds of policymakers. The world faced a struggle between East and West but was being steered from different centers in the South that fought against domination from the North. "Africans" regarded "Cold War issues as problems" from which they remained "aloof and unaffected," a US study of African attitudes in 1965 revealed. "Even when the Cold War appears in their midst, they are reluctant to identify it as such."[120] Instead, newly independent countries focused on the material promises of modernization, which proved to be difficult to fulfill alone, leading to the formation of groups of countries, such as the NIEO and the EAF, that could provide shelter from shrill foreign economic winds. Paradoxically, the dependency narrative, which encouraged the grouping of countries, also became hijacked by the Global North. LBJ's "regionalism" had to persuade Africans of the need for regional integration and deal with the supposedly "frustrating" effects of nationalism and modernization.[121] In Europe, the creation of postnational structures together with the former colonies not only provided a means for continued influence but also had to continue the optimistic modernization project, which had now become too challenging for any one nation to tackle on its own.

With so much doubt, a new generation of African leaders also began to look for new solutions to the development problem, preferring Communist or capitalist modernization programs over the liberationist path to modernity. The resources the superpowers could marshal made them more appealing options in the ideological scramble for Africa. In the 1970s, federations of liberation were swallowed whole by the unbridled need for material development and no longer represented an alternative international order.

Conclusion
How Decolonization Made Our Times

"The air over Africa is full of angry voices," a group of British visitors concluded in November 1960. "Cairo's Voice of the Arabs," Moscow, China, Washington, the French, and a "host of radio stations that are springing up in the new African countries" were all offering their listeners alternative visions of modernity.[1] In spite of this scramble for African hearts and minds in the 1950s and 1960s, decolonization is still assumed to have taken place within the bounds of a Cold War international system, with limited options for development. However, this book argues that the Cold War international system was not exported from Europe to the Global South and that nationalist leaders were not forced to make a choice between capitalism and Communism. Rather, liberationists sought to correct European modernity, which included the US and Soviet versions, by eliminating racism and disdain for precolonial culture while promoting their own anticolonial modernization project that saw precolonial ideas not as an obstacle but as a precondition for effective development.

After 1945, liberationists, imperialists, Communists, and capitalists became locked in an ideological struggle over the meaning of European modernity and the Enlightenment values that had justified it: reason, science, progress, development, and civilization.[2] Liberationists—Kwame Nkrumah principally among them—wanted to jump-start modernization by accepting economic aid to boost industrialization or agricultural production while rejecting outside ideologies, which had been conceived of as a package deal by Communists, capitalists, and imperialists.[3] Liberationists wanted to rid the world of a type of modernity that had been reserved for nonwhites and change the international system through the creation of federations to guard against empires of exploitation, liberty, and equality. This liberationist conception of international politics, born out of the legacy of Toussaint Louverture's revolt against French rule, was shared among postcolonial leaders in the 1950s and 1960s.

The fruits of modernity had been bruised from the inception. While Enlightenment philosophers did write about liberty and equality, thinkers such as Immanuel Kant also created a racial taxonomy that claimed "humanity" existed "in its greatest perfection in the white race."[4] Consequently, the liberationist critique of modernity became an unavoidable feature of an international system obsessed with progress. Liberationist arguments gained traction after World War II, as newly independent states such as Ghana intensified their ideological campaign. Unlike Communists and capitalists, anticolonial activists who critiqued European modernity had to make the more fundamental case that they also possessed the human capacity for "reason" and consequently had the ability to craft an alternative and better road map for human improvement and societal advancement. Nonwhites were also capable of harvesting the fruits of reason and building modernity, a task Bandung Conference delegates took on for the first time in 1955 as they tried to succeed where empires had failed and deliver on the promise of development.

From the vantage point of the Global South, it becomes clear the Cold War was only one of two international ideological struggles. The Soviets and the Americans were not the only ones with "higher motives for their expansion." They were not alone in their desire to "spread ideas of enterprise and social organization" in order "to save souls," while the British and French were not just "searching for resources and commercial advantage."[5] The clash between the Soviet gospel of equality and the US message of liberty was a battle for hearts and minds that unfolded alongside another struggle with nineteenth-century roots: the fight between imperial modernity, characterized by racial difference and technocracy, and anticolonial modernity, which embraced culture and history and rejected the psychological intrusion of the colonial project.

The International System Anticolonial Modernity Made

The battle between imperialism and anticolonialism shaped international relations, in the sense that in the 1950s and 1960s, all powers had to take a stance regarding liberation. Principally, people and leaders in the Global South were not forced to "take what was available"—Communism or capitalism—but had a much wider range of ideological options to reach the highly coveted horizon of modernity. Besides development models in the North, anticolonial road maps with varying degrees of state involvement and different relationships to the former colonizer were also on offer in the Global South, as exemplified by the disagreements between Léopold Senghor, Nkrumah, and Julius Nyerere over African Socialism.[6] The common denominator of these anticolonial schemes for progress was their emphasis on a reinvigorated relationship with the precolonial past and its culture. The attempts by different African nationalists to influence liberation fighters elsewhere on the continent also led to a deepening of political and ethnical conflicts. In South Africa, for instance, the African National Congress and the Pan Africanist Congress fought over the role race had to play in their fight against Apartheid, in light of different interpretations of Pan-Africanism. In Sudan, Ibrahim Abboud played Gamal Abdel Nasser and Nkrumah against each other. It was not only superpower intervention that helped put countries in the Global South in "a state of semipermanent civil war"; interventionist African leaders also had their part.[7]

The drive to project anticolonial modernity reconfigured the international system into a patchwork of federative and regional units, which slowed down the creation of a bipolar world. Instead of a superpower competition for the allegiance of newly independent nation states, international relations constituted a situation in which old and new empires were competing with many different federations of liberation. Decolonization was not "the collapse of colonial empires and the creation of new nation-states."[8] Rather, the post-1945 wave of independence created a world of federations that jockeyed for the loyalty of other countries, an international system that even staunch cold warrior Walt Rostow acknowledged existed at the end of the 1960s.[9] What has been coined the "federal moment" was not a fleeting feature of decolonization or a failed utopian project but a consecutive element of the postwar international order that cut across North-South and East-West lines, with mapmakers, politicians, and journalists trying to figure out what the zones of influence of liberationist ideologies were.[10] The existence of an attractive anticolonial alternative to Soviet and US modernity helps explain why many of the "public diplomacy" efforts of both superpowers failed in the Global South. The Cold War became "more ideological" and "more multipolar" in the Global South because of a surge of anticolonial ideologies.[11]

Pan-Africanism was only one of many "pan"-isms that sought the modernization of member states; these emerged in the nineteenth century, acquired political meaning after World War I, and were revived in some way after World

War II. Besides smaller federations, such as the United Arab Republic, the Ghana-Guinea Union, the Fédération du Mali, the Zanzibar-Tanganyika Union, and the Arab-Maghreb Union, larger visions had a global impact. Pan-Arabists wanted unification to reclaim the grandeur lost during Ottoman and Western occupation.[12] Pan-Asian enthusiasts sought to build a federation of liberation to guard against Chinese or Japanese aggression. Pan-Americanism led to the Pan-American Union in 1890, which aspired to increase cooperation between the United States and Latin America, but was adopted by *el libertador* Simón Bolívar, who conceived of it as an anti-US line of defense.[13] Even Pan-Europeanism drew strength from a fight against US domination and evolved in the course of the 1970s as Portugal, Spain, Ireland, and Eastern Europe all came to see the European Economic Community as a federation of democracy they wanted to join.[14]

In the 1960s, federations lost their liberationist appeal and became modernization tools. Within this international system, the end of the Third World project was not primarily the outcome of Cold War pressures but the result of a contradiction within liberationist ideologies: nationalists sought to remake other societies and thus violated their own basic principle of ideological noninterference, which harmed Afro-Asian and inter-African solidarity as well as Africa's relationship with Latin America.[15]

A Liberationist Retelling of Post-1945 International History

Through a liberationist lens, it is clear that policymakers in North and South crafted their foreign policies in the 1950s and 1960s with an eye on the anticolonial challenge. Colonial imaginings that had cast nonwhites as inferior became unnerving as the Pan-African critique on the hypocrisy of the civilizing mission was strengthened in the echo chamber of World War II. As a result, officials in the Global North in the late 1940s came to reject imperialism not on grounds of principle but on the basis that imperialism was ineffective in developmental terms. The colonial obsession with order was repackaged in technocratic terms in the 1950s and transformed into a concern over the supposed psychological instability of African subjects. This new psychological justification of control was confirmed by the outcome of the Bandung Conference, which diplomats in the Global North understood as a call for better development aid. While Bandung's participants had tried to agree on a joint strategy to sustain liberation through economic and cultural assistance, a clear-cut anticolonial modernization program did not come about. Ghanaian independence in March 1957 was a turning point because its leaders established a Pan-African anticolonial modernization project that accepted technocratic aid but resisted the import of ideas. Moreover, Accra's plea for African unity irreversibly placed a federation of liberation in the realm of international politics, realizing Louverture's call to resist those who "provoke" "disunity."[16] In 1959, the increased impact of anticolonial activism crystallized in the course of the Ghanaian and Nigerian battle against the French atomic bomb tests in the Sahara and forced the British and Belgian authorities to come to the table to negotiate a settlement with anticolonial activists in the Belgian Congo and the Central African Federation.

Routes to futures built on total equality, individual liberty, colonial civilization, or nonracial liberation became more punctuated after the first phase of the Congo Crisis of 1960–61. The descent into chaos triggered fears about the consequences of an unstable postcolonial state in the North and raised the menacing specter of a divided Africa in the South. The crisis made diplomats frantically search for new ways to create a more favorable postcolonial order. When Patrice Lumumba gave his inflammatory indictment of Belgian colonialism on Independence Day, he unknowingly confirmed the Northern cliché of the African strong man, sealing his fate while strengthening liberationist hopes. His murder taught the diplomatic corps, from Flagstaff House to the White House, that their interpretation of Africa's position in the international system—in dire need of guidance—had been correct, but the road toward it had been misguided and required modification. The riots in Léopoldville and Katanga effectively ended an internationally shared discourse of psychological modernization.

African hearts and minds, assertive and uncontrollable after 1960, became a threat rather than an opportunity in Africa's modernization. In their search for solutions, officials in the Global North embraced researchers in anthropology and the social sciences who warned against the adverse psychological effects of programs of technical change. All the while, officials in the Global South worked to immunize their populations against the ideas that could potentially accompany the much-needed economic aid. On a continent that was preoccupied with cultural uniqueness, cultural centers became battlegrounds and cultural officers the bearers of dangerous ideas as vocal anticolonialism came to be seen as a psychological consequence of the modernization process. Similarly, in southern Africa, racism was considered by African nationalists and by observers in the Global North as a psychological defect. By the mid-1960s, liberationist anticolonial modernity delivered disappointing results, since the material self-interest of postcolonial citizens was not being met. Officials increasingly began to reject cultural methods and instead relied on regionalism to turbocharge their development effort. The Organisation of African

Unity was created, and older imperial structures such as the Commonwealth were retooled to take on the seemingly insurmountable task of building modern societies.

By the early 1970s, the stage had been set for an increased involvement of the Cold War superpowers. Disillusioned by liberationist ideologies, Global South elites embraced solutions that sought to tackle an unequal international order and turned to either the Soviet or the US form of high modernism, since these seemed to be the sole models capable of marshaling the resources to achieve the required leap to modernity. Changing views on the mechanisms behind modernization further accelerated the anticolonial turn to the Cold War superpowers. While leaders such as Senghor, Nkrumah, and Jomo Kenyatta had believed foreign aid could be accepted so long as ideological accompaniments were guarded against, a younger generation disappointed with the results of ideological immunization, consisting of Amílcar Cabral, Agostinho Neto, and Mengistu Haile Mariam in Ethiopia, came to view economic and cultural assistance as a package deal. Liberationists had believed modernization and industrialization were powerful tools that had simply been wielded by the wrong people. By the 1970s, politicians in the South understood that attaining a robust modernity had to entail the approval of a donor's principles.[17]

The story of the ideological scramble for Africa suggests that the chronology of twentieth-century international history, with its obsession over the fall of the Berlin Wall, should be rethought. In November 1989, international politics was not suddenly released from a bipolar straightjacket and hijacked by a "Rise of the Rest." Rather, one legacy of the Enlightenment, the battle between equality and freedom, came to an end while the critique of European modernity with roots in the Haitian Revolution, manifested in the debate over the role of race and federalism, only intensified as countries such as China and South Africa expanded their middle class and European societies saw more people from their old colonial possessions move into the former metropole. From the liberationist perspective, 1989 did not make much of a dent: one legacy was cut off, but the confrontation with liberation continued. As the memories of the Cold War fade, it becomes apparent that the liberation struggle of the 1970s and 1980 in Ethiopia, South Africa, Rhodesia, and Portuguese Africa, the time period on which most of our insights about the Global Cold War are based, was exceptional for its attention to the bipolar struggle. In the 1950s and 1960s, the superpower rivalry was minimal, while it was the cultural and psychological impact of colonization and decolonization that shaped international politics. African political claims were interpreted in the Global North as proof that Africa needed more development, while Northern diplomacy was understood to be a neocolonial product. Our own times—marked by disagreements about the equitable distribution of global wealth, the costs of climate change, refugees, and democracy—are informed by colonialism's wrongs, not the social and political upheavals of the 1970s and 1980s.

The "Rise of the Rest" thus has an identifiable history, which can be recovered by considering the legacy of the European Enlightenment project, warts and all.[18] An acknowledgment of that history also helps us better comprehend the enduring influence of the liberationist critique as expounded by countries that cry neocolonialism, such as China, the Democratic Republic of the Congo, and Brazil. We cannot begin to address global challenges such as climate change, pandemics, and immigration without having a better toolbox to analyze the vastly different views of the international system and the misunderstandings that mark diplomacy. How liberation shaped the North and how different iterations of liberation structured the South should therefore be at the heart of our study of international relations past and present.

Abbreviations

AA	Archives africaines
AAPC	All-African People's Conference
ABAKO	Alliance des Bakongos
ACA-UFS	Archives for Contemporary Affairs—University of the Free State
AEB	Archives de l'état en Belgique
AF	Alliance Française
AGRB	Archives générales du Royaume de Belgique
AHU	Arquivo Histórico Ultramarino
AMAE	Archives du ministère des affaires étrangères
Amcon	American consulate
Amembassy	American embassy
ANC	African National Congress
ANS	Archives nationales du Sénégal
AOF	Afrique occidentale française
ASPFAE	Archives de service public fédéral affaires
AUA	African Union Archives
AWF	Ann Whitman File
BAA	Bureau of African Affairs
BAHDMNE	Biblioteca e Arquivo Histórico Diplomático Ministério dos Negócios Estrangeiros
BBC	British Broadcasting Corporation
BBCWAC	British Broadcasting Corporation Written Archives Centre
BDEE	*British Documents on the End of Empire*
BHL	Bentley Historical Library
BIC	Belgian Information Centre
BL	British Library
BNA	British National Archives
CAOM	Centre des archives d'outre-mer
CCTA	Commission de coopération technique en Afrique au Sud du Sahara (Commission for Technical Cooperation in Africa South of the Sahara)

CD&W	Colonial Development and Welfare
CHAN	Centre historique des archives nationales
CIA	Central Intelligence Agency
CIAS	Conference of Independent African States
CID	Centre d'information et de documentation du Congo Belge et du Ruanda-Urundi
CIS	Center for International Studies at the Massachusetts Institute of Technology
CO	Colonial Office
COI	Central Office of Information
CPP	Convention People's Party
CPSU	Communist Party of the Soviet Union
CRO	Commonwealth Relations Office
CUOHRO	Columbia University Oral History Research Office
DA	Direction Amérique
DAL	Direction Afrique-Levant
DAM	Direction des affaires africaines et malgaches
DAO	Direction de l'Asie et de l'Océanie
DDEL	Dwight D. Eisenhower Library
DDF	Documents diplomatiques français
DGACT	Direction générale des affaires culturelles et techniques
DGRC	Direction générale des relations culturelles
EAF	East African Federation
EEC	European Economic Community
FIDES	Fonds d'investissements pour le développement économique et social
FLING	Frente de Luta pela Independência Nacional da Guiné
FLN	Front de libération national
FNSP	Fondation nationale des sciences politiques
FO	Foreign Office
FRUS	Foreign Relations of the United States
GATT	General Agreement on Tariffs and Trade
GDR	German Democratic Republic
GPL	George Padmore Library
GPRA	Gouvernement provisoire de la République algérienne
GULSC	Georgetown University Library Special Collections
HAEC	Historical Archives of the European Commission
HAEU	Historical Archives of the European Union
HML	Hemeroteca Municipal de Lisboa
ICA	International Cooperation Administration

IISH	International Institute of Social History
IMEMO	Institut Mirovoi Ekonomiki i Mezhdunarodnykh Otnoshenii
Inbel	Institut belge d'information et de documentation
IPD	Information Policy Department
IRD	Information Research Department
JFK	John Fitzgerald Kennedy
JFKL	John Fitzgerald Kennedy Library
KADOC	Katholiek archief- en documentatiecentrum
KANU	Kenya African National Union
KNADS	Kenya National Archives and Documentation Service
KNII	Kwame Nkrumah Ideological Institute
LAC	Library and Archives Canada
LBJ	Lyndon Baines Johnson
LBJL	Lyndon Baines Johnson Library
LOC	Library of Congress
LSE	London School of Economics
LSEASC	London School of Economics Library Archives and Special Collections
MAE	Ministère des affaires étrangères
Memcon	Memorandum of conversation
Memdis	Memorandum of discussion
MIT	Massachusetts Institute of Technology
MNC	Mouvement national congolais
MPLA	Movimento Popular de Libertação de Angola
MSRC	Moorland-Spingarn Research Center at Howard University
NA-A	Národní archiv
NAC	National African Congress
NAE	National Archives of Ethiopia
NAM	Non-Aligned Movement
NAN	National Archives of Nigeria
NANTH	National Archives of the Netherlands, The Hague
NARA	National Archives and Records Administration
NASA	National Archives of South Africa
NATO	North Atlantic Treaty Organization
NAZ	National Archives of Zambia
NIEO	New International Economic Order
NP	National Party
NSC	National Security Council
NSF	National Security Files
OAU	Organisation of African Unity

OCAM	Organisation commune africaine et malgache
OCB	Operations Coordinating Board
PAAA	Politisches Archiv des Auswärtigen Amts
PAC	Pan Africanist Congress
PAIGC	Partido Africano da Independência de Guiné e Cabo Verde
PR	Public relations
PRAAD	Public Records Archives and Administration Department, Accra, Ghana
PRC	People's Republic of China
PSB	Psychological Strategy Board
RDA	Rassemblement démocratique africain
S.d.	Sine dato / without date
SALT	Strategic Arms Limitation Talks
SDECE	Service de documentation extérieure et de contre-espionnage
StateDept	State Department
TASS	Telegrafnoe agentstvo Sovetskogo Soiuza
TL	Truman Library
UAM	Union africaine et malgache
UAMCE	Union africaine et malgache de coopération economique
UAR	United Arab Republic
UCL	Université catholique de Louvain
UDI	Unilateral Declaration of Independence
UKIO	United Kingdom Information Office
UN	United Nations
UNCTAD	United Nations Conference on Trade and Development
UNESCO	United Nations Educational, Scientific and Cultural Organization
UNIP	United National Independence Party
UNOC	United Nations Operation in the Congo
USAID	United States Agency for International Development
USIA	United States Information Agency
USIS	United States Information Service
USSR	Union of Soviet Socialist Republics
WH Office	White House Office
ZANU	Zimbabwe African National Union
ZAPU	Zimbabwe African People's Union
ZBC	Zambia Broadcasting Corporation

Notes

Introduction

1. Archives nationales du Sénégal, Dakar (hereafter ANS), FM024, f: Recherches de solutions au problème Congo, Hebodomadaire No. 91, lettre de Brazzaville, 14 March 1961.

2. Luc De Vos, Emmanuel Gerard, Philippe Raxhon, and Jules Gérard-Libois, *Lumumba: De Complotten? De Moord* (Leuven: Davidsfonds, 2004), 69–135; "MI6 'Arranged Cold War killing' of Congo Prime Minister," *Guardian*, 10 April 2013.

3. Memorandum of Discussion (hereafter memdis) at 452nd Meeting of the NSC, 21 July 1960, *Foreign Relations of the United States* [hereafter FRUS] *1958–1960*, vol. 14, *Africa*, 338–41; memdis at the 456th Meeting of the NSC, 18 August 1960, *FRUS 1958–1960*, vol. 14, *Africa*, 421–24.

4. Edward Crankshaw, "A Crowded Safari," *Observer*, 24 January 1960; "The Observer's Guide to the 'Isms' of Africa," *Observer*, 10 January 1960, 10.

5. G. R. Coulthard, "The French West Indian Background of 'Négritude,'" *Caribbean Quarterly* 7, no. 3 (1961): 128–36; Leslie James, *George Padmore and Decolonization from Below: Pan-Africanism, the Cold War, and the End of Empire* (London: Palgrave Macmillan, 2014); Robert L. Tignor, *W. Arthur Lewis and the Birth of Development Economics* (Princeton, NJ: Princeton University Press, 2006).

6. Lyndon Baines Johnson Library (hereafter LBJL), WH central file, confidential file, box 8 (1 of 2), f: Congo, Republic of (1964), R. W. Komer, memorandum for Bill Moyers, 18 December 1964.

7. Frederick Cooper, "Reconstructing Empire in British and French Africa," in *Post-War Reconstruction in Europe: International Perspectives, 1945–1949*, ed. Mark Mazower, Jessica Reinisch, and David Feldman (Oxford: Oxford University Press, 2011), 197; Jennifer E. Sessions, *By Sword and Plow: France and the Conquest of Algeria* (Ithaca, NY: Cornell University Press, 2014).

8. Odd Arne Westad, *The Cold War: A World History* (New York: Basic Books, 2017), 627.

9. Kevin C. Dunn and Pierre Englebert, *Inside African Politics* (Boulder, CO: Lynne Rienner Publishers, 2019), 351; Odd Arne Westad, *The Global Cold War: Third World Interventions and the Making of Our Times* (Cambridge: Cambridge University Press, 2005), 4.

10. John Patrick Walsh, *Free and French in the Caribbean: Toussaint Louverture, Aimé Césaire, and Narratives of Loyal Opposition* (Bloomington: Indiana University Press, 2013), 102.

11. C. L. R. James, *The Black Jacobins: Toussaint L'Ouverture and the San Domingo Revolution* (New York: Vintage, 1989), 397, 291, 402 (Kenyatta quote is on p. 397); Gary Wilder, *Freedom Time: Negritude, Decolonization, and the Future of the World* (Durham, NC: Duke

University Press Books, 2015), 106; Walsh, *Free and French in the Caribbean*, 106; Aimé Césaire, *Toussaint Louverture: La Révolution Française et Le Problème Colonial* (Paris: Présence Africaine, 1961), 309.

12. Wilder, *Freedom Time*, 37–38.

13. Bill Ashcroft, Gareth Griffiths, and Helen Tiffin, *Post-Colonial Studies: The Key Concepts* (London: Routledge, 2000), 79; Nils Gilman, *Mandarins of the Future: Modernization Theory in Cold War America* (Baltimore: Johns Hopkins University Press, 2004), 170, 73–97; John C. Carothers, *The African Mind in Health and Disease: A Study in Ethnopsychiatry* (Geneva: World Health Organization, 1955); Louis S. B. Leakey, *Defeating Mau Mau* (London: Methuen, 1954); Louis S. B. Leakey, *Mau Mau and the Kikuyu* (London: Methuen, 1952); David McClelland, *The Achievement Motive* (New York: Appleton Century Crofts, 1953), 110.

14. Tony Chafer and Emmanuel Godin, *The End of the French Exception?: Decline and Revival of the "French Model"* (London: Palgrave Macmillan, 2010), 14, 15; Frederick Cooper, *Colonialism in Question: Theory, Knowledge, History* (San Francisco: University of California Press, 2005), 9; Priyamvada Gopal, *Insurgent Empire: Anticolonial Resistance and British Dissent* (London: Verso Books, 2020), 331. Even in the 1990s, African historians such as Agyeman turned to the French policy of assimilation to explain the "preference for colonial servitude": see Opoku Agyeman, *Nkrumah's Ghana and East Africa: Pan-Africanism and African Interstate Relations* (Teaneck, NJ: Fairleigh Dickinson University Press, 1992), 51.

15. Frantz Fanon, *Black Skin, White Masks*, trans. Richard Philcox (New York: Grove Press, 1967), 73; Tony Chafer, *The End of Empire in French West Africa: France's Successful Decolonization?* (New York: Berg Publishers, 2002), 48–49; Matthew M. Heaton, *Black Skin, White Coats: Nigerian Psychiatrists, Decolonization, and the Globalization of Psychiatry* (Athens: Ohio University Press, 2013), 12.

16. Dwight D. Eisenhower Library, Abilene, Kansas (hereafter DDEL), OCB Central File, WH Office, NSC Staff Papers 1948–1961, box 86, f: OCB 092.3 (File #2) (2) [estimated date: April–November 1955] (hereafter April–November 1955), memorandum for the Operations Coordinating Board (hereafter OCB), "Bandung Conference of April, 1955," 12 May 1955, 3–4.

17. Gilman, *Mandarins*, 155–202; David Ekbladh, *The Great American Mission: Modernization and the Construction of an American World Order* (Princeton, NJ: Princeton University Press, 2009), 173; Walt W. Rostow, *Eisenhower, Kennedy, and Foreign Aid* (Austin: University of Texas Press, 1985), 43–44.

18. Adom Getachew, *Worldmaking after Empire: The Rise and Fall of Self-Determination* (Princeton, NJ: Princeton University Press, 2019), 145.

19. Christopher R. W. Dietrich, *Oil Revolution: Anticolonial Elites, Sovereign Rights, and the Economic Culture of Decolonization* (Cambridge: Cambridge University Press, 2017), 4; Christopher Dietrich, "Strategies of Decolonization: Economic Sovereignty and National Security in Libyan–US Relations, 1949–1971," *Journal of Global History*, 2021, https://doi.org/10.1017/S1740022821000140.

20. Nicholas J. Cull, *The Cold War and the United States Information Agency: American Propaganda and Public Diplomacy, 1945–1989* (Cambridge: Cambridge University Press, 2009), x, 8.

21. Su Lin Lewis and Carolien Stolte, "Other Bandungs: Afro-Asian Internationalisms in the Early Cold War," *Journal of World History* 30, no. 1 (2019): 18.

22. Charles Tilly and Gabriel Ardant, *The Formation of National States in Western Europe* (Princeton, NJ: Princeton University Press, 1975), i–xiv.

23. Dwight D. Eisenhower: "Address and Remarks at the Baylor University Commencement Ceremonies, Waco, Texas," 25 May 1956, *The American Presidency Project*, ed. Gerhard Peters and John T. Woolley, accessed 5 March 2019, http://www.presidency.ucsb.edu/ws/?pid=10499.

24. National Archives and Records Administration, College Park, Maryland (hereafter NARA), RG. 360, P249, box 1, f: English Teaching, report on Proceedings Sessions I and II, "Anglo-American Conference Ditchley Park: The Future of the English Language Abroad" [November 1965], 249.

25. British National Archives, Kew (hereafter BNA), BW1/329, "Report on Anglo-French Discussions on Education, Cultural and Information Questions concerning Africa Held in Paris," 8 January 1960.

26. The existence of cultural assistance also holds important implications for the easily deployed dichotomy between hard and soft power: Joseph S. Nye, "Soft Power," *Foreign Policy*, no. 80 (1990): 160.

27. James H. Meriwether, *Proudly We Can Be Africans: Black Americans and Africa, 1935–1961* (Chapel Hill: University of North Carolina Press, 2002), 67; Minkah Makalani, "An Incessant Struggle against White Supremacy: The International Congress against Imperialism and the International Circuits of Black Radicalism," in *Outside In: The Transnational Circuitry of US History*, ed. Andrew Preston and Doug Rossinow (Oxford: Oxford University Press, 2017), 182–203; Richard H. King, *Race, Culture, and the Intellectuals: 1940–1970* (Washington, DC: Woodrow Wilson Center Press, 2004), 245.

28. Brenda Gayle Plummer, *In Search of Power: African Americans in the Era of Decolonization, 1956–1974* (Cambridge: Cambridge University Press, 2012); Meriwether, *Proudly We Can Be Africans*; Jason Parker, "Cold War II: The Eisenhower Administration, the Bandung Conference, and the Reperiodization of the Postwar Era," *Diplomatic History* 30, no. 5 (2006): 867–92; Jason Parker, "Ideology, Race and Nonalignment in US Cold War Foreign Relations: Or, How the Cold War Racialized Neutralism without Neutralizing Race," in *Challenging US Foreign Policy: America and the World in the Long Twentieth Century*, ed. Bevan Sewell and Scott Lucas (London: Palgrave Macmillan, 2011), 75–98; Naaborko Sackeyfio-Lenoch, "Women's International Alliances in an Emergent Ghana," *Journal of West African History* 4, no. 1 (2018): 27–56.

29. Immanuel Wallerstein, *Africa, the Politics of Independence: An Interpretation of Modern African History* (New York: Random House, 1961), 119.

30. Homi K. Bhada, in a foreword to the 2004 edition of Frantz Fanon's *The Wretched of the Earth*, claims the "global aspirations of the Third World 'national' thinking belonged to the internationalist traditions of socialism, Marxism and humanism"; see Frantz Fanon, *The Wretched of the Earth*, trans. Constance Farrington (New York: Grove Press, 2004 [1963]), xi.

31. Claude Liauzu, *L'enjeu tiersmondiste débats et combats* (Paris: l'Harmattan, 1987); Immanuel Wallerstein, *The Politics of the World-Economy: The States, the Movements, and the Civilizations; Essays* (Cambridge: Cambridge University Press, 1984), 1–15; Robert J. McMahon, "Introduction," in *The Cold War in the Third World*, ed. Robert J. McMahon (Oxford: Oxford University Press, 2013), 3; H. E. Shridath, S. Ramphal, and Indira Gandhi, "Third World Lecture 1982: South-South Option," *Third World Quarterly* 4, no. 3 (1982): 434.

32. For the conception of the Third World as created by the Cold War: Amanda Kay McVety, *Enlightened Aid: U.S. Development as Foreign Policy in Ethiopia: U.S. Development as Foreign Policy in Ethiopia* (Oxford: Oxford University Press, 2012), 120–22.

33. Fanon, *The Wretched of the Earth*, 143, 314, 238. Vijay Prashad has used Fanon's definition in an uncritical way and describes the different anticolonial conferences as expressions of the Third World project; see Vijay Prashad, *The Poorer Nations: A Possible History of the Global South* (London: Verso, 2012), 1–13; Vijay Prashad, *The Darker Nations: A People's History of the Third World* (New York: New Press, 2007), xv–1.

34. Prashad has used Fanon's definition in an uncritical way and describes the different conferences that dealt with an anticolonial theme—for instance in Brussels in 1928, Bandung in 1955, and Belgrade in 1961—as expressions of the same Third World project; see Fanon, *The Wretched of the Earth*, 314; Prashad, *The Poorer Nations*, 1–13; Prashad, *The Darker Nations*, xv–1.

35. Global Cold War historians acknowledge the diverse origins of the Third World concept, but see its political importance only in relation to the Cold War; see Westad, *The Global Cold War*, 111; McMahon, "Introduction," 3; Jason Parker, *Hearts, Minds, Voices: US Cold War Public Diplomacy and the Formation of the Third World* (Oxford: Oxford University Press, 2016), 29. The often-cited definition of French demographer Alfred Sauvy, who in 1952 drew a parallel with the so-called "third estate" of the French revolution, however, already hints at the concept's project-like nature.

36. Gregg A. Brazinsky, *Winning the Third World: Sino-American Rivalry during the Cold War* (Chapel Hill: University of North Carolina Press, 2017), 325–26.

37. Prashad, *The Darker Nations: A People's History of the Third World*, xvii.

38. Some historians have argued there already is a grand narrative of the Global South but point only to episodic political clashes at Bandung or Belgrade; see Pamila Gupta, Christopher J. Lee, Marissa J. Moorman, and Sandhya Shukla, "Editors' Introduction," *Radical History Review* 2018, no. 131 (2018): 3–4.

39. Europe at the center of the Cold War: Federico Romero, *Storia della guerra fredda: L'ultimo conflitto per l'Europa* (Turin: Einaudi Storia, 2009); Federico Romero, "Cold War Historiography at the Crossroads," *Cold War History* 14, no. 4 (2014): 697. Cold War as a US project: Anders Stephanson, "Fourteen Notes on the Very Concept of the Cold War," *H-Diplo*, February 2007, http://www.h-net.org/~diplo/essays/PDF/stephanson-14notes.pdf; Anders Stephanson, "Cold War Degree Zero," in *Uncertain Empire: American History and the Idea of the Cold War*, ed. Joel Isaac and Duncan Bell (Oxford: Oxford University Press, 2012), 26; Odd Arne Westad, "Exploring the Histories of the Cold War," in *Uncertain Empire: American History and the Idea of the Cold War*, ed. Joel Isaac and Duncan Bell (Oxford: Oxford University Press, 2012), 52; Westad, *The Cold War*, 617; Marco Wyss, *Postcolonial Security: Britain, France, and West Africa's Cold War* (Oxford: Oxford University Press, 2021), 5.

40. Romero, "Cold War Historiography at the Crossroads," 687; Sara Lorenzini, *Global Development: A Cold War History* (Princeton, NJ: Princeton University Press, 2019), 3.

41. Lorenz M. Lüthi, *Cold Wars: Asia, the Middle East, Europe* (Cambridge: Cambridge University Press, 2020), 67; Tony Smith, "New Bottles for New Wine: A Pericentric Framework for the Study of the Cold War," *Diplomatic History* 24, no. 4 (2000): 567–91; Asher Orkaby, *Beyond the Arab Cold War: The International History of the Yemen Civil War, 1962–68* (Oxford: Oxford University Press, 2017), 5; Heonik Kwon, *The Other Cold War* (New York: Columbia University Press, 2010), 6; Wyss, *Postcolonial Security*, 14.

42. Westad, *The Cold War*, 617; Mark Philip Bradley, "Decolonization, the Global South and the Cold War, 1919–1962," in vol. 1, *The Cambridge History of the Cold War*, ed. Melvyn P. Leffler and Odd Arne Westad (Cambridge: Cambridge University Press, 2010), 464–85; Lüthi, *Cold Wars*, 261; Nathan J. Citino, *Envisioning the Arab Future: Modernization in US-Arab Relations, 1945–1967* (Cambridge: Cambridge University Press, 2017), 3.

43. Westad, *The Global Cold War*, 364–95, 5.

44. Jennifer Wenzel, *Bulletproof: Afterlives of Anticolonial Prophecy in South Africa and Beyond* (Chicago: University of Chicago Press, 2010); Nils Gilman, "The New International Economic Order: A Reintroduction," *Humanity* 6, no. 1 (2015): 10; Frederick Cooper, *Citizenship between Empire and Nation: Remaking France and French Africa, 1945–1960* (Princeton, NJ: Princeton University Press, 2014), 440.

45. Wilder, *Freedom Time*; Priya Lal, *African Socialism in Postcolonial Tanzania: Between the Village and the World* (Cambridge: Cambridge University Press, 2015), 10; Jean Allman, "Nuclear Imperialism and the Pan-African Struggle for Peace and Freedom: Ghana, 1959–1962," *Souls* 10, no. 2 (2008): 97.

46. Ryan Irwin, *Gordian Knot: Apartheid and the Unmaking of the Liberal World Order* (Oxford: Oxford University Press, 2012), 188–89.

47. Michael Collins, "Decolonisation and the 'Federal Moment,'" *Diplomacy & Statecraft* 24, no. 1 (2013): 21–40; Westad, *The Global Cold War*, 3; Cooper, *Colonialism in Question*, 115–16.

48. Steven Belletto, "Inventing Other Realities: What the Cold War Means for Literary Studies," in *Uncertain Empire: American History and the Idea of the Cold War*, ed. Joel Isaac and Duncan Bell (Oxford: Oxford University Press, 2012), 75–90.

49. Walter D. Mignolo and Catherine E. Walsh, *On Decoloniality: Concepts, Analytics, Praxis* (Durham, NC: Duke University Press, 2018), 234.

50. Quintin Hoare, ed., *Antonio Gramsci, Selections from Political Writings (1921–1926)* (London: Lawrence and Wishart, 1978), 2; Sinah Theres Kloß, "The Global South as Subversive Practice: Challenges and Potentials of a Heuristic Concept," *Global South* 11, no. 2 (2017): 1–17.

51. Carl Oglesby, "Vietnamism Has Failed . . . the Revolution Can Only Be Mauled, Not Defeated," *Commonweal*, 1969; Carl Oglesby, "Notes on a Decade," *Liberation*, September 1969.

52. Julius K. Nyerere, "Unity for a New Order," *Black Scholar* 11, no. 5 (1980): 62; Michael Franczak, *Global Inequality and American Foreign Policy in the 1970s* (Ithaca, NY: Cornell University Press, 2022), 10.

53. See particularly Westad, *The Global Cold War*, 396–407; Kwon, *The Other Cold War*, 1–10. David Anderson has narrowed the Cold War to a series of violent events: Daniel Branch and Benedict Anderson, eds., *Allies at the End of Empire: Loyalists, Nationalists and the Cold War, 1945–76* (London: Routledge, 2018).

54. Quoted in Allman, "Nuclear Imperialism," 97; Elizabeth Schmidt, *Foreign Intervention in Africa: From the Cold War to the War on Terror* (Cambridge: Cambridge University Press, 2013); Kate Skinner, "A Different Kind of Union: An Assassination, Diplomatic Recognition, and Competing Visions of African Unity in Ghana-Togo Relations, 1956–1963," in *Visions of African Unity: New Perspectives on the History of Pan-Africanism and African Unification Projects*, ed. Matteo Grilli and Frank Gerits (London: Palgrave Macmillan, 2020), 23–48.

55. Jean Allman, "Kwame Nkrumah, African Studies and the Politics of Knowledge Production in the Black Star of Africa," *International Journal of African Historical Studies* 46, no. 2 (2013): 201; Jeffrey S. Ahlman, *Living with Nkrumahism: Nation, State, and Pan-Africanism in Ghana* (Athens: Ohio University Press, 2017), 1–28; Frederick Cooper, "Conflict and Connection: Rethinking Colonial African History," in *The Decolonization Reader*, ed. James D. Le Sueur (New York: Routledge, 2003), 157; Lewis and Stolte, "Other Bandungs"; Michele Louro, Carolien Stolte, Heather Streets-Salter, Sana Tannoury-Karam, eds., *The League Against Imperialism: Lives and Afterlives* (Leiden: Leiden University Press, 2020).

56. Glenda Sluga, *Internationalism in the Age of Nationalism* (Philadelphia: University of Pennsylvania Press, 2015), 125; Alanna O'Malley, *The Diplomacy of Decolonisation: America, Britain and the United Nations during the Congo Crisis 1960–64* (Manchester: Manchester University Press, 2018), 2; Mark Mazower, *No Enchanted Palace: The End of Empire and the Ideological Origins of the United Nations*, Lawrence Stone Lectures (Princeton, NJ: Princeton University Press, 2009), 189; Mark Mazower, *Governing the World: The History of an Idea, 1815 to the Present* (New York: Penguin Books, 2013), 272.

57. Kathleen Wilson, ed., *A New Imperial History: Culture, Identity, and Modernity in Britain and the Empire, 1660–1840* (Cambridge: Cambridge University Press, 2004).

58. Guy Vanthemsche, *Congo: De Impact van de Kolonie Op België* (Tielt: Lannoo, 2007), 129; Gopal, *Insurgent Empire*, 422.

59. Kwon, *The Other Cold War*, 130; Partha Chatterjee, *Nationalist Thought and the Colonial World: A Derivative Discourse* (London: Zed Books, 1986); Dipesh Chakrabarty, *Provincializing Europe: Postcolonial Thought and Historical Difference* (Princeton, NJ: Princeton University Press, 2007).

60. "A more sophisticated . . . historical agency indicates that both intervention and resistance had complicated sources," see Jeremi Suri, "The Cold War, Decolonization, and Global Social Awakenings: Historical Intersections," *Cold War History* 6, no. 3 (2006): 352–63, 358.

61. Frederick Cooper, "Possibility and Constraint: African Independence in Historical Perspective," *Journal of African History* 49, no. 2 (2008): 187; Christopher S. Clapham, *Africa and the International System: The Politics of State Survival* (Cambridge: Cambridge University Press, 1996); Ahlman, *Living with Nkrumahism*, 1–10.

62. Stephen Howe, "Introduction: New Imperial Histories," in *The New Imperial Histories Reader*, ed. Stephen Howe (London: Routledge, 2016), 2.

63. Ali Mazrui, *Towards a Pax Africana: A Study of Ideology and Ambition* (Chicago: University of Chicago Press, 1967); Ian R. Phimister, *An Economic and Social History of Zimbabwe, 1890–1948: Capital Accumulation and Class Struggle* (London: Longman, 1988); Terence O. Ranger, *Revolt in Southern Rhodesia, 1896–7: A Study in African Resistance* (London: Heinemann, 1967); Elizabeth Schmidt, *Cold War and Decolonization in Guinea, 1946–1958* (Athens: Ohio University Press, 2007); Schmidt, *Foreign Intervention in Africa*, 1–10.

64. Jeffrey James Byrne, *Mecca of Revolution: Algeria, Decolonization, and the Third World Order* (Oxford: Oxford University Press, 2016), 293; Matthew Connelly, "Rethinking the Cold War and Decolonization: The Grand Strategy of the Algerian War for Independence," *International Journal of Middle East Studies* 33, no. 2 (2001): 239, 222; Jeffrey James Byrne, "Our Own Special Brand of Socialism: Algeria and the Contest of Modernities in the 1960s," *Diplomatic History* 33, no. 3 (2009): 429.

65. Christy Thornton, *Revolution in Development: Mexico and the Governance of the Global Economy* (Berkeley: University of California Press, 2020), 12, 8, 198.

66. Lewis and Stolte, "Other Bandungs," 18.

67. Gerard McCann, "From Diaspora to Third Worldism and the United Nations: India and the Politics of Decolonizing Africa," Supplement, *Past & Present* 218, no. 8 (2013): 259–60; Similarly: George Roberts, *Revolutionary State-Making in Dar Es Salaam: African Liberation and the Global Cold War, 1961–1974* (Cambridge: Cambridge University Press, 2021), 8, 276–77.

68. Steven Jensen, *The Making of International Human Rights: The 1960s, Decolonization and the Reconstruction of Global Values* (Cambridge: Cambridge University Press, 2016); Mazower, *Governing the World*, 13–30; Irwin, *Gordian Knot*, 6; Cindy Ewing, "The Colombo Powers: Crafting Diplomacy in the Third World and Launching Afro-Asia at Bandung," *Cold War History* 19, no. 1 (2019): 1–19.

69. Gayatri Chakravorty Spivak, *A Critique of Postcolonial Reason: Toward a History of the Vanishing Present* (Cambridge, MA: Harvard University Press, 1999); Toyin Falola, *Nationalism and African Intellectuals* (Rochester, NY: University of Rochester Press, 2001); Brenda Cooper and Robert Morrell, eds., *Africa-Centred Knowledges: Crossing Fields and Worlds* (Woodbridge, UK: James Currey, 2014).

70. Patrick Chabal, *Africa: The Politics of Suffering and Smiling* (London: Zed Books, 2009); Clapham, *Africa and the International System*, 1–10; Getachew, *Worldmaking after Empire*, 28, 30, 76, 78, 100, 105, 178.

71. Stephen Ellis, "Writing Histories of Contemporary Africa," *Journal of African History* 43, no. 1 (2002): 7, 25; Idesbald Goddeeris and Sindani E. Kiangu, "Congomania in Academia: Recent Historical Research on the Belgian Colonial Past," *Low Countries Historical Review* 126, no. 4 (2011): 54–74; Mahmood Mamdani, "The African University," *London Review of Books* 40, no. 14 (July 19, 2018): 29–32; Paul E. Lovejoy, "Nigeria: The Ibadan School and Its Critics," in *African Historiographies: What History for Which Africa?*, ed. Bogumil Jewsiewicki and David Newbury (Beverly Hills: Sage Publications, 1986), 197–205; Saida Yahya-Othman, *Development As Rebellion: A Biography of Julius Nyerere, the Making of a Philosopher Ruler*, vol. 1 (Dar es Salaam: Mkuki Na Nyota Publishers, 2020), xviii–xix.

72. Quote from McMahon, "Introduction," 9; Natasa Miskovic, "Introduction," in *The Non-Aligned Movement and the Cold War: Delhi—Bandung—Belgrade*, ed. Natasa Miskovic, Harald Fischer-Tiné, and Nada Boskovska (London: Routledge, 2014), 1–18.

73. How the Cold War influenced decolonization is the focal point for historians, see "Cold War first slowed and then quickened a historical process already underway," Jason Parker, *Brother's Keeper: The United States, Race, and Empire in the British Caribbean, 1937–1962* (Oxford: Oxford University Press, 2008), 14.

74. Jamie Miller, *An African Volk: The Apartheid Regime and Its Search for Survival* (Oxford: Oxford University Press, 2016), 18; Poppy Cullen, "'Playing Cold War Politics': The Cold War in Anglo-Kenyan Relations in the 1960s," *Cold War History* 18, no. 1 (2017): 39–40.

75. John Lewis Gaddis, *We Now Know: Rethinking Cold War History* (Oxford: Oxford University Press, 1998).

76. Kenya National Archives and Documentation Services, Nairobi (hereafter KNADS), AHC/1/33, memorandum, D. N. Ndegwa, "Destruction of Cabinet Documents," 7 April 1965.

77. National Archives of Nigeria, Ibadan (hereafter NAN), PX/D1 Federal Nigeria 1960–62, "Federal Nigeria: Being a Record of Progress and Development in the Federation of Nigeria," vol. 3, no.7, July 1960, 3.

78. Jordanna Bailkin, "Where Did the Empire Go? Archives and Decolonization in Britain," *American Historical Review* 120, no. 3 (2015): 884–99; Omnia El Shakry, "'History without Documents': The Vexed Archives of Decolonization in the Middle East," *American Historical Review* 120, no. 3 (2015): 920–34; Jean Allman, "AHR Forum Phantoms of the Archive: Kwame Nkrumah, a Nazi Pilot Named Hanna, and the Contingencies of Postcolonial History-Writing," *American Historical Review* 118, no. 1 (2013): 104–29; Samuel Fury Childs Daly, "Archival Research in Africa," *African Affairs* 116, no. 463 (2017): 311–20.

79. Jonathon Glassman, *War of Words, War of Stones: Racial Thought and Violence in Colonial Zanzibar* (Bloomington: Indiana University Press, 2011), 7.

80. Daniel Bessner and Frederik Logevall, "Recentering the United States in the Historiography of American Foreign Relations," *Texas National Security Review* 3, no. 2 (2020): 38–55; Mario Del Pero, "On the Limits of Thomas Zeiler's Historiographical Triumphalism," *Journal of American History* 95, no. 4 (2009): 1079–82.

1. A Foreign Policy of the Mind, 1945–1954

1. Elspeth Huxley, "Two Revolutions That Are Changing Africa," *New York Times Magazine*, May 19, 1957; NARA, RG.306, UD-WW285, FRC2, f: Regional, Argus Tresridder, "A Study of the Cultural Program in Africa with Especial Reference to Education," October 1957, 2; Archives du ministère des affaires étrangères, La Courneuve (hereafter AMAE), Direction Afrique-Levant (hereafter DAL), Ghana 50QO/15, f: Politique intérieure, Service de presse et d'information, 19 May 1957; Archives de service public fédéral affaires étrangères, Brussels (hereafter ASPFAE), Archives africaines (hereafter AA), 14563, 1494, "Comité pour l'étude des relations économiques avec l'Afrique: The Next-to-Last Act in Africa by Elspeth Huxley," 10 July 1961; BNA, BW95/3, Richard Frost, "Visit to District Commissioners in Western Kenya," 4 September 1950, 6–8.

2. Christopher G. Thorne, *Allies of a Kind: The United States, Britain, and the War against Japan, 1941–1945* (Oxford: Oxford University Press, 1978), 669, 725, 750; Ronald Hyam, "Churchill and the Colonial Empire," in *Understanding the British Empire* (Cambridge: Cambridge University Press, 2010), 335.

3. Tony Chafer, *The End of Empire in French West Africa: France's Successful Decolonization?* (New York: Berg Publishers, 2002), 5, 12; Joseph-Roger de Benoist, *L'Afrique Occidentale Française de La Conférence de Brazzaville (1944) à l'Indépendance (1960)* (Dakar: Les Nouvelles Éditions Africaines, 1982); Maurice Obi Nwankwor, "French and Cultural Diplomacy: The African Experience," *International Affairs and Global Strategy* 10 (2013): 1–4.

4. Elizabeth Buettner, *Europe after Empire: Decolonization, Society, and Culture* (Cambridge: Cambridge University Press, 2016), 194; Jacob Mundy, "The Geopolitical Functions of the Western Sahara Conflict: US Hegemony, Moroccan Stability and Sahrawi Strategies of Resistance," in *Global, Regional and Local Dimensions of Western Sahara's Protracted Decolonization: When a Conflict Gets Old*, ed. Raquel Ojeda-Garcia, Irene Fernández-Molina, and Victoria Veguilla (London: Palgrave Macmillan, 2016), 57.

5. Miguel Bandeira Jéronimo, *The "Civilising Mission" of Portuguese Colonialism, 1870–1930* (London: Palgrave Macmillan, 2015), 195; Nelson Ribeiro, "Broadcasting to the

Portuguese Empire in Africa: Salazar's Singular Broadcasting Policy," *Critical Arts* 28, no. 6 (2014): 934; Miguel Bandeira Jerónimo and José Pedro Monteiro, "Internationalism and the Labours of the Portuguese Colonial Empire (1945–1974)," *Portuguese Studies* 29, no. 2 (2013): 142–63; Rik Coolsaet, *België En Zijn Buitenlandse Politiek 1830–2000* (Leuven: Van Halewyck, 2001), 421.

6. Jason Parker, *Hearts, Minds, Voices: US Cold War Public Diplomacy and the Formation of the Third World* (Oxford: Oxford University Press, 2016), 17; Vernon McKay, *Africa in World Politics* (New York: Harper & Row, 1963); Philip E. Muehlenbeck, *Betting on the Africans: John F. Kennedy's Courting of African Nationalist Leaders* (New York: Oxford University Press, 2012); Walt W. Rostow, *Eisenhower, Kennedy, and Foreign Aid* (Austin: University of Texas Press, 1985), 75–109. Quote taken from Thomas Borstelmann, *The Cold War and the Color Line: American Race Relations in the Global Arena* (Cambridge, MA: Harvard University Press, 2003), 116.

7. Sergey Mazov, *A Distant Front in the Cold War: The USSR in West Africa and the Congo, 1956–1964* (Stanford, CA: Stanford University Press, 2010), 15–16; Alessandro Iandolo, "Soviet Policy in West Africa, 1957–64" (PhD diss., University of Oxford, 2011), 17; Robert Legvold, *Soviet Policy in West Africa* (Cambridge, MA: Harvard University Press, 1970), 1–20.

8. ASPFAE, AD, AFRI372, "Garde de la legation belge a Pekin," s.d.; Judith Byfield, Carolyn Brown, Timothy Parsons, and Ahmad Alawad Sikainga, eds., *Africa and World War II* (Cambridge: Cambridge University Press, 2015); Sarah Ann Frank, *Hostages of Empire: Colonial Prisoners of War in Vichy France* (Lincoln: University of Nebraska Press, 2021); Luís Nuno Rodrigues, "'For a Better Guinea': Winning Hearts and Minds in Portuguese Guinea," in *Race, Ethnicity, and the Cold War*, ed. Philip E. Muehlenbeck (Nashville: Vanderbilt University Press, 2012), 118.

9. For an overview of the US debates: Frank Gerits, "Hungry Minds: Eisenhower's Cultural Assistance to Sub-Saharan Africa, 1953–1961," *Diplomatic History* 41, no. 3 (2017): 594–619; James Meriwether, *Tears, Fire, and Blood: The United States and the Decolonization of Africa* (Chapel Hill: University of North Carolina Press, 2021), 1–25; Jennifer M. Dueck, "International Rivalry and Culture in Syria and Lebanon under the French Mandate," in *Searching for a Cultural Diplomacy*, ed. Jessica C. Gienow-Hecht and Mark C. Donfried (New York: Berghahn Books, 2010), 151; Alain Dubosclard, *L'action artistique de la France aux États-Unis, 1915–1969* (Paris: CNRS, 2003), 350–51; Coolsaet, *België En Zijn Buitenlandse Politiek*; Ludo De Witte, *Huurlingen, Geheimagenten En Diplomaten* (Leuven: Van Halewyck Uitgeverij, 2015); Matthew G. Stanard, "De koloniale propaganda: Het ontwaken van een Belgisch koloniaal bewustzijn?," in *Koloniaal Congo: Een Geschiedenis in Vragen*, ed. Idesbald Goddeeris, Amandine Lauro, and Guy Vanthemsche (Antwerp: Polis, 2020), 325–37; Matthew G. Stanard, *Selling the Congo: A History of European Pro-Empire Propaganda and the Making of Belgian Imperialism* (Lincoln: University of Nebraska Press, 2012); Mathieu Zana Etambala, *Veroverd, Bezet, Gekoloniseerd Congo 1876–1914* (Gorredijk: Sterck & De Vreese, 2020), 24.

10. "Rival ideologies of empire often share key assumptions about the nature of the social world," Duncan Bell, *Reordering the World: Essays on Liberalism and Empire* (Princeton, NJ: Princeton University Press, 2016), 94.

11. Although political science distinguishes between state building, the construction of a functioning state, and nation building, with a focus on identity, both concepts were used interchangeably in the 1950s: Charles Tilly and Gabriel Ardant, *The Formation*

of National States in Western Europe (Princeton, NJ: Princeton University Press, 1975), i–xiv; Nils Gilman, *Mandarins of the Future: Modernization Theory in Cold War America* (Baltimore: Johns Hopkins University Press, 2004), 170.

12. Mark Mazower, *Hitler's Empire: How the Nazis Ruled Europe*, reprint ed. (New York: Penguin Books, 2009), 12; Frederick Cooper, "Reconstructing Empire in British and French Africa," in *Post-War Reconstruction in Europe: International Perspectives, 1945–1949*, ed. Mark Mazower, Jessica Reinisch, and David Feldman (Oxford: Oxford University Press, 2011), 197.

13. AMAE, DAL, Généralités, 1944–1955, 49QO/94, Senghor to DAL, "Exposé relative de la situation actuelle du poste national de Radio Brazzaville," 7 June 1950, 3; Chafer, *The End of Empire in French West Africa*, 55–56, 61–62; Frédéric Turpin, "La Communauté française: Un avenir pour la république?," in *Pierre Mendès-France et les outre-mers*, ed. Frédéric Turpin and Jacques Frémeaux (Paris: Les Indes savantes, 2012), 59; Chafer, *The End of Empire in French West Africa*, 133; Louisa Rice, "Cowboys and Communists: Cultural Diplomacy, Decolonization and the Cold War in French West Africa," *Journal of Colonialism and Colonial History* 11, no. 3 (2010), http://0-muse.jhu.edu.biblio.eui.eu/journals/journal_of_colonialism_and_colonial_history/v011/11.3.rice.html.

14. AMAE, DAL, Généralités, 49QONT/64, f: CB-V-7 Communisme, "La jeunesse de l'union française et l'assemblee mondiale de la jeunesse," [1953].

15. Kwesi Armah, *Peace without Power: Ghana's Foreign Policy 1957–1966* (Accra: Ghana University Press, 1998), 165; BNA, CO1027/40, Colonial Office, "Public Relations: Kenya," 23 October 1952.

16. Simon J. Potter, *Broadcasting Empire: The BBC and the British World, 1922–1970* (Oxford: Oxford University Press, 2012), 3–4; Harold Innis, *Empire and Communications* (Toronto: Dundurn Press, 2007), 1–31; BNA, BW154/1, "Notes of a Meeting Held at the British Council to Hear a Report from Mr. Fowells on His Visit to the Congo," 8 September 1960.

17. Andrew Defty, *Britain, America and Anti-Communist: The Information Research Department* (New York: Routledge, 2007), 243; BNA, CO1027/70, J. Boyd-Carpenter to David Maxwell Fyfe, 20 January 1954, memorandum, [1954]; James Vaughan, *The Failure of American and British Propaganda in the Arab Middle East, 1945–57: Unconquerable Minds* (London: Palgrave Macmillan, 2005), 16; Potter, *Broadcasting Empire*, 47; BNA, BW151/15, "Report on the Work of the British Council," 31 March 1954, 4–11; BNA, BW151/14, "Report on the Work of the British Council," 31 March 1953, 32.

18. Erik Linstrum, *Ruling Minds: Psychology in the British Empire* (Cambridge, MA: Harvard University Press, 2016); Joseph Morgan Hodge, *Triumph of the Expert: Agrarian Doctrines of Development and the Legacies of British Colonialism* (Athens: Ohio University Press, 2007), 136; Richard Hughes, *Capricorn: David Stirling's African Campaign* (London: Radcliffe Press, 2003), 1–2, 88; Alice Conklin, *A Mission to Civilize: The Republican Idea of Empire in France and West Africa, 1895–1930*, 1st ed. (Stanford, CA: Stanford University Press, 2000), 6, 248.

19. Chafer, *The End of Empire in French West Africa*, 48–49.

20. Aimé Césaire, "Poésie et Connaissance," in *Aimé Césaire: Poésie, Théâtre, Essais et Discours*, ed. Albert James Arnold (Paris: CNRS Éditions, 2013), 1373–96; Jackqueline Frost, "'The Red Hour': Poetic Violence and the Time of Transformation in Aimé Césaire's *Et les chiens se taisaient*," *Global South* 11, no. 1 (2017): 60.

21. Lauren L. Nelson, "Suzanne Césaire's Posthumanism: Figuring the Homme-Plante," *Feminist Modernist Studies* 3, no. 2 (2020): 162–79; Annette K. Joseph-Gabriel, *Reimagining Liberation: How Black Women Transformed Citizenship in the French Empire* (Champaign: University of Illinois Press, 2019), 29–56.

22. Frantz Fanon, *Black Skin, White Masks*, trans. Richard Philcox (New York: Grove Press, 1967), 180.

23. Matthew M. Heaton, *Black Skin, White Coats: Nigerian Psychiatrists, Decolonization, and the Globalization of Psychiatry* (Athens: Ohio University Press, 2013), 12.

24. Ali Mazrui, "Racial Self-Reliance and Cultural Dependency: Nyerere and Amin in Comparative Perspective," *Journal of International Affairs* 27, no. 1 (1973): 106; Joseph W. Nasongo and Lydiah L. Musungu, "The Implications of Nyerere's Theory of Education to Contemporary Education in Kenya," *Educational Research and Reviews* 4, no. 4 (2009): 111, 114; Linstrum, *Ruling Minds*, 213.

25. Harry S. Truman, *Memoirs by Harry S. Truman: Years of Trial and Hope* (New York: Doubleday and Company, 1956), 242, 246, 248; Memorandum of Conversation (hereafter memcon), by the Secretary of State, secret, 13 October 1949, *FRUS 1949*, vol. 6, *The Near East, South Asia and Africa, 1750–1752*.

26. Melvyn P. Leffler, *For the Soul of Mankind: The United States, the Soviet Union, and the Cold War*, 1st ed. (New York: Hill and Wang, 2008), 37.

27. Quoted in Amanda Kay McVety, "Pursuing Progress: Point Four in Ethiopia," *Diplomatic History* 32, no. 3 (2008): 386. Arthur Lewis also argued Truman claimed "technical assistance is what the under-developed chiefly need"; see Arthur W. Lewis, *The Theory of Economic Growth* (London: George Allen & Unwin, 1955), 19.

28. The argument of drama in Hannah Nicole Higgin, "Disseminating American Ideals in Africa, 1949–1969" (PhD diss., Cambridge University, 2014), 29–30; Harry S. Truman Library Presidential Library and Museum, Independence, MO (hereafter TL), Truman Papers, David Lloyd Files, box 20, f: Point IV Conference, "Outline of Remarks by Secretary Dean Acheson before the National Conference on International Economic and Social Development," 8 April 1952.

29. Dean Acheson, "What Is Point Four?," *Department of State Bulletin*, vol. XXVI, 4 February 1952, 155; TL, Dean Acheson Oral History (June 30, 1971), pp. 6–7; TL, PSB files, box 5, f: 091 Africa, Draft, Security Information, "Psychological Annex," 29 May 1953.

30. National Archives of Nigeria, Ibadan (hereafter NAN), BTS 1/33/6/6C, box 11, f: Point 4, "Address by the Honorable Henry A. Byroade, before the World Affairs Council of Northern California," 11 January 1954; Patrick O'Donovan, "The Magic of Nationalism: An Entire Continent Is Watching Nkrumah of the Gold Coast, the First Negro to Lead the Government of an African Colony," *Reporter*, 18 September 1951.

31. Howland H. Sargeant, "The Key to a Free World: Unity of Purpose and Action," *Department of State Bulletin*, vol. XXVI, no. 659, 11 January 1952, 202.

32. Paper Prepared in the Bureau of Near Eastern, South Asian, and African Affairs, Dean Acheson, "Regional Policy Statement on Africa South of the Sahara," 29 December 1950, *FRUS 1951*, vol. 5, *The Near East and Africa*, 119–1211; George C. McGhee, *Envoy to the Middle World: Adventures in Diplomacy* (New York: Harper & Row, 1984), 127.

33. TL, Truman Papers, David Lloyd Files, box 20, f: Point IV [1 of 3], "Report, Advisory Committee on Technical Assistance," 27 July 1949; "Harry S. Truman, Remarks to a Group of Point 4 Agricultural Trainees," *The American Presidency Project*, ed.

Gerhard Peters and John T. Woolley, accessed 5 March 2019, https://www.presidency.ucsb.edu/node/231082; NARA, RG.59, Lot Files, Office Files of George C. McGhee, f: Africa-1948-Memoranda, McGhee to the Secretary, "Summary of Conclusions and Recommendations Reached at Lourenco Marques Conference," 12 April 1950.

34. Vernon McKay, "Needs and Opportunities in Africa," *Annals of the American Academy of Political and Social Science* 268 (1950): 75–84.

35. TL, PSB Files, box 6, f: 091 India, memcon, 17 January 1952, Teg C. Grondahl, Chief Public Affairs Officer, "The Urgent Need for a Program to Cope with the Present Wave of Cynicism and Frustration among Indian Intellectuals and University Students," 28 April 1952.

36. Dean Acheson, "What Is Point Four?," *Department of State Bulletin*, vol. XXVI, 4 February 1952, 155.

37. Gilman, *Mandarins*, 35.

38. Hodge, *Triumph of the Expert*, 141.

39. Gilman, *Mandarins*, 94–95; Artemy M. Kalinovsky, *Laboratory of Socialist Development: Cold War Politics and Decolonization in Soviet Tajikistan* (Ithaca, NY: Cornell University Press, 2018), 1–18; Joseph Stalin, *Marxism and the National and Colonial Question* (Moscow: Co-operative Publishing Society of Foreign Workers in the USSR, 1935).

40. Mazov, *A Distant Front in the Cold War*, 12; Radoslav A. Yordanov, *The Soviet Union and the Horn of Africa during the Cold War: Between Ideology and Pragmatism* (Cambridge, MA: Harvard University Press, 2017), 4; Sergius Yakobson, "Soviet Concepts of Point Four," *Annals of the American Academy of Political and Social Science* 268, no. 1 (1950): 129–39.

41. KNADS, MAC/UGA/119/3, "Open Letter to Truman, President of the U.S. Government," 28 March 1949; AMAE, DAL, Généralités 49QO/55, f: les Etats-Unis et les questions coloniaux (March 1948–Dec. 1952), Henri Bonnet to DAL, "Brochure publiée par la 'Foreign Policy Association' sur les possessions britanniques en Afrique Occidentale," 13 April 1948; AMAE, DAL, Généralités 1944–1952, 49QO/57, Henri Bonnet to Robert Schuman, "Effort culturel des Etats-Unis en Afrique," 30 March 1950, 3; AMAE, Direction Amérique (hereafter DA), Etats-Unis 1952–1963, 91QO/433, Henri Bonnet to Georges Bidault, "Les Etats-Unis, les Nations-Unies et l'Afrique: Copie d'un article de M. Vernon McKay," 8 April 1953; Bonnet confirms Marc Michel's scholarship. Michel doubted "whether all French officials suspected collusion between the nationalists and the communists," Marc Michel, "The Decolonization of French Africa and the United States and Great Britain, 1945–58," in *Imperialism, Decolonization, and Africa: Studies Presented to John Hargreaves: With an Academic Memoir and Bibliography*, ed. John D Hargreaves and Roy C. Bridges (New York: St. Martin's Press, 2000), 164; NASA, BTS 1/33/8/3, vol. 3, "The Impact of Africa on International Relations by Vernon McKay," 1960.

42. Ribeiro, "Broadcasting to the Portuguese Empire in Africa," 921.

43. ASPFAE, AA, AII3274, f: Etats-Unis Amérique, Pierre Wigny, "Voyage aux Etats-Unis 7 mars–23 avril 1952," 23 April 1952; Frank Gerits, "'Défendre l'oeuvre que nous réalisons en afrique': Belgian Public Diplomacy and the Global Cold War (1945–1966)," *Dutch Crossing: Journal of Low Countries Studies* 40, no. 1 (2016): 70; Miguel Bandeira Jerónimo and José Pedro Monteiro, "Colonial Labour Internationalized: Portugal and the Decolonization Momentum (1945–1975)," *International History Review* 42, no. 3 (2020): 12.

44. AMAE, DAL, Généralités, 49QO/56, Henry Hauck, "L'aide aux pays insuffisamment développés, le rôle de la France et celui des pays signataires du Traité de Bruxelles," 18 March 1949, 6; ASPFAE, AA, INFO(36), "Raisons et moyens de faire de la propagande ideologique coloniale aux Etats-Unis," 4 July 1951; ASPFAE, AA, AII3274, "Note sur l'extension de la propagande coloniale belge aux Etats-Unis, par Jan-Albert Goris," 15 April 1952, Pierre Ryckmans, "Propagande aux États-Unis," 24 August 1952.

45. The political aspect of the plan was thus not implicit as argued in Guy Vanthemsche, *Genèse et portée du "Plan décennal" du Congo belge (1949–1959)*, Académie royale des sciences d'outre-mer, Classe des sciences morales et politiques, Mémoires in-8. N. S. 51, 4 (Brussels: Académie royale de Belgique, 1994), 32.

46. ASPFAE, INFO(94), "Reportage photographique de la visite du Mwami de l'Urundi en Belgique," 4 September 1950; ASPFAE, INFO(37), "De Afrikaanse maskers," 4 November 1949.

47. Peo Hansen and Stefan Jonsson, *Eurafrica: The Untold History of European Integration and Colonialism* (London: Bloomsbury Academic, 2014), 7; Coolsaet, *België En Zijn Buitenlandse Politiek*, 424; Pierre Wigny, "Les Etats-Unis et le Congo," *Revue Générale Belge* 87 (1952): 146; NASA, BTS 1/33/6/6C, f: USA Aid to Underdeveloped Countries, J. S. F. Botha, "Point IV: Discussion by the American Academy of Political and Social Science," 21 April 1950, 1; NASA, BEV, box 9, f: Belgian Congo economic development general, Die Sekretaris van Buitelandse Sake, "Goewermentsraad van die Kongo: Openingrede van die Goewerneur-Generaal," 11 September 1952.

48. ASPFAE, AA, AII3274, Wigny, "Voyage aux Etats Unis," 5.

49. ASPFAE, INFO(94), Marcel-Henri Jaspar to van Zeeland, 5 April 1950.

50. Vanthemsche calls on historians to link colonial and Belgian foreign policy, in Guy Vanthemsche, *Congo: De Impact van de Kolonie Op België* (Tielt: Lannoo, 2007), 99; Zana Aziza Etambala, *De Teloorgang van Een Modelkolonie: Belgisch Congo (1958–1960)* (Leuven: Acco, 2008), 9; Idesbald Goddeeris and Sindani E. Kiangu, "Congomania in Academia: Recent Historical Research on the Belgian Colonial Past," *Low Countries Historical Review* 126, no. 4 (2011): 54–74; Guy Vanthemsche, "The Historiography of Belgian Colonialism in the Congo," in *Europe and the World in European Historiography*, ed. Csaba Lévai (Pisa: Pisa University Press, 2006), 89–119.

51. Pierre Wigny, "Methods of Government in the Belgian Congo," *African Affairs* 50, no. 201 (1951): 310–11; ASPFAE, AA, AII3274, Wigny, rapport de mission, "Voyage aux Etats-Unis," 5.

52. "Onwetendheid" "kwadertrouw," NASA, BEV, box 9, f: Belgian Congo economic development general, Die Sekretaris van Buitelandse Sake, "Goewermentsraad van die Kongo. Openignrede van die Goewerneru-Generaal," 11 September 1952; ASPFAE, EC (4363), "De Huidige Strekkingen van onze koloniale politiek," [1950s]; ASPFAE, AA, AII3274, f: Etats-Unis Amérique, Wigny, rapport de mission, "Voyage aux Etats-Unis," 5; Wigny, "Les Etats-Unis et Le Congo," 144.

53. ASPFAE, AA, AII3274, Ambassadeur de Belgique to van Zeeland, "Réactions à l'égard du rapport confidentiel de la délégation belge auprès de l'O.N.U. sur l'anticolonialisme aux Nations Unis," 14 April 1952, 2.

54. Heriberto Cairo, "Portugal Is Not a Small Country: Maps and Propaganda in the Salazar Regime," *Geopolitics* 11, no. 3 (2006): 371; Márcia Gonçalves, "Of Peasants and Settlers: Ideals of Portugueseness, Imperial Nationalism and European Settlement in

Africa, c. 1930–c. 1945," *European Review of History: Revue Européenne d'histoire* 25, no. 1 (2018): 174–77; Daniel Melo, *Salazarismo e Cultura Popular (1933–1958)* (Lisbon: Imprensa de Ciências Sociais, 2001).

55. Quoted in Tom Gallagher, *Salazar: The Dictator Who Refused to Die* (London: Hurst, 2020), 176; António Tomás, *Amílcar Cabral: The Life of a Reluctant Nationalist* (London: Hurst, 2021), 48.

56. Biblioteca e Arquivo Histórico Diplomático Ministério dos Negócios Estrangeiros, Lisbon, Portugal (hereafter BAHDMNE), AHD/MU/GM/GNP/RNP/0520/01619, "Estudo da imigração indígena em Moçambique pelo Inspector Superior Henrique Galvão," 1947.

57. Jeanne Marie Penvenne, *African Workers and Colonial Racism: Mozambican Strategies and Struggles in Lourenco Marques, 1877–1962* (Woodbridge, UK: James Currey, 1995), 6.

58. Ribeiro, "Broadcasting to the Portuguese Empire in Africa," 929; Jerry Dávila, *Hotel Trópico: Brazil and the Challenge of African Decolonization, 1950–1980* (Durham, NC: Duke University Press, 2010), 9, 11.

59. Placide Tempels, *Bantoe-Filosofie* (Antwerp: De Sikkel, 1946), 107–8.

60. Jean Roussel and J. Croux, trans., *Koloniale Plichtenleer* (Namen: Ad. Wesmael-Charlier, 1953), 170, 232; ASPFAE, AD, 2889, Herpin, "Conférence diplomatique à Leopoldville," 20 February 1958.

61. Sociology was important, but psychology was more influential, contrary to: George Steinmetz, "Sociology and Colonialism in the British and French Empires, 1945–1965," *Journal of Modern History* 89, no. 3 (31 August 2017): 601–48.

62. Linstrum, *Ruling Minds*, 163; Gordon Cumming, *Aid to Africa: French and British Policies from the Cold War to the New Millennium* (Aldershot: Ashgate, 2001), 59; Chafer, *The End of Empire*, 133.

63. Katholiek archief- en documentatiecentrum, Leuven (hereafter KADOC), Archief Jef van Bilsen, box 16, f: 5.2.4/2, N. De Cleene, "Jozef van Wing 1 april 1884–30 July 1970," 1970, 3; ASPFAE, AA, INFO(92), speech transcript, "C'est a une élite que je m'addresse," speech transcript, "Opening van de cursussen," 1951, "Politiek, geestelijk en moreel voogd," speech transcript, "Premier Session," 1952; Guy Vanthemsche, *Genèse et portée du "Plan décennal" du Congo belge (1949–1959)*, Académie royale des sciences d'outre-mer, Classe des sciences morales et politiques, Mémoires in-8. N. S. 51,4 (Brussels: Académie royale de Belgique, 1994), 7–11; ASPFAE, AA, INFO(38), "Aspects du Plan," s.d., 8; Eduardo De Sousa Ferreira, *Portuguese Colonialism in Africa: The End of an Era*, 1st ed. (Paris: UNESCO Press, 1974), 67.

64. Alessandro Iandolo, "De-Stalinizing Growth: Decolonization and the Development of Development Economics in the Soviet Union," in *The Development Century: A Global History*, Global and International History, ed. Erez Manela and Stephen J. Macekura (Cambridge: Cambridge University Press, 2018), 203.

65. Quoted in TL, PSB Files, box 5, f: 091 Africa, "Psychological Annex," 29 May 1953, 1; quoted in TL, Stanley Andrews Oral History (31 October 1970), pp. 43–5; quoted in Dean Acheson, *Present at the Creation: My Years in the State Department* (New York: Norton, 1969), 266; quoted in Jonathan B. Bingham, *Shirt-Sleeve Diplomacy: 4 Points in Action* (New York: John Day Company, 1954), 280; TL, Dean Acheson Oral History (30 June 1971), pp 6–7; for the argument of the indifferent Acheson, Higgin, "Disseminating American Ideals in Africa, 1949–1969," 34.

66. Gilman, *Mandarins*, 97; David McClelland, *The Achievement Motive* (New York: Appleton Century Crofts, 1953), 110; TL, Papers of Benjamin H. Hardy, Subject File, box 1, Preface "President Truman's Point 4," s.d..

67. Boyd van Dijk, "Internationalizing Colonial War: On the Unintended Consequences of the Interventions of the International Committee of the Red Cross in South-East Asia, 1945–1949," *Past & Present* 250, no. 1 (2021): 243; David A. Percox, *Britain, Kenya and the Cold War: Imperial Defence, Colonial Security and Decolonisation* (London: I.B. Tauris, 2004); Robert L. Tignor, "The Cold War Dimension of Kenyan Decolonization," *Journal of African History* 46, no. 2 (2005): 360–61; Susan Lisa Carruthers, *Winning Hearts and Minds: British Governments, the Media and Colonial Counter-Insurgency, 1944–1960* (Leicester: Leicester University Press, 1995); Benjamin Grob-Fitzgibbon, *Imperial Endgame: Britain's Dirty Wars and the End of Empire* (London: Palgrave Macmillan, 2011); Daniel Branch, *Defeating Mau Mau, Creating Kenya: Counterinsurgency, Civil War, and Decolonization* (Cambridge: Cambridge University Press, 2009); Gerald Horne, *Mau Mau in Harlem?: The U.S. and the Liberation of Kenya* (London: Palgrave MacMillan, 2009).

68. Caroline Elkins, *Britain's Gulag* (London: Jonathan Cape, 2005), 1–30.

69. BNA, CO1027/40, memorandum, CO, "Public relations: Kenya," 23 October 1952, "Kenya Colony Annual Report—1952 African Information Services," [1952], Harold Evans to Charles Crawford, 11 August 1953, E.B. David to Crawford, 29 July 1953.

70. Dwight D. Eisenhower, *Waging Peace: 1956–1961* (London: Heinemann, 1965), 572.

71. Gerits, "Hungry Minds," 594–96.

72. DDEL, Papers as President Ann Whitman File (hereafter AWF), DDE Diary Series, box 8, Eisenhower to Grunther, 30 November 1954.

73. DDEL, box 19, Eisenhower to Churchill, 22 July 1954, 2, 3; Eisenhower's frustration about Pierre Mendès France in Matthew Connelly, *A Diplomatic Revolution: Algeria's Fight for Independence and the Origins of the Post-Cold War Era* (Oxford: Oxford University Press, 2003), 64.

74. Roland Quinault, "Churchill and Black Africa," *History Today* 55, no. 6 (June 2005): 31–36; DDEL, AWF, DDE Diaries Series, box 1, Diary Entry on Tuesday, 6 January 1953, 3–5.

75. Connelly, *A Diplomatic Revolution*, 64; DDEL, AWF, DDE Diary Series, box 8, Eisenhower to Alfred M. Grunther, 30 November 1954.

76. NARA, RG.59, CDF1960-63, 611.53/11-960–611.539/2-1260, memcon, Dwight Eisenhower, John Eisenhower, C. Burke Elbrick, "US-Portugal Relations," 9 November 1960; counter the argument that Eisenhower feared Portugal with its meager economic resources would be unable to maintain its position in Africa, see Luís Nuno Rodrigues, *Salazar-Kennedy: A Crise de Uma Aliança* (Lisbon: Notícias editorial, 2002), 31.

77. BNA, CO10247/40, notes, 27 July 1953.

78. BNA, CO1027/40, Harold Evans to Charles, 11 August 1953, E. B. David, 29 July 1953, BNA, CO1027/83, notes in the file, Carstairs, 30 March 1955.

79. Quoted in Richard Toye, *Churchill's Empire: The World That Made Him and the World He Made* (London: Pan Books, 2010), x.

80. BNA, CO1027/74, minutes, Watrous for Evans, 16 March 1954; KNADS, AHC/10/12, W.A. Roberts, "The Technical Development of Broadcasting in Colonial Territories, Kenya," May 1953.

81. AMAE, 49QONT/65, f: AFR-XI-8 Institut français, note, DAL to DGRC, "Politique culturelle française en Afrique Noire," 11 October 1954, Memorandum, J. Révil, "Possibilités de notre action culturelle en Afrique Occidentale Britannique," 25 October 1955, note pour la DGRC, DAL to DGRC, "Effort culturel français en Afrique," 30 December 1954, Généralités 1953–1959; AMAE, 54QO/40, "Répercussions du Mau Mau en Gold Coast," 4 December 1952.

82. ASPFAE, AD, AFRI121, "Eventualité d'un mouvement nationaliste au Congo et influence des Mau-Mau, de Brazzaville, de la Côte d'Or et des communistes," [1953]; ASPFAE, AA, 3283, AE-2, no. 1801ter, "Note," by L. Smolderen, 31 August 1954; ASPFAE, INFO (25), f: 16, "L'armée-La nation / Het leger-De natie"—no. spécial consacré au Congo belge," 1952; "Het leger de natie: Het Belgische beschavingswerk Kongo," Een Blik op Kongo, 15 January 1953.

83. KADOC, Pholien, box 574, "Résumé de l'exposé de Buisseret devant la commission des colonies du Sénat," 7 December 1954, 2–3.

84. ASPFAE, AA, AEII3211, Harold Eeman to Paul van Zeeland, "L'Islam et le Congo," 7 April 1954, Harold Eeman to Paul van Zeeland, "Musulmans congolais," 27 June 1953.

85. BNA, CO936/564, "Broad Lines of Future Educational Policy in Nigeria," August 1959; Frederick Cooper, Colonialism in Question: Theory, Knowledge, History (San Francisco: University of California Press, 2005), 37, 144.

86. DDEL, AWF, DDE Diaries Series, box 1, diary entry on Tuesday, 6 January 1953, 3–5.

87. DDEL, box 12, Washburn Papers, f: Educational Development 1961 (6), report, Harold Hoskins, "Report on American Overseas Education," 29 October 1954; G. Lewis Schmidt, "Interview with Earl Wilson, 1988, The Foreign Affairs Oral History Collection of the Association for Diplomatic Studies and Training," accessed November 4, 2021, https://www.loc.gov/item/mfdipbib001273/; Georgetown University Library Special Collections Research Center, Washington, DC (hereafter GULSC), Wilson Earl J. Papers, box 1, f: Correspondence 12/17/1957–06/14/1983, Saxton Bradford to Earl Wilson, December 1957.

88. DDEL, Washburn Papers, box 12, f: Educational Development 1959–60 (1), James Halsema to Washburn, "Role of USIA in Overseas Education," 15 December 1960.

89. Robert Bowie and Richard Immerman, Waging Peace: How Eisenhower Shaped an Enduring Cold War Strategy (New York: Oxford University Press, 1998), 44; Kenneth Osgood, Total Cold War: Eisenhower's Secret Propaganda Battle at Home and Abroad (Lawrence: University Press of Kansas, 2006), 73; the claim that Eisenhower's requests for speeches were propaganda, Ebere Nwaubani, The United States and Decolonization in West Africa, 1950–1960 (Rochester, NY: University of Rochester Press, 2001), 39.

90. This conclusion rejects the notion that the Eisenhower administration was unwilling to educate Africans, see Brenda Gayle Plummer, In Search of Power: African Americans in the Era of Decolonization, 1956–1974 (Cambridge: Cambridge University Press, 2012), 65.

91. Winston Churchill, The River War, 2nd ed. (London: Eyre & Spottiswoode, 1933), 7.

92. Turpin, "La Communauté française," 59; Chafer, The End of Empire, 226.

93. Alan K. Smith, "António Salazar and the Reversal of Portuguese Colonial Policy," Journal of African History 15, no. 4 (1974): 653–67; Oliveira Salazar, Centro Católico Português: Princípios e Organização (Coimbra: Coimbra editora limitada, 1922).

94. Paul-Henri Spaak, "L'Alliance occidentale et le destin de l'Europe. In: Mars et Mercure. 25-02-1957. Mars 1957, no. 3, pp. 7–9," accessed August 23, 2021, https://www.cvce.eu/s/fh.

95. Kalinovsky, *Laboratory of Socialist Development*, 2.

96. Elwood Dunn, *Liberia and the United States during the Cold War: Limits of Reciprocity* (London: Palgrave Macmillan, 2009), 34; Jonathan Zimmerman, *Innocents Abroad: American Teachers in the American Century* (Cambridge, MA: Harvard University Press, 2008), 34; Adebayo Oyebade and Toyin Falola, "West Africa and the United States in Historical Perspective," in *The United States and West Africa: Interactions and Relations*, ed. Alusine Jalloh and Toyin Falola (Rochester, NY: University of Rochester Press, 2008), 17–37; Borstelmann argues Eisenhower made no distinction between racial conflict abroad and at home, Borstelmann, *The Cold War*, 5.

97. Stephen E. Ambrose, *Eisenhower: Soldier, General of the Army, President-Elect, 1890–1952* (New York: Simon & Schuster, 1983), 101–4, 106, 109.

98. DDEL, AWF, NSC Series, box 11, memorandum of the 397th Meeting of the NSC, February 26, 1959; DDEL, AWF, NSC Series, box 12, memdisc of the 432nd Meeting of the NSC, 14 January 1960; DDEL, AWF, NSC Series, box 11, Discussion at the 410th Meeting of the NSC, Thursday, 18 June 1959, 4; memcon, July 24, 1958, *FRUS 1958–1960*, vol. 14, *Africa*, 647–652.

99. KNADS, CS/2/8/4, M. F. Hill, "A Record of a Meeting of a Sub-Committee appointed by the Conference of Information Officers to Consider the Matter of Broadcasting Policy and Practice," 11 February 1941; National Archives of Nigeria, Ibadan (hereafter NAN), FISL/626, "Annual Report on the Public Relations Office for the Year 1944," [1945]; NAN, FISL/141, G.A.J. Bieneman, "Folklore," 15 January 1942; Philip Muehlenbeck, *Czechoslovakia in Africa, 1945–1968* (London: Palgrave Macmillan, 2015), 18; Gerits, "'Défendre l'oeuvre que nous réalisons en Afrique,'" 68.

100. Tomás, *Amílcar Cabral*, 48; Hemeroteca municipal de Lisboa, Lisbon, Carlos Alberto Garcia Alves Roçadas, "Recomecemos," *Boletim de Propaganda e Informação de Cabo Verde*, October 1, 1949; Amílcar Cabral, "Algumas considerações acêrca das chuvas," *Boletim de Propaganda e Informação de Cabo Verde*, October 1, 1949.

101. Arquivo Histórico Ultramarino, Lisbon (hereafter AHU), SR.A11, Cx043, report, José António Fernandes, 28 August 1952.

102. AMAE, DAL, Nord Est Afrique 1960–1965, 35QO/8, report, Jean Desparmet to DAL, "Mission d'etude des moyens d'information français en afrique centrale et orientale," 6 May 1964, 33; AMAE, DAL, Ghana 1960–1965, 50QO/72, Guiringaud to DAL, "Information Politique," 14 May 1960, 4; Vaughan, *The Failure of American and British Propaganda in the Arab Middle East, 1945–57*, 16; Kate Morris, *British Techniques of Public Relations and Propaganda for Mobilizing East and Central Africa during World War II* (Lewiston, NY: Edwin Mellen Press, 2000), 445.

103. NARA, RG.306, A1-1072, box 9, f: African Program, Historical Background, draft, Peter L. Koffsky, "The United States Information Program in Africa, 1945–1970: A History & Interpretation," 2-1; BNA, CO1027/83, Harold Evans to W. T. A. Cox, February 1956; BNA, CO1027/72, draft paper, "The Overseas Information Services Prospects for Expansion in 1956/1957," [1955]; BNA, INF12/978, Colonial Office, "Information Activities Undertaken by the Colonial Office in the African Territories," [1958]; AMAE,

DAL, généralités, 49QONT/51, f: Conversations franco-britanniques sur l'Afrique, memcon, "United States Information Agency," 14 May 1954.

104. NARA, RG.84 Ghana Post Files, box 1, f: USIS-Accra Prior to 1952–1956, Eugene Sawyer to USIA, "Activities of Regional Cultural Affairs Officer," 15 November 1955.

105. For instance, Karen Bell, "Developing a 'Sense of Community': U.S. Cultural Diplomacy and the Place of Africa during the Early Cold War Period 1953–54," in *The United States and West Africa: Interactions and Relations*, ed. Alusine Jalloh and Toyin Falola (Rochester, NY: University of Rochester Press, 2008), 139.

106. NARA, RG.59, CDF1950–1954, 511.45K3/10-1254–511.45R3/7-2850, Hyman Bloom to State Department (hereafter StateDept), "USIE: Need, in All Media, for Greater Emphasis on Affairs of U.S. Negroes," 2 April 1951; NARA, RG.59, A1-3112-J, box 1, f: Ford Foundation, memcon, StateDept, "Interest of Various Foundations in Africa South of the Sahara, June 29–July 1 1955," 2 July 1955.

107. John Fitzgerald Kennedy Library, Boston (hereafter JFKL), Papers President Kennedy, National Security Files (hereafter NSF), box 2, f: Africa: General, 9/29/61-10/31/61, Summary, George Ball, "Report to the President on Sub-Sahara African Student Programs," 13 October 1961.

108. RG.306, P253, box 3, f: Reports to NSC, Semi-Annual Report to NSC, "The Near East, South Asia and Africa (NEA)," 16 July 1954, 6–7; BNA, CO1035/120, secret report, "Communism in the Gold Coast," [1954].

109. NARA, vol. 2, no. 1, 10, RG.306, P46, box 90, f: Accra American Outlook 1952–1957 (folder 2 of 2), pamphlet, *American Outlook*, January 1956.

110. "Propaganda mediocre mais luxieuse": AMAE, DAL, Généralités 1944–1952, 94QO/96, Monod to direction du personnel, "Représentation française en Afrique Noire," 20 April 1945, 27; AMAE, DAL, Nord-Est Afrique 1960–1965, 35QO/17, DAL, "Représentation consulaire américaine," 13 May 1949, 4; AMAE, DAL, AOF 1944–1959, 34QO/4, Haut-Commissaire to ministre d'outre-mer, 6 September 1950, ministre de la France d'outre-mer to direction Afrique-Levant, "Activité Consul des USA Jester à Dakar," 15 September 1950; Louisa Rice does not mention the conflict between Jester and France, Rice, "Cowboys and Communists."

111. NARA, RG.84 Ghana Post Files, box 1, f: USIS-Accra Prior to 1952–1956, A. Q. Smart-Abbey to Department of Social Welfare and Community Development, 27 March 1954, H. E. Lorini to R. P. Ross, 17 March 1952, American consulate to StateDept, "IE: Motion Pictures—Request for prints of the Disney health films," 7 November 1951.

112. ASPFAE, INFO(89), J. van den Haute, "Rapport de Mission," 6 August 1949, 2–3, 11, "Procés-verbal de la réunion du Comité de Direction," 10 November 1949; L. Van Bever, *Le cinéma pour Africains* (Brussels: G. Van Campenhout, 1950), 31; ASPFAE, INFO(94), f: Propagande Belge au Congo 4, Gerard De Boe to André Dequae, 3 July 1951, le Vice Gouverneur-General, "Réalisation en Belgique de films pour Congolais," 16 October 1951.

113. NARA, RG.59, CDF1950-54, 511.553/1-454–511.55A5, Charles K. Bevilacqua to StateDept, "Transmittal Report on Belgian Congo and French Equatorial Africa—USIS," 15 December 1952, 8–9.

114. NARA, RG.306, UD-WW285, USIS-Leopoldville to USIA, "Covering Despatch for USIA Classified Despatch No. 30," 30 June 1954, 4.

115. Archives d' Alliance Française, Paris (hereafter AF), Afrique Pays A à D 47–57, f: Congo-belge, Paul Lorion to Georges Bidault, "Alliance Française au Congo Belge," 7 April 1954.

116. Memdis at 375th NSC meeting, August 7, 1958, *FRUS 1958–1960*, vol. 14, *Africa*, 21.

117. Odd Arne Westad, *The Global Cold War: Third World Interventions and the Making of Our Times* (Cambridge: Cambridge University Press, 2005), 5.

2. Offering Hungry Minds a Better Development Project, 1955–1956

1. NARA, RG.306, UD-WW285, FRC5, f: General—Bandung Conf, Cable, "Bandung US info," 17 April 1955; Homer Alexander Jack, *Bandung: An On-the-Spot Description of the Asian-African Conference, Bandung, Indonesia, April, 1955* (Chicago: Toward Freedom, 1955), 1.

2. Dipesh Chakrabarty, "The Legacies of Bandung: Decolonization and the Politics of Culture," in *Making a World after Empire: The Bandung Moment and Its Political Afterlives*, ed. Christopher J. Lee (Athens: Ohio University Press, 2010), 50.

3. BNA, DO35/4665, Commonwealth Relations Office (hereafter CRO), "Proposed Afro-Asian Conference to be held at Djakarta about February/March 1955," 17 November 1955.

4. Naoko Shimazu, "Diplomacy as Theatre: Staging the Bandung Conference of 1955," *Modern Asian Studies* 48, no. 1 (2013): 225–52; Robert Vitalis, "The Midnight Ride of Kwame Nkrumah and Other Fables of Bandung (Ban-Doong)," *Humanity* 4, no. 2 (2003): 263; Cindy Ewing, "The Colombo Powers: Crafting Diplomacy in the Third World and Launching Afro-Asia at Bandung," *Cold War History* 19, no. 1 (2019): 1–19; Hao Chen, "Resisting Bandung? Taiwan's Struggle for 'Representational Legitimacy' in the Rise of the Asian Peoples' Anti-Communist League, 1954–57," *International History Review* 43, no. 2 (2021): 244–63.

5. The hyphenated forms for "non-aligned" and "non-alignment" are used here since these were the forms that were most widely used in the 1960s, including in the official documents of the first two conferences of non-aligned countries in 1961 and 1964, see Simon Stevens, "Stevens on Rakove, 'Kennedy, Johnson, and the Nonaligned World,'" "H-1960s," *H-Net: Humanities and Social Sciences Online*, accessed January 4, 2022, https://networks.h-net.org/node/19474/reviews/37373/stevens-rakove-kennedy-johnson-and-nonaligned-world.

6. Vijay Prashad, *The Darker Nations: A People's History of the Third World* (New York: New Press, 2007), 14; Mark Philip Bradley, "Decolonization, the Global South and the Cold War, 1919–1962," in *The Cambridge History of the Cold War*, ed. Melvyn P. Leffler and Odd Arne Westad, vol. 1 (Cambridge: Cambridge University Press, 2010), 14, 34; Odd Arne Westad, *The Global Cold War: Third World Interventions and the Making of Our Times* (Cambridge: Cambridge University Press, 2005), 98; Lorenz M. Lüthi, *Cold Wars: Asia, the Middle East, Europe* (Cambridge: Cambridge University Press, 2020), 278–81; Jeffrey James Byrne, "From Bandung to Havana: Institutionalizing the Contentions of Postcolonial Internationalism," in *The League Against Imperialism: Lives and Afterlives*, ed. Michele Louro, Carolien Stolte, Heather Streets-Salter, and Sana Tannoury-Karam (Leiden: Leiden University Press, 2020), 371–96.

7. Adom Getachew, *Worldmaking after Empire: The Rise and Fall of Self-Determination* (Princeton, NJ: Princeton University Press, 2019), 87–88; Christopher R. W. Dietrich, *Oil Revolution: Anticolonial Elites, Sovereign Rights, and the Economic Culture of Decolonization* (Cambridge: Cambridge University Press, 2017), 66; see Seng Tan and Amitav Acharya, *Bandung Revisited: The Legacy of the 1955 Asian-African Conference for International Order* (Honolulu: University of Hawaii Press, 2009), 3–4.

8. Cary Fraser, "An American Dilemma: Race and Realpolitik in the American Response to the Bandung Conference, 1955," in *Window on Freedom: Race, Civil Rights, and Foreign Affairs, 1945–1988*, ed. Brenda Gayle Plummer (Chapel Hill: University of North Carolina Press, 2003), 115–40; Kevin Gaines, *American Africans in Ghana* (Chapel Hill: University of North Carolina Press, 2006); Brenda Gayle Plummer, "Introduction," in Plummer, ed., *Window on Freedom*, 1–20.

9. Arlene B. Tickner and Karen Smith, eds., *International Relations from the Global South: Worlds of Difference* (New York: Routledge, 2020).

10. Michele Louro, *Comrades against Imperialism: Nehru, India, and Interwar Internationalism* (New York: Cambridge University Press, 2018), 27.

11. DDEL, OCB Central File, WH Office, NSC Staff Papers 1948–1961, box 86, f: OCB 092.3 (File #2) (2) [April-November 1955], "Speech of Prime Minister Ali Sastroamidjojo of Indonesia," 12 May 1955, 4–5.

12. Frantz Fanon, *The Wretched of the Earth*, trans. Constance Farrington (New York: Grove Press, 2004 [1963]), 314; Prashad, *The Darker Nations*, xv–1.

13. Aimé Césaire, *Discourse on Colonialism*, trans. Joan Pinkham (New York: Monthly Review Press, 1972), 21–23.

14. David C. Engerman, *The Price of Aid: The Economic Cold War in India* (Cambridge, MA: Harvard University Press, 2018), 23; Brij Kishore Sharma, "Jawaharalal Nehru's Model of Development," *Proceedings of the Indian History Congress* 73 (2012): 1292–1302; Odd Arne Westad, *The Cold War: A World History* (New York: Basic Books, 2017), 424.

15. W. Arthur Lewis, *The Theory of Economic Growth* (London: George Allen & Unwin, 1955), 19–20; W. Arthur Lewis, "Report on Industrialisation and the Gold Coast" (Accra: Government Printing Department, 1953), 12; Robert L. Tignor, *W. Arthur Lewis and the Birth of Development Economics* (Princeton, NJ: Princeton University Press, 2006), x.

16. DDEL, OCB Central File, White House Office, NSC Staff Papers 1948–1961, box 86, "Bandung Conference of April, 1955," 12 May 1955, 3–4; Jack, *Bandung*, 5; "World Press Opinion," *Asian-African Conference Bulletin*, March 1955, 16.

17. Angadipuram Appadorai, "The Bandung Conference," *India Quarterly* 11, no. 3 (1955): 216.

18. Ewing, "The Colombo Powers," 5; Lüthi, *Cold Wars*, 267–268.

19. Antoinette Burton, "The Solidarities of Bandung: Toward a Critical 21st-Century History," in *Making a World after Empire: The Bandung Moment and Its Political Afterlives*, ed. Christopher J. Lee (Athens: Ohio University Press, 2010), 354; DDEL, OCB Central File, WH Office, NSC Staff Papers 1948–1961, box 86, f: OCB 092.3 (File #2) (2) [April-November 1955], "Speech of President Sukarno," 12 May 1955, 3/4; KNADS, AHC/1/33, memorandum, Minister of Information Broadcasting and Tourism, 22 October 1963.

20. Ashwin Desai and Goolam Vahed, *The South African Gandhi: Stretcher-Bearer of Empire* (Stanford, CA: Stanford University Press, 2016), 297.

21. Lydia Walker, "Decolonization in the 1960s: On Legitimate and Illegitimate Nationalist Claims-Making," *Past & Present* 242, no. 1 (2019): 244.

22. "Addresses by the Heads of Delegations," *Afro-Asian Conference Bulletin*, vol. 4, 19 April 1955; DDEL, OCB Central File, WH Office, NSC Staff Papers 1948–1961, box 86, "Speech of Prime Minister Ali Sastroamidjojo of Indonesia," 12 May 1955, 3; Colin Legum, *Bandung, Cairo and Accra: A Report on the First Conference of Independent African States* (London: Africa Bureau, 1958), 5; Vitalis, "The Midnight Ride of Kwame Nkrumah," 274; "Address by Heads of Delegations," *Asian-African Conference Bulletin*, April 19, 1955.

23. International Institute of Social History, Amsterdam (hereafter IISH), COLL00241, Robert J. Moon, "A New Age, Atomic Energy and Moral Re-armament," 20 February 1955.

24. William Mulligan and Maurice Bric, *A Global History of Anti-Slavery Politics in the Nineteenth Century* (London: Palgrave Macmillan, 2013), 2; DDEL, OCB Central File, WH Office, NSC staff papers 1948–1961, box 86, f: OCB 092.3 (File #2) (2) [April–November 1955], "Speech of President Sukarno," 12 May 1955, 3–4, "Speech by Mohammed Fadhil Jamali, Chief Delegate of Iraq," 12 May 1955, 3, "Speech on Colonialism by Sir John Kotelawala, Prime Minister of Ceylon," 12 May 1955, 3; BNA, FO371/116981, UK High Commissioner in Ceylon to CRO, 18 April 1955; NARA, RG.306, UD-WW 285, FRC5, f: General—Bandung Conf., Oscar Morland to FO, 20 April 1955; BNA, DO35/6098, Singapore to FO, 19 April 1955, FO371/116984, Nehru to Eden, 29 April 1955, FCO141/5051, British Embassy Djakarta to FO, 5 May 1955.

25. Appadorai, "The Bandung Conference," 229–30.

26. Anticolonial diplomacy is seen as a methodology, Jeffrey James Byrne, *Mecca of Revolution: Algeria, Decolonization, and the Third World Order* (Oxford: Oxford University Press, 2016), 14.

27. George McTurnan Kahin, *The Asian African Conference, Bandung, Indonesia, April 1955* (Ithaca, NY: Cornell University Press, 1956), 73–75; Appadorai, "The Bandung Conference," 233.

28. Vitalis, "The Midnight Ride of Kwame Nkrumah," 272.

29. Quoted in Sulmaan Wasif Khan, "Cold War Co-Operation: New Chinese Evidence on Jawaharlal Nehru's 1954 Visit to Beijing," *Cold War History* 11, no. 2 (2011): 201.

30. BNA, FO371/116983, R. W. Parkes, "Some Impressions of the Bandung Conference April 18–24," [April 1955], 8.

31. Archives of the North Atlantic Treaty Organization, Evere (hereafter NATO Archives), NATO/CR(55)21, "Summary Record of a Meeting of the Council held at the Palais Chaillot, Paris, XVIe," 10 May 1955; BNA, FO371/116984, British embassy Djakarta to FO, 30 April 1955; ASPFAE, AA, 12966/1955, Willy Stevens to Spaak, "Indonésie: Politique intérieure," 20 January 1955.

32. Westad, *The Cold War*, 432.

33. Kahin, *The Asian-African Conference*, 74–77; AMAE, DAO, Généralités, 124QO/190bis, "Conférence afro-asiatique," 6 January 1955; BNA, FO371/116975, W. D. Allen to Alan Lennox-Boyd, "Afro-Asian Conference," 6 January 1954; AMAE, DE1956–1960, 22QO/118bis, "Conférence de M. NAEGELEN sur le problème algérien et islamique," 10 November 1956; BNA, DO35/6097, FO to Middleton, [February 1955]; BNA, DO35/6098, Embassy of Kathmandu to F. S. Tomlinson, South-East Asia Department Foreign Office, 14 April 1955.

34. ASPFAE, 13.192 II, Bayens to Van Zeeland, "Buitenlandse politiek in Indonesië," 17 March 1954.

35. Westad, *The Global Cold War*, 99; Bill V. Mullen, *Afro-Orientalism* (Minneapolis: University of Minnesota Press, 2004), 65–66; Desai and Vahed, *The South African Gandhi*, 297.

36. BNA, CO936/347, minutes, W. A. C Mathieson for Gorell Barness, 31 December 1954, Alan Lennox-Boyd to Eden, 11 January 1955; BNA, FO371/116975, minutes, W. D. Allen for FO, "Afro-Asian Conference," 1 January 1955, telegram, Washington to FO, 31 December 1954, minutes, J. E. Cable, 6 January 1955, minutes, W. D. Allen, "Afro-Asian Conference," 3 January 1955; ASPFAE, AA, 13.192 II, Le Marquis du Parc Locmaria to Spaak, 24 September 1954.

37. Minutes of a Meeting, Secretary's Office, Department of State, Washington, 7 January 1955, *FRUS 1955–1957*, vol. 21, *East Asian Security*, 1–5; Memorandum from the acting chief of the reports and operations staff (Gilman) to the secretary of state, "Main Points of Attached Status Report on Afro-Asian Working Group," 8 February 1955, *FRUS 1955–1957*, vol. 21, *East Asian Security*, 29–30; DDEL, AWF, NSC Series, box 6, f: 230th Meeting of NSC, memdisc, "230th Meeting of the NSC," 5 January 1955.

38. NARA, RG.59, A1-1586-C, Lot 62D430, box 35 f: Bandung, memorandum for the undersecretary, 12 January 1955, OCB, "Reactions to the Afro-Asian Conference (Compiled by the OCB Staff)," [1955]; DDEL, Jackson, C. D.: Papers, 1931–1967, box 78, f: N-Misc. (1), "The Bandung Conference Thoughts and Recommendations," [1955]; DDEL, Jackson, C. D.: Papers, 1931–1967, box 78, f: N-Misc. (1), "The Bandung Conference Thoughts and Recommendations," [1955]; Official File, 1953–1961, WH Central Files, f: OF II6ffAsian-African Conference, box 503, memorandum for Honorable James C. Hagerty, 6 April 1955, memorandum for Governor Sherman Adams, 6 April 1955, Official file, "Proposed Comments by the president on economic program for South and East Asia, 1953–1961," 31 March 1953, memorandum for Governor Adams, "Proposed Presidential Speech before the Bandung Conference," 31 March 1953.

39. Report prepared by the NSC, "(NSC 5509): Status of United States Programs for National Security as of December 31, 1954," March 2, 1955, *FRUS 1955–1957*, vol. 9, *Foreign Economic Policy, Foreign Information Program*, 504–21; DDEL, US President's Committee on Information Activities Abroad Records, 1959–61, box 27, f: Minutes (2), "Notes on Mr. Bissell's Presentation," 15 March 1960; Memorandum prepared in the Office of African Affairs, "The United States in Africa South of the Sahara," 3 August 1955, *FRUS 1955–1957*, vol. 18, *Africa*, 13–22; Kenneth Osgood, *Total Cold War: Eisenhower's Secret Propaganda Battle at Home and Abroad* (Lawrence: University Press of Kansas, 2006), 355.

40. Despite the explicit reference to sarcasm in the transcript, "facetiously," historians have taken Eisenhower's remark seriously. For one example, see the work from which this quote is taken, Carol Anderson, "The Cold War in the Atlantic World," in *The Atlantic World, 1450–2000*, ed. Toyin Falola and Kevin David Roberts (Bloomington: Indiana University Press, 2008), 300.

41. Archives for Contemporary Affairs, University of the Free State, Bloemfontein (hereafter ACA-UFS), PV 188, f. 46, du Plessis, "Draft of an uncompleted despatch," June 1954, 5–6.

42. BNA, CO936/348, R. Makins to FO, 28 February 1955; Augusto Espiritu, "'To Carry Water on Both Shoulders': Carlos P. Romulo, American Empire, and the Meaning of Bandung," *Radical History Review*, no. 95 (2006): 177; Jason Parker, "Cold War II:

The Eisenhower Administration, the Bandung Conference, and the Reperiodization of the Postwar Era," *Diplomatic History* 30, no. 5 (2006): 888.

43. BNA, FO371/16975, minutes, C. R. A. Rae, "Afro-Asian Conference," 31 December 1954, note, E. M. West to A. A. W. Landymore, 4 March 1955; Memorandum of a conversation, Department of State, Washington, "Participation of African States in Afro-Asian Conference," 1 February 1955, *FRUS 1955–1957*, vol. 18, *Africa*, 1–2; BNA, FCO141/5051, telegram, StateDept, 31 December 1954; FO371/16975, minutes, J. E. Cable, 3 January 1955, Parkes to FO, 3 January 1955; BNA, FO371/116977, "Afro-Asian Conference," [January 1955]; BNA, FO371/116978, memorandum, "Afro-Asian Conference," 2 March 1955.

44. BNA, FCO141/505, governor to secretary of state, 8 January 1955, 2, secretary of state to governor, 21 January 1955.

45. Nkrumah is described as someone who abided by British rules, Kweku Ampiah, *The Political and Moral Imperatives of the Bandung Conference of 1955: The Reactions of the US, UK and Japan* (Folkestone: Global Oriental, 2007), 128.

46. AMAE, DAO, Généralités, 124QO/190bis, M. C. Renner to ministre des affaires etrangeres, "Conférence Afro-Asiatique," 26 January 1955; BNA, FCO141/5051, "Afro-Asian Conference," 2 May 1955, memcon, F. E. Cumming-Bruce, "Record of Talk with Mr. Dei-Anang," 2 May 1955; Public Records Archives and Administration Department, Accra (hereafter PRAAD), RG.17/2/800, Nkrumah to Nehru, 17 March 1955.

47. Quoted in Dietrich, *Oil*, 65.

48. Tony Chafer, *The End of Empire in French West Africa: France's Successful Decolonization?* (New York: Berg Publishers, 2002), 29, 145; AMAE, DAL Généralités, 49QONT/32, f: 32/1, "Bulletin d'information du mois de July 1955, émanant de la Direction d'Afrique-Levant Sous-Direction d'Afrique," 1955; BNA, FO371/116975, W. D. Allen to Alan Lennox-Boyd, "Afro-Asian Conference," 6 January 1954; AMAE, DAO, Généralités, 124QO/190, note, "La première Conférence afro-asiatique, Bandung—(Indonésie) 18 April 1955 par le commandant Rousset," 6 April 1955, 5; AMAE, DAO, Généralités, 124QO/190bis, note, "Le menace l'Asie surpeuplée," [1955], note for direction général des affaires politiques, "Conférence afro-asiatique," [January 1955].

49. Matthew Connelly, *A Diplomatic Revolution: Algeria's Fight for Independence and the Origins of the Post-Cold War Era* (Oxford: Oxford University Press, 2003), 81.

50. AMAE, DAO, Généralités, 142QO/190ter, Auge, "De la part de M.P. Devinat," 26 March 1955, note for cabinet du ministre, "Voyage en Asie de M. Devinat," 14 March 1955; BNA, FO371/116980, H. S. Stephenson to F. S. Tomlinson, 4 April 1955; AMAE, DAO, Généralités, 124QO/190, P. H. Teitgen to DAO, "Conférence Afro-Asiatque de Bandoeng," 6 April 1955.

51. BNA, FO371/116977, "Afro-Asian Conference," [January 1955]; quote taken from Nicholas Tarling, "'Ah-Ah': Britain and the Bandung Conference of 1955," *Journal of Southeast Asian Studies* 23, no. 1 (1992): 86.

52. AMAE, DAO, Généralités, 124QO/190bis, consul de France à Singapour to DAO, "Entretien avec M. Dudley," 31 January 1955, 6; this contradicts Tarling, "'Ah, Ah,'" 110.

53. Jean Roussel and J. Croux, trans., *Koloniale Plichtenleer* (Namen: Ad. Wesmael-Charlier, 1953), 63.

54. ASPFAE, AA, 13.192 II, Bayens to Spaak, "La prochain conférence Afrique-Asie est une tentative de grouper tous les peuples de couleur autour des idéaux de paix mondiale

et d'anticolonialisme," 31 December 1954, Louis de San to Paul Henri Spaak, 2 September 1954.

55. ASPFAE, AA, 2912, Buisseret to Brussels, 23 March 1955, Stevens to Spaak, 16 March 1955.

56. Tom Gallagher, *Salazar: The Dictator Who Refused to Die* (London: Hurst, 2020), 175.

57. AHU, DG Administração e Política Civil, Cx 799, Chefe do Gabinete do Ministro do Ultramar to Ministério dos Negócios Estrangeiros Direcção Geral dos Negócios Políticos e da Administração Interna, 27 October 1955, 5 October 1955; Alessandro Iandolo, "Soviet Policy in West Africa, 1957–64" (PhD diss., University of Oxford, 2011), 78.

58. Memorandum of a Conversation between President Eisenhower and Prime Minister Nehru, 19 December 1956, *FRUS 1955–1957*, vol. 8, *South Asia*, 331–41.

59. Quote taken from William Glenn Gray, *Germany's Cold War: The Global Campaign to Isolate East Germany, 1949–1969* (Chapel Hill: University of North Carolina Press, 2003), 21; Quinn Slobodian, "Bandung in Divided Germany: Managing Non-Aligned Politics in East and West, 1955–63," *Journal of Imperial and Commonwealth History* 41, no. 4 (2013): 644–62.

60. ASPFAE, AA, 13.192 II, Arthur Wauter to Spaak, "La pression Soviétique sur les Neutres d'Asie," 24 September 1954.

61. BNA, FO371/116650, "Molotov, speech to the Supreme Soviet," February 1955.

62. Khrushchev's insistence that these leaders were still part of the bourgeoisie has most convincingly been argued by Iandolo, "Soviet Policy," 77; Philip Muehlenbeck, *Czechoslovakia in Africa, 1945–1968* (London: Palgrave Macmillan, 2015), 92; Sergey Mazov, *A Distant Front in the Cold War: The USSR in West Africa and the Congo, 1956–1964* (Stanford, CA: Stanford University Press, 2010), 13; Národní archiv, Prague (hereafter NA-A), Antonin Novotny, Egypt(SAR) 7, Příloha Kčj M-006530-1955, [1955].

63. "Report from the Asia Section, Chinese Foreign Ministry, 'On the Asian-African Conference,' 15 December 1954, History and Public Policy Program Digital Archive, PRC FMA 207-00085-17, 144–149. Obtained by Amitav Acharya and translated by Yang Shanhou," accessed 30 March 2020, https://digitalarchive.wilsoncenter.org/document /112442; "Report by the Chinese Foreign Ministry, 'Some Existing Issues in and Suggestions for the Asia-Africa Conference,' 1955, History and Public Policy Program Digital Archive, PRC FMA 207-00004-06, 59–62. Obtained by Amitav Acharya and translated by Yang Shanhou," accessed 30 March 2020, https://digitalarchive.wilsoncenter.org/docu ment/113179; "Summary of the Informal Discussion on Information Material Work during China's Preparation for the Asian-African Conference, January 17, 1955, History and Public Policy Program Digital Archive, PRC FMA 207-00020-01. Obtained by Amitav Acharya and translated by Yang Shanhou," accessed 30 March 2020, https://digita larchive.wilsoncenter.org/document/114635.

64. Sergei Khrushchev, ed., *Memoirs of Nikita Khrushchev*, vol. 3, *Statesman, 1953–1964* (University Park: Penn State University Press, 2013), 725, 727.

65. Alessandro Iandolo, *Arrested Development: The Soviet Union in Ghana, Guinea, and Mali, 1955–1968* (Ithaca, NY: Cornell University Press, 2022), 46.

66. BAHDMNE, PAA 214, f: Circular No. 14 Textos de Declaração e Resoluçao, "Conferência dos estados Africanos (Accra—Abril, 1958)," July 1958.

67. Telegram from Delegation at the North Atlantic Council Ministerial Meeting to the Department of State, May 11, 1955, *FRUS 1955–1957*, vol. 27, *Western Europe and Canada*, 442–443; ASPFAE, AA, 364, Roger Malengreau to Spaak, "La conference Afro-Asiatique de Bandung," 19 April 1955, 2–3; ASPFAE, AA, 1370, Direction Générale de la Politique Direction P.I./D No,Aff.Col./3060, "La Conference Afro-Asiatique de Bandoeng (18–22 Avril 1955)," 27 April 1955; ASPFAE, AA, 12966/1955, Stevens to Spaak, "La conférence de Bandung a condamné le colonialism," 27 April 1955.

68. AMAE, DAL Généralités, 49QONT/32, f: 32/1, "Bulletin d'information du mois de July 1955, émanant de la Direction d'Afrique-Levant Sous-Direction d'Afrique," 1955; DAO Généralités, 124QO/274, f: Chine, Conférence de Bandung, Affaire de Formose, note, "Conférence de Bandung Affaire de Formose," 6 May 1955.

69. BNA, FO371/116985, Roger Makins to FO, 12 May 1955; CO 936/350, notes, Geoffrey Caston, 24 May 1955; DDEL, WH Office, OCB central file, box 86, "Bandung Conference of April, 1955," 12 May 1955.

70. Quotes taken from BNA, FO371/116984, British Embassy Djakarta to FO, 5 May 1955; BNA, FCO141/5051, British Embassy Djakarta to FO, 5 May 1955, memcon, F. E. Cumming-Bruce, "Record of Talk with Mr. Dei-Anang," 2 May 1955; BNA, FO371/116981, Djakarta to FO, 22 April 1955; Tarling, "'Ah Ah,'" 109.

71. Westad argues the final communiqué's significance stemmed from the principles it prescribed, Westad, *The Global Cold War*, 102. Bandung generally generated little response in France: Parker, "Cold War II," 891–92; Tarling, "'Ah Ah,'" 108–11; Amady Aly Dieng, *Les grands combats de la Fédération des étudiants d'Afrique noire de Bandung aux indépendances, 1955–1960* (Paris: L'I Iarmattan, 2009), 1–15; Jack, *Bandung*, 1–10; Kahin, *The Asian-African Conference*, 1–38; Carlos P. Romulo, *The Meaning of Bandung* (Chapel Hill: University of North Carolina Press, 1956), 177.

72. "Nous ne pourrons éviter longtemps la confrontation. Si nous la refusons, elle se fera": AMAE, DAL, Généralités 1953–1959, 49QONT/66, Leopold Senghor, "Voyage officiel en Afrique occidentale britannique, du secrétaire d'état à la Présidence du Conseil 22 Septembre—7 October 1955," October 1955, 21; Babacar M'Baye, "Richard Wright and African Francophone Intellectuals: A Reassessment of the 1956 Congress of Black Writers in Paris," in *African Diaspora and the Metropolis: Reading the African, African American and Caribbean Experience*, ed. Fassil Demissie (New York: Routledge, 2013), 36–37.

73. Chafer, *The End of Empire*, 93, 16; Richard Watts, "Negritude, Présence Africaine, Race," in *Postcolonial Thought in the French-Speaking World*, ed. Charles Forsdick and David Murphy (Liverpool: Liverpool University Press, 2009), 227–37.

74. Khrushchev's insistence that nationalist leaders were still part of the bourgeoisie has most convincingly been argued by Iandolo, "Soviet Policy," 77, 116; Vladislav M. Zubok, *A Failed Empire: The Soviet Union in the Cold War from Stalin to Gorbachev* (Chapel Hill: University of North Carolina Press, 2008), 103; Khrushchev, *Memoirs of Nikita Khrushchev*, vol. 3, 723, 877; Iandolo, *Arrested Development*, 47–48; Natalia Telepneva, "Mediators of Liberation: Eastern-Bloc Officials, Mozambican Diplomacy and the Origins of Soviet Support for Frelimo, 1958–1965," *Journal of Southern African Studies* 43, no. 1 (2017): 71–72.

75. Gregg A. Brazinsky, *Winning the Third World: Sino-American Rivalry during the Cold War* (Chapel Hill: University of North Carolina Press, 2017), 104.

76. Vladislav M. Zubok, *A Failed Empire: The Soviet Union in the Cold War from Stalin to Gorbachev* (Chapel Hill: University of North Carolina Press, 2008), 103.

77. NARA, RG.59, A1-1587-M, box 63, f: Nationalism, memorandum for Andrew Berding, 9 May 1955; RG.306, UD-WW 285, FRC5, f: Afro-Asian Conference—1956, Circular, 22 May 1956; £271,560 for the BC, £133,850 for the COI, £130,000 for the BBC, £64,000 for the CRO, £27,500 for the Foreign Office Information Service, and £23,000 for the Colonial Office Information Service, see BNA, CO1027/72, draft paper for OIS (Official) Committee, "The Overseas Information Services Prospects for Expansion in 1956/1957," [1955]; David Goldsworthy, ed., "The Conservative Government and the End of Empire 1951–1957," *British Documents on the End of Empire* (hereafter *BDEE*), vol. 3, part 1, no. 169 (1994), 408–411; BNA, CO1027/72, Anthony Eden, "Colonial Publicity," 6 August 1954.

78. BNA, CO1027/72, H. T. Bourdillon to I. T. M. Pink, "Proposed General Assembly Speech Defending Colonialism," 24 September 1956.

79. H. T. Bourdillon to I. T. M. Pink, 30 October 1956, in Goldsworthy, "The Conservative Government and the End of Empire 1951–1957," 415 (no. 171); BNA, CO1027/74, minutes, Watrous for Evans, 16 March 1954; BNA, INF12/978, CO, "Information Activities Undertaken by the Colonial Office in the African Territories," [1958].

80. KNADS, AHC/10/83, Pamphlet, "If You Ask Me," November 1955, 161, vol. 4, no. 5, memorandum, director of information, 30 November 1955.

81. ASPFAE, AA, 12966/1955, Stevens to Spaak, 22 April 1955, Stevens to Spaak, 27 April 1955, "Sorte de libération nouvelle des griffes de l'accident," in Stevens to Spaak, 28 April 1955, 1, d'Aspermont Lynden to Spaak, 30 April 1955, 1.

82. BAHDMNE, SR.035 1957–1968, SR 035 1957–1968, Pt. 1, 1957/NOV/21–1964/ JUL/31, PAA 214, f: Circular No. 14 Textos de Declaração e Resoluçao, "Conferência dos estados Africanos (Accra—Abril, 1958)," July 1958; Jacob Mundy, "The Geopolitical Functions of the Western Sahara Conflict: US Hegemony, Moroccan Stability and Sahrawi Strategies of Resistance," in *Global, Regional and Local Dimensions of Western Sahara's Protracted Decolonization: When a Conflict Gets Old*, ed. Raquel Ojeda-Garcia, Irene Fernández-Molina, and Victoria Veguilla (London: Palgrave Macmillan, 2016), 53–78; Sara Marzagora, "Ethiopian Intellectual History and the Global: Käbbädä Mikael's Geographies of Belonging," *Journal of World Literature* 4, no. 1 (2019): 108.

83. Kate Morris, *British Techniques of Public Relations and Propaganda for Mobilizing East and Central Africa during World War II* (Lewiston, NY: Edwin Mellen Press, 2000), 210.

84. Memorandum from the Secretary of State to the President, May 14, 1956, *FRUS 1955–1957*, vol. 22, *Southeast Asia*, 267–268; Robert B. Rakove, *Kennedy, Johnson, and the Nonaligned World* (Cambridge: Cambridge University Press, 2012), 3; Egya Sangmuah, "Eisenhower and Containment in North Africa, 1956–1960," *Middle East Journal* 44, no. 1 (1990): 77.

85. Quoted in Vitalis, "The Midnight Ride of Kwame Nkrumah," 276; Scott Thompson, *Ghana's Foreign Policy, 1957–1966: Diplomacy, Ideology, and the New State* (Princeton, NJ: Princeton University Press, 1969), 46.

86. Legum, *Bandung, Cairo and Accra*, 6, 13.

87. Quoted in Ama Biney, *The Political and Social Thought of Kwame Nkrumah* (London: Palgrave Macmillan, 2011), 163.

88. KNADS, MAC/CON/181/5, Homer Jack, "Towards Freedom," vol. 8, no. 1, January 1959, 3.

89. Quoted in Gerard McCann, "Where Was the Afro in Afro-Asian Solidarity? Africa's 'Bandung Moment' in 1950s Asia," *Journal of World History* 30, no. 1–2 (2019): 118.

90. Michael Dei-Anang, *The Administration of Ghana's Foreign Relations, 1957–1965: A Personal Memoir* (London: Athlone Press, 1975), 20; Thompson, *Ghana's Foreign Policy*, 39.

91. NARA, RG.306, P249, box 10, f: Policy—French Atomic Tests [Folder 1/2], Washburn to African posts, "Emergency Conference For Peace and Security in Africa," 1 April 1960.

92. Kwame Nkrumah, *Ghana: The Autobiography of Kwame Nkrumah* (Edinburgh: T. Nelson, 1957), 46–47.

93. ACA-UFS, PV188, f. 46, Persoonlijk, du Plessis to Louw, 18 Augustus 1956; Marzagora, "Ethiopian Intellectual History and the Global," 107.

94. Ebere Nwaubani, *The United States and Decolonization in West Africa, 1950–1960* (Rochester, NY: University of Rochester Press, 2001), 99.

95. For a historiographical overview: Frank Gerits, "Hungry Minds: The Eisenhower Administration and Cultural Assistance in Sub-Saharan Africa (1953–1961)," *Diplomatic History* 1, no. 3 (2017): 4–5.

96. Mazov, *A Distant Front*, 254; David C. Engerman, *Modernization from the Other Shore: American Intellectuals and the Romance of Russian Development* (Cambridge MA: Harvard University Press, 2004).

97. Alain Dubosclard, *L'action artistique*, 350–51; Jennifer M. Dueck, "International Rivalry and Culture in Syria and Lebanon under the French Mandate," in *Searching for a Cultural Diplomacy*, ed. Jessica C. Gienow-Hecht and Mark C. Donfried (New York: Berghahn Books, 2010), 151–52; Jennifer M. Dueck, *The Claims of Culture at Empire's End: Syria and Lebanon Under French Rule* (Oxford: Oxford University Press, 2009), 4; Louis Dollot, *Les relations culturelles internationales* (Paris: Presses Universitaires de France, 1964); Carl Doka, *Les relations culturelles sur le plan international* (Neuchâtel: La Baconnière, 1959); Annie Angrémy, *La diplomatie culturelle de la France* (Strasbourg: Conseil de la coopération culturelle du Conseil de l'Europe, 1970); Suzanne Balous, *L'action culturelle de la France dans le monde: Préf. de Maurice Genevoix* (Paris: Presses universitaires de France, 1970), 175–177; Albert Salon, *L'action culturelle de la France dans le monde* (Paris: Fernand Nathan, 1983); Tony Shaw, *Eden, Suez and the Mass Media: Propaganda and Persuasion during the Suez Crisis* (London: I.B.Tauris, 1996), 169, 189–92; James Vaughan, *The Failure of American and British Propaganda in the Arab Middle East, 1945–57: Unconquerable Minds* (London: Palgrave Macmillan, 2005), 248–49.

98. Matthew Connelly, "Taking Off the Cold War Lens: Visions of North-South Conflict during the Algerian War for Independence," *American Historical Review* 105, no. 3 (2000): 739–40.

99. ACA-UFS, PV188, f: 46, W. C. du Plessis, "Draft of an Uncompleted Despatch," June 1954, 3.

100. Dwight D. Eisenhower, "Address and Remarks at the Baylor University Commencement Ceremonies, Waco, Texas," 25 May 1956, *The American Presidency Project*, ed. Gerhard Peters and John T. Woolley, accessed 5 March 2019, http://www.presidency.ucsb.edu/ws/?pid=10499.

101. NARA, RG.306, UD-WW 285, box 1, f: country objectives, Robert G. McGregor to USIA, "Country Objectives," s.d.; NARA, RG.59, A1-3112-J, box 1, f: Correspondence Reg, Robert G. McGregor to George V. Allen, 21 March 1956; NARA, RG.306, A1-1072, box 9, f: African Program, Historical Background 1970, Peter L. Koffsky, "The United States Information Program in Africa, 1945–1970: A History & Interpretation," 2-1.

102. NARA, RG.306, A1-1072, box 8, J. L. Morril, "A Proposal for the Coordination of the Exchange of Persons Programs of the International Educational Exchange Service and of the International Cooperation Administration," 1 May 1956; NARA, RG.306, P257, box 2, f: ICA Memoranda (IAN) 1953–1956, Andrew Berding and William J. Handley, "USIS-ICA Cooperation in the NEA Area," 19 December 1955; NARA, RG.306, UD-WW285, FRC 2, f: ICA, D. G. MacDonald, executive secretary, "Conference of African and European Missions Directors, Program Officers and Executive Officers— Madrid," 12 March 1960.

103. BNA, CO1035/17, confidential memorandum, IRD, 1 August 1956; BNA, CO1035/126, "Soviet Penetration of Africa," February 1956, minutes, Mr. Watson, Mr. Carstairs, 10 May 1956.

104. Renner admitted the Soviet influence was negligible, see AMAE, DAL, Ghana 1953–1965, 50QO/6, Renner to DAL, "Congrès anti-colonial," 25 March 1955; BNA, CO1035/120, Gladwyn Jebb to Selwyn Lloyd, 31 October 1956.

105. AMAE, DAL, Généralités 1953–1959, 49QONT/66, Senghor, "Voyage officiel en Afrique," 21, 2; Connelly, A Diplomatic Revolution, 92–93.

106. Filipe Ribeiro de Meneses, Salazar: A Political Biography (New York: Enigma Books, 2010), 450.

107. ASPFAE, AA, 2912, Eeman to Spaak, "Soudan," 24 February 1955.

108. BNA, CO1035/126, Note for C.Y. Carstairs, 2 July 1956.

109. AMAE, DAL, Généralités 1953–1959, 49QONT/66, Paul Raymond to DAL, "Requitte adressée à M. Senghor," 12 November 1955; AMAE, DAL, Généralités 1953–1959, 49QONT/52, memcon, "Relations culturelles entre les territoires d'Afrique Occidentale Française et les Territoires Britanniques," 30 November 1955; Watts, "Negritude, Présence Africaine, Race," 227–29.

110. ANS, Dossier Senghor, f: 1945–1955 Extraits du Rapport présenté par L. S. Senghor Secrétaire à la Présidence du Conseil à la suite de sa mission dans les territoires l'Afrique sans centre britannique (22 sept–6 oct 1955), report, s.d., 2; "L'indépendance de l'esprit, l'indépendance culturelle, est le préalable nécessaire aux autres indépendances: politique, économique et sociale," in ANS, Dossier Senghor, Dossier 1 1937–1960, f: unnamed, "La Foie Africaine de Socialisme (Essai de définition) par Léopold Sedar Senghor," s.d.

111. AMAE, DAL, Généralités 1953–1959, 49QONT/66, Senghor, "Voyage officiel en Afrique," 14.

112. Alain Dubosclard, Histoire de la fédération des Alliances Françaises aux Etats-Unis (Paris: L'Harmattan, 1998), 155; AMAE, DAL, Généralités 1952–1959, 94QONT/66, Pinay to Senghor, "Voyage officiel de M. Senghor en Afrique Occidentale Britannique," 23 December 1955, DGRC to DAL, "Récente mission de M. Senghor en Afrique Occidentale Britannique," 26 November 1955, 1.

113. ANS, Dossier Senghor, f: 1945–1955 Extraits du Rapport présenté par L. S. Senghor Secrétaire à la Présidence du Conseil à la suite de sa mission dans les territoires l'Afrique sans centre britannique (22 sept—6 oct 1955), untitled document, s.d., 3.

114. Eisenhower to Barbara Bates Gunderson, 7 June 1956, Louis Galambos and Daun Van Ee, *The Papers of Dwight David Eisenhower* (Baltimore: John Hopkins University Press, 2001), vol. 17, 218; quote in Eisenhower, "Address and Remarks at the Baylor University."

115. Eisenhower, "Address and Remarks at the Baylor University." On Eisenhower's Wilsonianism: Steven Metz, "Eisenhower and the Planning of American Grand Strategy," *Journal of Strategic Studies* 14, no. 1 (1991): 49.

116. Samuel Hale Butterfield, *U.S. Development Aid—An Historic First: Achievements and Failures in the Twentieth Century* (Westport, CT: Praeger, 2004), 51; Hannah Nicole Higgin, "Disseminating American Ideals in Africa, 1949–1969" (PhD diss., Cambridge University, 2014), 25; Sergei Y. Shenin, *The United States and the Third World: The Origins of Postwar Relations and the Point Four Program* (New York: Nova Science Publishers, 1999), 23.

117. ACA-UFS, PV 188, f. 46, du Plessis to Louw, 18 August 1956.

118. KNADS, MAC/CON/193/1, "Address by His Excellency Professor Raden Supomo, Indonesian Ambassador in London Given at the Islamic Cultural Centre," 6 August 1955, 5.

119. Memdisc at the 226th meeting of the NSC, December 1, 1954, *FRUS 1952–1954*, vol. 24, part 1, *China and Japan*, 971–5; memdisc at the 273rd meeting of the NSC, 18 January 1956, *FRUS 1955–1957*, vol. 10, *Foreign Economic Policy*, 64–68.

120. Report by the Executive Secretary to the NSC on Basic NSC Security Policy NSC 162/2, 30 October 1953, *FRUS 1952–1954*, vol. 2, part 1, *National Security Affairs*, 577–97.

121. Memorandum prepared in the Office of African Affairs, "The United States in Africa South of the Sahara," 4 August 1955, *FRUS 1955–1957*, vol. 18, *Africa*, 21.

122. NARA, RG.469, P206, box 13, f: Aid for Africa South of the Sahara (Randall Report), memorandum to Council on Foreign Economic Policy, "CFEP 568—United States Foreign Economic Policy for Africa South of the Sahara," 5 June 1958, 2; Michael R. Adamson, "'The Most Important Single Aspect of Our Foreign Policy'?: The Eisenhower Administration, Foreign Aid, and the Third World," in *The Eisenhower Administration, the Third World, and the Globalization of the Cold War*, ed. Kathryn C. Statler and Andrew L. Johns (Lanham, MD: Rowman & Littlefield, 2006), 63.

123. KNADS, AHC 29/11, Robert W. C. Brown to Alistair Metheson, 14 January 1956; David E. Apter, *Ghana in Transition* (New York: Atheneum, 1955), 3.

124. Vaughan makes the opposite argument; see Vaughan, *The Failure of American and British Propaganda in the Arab Middle East*, 247; BNA, BW151/17, "The British Council: Annual Report 1955–1956," 1956, 25; BNA, CO1027/72, "The Overseas Information Services Prospects for Expansion in 1956/1957," [1956].

125. It was admitted that only twenty-two Europeans and thirty-three Africans in the Gold Coast had a known connection with Communism; BNA, PREM11/1367, minutes, Prime Minister, 1 September 1955; BNA, CO1035/120, "Communism in the Gold Coast," s.d.

126. Jef Van Bilsen, *Kongo 1945–1965: Het Einde van Een Kolonie* (Leuven: Davidsfonds, 1993), 108; Jef Van Bilsen, "Een Dertigjarenplan Voor de Politieke Ontvoogding van Belgisch Afrika," *De Gids Op Maatschappelijk Gebied* 12 (1955): 999–1028; Vanthemsche, *Congo*, 86; Université catholique du Louvain, Louvain-la-Neuve (hereafter UCL), Van Zeeland, box 807, Van Zeeland, "Impressions recuellies au cours d'un voyage au Congo, du 14 décembre 1956 au 17 janvier 1957," January 1957.

127. ASPFAE, AA, INFO(59), "Note sur la création du 'Centre Culturel du Congo Belge,'" [1956]; Miguel Bandeira Jéronimo, *The "Civilising Mission" of Portuguese Colonialism, 1870–1930* (London: Palgrave Macmillan, 2015), 96.

128. Filipe Ribeiro De Meneses and Robert McNamara, *The White Redoubt, the Great Powers and the Struggle for Southern Africa, 1960–1980* (London: Palgrave Macmillan, 2018), 10; Centre des archives d'outre-mer, Aix-en-Provence (hereafter CAOM), 2261/2, Affaires Politiques, memcon, "Proces Verbal de la Conférence Interterritoriale sur les principaux problèmes Musulmans," 31 January 1955, Ministère de la France d'outre-mer, "La propaganda islamique dans les milieux africains," 11 June 1955; AMAE, DAL, Ghana 1953–1959, 50QO/8, Victor Gares to DAL, "Voyage à Abidjan des élèves de l'Ecole Secondaire de Tamale, Gold Coast," 6 August 1956, note pour le Secrétaire General, "Création à Accra du poste d'information," 5 April 1956; AMAE, DGRCST, Echanges Culturels, 1956–1959, 241QO/254, P. Barbusse to Alioune Diop, 15 September 1956.

129. BNA, CO1027/74, minutes, Watrous for Evans, 16 March 1954; BNA, CO1027/72, "The Overseas Information Services Prospects for Expansion in 1956/1957," [1955]; BNA, INF12/978, CO, "Information activities undertaken by the Colonial Office in the African territories," [1958]; BNA, BW151/17, "The British Council Annual Report 1955–1956," 1956, 8.

130. BNA, CO1027/74, "Working Party on Future Development Finance," [1956]; NARA, RG.59, CDF1950–1954, 511.45K/12-2656–511.45R5/8-1255, "Thematic Cooperation VOA and British Broadcasting Facilities," 8 May 1956; Karen Bell, "Developing a 'Sense of Community': U.S. Cultural Diplomacy and the Place of Africa during the Early Cold War Period 1953–54," in *The United States and West Africa: Interactions and Relations*, ed. Alusine Jalloh and Toyin Falola (Rochester, NY: University of Rochester Press, 2008), 132.

131. Quote taken from Mazov, *A Distant Front*, 26; Philipp Casula, "The Soviet Afro-Asian Solidarity Committee and Soviet Perceptions of the Middle East during Late Socialism," *Cahiers du monde russe* 59, no. 4 (2018): 499.

132. DDEL, Washburn Papers, f: Educational Development 1961 (3), box 12, President's Committee on Information Activities Abroad, "A Program for International Educational Development," August 8, 1960, 1, 5; NARA, RG.59, A1-5082, box 3, f: Educational & Cultural Exchange, "Progress Report on Activities of the OCB Inter-Agency Committee on the President's Baylor Proposals," 26 June 1957, 1–2, 4, 7; NARA, RG.59, A1-5082, box 3, f: Educational & Cultural Exchange, Charles Johnson, "Progress Report on Activities of the OCB Inter-Agency Committee on the President's Baylor Proposals," 17 July 1957.

133. NARA, RG.59, A1-5082, box 3, f: Educational & Cultural Exchange, Paul Geren, "Conference on Implementation of the Baylor Proposal," 1956, 3, 8.

134. NARA, RG.306, UD-WW285, FRC 2, f: ICA, Marcus Gordon, "Activities of the ICA in Africa in the Education and Cultural Fields," 23 November 1959, 13; NARA, RG.306, UD-WW285, FRC 2, f: Regional, Saxton Bradford to John Noon, "Exchange of Information on Activities in the Educational and Cultural Field in Africa," 17 December 1959, 1–3.

135. Adamson, "'The Most Important Single Aspect of Our Foreign Policy'?," 63, 51; DDEL, AWF, NSC Series, box 11, f: 410th, memdisc of the 410th Meeting of the NSC, 18 June 1959, 4; JFKL, Africa: General, 9/29/61–10/31/61, National Security Files, Papers

as President, box 2, George Ball, "Report to the President on Sub-Sahara African Student Programs," 13 October 1961; NARA, RG.469, P206, box 13, f: Aid for Africa South of the Sahara, "CFEP 568—United States Foreign Economic Policy for Africa South of the Sahara," 5 June 1958, 2.

136. Ray Takeyh, *The Origins of the Eisenhower Doctrine: The US, Britain and Nasser's Egypt, 1953–57* (New York: Macmillan Press, 2000), ix–26.

137. Salim Yaqub, *Containing Arab Nationalism: The Eisenhower Doctrine and the Middle East* (Chapel Hill: University of North Carolina Press, 2004), 1–2.

138. DDEL, AWF, Papers as President 1952–1961, NSC Series, box 8, f: 302nd Meeting of the NSC, memdisc at the 302nd Meeting of the NSC, 1 November 1956.

139. NARA, RG.306, P253, box 2, Mr. Damon and William J. Handley, "Psychological Implementation of Eisenhower Doctrine," 2 January 1957; AMAE, DA, Etats-Unis 1952–1963, 91QO/433, Charles Luce to Christian Pineau, "Doctrine Eisenhower et l'Afrique," 5 April 1957, 10–11.

140. NARA, RG.469, P206, box 15, f: Africa (Uganda—Delgado Trades—1958-Contract) Technical Inst., Sudan Government and Communism Statement by Foreign Minister, 19 September 1957.

141. ACA-UFS, PV188, f. 46, du Plessis to Louw, 18 August 1956.

142. Paul Hoffman, "Blueprint for Foreign Aid," *New York Times Magazine*, February 17, 1957, 38; Secretary of the Treasury (Humphrey) to the Chairman of the Council on Foreign Economic Policy, March 20, 1957, *FRUS 1955–1957*, vol. 10, *Foreign Aid and Economic Defense Policy*, 177.

143. Eisenhower to Humphrey, March 27, 1957, *The Papers of Dwight David Eisenhower*, vol. 17, 115–117; Eisenhower to Frank Altschul, October 25, 1957, *The Papers of Dwight David Eisenhower*, vol. 18, 512; Hoffman, "Blueprint for Foreign Aid," 43; Max F. Millikan and Walt W. Rostow, *A Proposal: Key to an Effective Foreign Policy* (New York: Harper, 1957), 38.

144. Stephen E. Ambrose, *Eisenhower: The President 1952–1959* (London: George Allen & Unwin, 1948), 2, 387.

145. DDEL, AWF, NSC Series, box 12, memdisc of the 432nd Meeting of the NSC, 14 January 1960; NARA, RG.306, A1-1072, box 9, f: African Program, Historical Background 1970, Peter L. Koffsky, "The United States Information Program in Africa, 1945–1970: A History & Interpretation," p. 2-1; NARA, CDF1955–59, 611.451/2-955–611.47231/3-3058, USLO Khartoum, "U.S. Policy Towards the Sudan," 16 August 1955.

146. Sergei Y. Shenin, *America's Helping Hand: Paving the Way to Globalization (Eisenhower's Foreign Aid Policy and Politics)* (New York: Nova Publishers, 2005), 201; NARA, RG.469, P36, box 3, f: Africa Fund, Arthur L. Richards and Jane M. Alden, "Relations of Mutual Security Act Amendment to the President's Baylor Proposals," s.d.

147. Centre historique des archives nationales, Cedex, Paris (hereafter CHAN), Ministère de la coopération, direction de la coopération technique et culturelle, 19810443/57, "Coopération interafricaine: Dixième anniversaire CCTA/CSA—FAMA," 1960.

148. Michael Goebel, *Anti-Imperial Metropolis: Interwar Paris and the Seeds of Third World Nationalism* (New York: Cambridge University Press, 2015), 283.

149. Walt W. Rostow, *The Stages of Economic Growth: A Non-Communist Manifesto* (Cambridge: Cambridge University Press, 1960), 27.

3. The Pan-African Path to Modernity, 1957–1958

1. British Broadcasting Corporation Written Archives Centre, Caversham (hereafter BBCWAC), E1/1,433/1, A. R. Phillips to C. G. Johnson, 28 February 1957, Ghana Information Services, "The World Press and Ghana Independence," 23 March 1957; information professionals in Accra were E. Sawyer of USIA, H. Andrews of the Liberian Bureau of Information, L. Fleming of the BBC, Jack Allen from Reuters, Claude Wauthier of Agence-France-Presse, Vasily Kisselev of *Pravda*, Alex Riveria of the *Pittsburgh Courier*, and Akim Emiola of *Nigeria Tribune*.

2. BBCWAC, E1/1,433/1, J. B. Millar to Bernard Moore, 25 March 1957, Ghana Information Services, "The World Press and Ghana Independence," 23 March 1957, Director of Information Services, "Ghana Independence Celebrations: List of Fully Accredited Overseas and Local Correspondents," 6 March 1957, draft, "Opening Announcement for 'The Birth of Ghana,'" s.d.

3. BBCWAC, E1/1,435/1, note, director general BBC London, 5 November 1958.

4. That same night he opened the Ghana Museum; Moorland-Spingarn Research Centre, Howard University, Washington, DC (hereafter MSRC), Nkrumah Papers, box 154-38, f: 21, transcript, "Prime Minister's Midnight Speech on the Eve of Independence," 6 March 1957; "Ghana's Foreign Policy Will Not Be Dictated by the Need for Aid," *Ghana Today*, March 20, 1957, vol. 1, no. 2, 2; George P. Hagan, "Nkrumah's Cultural Policy," in *The Life and Work of Kwame Nkrumah: Papers of a Symposium Organized by the Institute of African Studies, University of Ghana, Legon*, ed. Kwame Arhin (Trenton, NJ: Africa World Press, 1993), 1.

5. Scott Thompson, *Ghana's Foreign Policy, 1957–1966: Diplomacy, Ideology, and the New State* (Princeton, NJ: Princeton University Press, 1969), 418; Ebere Nwaubani, *The United States and Decolonization in West Africa, 1950–1960* (Rochester, NY: University of Rochester Press, 2001), 119–63.

6. Kofi Batsa, *The Spark: From Kwame Nkrumah to Hilla Limann* (London: Rex Collings, 1985); Michael Dei-Anang, *The Administration of Ghana's Foreign Relations, 1957–1965: A Personal Memoir* (London: Athlone Press, 1975); Kwesi Armah, *Africa's Golden Road* (London: Heinemann, 1965); J. H. Frimpong-Ansah, *The Vampire State in Africa: The Political Economy of Decline in Ghana* (Trenton, NJ: Africa World Press, 1991); Opoku Agyeman, *Nkrumah's Ghana and East Africa: Pan-Africanism and African Interstate Relations* (Teaneck, NJ: Fairleigh Dickinson University Press, 1992); Kofi Buenor Hadjor, *Nkrumah and Ghana: The Dilemma of Post-Colonial Power* (London: Kegan Paul International, 1988), 99–105; David Rooney, *Kwame Nkrumah: Vision and Tragedy* (Accra: Sub-Saharan Publishers, 2007); Basil Davidson, *Black Star: A View of the Life and Times of Kwame Nkrumah* (London: Allen Lane, 1973), 1–15.

7. Boni Yao Gebe, "Ghana's Foreign Policy at Independence and Implications for the 1966 Coup d'état," *Journal of Pan African Studies* 2, no. 3 (2008): 160–86; Ama Biney, *The Political and Social Thought of Kwame Nkrumah* (London: Palgrave Macmillan, 2011); Ama Biney, "The Legacy of Kwame Nkrumah in Retrospect," *Journal of Pan African Studies*, no. 2 (2008); David Birmingham, *Kwame Nkrumah: The Father of African Nationalism* (Athens: Ohio University Press, 1998); Aremu Johnson Olaosebikan, "Kwame Nkrumah and the Proposed African Common Government," *African Journal of Political Science and International Relations* 5, no. 4 (2011): 218–28; Marika Sherwood, *Kwame Nkrumah and the*

Dawn of the Cold War: The West African National Secretariat, 1945–48 (London: Pluto Press, 2019); Ahmad Rahman, *The Regime Change of Kwame Nkrumah: Epic Heroism in Africa and the Diaspora* (London: Palgrave Macmillan, 2007), 177, 189, 191; Kwame Nkrumah, *I Speak of Freedom: A Statement of African Ideology* (London: William Heinemann, 1961), 201.

8. Jeffrey S. Ahlman, "A New Type of Citizen: Youth, Gender, and Generation in the Ghanain Builders Brigade," *Journal of African History* 53, no. 1 (2012): 87–105; Jeffrey S. Ahlman, "Road to Ghana: Nkrumah, Southern Africa and the Eclipse of a Decolonizing Africa," *Kronos* 37, no. 1 (2011): 23–40; Jeffrey S. Ahlman, "The Algerian Question in Nkrumah's Ghana, 1958–1960: Debating 'Violence' and 'Nonviolence' in African Decolonization," *Africa Today* 57, no. 2 (2010): 67–84; Jean Allman, "Nuclear Imperialism and the Pan-African Struggle for Peace and Freedom: Ghana, 1959–1962," *Souls* 10, no. 2 (2008): 83–102.

9. Colin Legum, *Pan-Africanism: A Short Political Guide* (London: Pall Mall Press, 1962), 15.

10. MSRC, Nkrumah Papers, box 154–38, f: Afari-Gyan, research paper, K. Afari-Gyan, "The Problems of Mental Decolonization," [1964]; Kwame Nkrumah, *Consciencism: Philosophy and Ideology for De-colonization* (London: Heinemann, 1964), 3.

11. Toyin Falola, *Nationalism and African Intellectuals* (Rochester, NY: University of Rochester Press, 2001), 156–58; Kwame Nkrumah, *Ghana: The Autobiography of Kwame Nkrumah* (Edinburgh: T. Nelson, 1957), 24–26; Kwame Nkrumah, *Towards Colonial Freedom: Africa in the Struggle Against World Imperialism* (London: Heinemann, 1947), 1.

12. Ayo J. Langley, ed., *Ideologies of Liberation in Black Africa 1856–1970: Documents on Modern African Political Thought from Colonial Times to the Present* (London: Rex Collings, 1979), 24, 423–32; Adom Getachew, *Worldmaking after Empire: The Rise and Fall of Self-Determination* (Princeton, NJ: Princeton University Press, 2019), 7.

13. Leslie Elaine James, "'What We Put in Black and White': George Padmore and the Practice of Anti-Imperial Politics" (PhD. Diss., London School of Economics, 2012), 156; K. Afari-Gyan, "Nkrumah's Ideology," in *The Life and Work of Kwame Nkrumah*, ed. Kwame Arhin (Trenton, NJ: Africa World Press, 1993), 166.

14. George Padmore, *Pan-Africanism or Communism? The Coming Struggle for Africa* (London: Dennis Dobson, 1956), 12.

15. MSRC, Nkrumah Papers, box 154–38, f: 21, "Prime Minister's Midnight Speech on the Eve of Independence," 6 March 1957.

16. ASPFAE, AD, 14563, Geoffroy d'Aspremont Lynden to Victor Larock, "Passage par Delhi de deux Ministres de Ghana," 20 September 1957; KNADS, MAC/CON/181/5, "Steering-Committee of the All-African People's Conference, Tunis," 31 May 1959.

17. "Lamine Senghor, The Negro's Fight for Freedom," *Black Past*, 11 August 2009, https://www.blackpast.org/global-african-history/1927-lamine-senghor-negro-s-fight-freedom/; Minkah Makalani, "An Incessant Struggle against White Supremacy: The International Congress against Imperialism and the International Circuits of Black Radicalism," in *Outside In: The Transnational Circuitry of US History*, ed. Andrew Preston and Doug Rossinow (Oxford: Oxford University Press, 2017), 190.

18. KNADS, MAC/KEN/74/3, Padmore to Murumbi, 24 March 1958.

19. Arthur W. Lewis, *The Theory of Economic Growth* (London: George Allen & Unwin, 1955), 19–20; Robert L. Tignor, *W. Arthur Lewis and the Birth of Development Economics* (Princeton, NJ: Princeton University Press, 2006), 152; *All-African People's Conference:*

Speeches by the Prime Minister of Ghana at the Opening and Closing Sessions on December 8th and 13th, 1958 (Accra: Community Centre, 1958), 6.

20. Thompson, *Ghana's Foreign Policy*, 418; PRAAD, SC/BAA/499A, Archbishop Makarios to Nkrumah, 4 May 1965.

21. Quoted in Obed Asamoah, "Nkrumah's Foreign Policy 1951–1966," in *The Life and Work of Kwame Nkrumah*, ed. Kwame Arhin (Trenton, NJ: Africa World Press, 1993), 248; Thompson, *Ghana's Foreign Policy*, 110, 177–83, 279–90; Priya Lal, *African Socialism in Postcolonial Tanzania: Between the Village and the World* (Cambridge: Cambridge University Press, 2015), 56.

22. ANS, VP 194, J.M. Calvel to Ministre des Affaire Etrangères, "L'Afrique, La Doctrine de Monroe et les grandes puissances," 4 November 1960.

23. Afari-Gyan, "Nkrumah's Ideology," 168; Asamoah, "Nkrumah's Foreign Policy 1951–1966," 242.

24. MSRC, Nkrumah Papers, box 154–38, f: 21, transcript, "Prime Minister's Midnight Speech on the Eve of Independence," 6 March 1957.

25. Kwame Nkrumah, *Neo-Colonialism, The Last Stage of Imperialism* (London: Panaf Books, 1965), 239; Birmingham, *Kwame Nkrumah*, 3; PRAAD, SC/BAA/136, transcript, "Conference of Independent African States," 15 April 1958, 5–6.

26. National Archives of Zambia, Lusaka (hereafter NAZ), box Bulletin of African Affairs, W. E. B. Dubois, "Pan Africa 1919–1958," December 1958, 1.

27. "Africa Had Scholars before Europe," *Evening News*, September 4, 1963; Nkrumah, *I Speak of Freedom*, 125; Biney, *The Political and Social Thought of Kwame Nkrumah*, 120; Samuel Obeng, ed., "Opening of the Institute of African Studies, Legon October 25, 1963," in *Selected Speeches of Kwame Nkrumah*, vol. 2 (Accra: Afram Publications, 2009), 120.

28. George Padmore Library, Accra (hereafter GPL), BAA/RLAA/370, "Ghana's Role in Emergent Africa," 25 July 1960; Agyeman, *Nkrumah's Ghana and East Africa*, 79–89; Hadjor, *Nkrumah and Ghana*, 91–98; "Pan-African Freedom Movement of East and Central Africa (PAFMECA)," *International Organization* 16, no. 2 (1962): 446–48.

29. Emma Kluge, "West Papua and the International History of Decolonization, 1961–69," *International History Review* 42, no. 6 (2020): 1155–72; Meredith Terretta, "Cameroonian Nationalists Go Global: From Forest 'Maquis' to a Pan-African Accra," *Journal of African History* 51, no. 2 (2010): 189–212.

30. C. L. R. James and Robin D. G. Kelley, *A History of Pan-African Revolt* (Oakland: PM Press, 2012), 27–28.

31. Ray Gildea, *Kwame Nkrumah and the West Indies, 1962* (San Juan: Vedic Enterprises, 1962).

32. MSRC, Nkrumah Papers, box 154–41, f: Correspondence 1952–1957, Padmore to Nkrumah, 24 July 1956: NARA, RG.59, CDF1955–59, 645.5694/2-1756, American Embassy (hereafter Amembassy) Accra to StateDept, "Prime Minister Makes Foreign Policy Speech," 19 July 1958, Amembassy Accra to StateDept, "Changes Made by the Prime Minister in the Delivery of his Policy Speech in the Legislative Assembly," 19 March 1957; Nkrumah, *Ghana: The Autobiography of Kwame Nkrumah*, x; Leslie James, *George Padmore and Decolonization from Below: Pan-Africanism, the Cold War, and the End of Empire* (London: Palgrave Macmillan, 2014), 145.

33. KNADS, MAC/KEN/78/1, Murumbi to Mboya, 13 June 1957; also see Ismay Milford and Gerard McCann, "African Internationalisms and the Erstwhile Trajectories of Kenyan Community Development: Joseph Murumbi's 1950s," *Journal of Contemporary History* 57, no. 1 (January 2022): 18, https://doi.org/10.1177/00220094211011536.

34. MSRC, Gizenga Papers, box 128-6, f: Nkrumah Foreign Relations—the UN, transcript, Daniel Chapman, "Statement by Ambassador Daniel Chapman Permanent Representative of Ghana to the United Nations before the Committee on Information from Non-self-governing Territories," 23 April 1959; Samuel Obeng, ed., "Step to Freedom: Nationalists' Conference of African Freedom Fighters," in *Selected Speeches of Kwame Nkrumah*, vol. 2 (Accra: Afram Publications, 2009), 44.

35. BNA, PREM11/1367, statement by the secretary of state for the colonies, 11 May 1956, 3; AMAE, DAL, Ghana 1953–1959, 50QO/8, "Declaration sur les Affaires Exterieures du premier ministre de la Gold Coast a l'Assemblee Legislative," 3 September 1956, "Formation des Candidats a la Carriere Diplomatique de la Gold Coast," 23 July 1954.

36. MSRC, Gizenga Papers, box 128-5, f: Nkrumah Speeches—Addresses to the UN, 1953–1957, 1958, 1960, transcript, "Address Delivered by the Prime Minister of Ghana to the Afro-Asian Group at United Nations Headquarters, New York on Tuesday, July 29th, 1958," October 1958.

37. MSRC, Gizenga Papers, box 128-5, f: Kwame Nkrumah Speeches—Addresses to the UN, 1957, 1958, 1960, transcript, "Television Recording made by Dr. Kwame Nkrumah, Prime Minister of Ghana at the United Nations," 29 July 1958.

38. Batsa, *The Spark*, 13; GPL, BAA/RLAA/348, Alphonse Ebassa to Aloysius K. Barden, 22 August 1960; Nkrumah to Milne, 18 May 1966, quoted in June Milne, ed., *Kwame Nkrumah: The Conakry Years, His Life and Letters* (Bedford: Panaf Books, 1990), 43–44.

39. S. E. Quarm, *Diplomatic Offensive: An Overview of Ghana's Diplomacy under Dr. Kwame Nkrumah* (Accra: Afram Publications, 1997), 20.

40. PRAAD, SC/BAA/251, "Minutes of the 5th Meeting of the African Affairs Committee held on November 19th 1959 at Flagstaff House," 19 November 1959.

41. ASPFAE, AA, AEII3211, memcon, Jean van den Bosch to Victor Larock, "Entretien avec le président Nasser," 12 April 1958; M. Abdel-Kader Hatem, *Information and the Arab Cause* (London: Longman Group Ltd., 1974), 6.

42. DDEL, WH Office, NSC Series, Policy Papers Subseries, box 25, f: NSC5818, S. Everett Gleason, "U.S. Policy toward Africa South of the Sahara Prior to Calendar Year 1960," 26 August 1958, 4; BNA, FO371/137966, "Summary Record of the First Meeting at Ambassadorial Level," 16 April 1959, 2.

43. Peo Hansen and Stefan Jonsson, *Eurafrica: The Untold History of European Integration and Colonialism* (London: Bloomsbury Academic, 2014), 267.

44. KNADS, MAC/ZAN/118/1(B), "Whiter Zanzibar?," s.d.; BNA, CO822/1349, letter to Mark E. Allen, E. G. Le Tocq, 12 December 1958; BAHDMNE, PAA 220, newspaper, "Le Progres Egyptien," numéro special, January 1958, 24; Politisches Archiv des Auswärtigen Amts, Berlin Germany (hereafter PAAA), 600–82.01/22, B 90 745, "Betr. Errichtung eines "Cultural Centre" der Vereinigten Arabischen Republik in Accra," 26 November 1958.

45. NARA, RG.59, CDF1955–59, 645.5694/2-1756–645U.86B322/1-2959, Peter Rutter to Amembassy Accra, "Ghana's Relations with Egypt," 16 May 1957; Elwood Dunn, *Liberia and the United States during the Cold War: Limits of Reciprocity* (London: Palgrave Macmillan, 2009), 81–85; NARA, RG.59, CDF1955–59, 6519.00/9-2958–65/W.61/1-2159, "Ghanaian-Liberian Relations in the First Year of Ghana's Independence," 19 May 1958, Richard L. Jones, "Prospects for Guinean-Liberian Relations on the Eve of Touré's Visit to Monrovia," 17 November 1958, Amcon Lagos to StateDept, "Newly Assigned Liberian ConGen Making Determined Public Relations Campaign," 14 July 1959; NARA, RG.59, CDF1955–59, 645.5694/2-1756–645U.86B322/1-2959, transcript, "Broadcasts Made by the Liberian Consul General to Nigeria over NBC," 3 July 1959; Nkrumah, *Ghana: The Autobiography of Kwame Nkrumah*, 180.

46. "France. Service de documentation extérieure et de contre-espionnage. La Conférence de l'unité maghrébine (Tanger, 27–30 avril 1958). 02-05-1958," accessed August 23, 2021, https://www.cvce.eu/s/4c.

47. Classic works on African Socialism include William H. Friedland and Carl G. Rosberg Jr., eds., *African Socialism* (Stanford, CA: Stanford University Press, 1964); Abdul Rahman Mohamed Babu, *African Socialism or Socialist Africa* (London: Zed Press, 1981).

48. ANS, Dossier Senghor, f: L. S. Senghor 1949–1955, "Extrait de Marches Coloniaux," 14 May 1955; KNADS, MAC/CON/181/1, "Conference du Rassemblement des Peuples Africains, 5–12 December 1958, Allocation à la conférence Le Pan-Africanisme, de 1919 à 1958 par W. E. B. Du Bois," [1958]; Langley, *Ideologies of Liberation*, 49.

49. Getachew Metaferia, "The Ethiopian Connection to the Pan-African Movement," *Journal of Third World Studies* 12, no. 2 (1995): 302; Monique Bedasse, *Jah Kingdom Rastafarians, Tanzania, and Pan-Africanism in the Age of Decolonization* (Chapel Hill: University of North Carolina Press, 2017), 4.

50. BAHDMNE, PAA 214, f: Circular No.14 Textos de Declaração e Resoluçao, "Ethiopia Observer Dedicated to the Conference of Independent African States," April 1958, 89.

51. NAZ, MFA1/1/500/52, report No. ADD/12/66 (supplementary and special) for period September 15–30, 1966; Vijay Prashad, *The Darker Nations: A People's History of the Third World* (New York: New Press, 2007), 264.

52. Ahlman, "Road to Ghana," 27.

53. PRAAD, SC/BAA/136, transcript, "Conference of Independent African States," 15 April 1958.

54. KNADS, MAC/CON/183/1, A. K. Barden, "Awakening Africa," s.d., 14.

55. PRAAD, SC/BAA/136, "Conference of Independent African States, April 15 to April 23," [1958], 3, "Conference of Independent African States," 15 April 1958, "Conference of African States," [1958]; Nkrumah, *Towards Colonial Freedom*, 1–3.

56. BAHDMNE, PAA 214, f: Conferencias e Congressos Internactionais, A Bem de Nação Director Geral, 18 Outubro de 1958, "Accra en visite à Rio," 2, 10, 1958.

57. "Larock nous parle des fêtes de l'indépendance du Ghana," *Le Peuple*, 9 March 1957.

58. Nkrumah, *Consciencism*, 6; BNA, CO936/578, top secret minutes, "Meeting held at 12, Carlton House Terrace, to discuss the projected Pan-African Conference in Ghana," 20 February 1958; NARA, RG.59, CDF1955–1959, 645.5694/2-1756–645U.86332/1-2959,

Flake to StateDept, 23 August 1958; BNA, FO371/108193, W. L. Gorell Barnes to Charles Arden-Clarke, 6 November 1954.

59. BNA, CO936/576, Khartoum to FO, 26 March 1957; Thompson, *Ghana's Foreign Policy*, 32.

60. NASA, BEV, box 12, f: Ghana, Strijdom to Nkrumah, 5 November 1957.

61. BNA, INF12/863, Washington to FO, 10 April 1958, extract from letter, N. A. Leadbitter UKIO to R. I. Hall CRO, 23 April 1958; AMAE, DAL Généralités, 49QONT/43, f: Première Conference d'Accra documents (mars 1957–avril 1958), Henri-Francis Mazoyer to DAL, "S.e.: L'opinion et la conférence d'Accra," 25 April 1958, 5.

62. PRAAD, SC/BAA/122, "Ghana's Role in the Committee on Information from Non-self-governing Territories," 12 May 1959; Ahlman, "The Algerian Question in Nkrumah's Ghana," 73; Rooney, *Kwame Nkrumah*, 209; Thompson, *Ghana's Foreign Policy*, 31–39.

63. Sergey Mazov, *A Distant Front in the Cold War: The USSR in West Africa and the Congo, 1956–1964* (Stanford, CA: Stanford University Press, 2010), 24; Andrei Gromyko, *Memoirs* (New York: Doubleday, 1989), 263–65.

64. "Infiltration psychologique": AMAE, DAL Généralités, 49QONT/43, f: Première Conference d'Accra documents (mars 1957–avril 1958), Henri-Francis Mazoyer to DAL, "Commentaires de presse sur la conférence d'Accra," 30 July 1958; ASPFAE AD, 14563, Le Baron Silvercruys to Victor Larock, "Conférence des Etats indépendants africains à Accra," 2 May 1958; Archives générales du Royaume de Belgique, Brussels (hereafter AGRB), I528 D'Aspremont Lynden, f: 3, "Action politique de l'Institut de Sociologie Solvay au Congo," 28 June 1960.

65. BNA, CO936/579, minutes, R. N Posnett to Mr. Watson and Mr. Jerrom, 13 August 1958, minutes for secretary of state, 25 July 1958, W. D. Allen to N. D. Watson, 30 September 1958, secret draft, A. W. Snelling for Mr. Eastwood, [July 1958].

66. Memcon, 23 July 1958, Memcon, July 24, 1958, *FRUS 1958–1960*, vol. 14, *Africa*, 647–652; NARA, RG.306, P74, box 17, f: Ghana 1959, USIS-Accra to USIA, "USIS Coverage of the All African Peoples Conference," 16 December 1958.

67. Library and Archives Canada, Ottawa (hereafter LAC), RG.203, E. W. T. Gill to Secretary of State, Ottawa, "Conference of Independent African States," 28 April 1958, 6.

68. BAHDMNE, SR.035 1957–1968, SR 035 1957–1968, Pt 1. 1957/NOV/21–1964/JUL/31, Ministerio do Ultramar, 17 Maio de 1958, PAA 214, f: Circular No. 14 Textos de Declaração e Resolução, "Conferência de Ghana," 23 March 1958, "Conferência dos estados Africanos (Accra—Abril, 1958)," July 1958, Antonio de Siqueira Freire, "Conferência de Accra," 4 May 1958.

69. BNA, CO936/579, F. R. MacGennis to R. S. Faber, 11 August 1958, secret, "Extract from the record of the Quadripartite Discussion on Africa Lisbon 1958," [1958]; AMAE, DA, Etats-Unis, 91QO/433, Herve Alphand to Christian Pinau, "Conférence d'Accra, A. S. Entretien avec M. Julius Holmes," [1958].

70. NARA, RG.59, CDF1955–1959, 645.5694/2-1756–645U.86332/1-2959n, Accra to secretary of state, 25 July 1958.

71. *Resolutions of the All African People's Conference Held at Accra, Ghana December 5–13, 1958* (Accra: Community Centre, 1959), 7.

72. KNADS, MAC/CON/181/1, "Free Jomo Kenyatta Now!," [1958], "Resolution on Kamerun Adopted by the First Committee—on Imperialism and Colonialism of the

All African Peoples Conference," s.d.; KNADS, MAC/CON/184/3, "Resolutions to All African Peoples Conference Rev. Michael Scott—South West Africa," s.d.; KNADS, MAC/CON/181/5 AAPC, Homer Jack, "Towards Freedom," vol. 8, no. 1, January 1959, 3; NARA, RG.59, CDF1955–1959, 645.5694/2-1756–645U.86332/1-2959, Accra to secretary of state, 25 July 1958; Mboya quoted in BAHDMNE, PAA 215, "2e Conferencia dos Estados Africanos Independentes Addis-Abeba, de 14 a 26 de Junho de 1960," 26 June 1960, 18; Ahlman, "The Algerian Question in Nkrumah's Ghana," 74; António Tomás, *Amílcar Cabral: The Life of a Reluctant Nationalist* (London: Hurst, 2021), 109; Alex Marino, "The United States and Portuguese Angola: Space, Race, and the Cold War in Africa" (PhD diss., University of Arkansas, 2021), 83–84.

73. *All-African People's Conference: Speeches by the Prime Minister of Ghana at the Opening and Closing Sessions on December 8th and 13th, 1958* (Accra: Community Centre, 1958), 2; "Ideas and Courage, Not Guns," *Ghana Today*, April 29, 1959, vol. 3, no. 5, 1.

74. Nkrumah to Milne, 18 May 1966, quoted in Milne, *Kwame Nkrumah*, 43–44.

75. *Nkrumah's Subversion in Africa: Documentary Evidence of Nkrumah's Interference in the Affairs of Other African States* (Accra: Ministry of Information, 1966), 6; Ahlman, "Road to Ghana," 1, 36; Ahlman, "The Algerian Question in Nkrumah's Ghana," 76.

76. Frantz Fanon, *The Wretched of the Earth*, trans. Constance Farrington (New York: Grove Press, 1963), 36.

77. Frantz Fanon, *Toward the African Revolution: Political Essays*, trans. Haakon Chevalier (New York: Grove Press, 1988), 178.

78. Milne, *Kwame Nkrumah*, 174; Peter Worsley also claimed "Fanon's writing" was "not always worked through," see Peter Worsley, "Frantz Fanon and the 'Lumpenproletariat,'" *Socialist Register* 9 (1972): 193.

79. *All-African People's Conference: Speeches by the Prime Minister of Ghana at the Opening and Closing Sessions on December 8th and 13th, 1958*, 4; *Resolutions of the All African People's Conference Held at Accra, Ghana December 5–13, 1958* (Accra: Community Centre, 1959), 6; Samuel Obeng, ed., "Positive Action Conference for Peace and Security in Africa, Accra, April 7, 1960," in *Selected Speeches of Kwame Nkrumah*, vol. 1 (Accra: Afram Publishing, 1979), 54.

80. Nkrumah, *Ghana: The Autobiography of Kwame Nkrumah*, vii–viii.

81. Fanon, *The Wretched of the Earth*, 94.

82. Kwame Nkrumah, *What I Mean by "Positive Action"* (Accra: Convention People's Party, 1950), 3; GPL, BAA/RLAA/423, "Development of the Kwame Nkrumah Institute, Winneba, as the Institute of Political Science," [1961].

83. *Resolutions of the All African People's Conference Held at Accra, Ghana December 5–13, 1958*, 7.

84. Thompson, *Ghana's Foreign Policy*, 107; PRAAD, SC/BAA/251, "Minutes of the 3rd Meeting of the African Affairs Committee held on Thursday," 22 October 1959; *Resolutions of the All African People's Conference Held at Accra, Ghana December 5–13, 1958*, 7; James, *George Padmore and Decolonization from Below*, 164.

85. GPL, BAA/RLAA/370, Kofi Baako to Nkrumah, "Operation Independence Transfer of Financial aid to Freedom Fighters," [1960].

86. PRAAD, SC/BAA/357, Barden to Nkrumah, 20 May 1964; Interview with K. B. Asante by Frank Gerits on March 13, 2012, in Labadi, Accra, Ghana.

87. GPL, BAA/RLAA/430, "Bureau of African Affairs," [1964]; GPL, BAA/RLAA/247 1962 Receipts: Bills, Correspondence (BAA), Barden to the Acting Secretary to the Prime Minister, 30 January 1959, Padmore to the Acting Secretary to the Prime Minister, Government House Accra, 9 April 1959, A. K Barden to the Acting Secretary to the Prime Minister, Government House Accra, 18 March 1959, bill for MLN, 11 April 1959.

88. GPL, BAA/RLAA/370, Kofi Baako to Nkrumah, "Operation Independence Transfer of Financial Aid to Freedom Fighters," [1960]; PRAAD, RG.17/2/501, minutes of meeting, "Sixth Meeting of the African Affairs committee held at Flagstaff House at 1 P.M. on Friday, 4th December, 1959," 4 December 1959.

89. GPL, BAA/RLAA/370, BAA chairman to Nkrumah, "Operation Independence Transfer of Financial aid to Freedom Fighters," [1960].

90. GPL, BAA/RLAA/413, Padmore to Jian, *Times of India*, and Nkrumah, 6 September 1959.

91. GPL, BAA/RLAA/455, "Resolutions of the All African People's Conference held at Accra, Ghana December 5–13, 1958," 19 January 1959, 6.

92. GPL, BAA/RLAA/437, "The Ghana Young Pioneers," s.d.

93. *Nkrumah's Subversion in Africa: Documentary Evidence of Nkrumah's Interference in the Affairs of Other African States*, 44.

94. GPL, BAA/RLAA/1038A, Permanent Secretary Ministry of Education W. W. K. Vanderpuye to Padmore, "Suggested Scholarships Awards to Liberian Citizens," 29 September 1958; Jeffrey S. Ahlman, *Living with Nkrumahism: Nation, State, and Pan-Africanism in Ghana* (Athens: Ohio University Press, 2017), 190; Ahlman, "A New Type of Citizen," 87; NARA, RG.469, P65, box 1, f: Ghana Reports (Builders Brigade), Hemmerich to ICA, "Builders Brigade: Further ICA Technical Assistance," 10 March 1958, Bernstein, "US Assistance for Builders Brigade in Africa," [1957–1958].

95. GPL, BAA/RLAA/247, Colfecumer to Acting Secretary to the Prime Minister, 28 January 1959.

96. AMAE, DAL Ghana, 50QO/19, f: Relations du Pays avec la France, Louis de Guiringaud to DAL, "Nationalisme et négritude," 4 July 1958.

97. NARA, RG.306, UD-WW285, f: IPS, presentation, Olcott H. Deming, public affairs adviser for African affairs, 15 December 1959; NARA, RG.306, P74, box 17, f: Ghana 19, USIS-Accra to USIA, "Requests of Prime Minister's Advisor on African Affairs," 9 July 1958.

98. James H. Meriwether, *Proudly We Can Be Africans: Black Americans and Africa, 1935–1961* (Chapel Hill: University of North Carolina Press, 2002), 150–153; Amy Bass, *Those About Him Remained Silent: The Battle Over W. E. B. Du Bois* (Minneapolis: University of Minnesota Press, 2009), viii; Birmingham, *Kwame Nkrumah*, 129; Jonathan Fenderson, "Evolving Conceptions of Pan-African Scholarship: W. E. B. Du Bois, Carter G. Woodson, and the 'Encyclopedia Africana,' 1909–1963," *Journal of African American History* 95, no. 1 (2010): 71–91; Jean Allman, "Kwame Nkrumah, African Studies and the Politics of Knowledge Production in the Black Star of Africa," *International Journal of African Historical Studies* 46, no. 2 (2013): 181–183.

99. BBCWAC, E1/1,3791,1, "Proposed Scheme for the International Service of the Ghana Broadcasting System by A. L. Pidgeon and J. L. Marshall of the Canadian Broadcasting Corporation," 14 March 1958, "Government Statement on the Report on External

Broadcasting by Messrs. A. L. Pidgeion and J. L. Marshall," 14 March 1958; "Radio Ghana Increases Local Programming," *Ghana Today*, July 10, 1957, vol. 1, no. 10, 2.

100. PRAAD, RG.17/2/501, minutes of meeting, "Sixth Meeting of the African Affairs committee held at the Flagstaff House at 1 P.M. on Friday, 4th December, 1959," 4 December 1959; KNADS, MAC/CON/183/1, A. K. Barden, "Awakening Africa," 1958, 20.

101. AMAE, DAL Généralités, 49QONT/69, memcon, "Proces—Verbaux de la Première Conférence: Des directeurs de Radiodiffusion Africaine: tenue a Rabat du 23 au 26 Mai 1960," 26 May 1960, 1, 8.

102. PRAAD, SC/BAA/357, Nkrumah to T. Makonnen, "African Affairs Centre," 17 June 1960, Makonnen to Nkrumah, 22 June 1960; PRAAD, RG.17/2/501, minutes of meeting, "7th Meeting of the African Affairs committee on Thursday 17th December 1959," 4 December 1959; PRAAD, RG.17/2/796, "Miss Evelyn Molabatsi—Drunkenness," [7 February 1966]; GPL, BAA/RLAA/393, anonymous letter to Nkrumah, s.d.

103. GPL, BAA/RLAA/370, A. K. Barden to Nkrumah, "Special Mission to East and Central Africa," 28 November 1960.

104. NARA, RG.59, CDF1955–59, 611.70/10-158–611.7194/12-457, Amembassy Paris to StateDept, 6 January 1959.

105. ASPFAE, AD, AF/I/1/1959, André de Staercke, "V. Comité sur l'Afrique," [1959].

106. Mazov, *A Distant Front*, 23; Alessandro Iandolo, *Arrested Development: The Soviet Union in Ghana, Guinea, and Mali, 1955–1968* (Ithaca, NY: Cornell University Press, 2022), 70.

107. ASPFAE, AD, 14563, André Chaval to Pierre Wigny, "Kwamé N'Krumah," 4 February 1959; in spite of what historians have written: Zana Aziza Etambala, *De Teloorgang van Een Modelkolonie: Belgisch Congo (1958–1960)* (Leuven: Acco, 2008), 36.

108. AMAE, DAL, 50QO/15, f: Politique Intérieure, M. C. Renner to minister of foreign affairs, "Marriage de M. Nkrumah," 2 January 1958; BNA, INF12/863, R. H. K. Marett, "Report on visit to East Africa by R. H. K," March/November 1960, 12; the ICA described Nkrumah's Pan-African conference as a first step toward African economic cooperation: NARA, RG.469, P36, box 11, f: Africa Advisory Conference, memcon, "International Cooperation Administration: Advisory Conference on Africa May 17–27, 1960: Pan-Africanism," 27 May 1960, 2.

109. NASA, BTS 1/33/8/3 vol. 1, S. E. D. Brown, "The South African Observer," January 1959, 1.

110. NARA, RG.59, CDF1955–59, 611.70/10-158–611.7194/12-457, "Address by the Honorable Joseph C. Satterthwaite, Assistant Secretary of State for African Affairs before the Southern Assembly (Tulane University): The United States and the New Africa," 17 January 1959; BNA, CO822/1349, letter, E. G. Le Tocq to Mark E. Allen, 12 December 1958; BNA, FO371/137966, "Summary Record of the First Meeting at Ambassadorial Level," 16 April 1959, 2.

111. Quote taken from Ronald Hyam, *Britain's Declining Empire: The Road to Decolonisation, 1918–1968* (Cambridge: Cambridge University Press, 2007), 242; David Birmingham, *The Decolonization of Africa* (Athens: Ohio University Press, 1995), 13; Alistair Horne, *Macmillan: The Official Biography* (Basingstoke: Pan Macmillan, 2008), 260–90;

quote taken from Guia Migani, "De Gaulle and Sub-Saharan Africa: From Decolonization to French Development Policy, 1958–1963," in *Globalizing de Gaulle: International
Perspectives on French Foreign Policies, 1958–1969*, ed. Christian Nuenlist, Anna Locher, and
Martin Garret (Lanham: Lexington Books, 2010), 254; Guia Migani, "Sékou Touré et la
contestation de l'ordre colonial en Afrique sub-saharienne, 1958–1963," *Monde(s)* 2,
no. 2 (2012): 272–73; for a historiographical overview: Frank Gerits, "The Postcolonial
Cultural Transaction: Rethinking the Guinea Crisis within the French Cultural Strategy
for Africa, 1958–60," *Cold War History* 19, no. 3 (2019): 1743–7962.

112. CHAN, 5AG1/765 Fonds de la présidence de la République de Charles de Gaulle,
f: Notes et Entretiens (1958–1959), "Entretien du Général de Gaule avec Monsieur
Black," 21 October 1958; Elizabeth Schmidt, *Foreign Intervention in Africa: From the Cold
War to the War on Terror* (Cambridge: Cambridge University Press, 2013), 174; Georges
Chaffard, *Les carnets secrets de la décolonisation II* (Paris: Calmann-Lévy, 1967), 189.

113. Elizabeth Schmidt, *Cold War and Decolonization in Guinea, 1946–1958* (Athens:
Ohio University Press, 2007), 166; BNA, FO371/138838, H. Carr CRD to A. C. Cam-
eron BC, 27 October 1959.

114. NARA, RG.306, UD-WW285, FRC 1, f: Briefing Paper, Nixon, "The Emergence
of Africa: Report to the President by Vice President Nixon on His Trip to Africa: February 28–March 21, 1957," [March 1957], 1–2; memdisc at 375th NSC meeting, August 7,
1958, *FRUS 1958–1960*, vol. 14, *Africa*, 21.

115. "Eisenhower, Dwight D. to George Magoffin Humphrey, 27 March 1957. In *The
Papers of Dwight David Eisenhower*, ed. L. Galambos and D. van Ee, doc. 90. World Wide
Web facsimile by the Dwight D. Eisenhower Memorial Commission of the print edition;
Baltimore: The Johns Hopkins University Press, 1996," accessed April 1, 2014, http://
www.eisenhowermemorial.org/presidential-papers/second-term/documents/90.cfm.

116. BNA, CO1027/252, Ralph Murray, "For Mr. Carstairs's signature," 26 May 1959;
BNA, CO967/337, minute, Alan Lennox-Boyd, 16 October 1958; NARA, RG 59
CDF1955–59, 611.70/10-158–611.7194/12-457, "Address by the Honorable Joseph C.
Satterthwaite, Assistant Secretary of State for African Affairs before the Southern As-
sembly," 17 January 1959, 8.

117. BNA, FO371/137940, draft record, Anglo-French talks, 1 December 1958; BNA,
FO371/116979, C. Steel to FO, 31 March 1955.

118. ANS, FM39 Congo, Transcript, "Radio Bamako—3 Fevrier 1961–12 H. 45," 3
February 1961, 14.

119. Thompson, *Ghana's Foreign Policy*, 68–69; Library of Congress, Washington DC
(hereafter LOC), Harriman Papers, box 543, airgram, 5 April 1964.

120. BNA, FO371/138170, "Le Colonial Office contre le Communauté," s.d.; CHAN,
Fonds de la présidence de la république de Charles de Gaulle 5AG1/765, f: Notes et Entretiens 1958–1959, aide memoire, 5 December 1958.

121. BNA, CO936/564, "Record of Anglo French Official Talks on Africa held in
London on December 7 and 8," 8 December 1958; AMAE, DAL, Guinee (sous déroga-
tion), 51QO/35, SDECE, "La Situation Interieure et les Relations Extérieures de la Re-
publique de Guinee (Oct.-Nov. 1958)," 2 December 1958, 27.

122. "Pour preparer psychologiquement le terrain": AMAE, DAL, Ghana 1960–1965,
50QO/72, de Guiringaud to DAL, "Information politique," 14 May 1960, 2; "effort culturel de notre part": AMAE, DAL, Congo belge 1953–1959, 44QO/41, de Guiringaud to

DGRC, "Passage de la troupe de l'Union française," 17 February 1954; AMAE, DAL, Ghana 1960–1965, 50QO/72, de Guiringaud to Monsieur le Ministre des Affaires Etrangères, "Enseignement du français au Ghana," 21 April 1960, 1.

123. AMAE, DAL, Guinee, 51QO/28, f: Education Relations culturelle, note pour le Ministre, de Guiringaud, "Présence culturelle et technique française en Guinée," 28 Novembre 1958.

124. ASPFAE, AA, 14563, Le Baron J. Guillaume to Wigny, "Création de l'Union entre le Ghana et la Guinée—Projet de Fédération des anciens Territoires d'Outre-Mer," 25 November 1958.

125. "Je comprends bien que n'ont pas ici le même éclairage qu'à Paris. . . . des Africaines français . . . ne sont pas nos ennemies," see Fondation Nationale des Sciences Politiques, Paris (hereafter FNSP), CM 7 1958, de Guiringaud to Couve de Murville, 11 December 1958.

126. "Ne pas se dérober à un entretien est une chose. Répondre à une convocation et rester pendant deux heures est une autre," see FNSP, CM 7 1958, Debré to de Guiringaud, 28 November 1958.

127. AMAE, DAL, Guinee, 50QO/36, f: Relations Guinnée-Ghana, Monsieur Daridan, ambassade de France au Ghana, 21 November 1958.

128. Nwaubani, The United States and Decolonization in West Africa, 206; Mazov, A Distant Front, 60.

129. Memdisc of the 432nd Meeting of the National Security Council, 14 January 1960, Papers as President, 1953–1961, NSC Series, box 12, f: 432nd Meeting of NSC, DDEL; Memcon, October 27, 1959, FRUS 1958–1960, vol. 14, Africa, 698–701.

130. Alessandro Iandolo, "Soviet Policy in West Africa, 1957–64" (PhD diss., University of Oxford, 2011), 141, 150; Mazov, A Distant Front, 134–35.

131. BNA, FO371/138170, A. T. Oldham, 14 January 1959; Kaba Lanciné, "From Colonialism to Autocracy: Guinea under Sékou Touré, 1957–1984," in Decolonization and African Independence: The Transfers of Power, 1960–1980, ed. Prosser Gifford and William Roger Louis (New Haven, CT: Yale University Press, 1988), 228; Fred Marte, Political Cycles in International Relations: The Cold War and Africa 1945–1990 (Amsterdam: VU Press, 1994), 148.

132. BNA, FO371/137966, "Summary Record of the Third Meeting at Ambassadorial Level Held on April 20," 28 April 1959, 2.

133. NARA, RG.59, A1-3112-B, box 1, Penfield to Ferguson, "Suggestions for Airgram to Paris and Conakry," 1 May 1959; NARA, RG.84, Ghana Post Files General Records 1952–58, box 2, f: D. Exchange of Persons, StateDept, "Educational Exchange: Proposed Fiscal Year 1960 Country Program," 13 May 1958.

134. AMAE, DAL Guinee 1958–1959 (sous dérogation), 51QO/35, "Comité d'action Psychologique," 16 June 1959; BNA, FO371/138837, letter, J. S. H. Shattock to J. H. A. Watson, 21 May 1959; Mairi Stewart MacDonald, "The Challenge of Guinean Independence, 1958–1971," (PhD. dissertation, University of Toronto, 2009), 101.

135. NARA, RG.59, CDF1955–1958, 870.461/8-1258–871.00/12-265, Amembassy London to StateDept, "Reported Interest of Sekou Touré, President of Guinea in Hiring an American as Public Relations Advisor," 18 November 1959; NARA, RG.469, P206, box 3, f: Guinea 1959–1960, Eugene B. Abrams, "FY 60 Contracts for Guinea," 29 June 1960.

136. The conversation can be found in Mazov, A Distant Front, 133.

137. BNA, FO111/138838, Wynn Hugh-Jones to FO, 2 September 1959; Elizabeth Schmidt's research explores Touré's pragmatic leadership style: Schmidt, *Cold War and Decolonization in Guinea*, 171, 174, 277; Charles de Gaulle, *Mémoires d'Espoire: Le Renouveau 1958–1962* (Plon: Librairie, 1970), 60.

138. NARA, RG.306, P249, box 10, f: English teaching, L. J. Saccio to Joseph C. Satterthwaite, "ICA Paper on US Assistance to Tropical Africa for Mr. Dillon," 25 March 1960, 8.

139. BNA, INF12/863, R. H. K. Marett, "Report on Visit to East Africa by R. H. K.," March/November 1960, 12.

140. BNA, FO111/138838, FO to Conakry, 28 August 1959.

141. BNA, INF12/863, R. H. K. Marett, "Report on Visit to East Africa by R. H. K.," March/November 1960, 12, 8; in his book, Marett repeats what he wrote in his report: Robert Marett, *Through the Back Door: An Inside View of Britain's Overseas Information Services* (Oxford: Pergamon Press, 1968), 196–99.

142. ANS, FM13, "Information diplomatique: Relations diplomatiques entre Bonn et Conakry," 6 Avril 1960.

143. Emphasis in the original: NARA, RG.59, CDF1960–63, 751.56311/1-760–751F.00/7-261, Department of State, "Communist Influence in Guinea," 9 March 1960.

144. Mazov, *A Distant Front*, 129.

145. NARA, RG.306, P249, box 10, f: English teaching, L. J. Saccio to Joseph C. Satterthwaite, "ICA Paper on US Assistance to Tropical Africa for Mr. Dillon," 25 March 1960, 9.

146. NARA, RG.469, P206, box 3, f: Guinea 1959–1960, John H. Morrow to StateDept, "Recommendation for Impact Project in Guinea," 15 February 1960.

147. BNA, DO35/9716, Notes, B. A Cockram, 10 May 1957; NARA, RG.306, UD-WW285, FRC 2, f: Regional, Argus Tresridder, "A Study of the Cultural Program in Africa with Especial Reference to Education: Program Development and Coordination Staff Information Center Service United States Information Agency," October 1957, 28, "Meeting of Representatives of Government Agencies on Africa," 16 October 1959.

148. FNSP, 2DE61, f: Juin 1958-février 1962, Note pour le premier ministre, "Conception et organisation d'ensemble de l'action culturelle et technique française à l'étranger," 8 October 1959, 1–3; Martin Garret, "Conclusion: A Gaullist Grand Strategy?," in *Globalizing de Gaulle: International Perspectives on French Foreign Policies, 1958–1969*, ed. Christian Nuenlist, Anna Locher, and Martin Garret (Lanham: Lexington Books, 2010), 302–303; Robert Frank, "La machine diplomatique culturelle française après 1945," *Relations Internationales*, no. 115 (2003): 332; Rice, "Cowboys and Communists."

149. "Veritable politique d'offre de services," FNSP, 2DE61, f: June 1958–February 1962, Note pour le premier ministre, "Conception et organisation d'ensemble de l'action culturelle et technique française à l'étranger," 8 October 1959, 1–3, 2.

150. DDEL, Papers as President, 1953–1961, NSC Series, box 12, f: 432nd Meeting of NSC, memdisc of the 432nd meeting of the National Security Council, 14 January 1960; AMAE, DAL Guinee, 51QO/28, note pour le Ministre, Guiringaud, "Présence culturelle et technique française en Guinée," 28 November 1958, f: Education Relations culturelle; AMAE, DAL Guinée, 51QO/61, f: Guinée: Education et relations culturelles, note pour le ministre, DGACT, Enseignement et Oeuvres, 10 May 1960; Chakrabarty, "The Legacies of Bandung," 53.

151. "Le problème du maintien de notre présence culturelle en Guinée se trouve donc posé. Si les professeurs qui sont ici refusent de demeurer dans leurs poste . . . revenir sur leur décidé . . . d'assurer la pérennité de la culture française dans ce pays d'Afrique," see AMAE, DAL Guinee, 51QO/67, f: Guinée: Education et relations culturelles, Siraud to Ministre des Affaires Etrangeres, "Situation des professeurs en Guinée," 21 May 1960, 3.

152. Schmidt, *Cold War and Decolonization in Guinea*, 176; AMAE, DAL Guinee, 51QO/67, f: Guinée: Education et relations culturelles, Seydoux to Chargé d'Affaires Conakry, "Mission de M. Mauffrais," 11 January 1960.

153. AMAE, DAL Généralités, 49QONT/65, memorandum, Roger Seydoux, 22 May 1959, Note, DAL, 13 August 1959; AMAE, DAL, Ghana 1953–1959 (sous déroga-tion), 50QO/28, f: Education—Question culturelles Bulletings S.D.E.C.E: June–July 1958, S.D.E.C.E bulletin, Présidence du conseil, "Ghana: Activités Pan-Africaines," 26 June 1958; NARA, RG.59, CDF1955–59, 550.60/6-958-556D.973/9-957, Amembassy Tunis, "The Alliance Française in Tunisia," 24 November 1958.

154. NARA, RG.469, P206, box 3, f: Guinea 1959–1960, Wilbert C. Petty to USIA, "English Teaching Potential," 27 October 1960, 2; BNA, FO1110/138838, memoran-dum, Christopher Ewart-Biggs, 29 September 1959; BNA, BW132/1, J. D. B. Fowells, "Report on Visit to Guinea, January 14th–26th 1960"; BNA, BW1/280, "British Council Work in Non-British West and Equatorial Africa," [1960].

155. Quotation taken from NARA, RG.306, A1-1072, box 194, f: English Language Teaching 1962, "N.E. Policy," [1961]; NARA, RG.469, P206, box 3, f: Guinea 1959–1960, Wilbert C. Petty to USIA, "English Teaching Potential," 27 October 1960, 1.

156. NARA, RG.469, P206, box 3, f: Africa-Guinea 1959–1960, Embassy Conakry to Dept of State, "USIA Program for Guinea, Particularly English-Teaching Program," 21 July 1959; NARA, RG.469, P206, box 3, f: Guinea 1959–1960, Wilbert C. Petty to USIA, "English Teaching Potential," 27 October 1960, 2; NARA, RG.469, P206, box 1, f: Africa-General 1/60-6/60, working paper, Verna Carley, "A Working Paper on Observations made of the Needs of Education in Africa, South of the Sahara," June 1960, 1.

157. ASPFAE, AD, AFRI (135), f: 186, M. Taymans, "Coup d'œil sur la Guinée: En-tretien avec l'archevêque expulsé de Conakry," 1 September 1961.

158. Patrick Chabal, *Amilcar Cabral: Revolutionary Leadership and People's War* (Cambridge: Cambridge University Press, 1983), 57.

4. Redefining Decolonization in the Sahara, 1959–1960

1. BNA, FO371/138609, Arnold Smith, "Afro Asian Solidarity Secretariat, Cairo: Anti Sahara Atomic Test Day," October 1959.

2. NAZ, MFA1/1/507/98, special report, Vernon Mwaanga, 28 March 1967.

3. Odd Arne Westad, *The Cold War: A World History* (New York: Basic Books, 2017), 627; Jean Allman, "Nuclear Imperialism and the Pan-African Struggle for Peace and Freedom: Ghana, 1959–1962," *Souls* 10, no. 2 (2008): 83–102; Abena Dove Osseo-Asare, *Atomic Junction: Nuclear Power in Africa after Independence* (Cambridge: Cambridge University Press, 2019), 21.

4. "United Nations General Assembly Fifteenth Session Official Records, 869th Plenary Meeting, Friday 30 September 1960 at 10:30 a.m., UN Documents," accessed September 22, 2021, https://undocs.org/en/A/PV.869.

5. Jensen, *The Making of International Human Rights*, 227; Tehila Sasson, "Milking the Third World? Humanitarianism, Capitalism, and the Moral Economy of the Nestlé Boycott," *American Historical Review* 121, no. 4 (2016): 1196–1224; Oona A. Hathaway and Scott J. Shapiro, *The Internationalists: How a Radical Plan to Outlaw War Remade the World* (New York: Simon & Schuster, 2017).

6. Scott Thompson, *Ghana's Foreign Policy, 1957–1966: Diplomacy, Ideology, and the New State* (Princeton, NJ: Princeton University Press, 1969), 91–92, 99, 111.

7. Gary Wilder, *Freedom Time: Negritude, Decolonization, and the Future of the World* (Durham, NC: Duke University Press Books, 2015), 1–10; Priya Lal, *African Socialism in Postcolonial Tanzania: Between the Village and the World* (Cambridge: Cambridge University Press, 2015), 10; Allman, "Nuclear," 97; Frederick Cooper, *Decolonization and African Society: The Labor Question in French and British Africa* (Cambridge: Cambridge University Press, 1996), 17; Vijay Prashad, *The Darker Nations: A People's History of the Third World* (New York: New Press, 2007), 24; Kate Skinner, "A Different Kind of Union: An Assassination, Diplomatic Recognition, and Competing Visions of African Unity in Ghana-Togo Relations, 1956–1963," in *Visions of African Unity: New Perspectives on the History of Pan-Africanism and African Unification Projects*, ed. Matteo Grilli and Frank Gerits (London: Palgrave Macmillan, 2020), 23–48; Vincent Intondi, *African Americans Against the Bomb: Nuclear Weapons, Colonialism, and the Black Freedom Movement* (Stanford, CA: Stanford University Press, 2015), 51; Yasu'o Mizobe, "An Overview of Japanese-African Relations and the 1960s Campaigns against the Atomic Bomb: Based on an Analysis of the 1962 Accra Assembly of the World without the Bomb," *Global Japanese Studies Review* 10, no. 1 (2018): 66.

8. Quotes taken from Archives de l'état en Belgique, Leuven (hereafter AEB), Archief Gaston Eyskens, 6069, "Verklaring Koning," 13 January 1959; Etambala points out that the declaration had been well prepared and was intended as a conservative and careful statement, see Aziza Etambala, *De Teloorgang van Een Modelkolonie: Belgisch Congo (1958–1960)* (Leuven: Acco, 2008), 194.

9. Paul Verhaegen, *De Psychologie van de Afrikaanse Zwarte* (Antwerp: Standaard, Katholieke Hogeschooluitbreiding, 1958).

10. ASPFAE, AD, AF/I/1 Mars-Juin 1959, No. d'ordre: 219, Le Compte Ph. De Liederke to P. Wigny, "Faible influence de Moscou et du Caire dans l'Est Africain à l'heure actuelle; l'effervescence est une conséquence directe d'Accra," 26 June 1959; ASPFAE, AF/I/1/1959, P Vanderstichelen to Wigny, "La déclaration du Gouvernement Belge relative à l'évolution politique du Congo Belge, et l'opinion sud-africaine," 19 January 1959; AGRB, I528 Pholien, box 575, R. Sergoynne, "Note sur la cause des troubles à Léopoldville des 3.4.5 Janvier 1959," [January 1959]. ASPFAE, AD, AF/I/1 March–June 1959, No. d'ordre: 219, Le Compte Ph. De Liederke Consul Général de Belgique to Monsieur P. Wigny, "Faible influence de Moscou et du Caire dans l'Est Africain à l'heure actuelle," 26 June 1959; KNADS, MAC/CON/181/5, "Nkrumah: the Myth and the Man by Russell Howe," 14 June 1959; ASPFAE, AD, AF/I/1/ 1959 January–February, R. van Meerbeke to Wigny, "Conférence panafricaine d'Accra," 20 February 1959; BAHDMNE, SR.66 Congo, Pt. 1, Leopoldville to Lisbon, 29 January 1959.

11. AGRB, I528 D'Aspremont Lynden, f: 58, Griffie, Kamer van Volksvertegenwoordigers, 31 March 1959; report, "Origines," [March 1959].

12. "Une soif d'indépendance et d'égalité avec les Blancs," see ASPFAE, AD, AF-1-1959, "Impressions d'un voyage au Congo Belge et au Ruanda-Urundi," [May 1959],

2–3; AGRB, I528 D'Aspremont Lynden, f:57, Proces-Verbal, "Declaration faite par le ministre du Congo Belge et du Ruanda-Urundi aux commissions réunies de la chambre et du senat," 24 February 1959; Etambala, *De Teloorgang*, 216.

13. BAHDMNE, SR.66 Congo, Pt. 1, unnamed author to Ministro dos Negócios Estrangeiros, 4 August 1959.

14. "Naar het hoofd stijgende sterke drank," see National Archives of the Netherlands, The Hague (hereafter NANTH), Archief Ambassade Congo-Kinshasa, 2.05.265, Nederlandse ambassade in Leopoldville, 1950–1974, inventarisnummer 145, Boreel to Luns, 25 February 1959.

15. AEB, Archief Gaston Eyskens, 6068, Sylvain Plasschaert to Eyskens, "Memorandum nopens de huidige politieke situatie in Congo," 10 June 1959.

16. ASPFAE, AD, AF/I/1/1959 July–October, "Compte rendu de la reunion de contact Belext-Minicoru-Inforcongo du 22 octobre 1959," 22 October 1959, 2.

17. Paul-Henri Spaak, "L'Alliance occidentale et le destin de l'Europe, address to the Mars et Mercure Industrial and Commercial Circle of Former Officers and Reserve Officers, 25 February 1957," accessed December 1, 2021, https://www.cvce.eu/en/obj /address_given_by_ paul_henri_spaak_on_nato_and_the_common_market_brussels _25_february_1957-en-6410340b-6469-42f7-ad5e-9c9437ee36d3.html.

18. AEB, Archief Gaston Eyskens, 6068, D'Aspermeont Lynden to Eyskens, 27 Août 1958.

19. AGRB, I528 Pholien, box 575, Commission du Congo Centrale, "Note sur la politique Belgo-Congolaise," 23 November 1959.

20. AEB, Archief Gaston Eyskens, 6066, Eyskens to J. Bogaert, 30 January 1959.

21. Quoted in Ludo De Witte, *De Moord Op Lumumba* (Antwerp: Van Halewyck, 2000), 336.

22. ASPFAE, AD, A1967F/I/1/1959 July–October, "Aide Mémoire concernant la politique belge en Afrique," 8 March 1959.

23. "Foule congolais," see AEB, Archief Gaston Eyskens, 6069, pamphlet, "L'action psychologique à la Force Publique par le lieutenant général Émile Janssens," 1959, 16, 10, 8.

24. AEB, Archief Gaston Eyskens, 6066, Vice Présidence Kamer van Volksvertegenwoordigers to Eyskens, 15 Januari 1960, 1.

25. AGRB, I528 D'Aspremont Lynden, box 53–80, f: 63, "La table ronde Belgo-Congolaise," [1959], 61–63; Guy Vanthemsche, *Congo: De Impact van de Kolonie Op België* (Tielt: Lannoo, 2007), 80; Thomas R. Kanza, *Conflict in the Congo: The Rise and Fall of Lumumba* (Harmondsworth: Penguin, 1972), 75.

26. AEB, Archief Gaston Eyskens, 6069, Jan de Meyer, "note a monsieur le premier ministre sur la conférence de la table ronde," 31 December 1959.

27. AGRB, I591 Wigny, box 1–7, f: 2, Pierre Wigny, "Memoires du Congo," s.d., 40.

28. AEB, Archief Gaston Eyskens, 6073, Eyskens, "Rede van de Heer Eerste Minister bij de opening van de Rondetafelconferentie," 20 January 1960, 3.

29. AEB, Archief Gaston Eyskens, 6077, M. van de Putte, "Preparation de la table ronde economique," 25 March 1960, 13–15.

30. AEB, Archief Gaston Eyskens, 6077, Banque nationale, 6 March 1960.

31. AEB, Archief Gaston Eyskens, 6073, note pour Monsieur le Ministre, "Société de développement," 21 January 1960.

32. BAHDMNE, SR. 66 Congo, Pt. 1, memorandum, 20 April 1960.

33. AGRB, I528 D'Aspremont Lynden, f: 87, "Economisch beleid van België ten opzichte van Congo," 31 March 1960, 2; AEB, Archief Gaston Eyskens, 6066, van Cauwelaert to Eyskens, 10 February 1960.

34. AGRB, I528 D'Aspremont Lynden, f: 87, "Rede van de heer eerste minister bij de opening van de economische rondetafelconferentie," 26 April 1960, 1.

35. AEB, Archief Gaston Eyskens, 6068, Sylvain Plasschaert to Prof. Eyskens, "Memorandum nopens de huidige politieke situatie in Congo," 10 June 1959.

36. Ludo De Witte, *Crisis in Kongo: De Rol van de Verenigde Naties, de Regering-Eyskens En Het Koningshuis in de Omverwerping van Lumumba En de Opkomst van Mobutu* (Leuven: Uitgeverij van Halewyck, 1996), 24.

37. AGRB, I528 D'Aspremont Lynden, box 53–80, f: 59, "Congo op de drempel der onafhankelijkheid," [1959], 29.

38. AGRB, I528 D'Aspremont Lynden, box 53–80, f: 61, "Le Congo à l'aube de l'indépendance," [1960].

39. AGRB, I528 D'Aspermeont Lynden, box 1–3, f: 3, "Action politique de l'Institut de Sociologie Solvay au Congo," 28 June 1960; AGRB, I591 Wigny, box 1–7, f: 2, Pierre Wigny, "Memoires du Congo," s.d., 40.

40. BAHDMNE, SR.66 Congo, Pt.1, "Relatório Pessoal Alcerca Do Congo Belga, Refernete a Fevereiro de 1960," [1960], 3.

41. Filipe Ribeiro de Meneses, *Salazar: A Political Biography* (New York: Enigma Books, 2010), 451.

42. ANS, VP144, f: Congo ex-belge, "Compte rendu d'écoute de Radio Conakry du 30 Janvier 1960 à 12h145," 30 January 1960.

43. Andrew Cohen, *The Politics and Economics of Decolonization in Africa: The Failed Experiment of the Central African Federation* (London: I.B. Tauris, 2017), 83, 87.

44. KNADS, MAC/CON/181/4, S. Paintsil, "Emergency meeting of the Steering committee of the AAPC held at Conakry, Republic of Guinea," 15 April 1959.

45. KNADS, MAC/CON/181/5, "Steering-Committee of the All-African People's Conference, Tunis," 31 May 1959.

46. KNADS, MAC/CAF/124/6, "Central Africa Committee," [1959].

47. NARA, RG.59, CDF1955–59, 645.5694/2-1756-645U.863322/1-2959, Stephen Gurney Gebelt to StateDept, "Ghana Government Statement Concerning Visit of Mr. Chipunza, Member of the Federal Government of Rhodesia and Nyassaland," 29 May 1959.

48. KNADS, MAC/CON/181/4, "Resolution the Steering committee of the All-African Peoples" Conference, AAPC Steering committee, 15-16-17 April 1959," [April 1959].

49. NAZ, Shelf 20, box 182 D, Northern Rhodesia Miscellaneous Reports 1950–59, "The Progress of Africans in Southern Rhodesia," April 1959, 32.

50. NARA, RG.59 CDF611.45A/2-955–611.47231/3-3058, Joseph Palmer to State Department, "Federal Prime Minister Attacks the United States and the United Kingdom," 13 November 1959.

51. The envoy the CO and the CRO had sent out to study French colonial management came back with a list of the radios, libraries, and information services that were operating in Dakar, rather than a close study of the French PR techniques; BNA, INF

12/978, CO, "Information activities undertaken by the Colonial Office in the African territories," [1958], A. P. Cullen, "Information Work in Africa South of the Sahara: Report of a Tour by Mr. A.P. Cullen from February 4 to June 25, 1958," [1958]; BNA, CO1027/252, Ralph Murray to FO, 26 May 1959, M. E. Allen to N. D. Watson, 24 April 1959.

52. BNA, PREM11/2588, memcon, Alec Douglas-Home, "Conversation with Dr. Nkrumah on Colonialism in Africa," 1 June 1959.

53. BNA, INF12/863, R. H. K. Marett, "Report on Visit to East Africa by R. H. K.," March/November 1960, 12; Robert Marett, *Through the Back Door: An Inside View of Britain's Overseas Information Services* (Oxford: Pergamon Press, 1968), 198–199; BNA, INF12/1339, CO, "The Objectives of United Kingdom Information Policy on Colonial Territories (with Special Reference to the East African Territories)," February 1959.

54. Quoted in Ronald Hyam, *Britain's Declining Empire: The Road to Decolonisation, 1918–1968* (Cambridge: Cambridge University Press, 2007), 256.

55. BNA, CAB134/1356, memorandum, Africa (Official) Committee, [1960].

56. AMAE, DAL Généralités 1960–1965, 49QONT/94, FO to MAE, "Anglo-French Talks on Information: Outline Record and Conclusions, The Foreign Office—July 4/5, 1960," 1960, 2; BNA, CO 936/545, "Brief for Anglo-US talks on Colonial Items at the 14th Session of the General Assembly: Washington, 14th and 15th September 1959," 14 September 1959; AMAE, DAL Guinee 1960–1965, 51QO/41, ambassade de France en Guinee to DAL, "Poste de radiodiffusion en Guinée," 26 January 1960, ambassade de France, la République fédérale d'Allemagne to Couve de Murville, "Projet de création d'un centre de radiodiffusion en Guinée," 27 July 1960.

57. NARA, RG.306, UD-WW285, FRC 2, f: IBS, James H. Logan, "Programming Objectives: African Service—IBS/RN," 12 February 1959, 1–2; Massachusetts Institute of Technology Archives (hereafter MIT Archives), MC 440 Ithiel de Sola Pool Papers, 1941–1984, box 134, f: Voice of America—Speech December 1961, Leon Festinger, "The Voice of America: Forum Lectures, The Theory of Cognitive Dissonance," [1961]; NARA, RG.306, UD-WW258, FRC 2, f: IBS, Handley (IAN), Henry Loomis (IBS), "Special African Project," 17 November 1959, Henry Loomis, "Report on Trip to Africa July-September 1959," [undated, 1959]; NARA, RG.306, UD-WW285, FRC 3, f: Letters General, "Extracts from a letter from Henry Loomis," 22 August 1959; NARA, RG.306, P249, box 10, f: Policy-Kampala Conference [folder 1/2], "African Conference on Department of State and US Information Agency Cultural Programs April 5–9, 1960," 9 April 1960, 1.

58. John Darwin, *The Empire Project: The Rise and Fall of the British World-System, 1830–1970* (Cambridge: Cambridge University Press, 2009), 620; BNA, INF12/867, A. D. C. Peterson, "Nyasaland in the London Times," 3 August 1959, John C. Hyde to E. C. R. Hadfield, 5 August 1959.

59. NAZ, Shelf 20, box 182D, Northern Rhodesia Miscellaneous Reports, 1950–1969, "Supplementary Report on the African Personality Tests," October 1959.

60. "Big UN Vote Calls on France to Drop Bomb Plan," *Times Saturday*, 21 November 1959; BNA, PREM 11/2694, New York to FO, 18 November 1959, secret minute, Macmillan, 30 October 1959.

61. LAC, RG.203, E. W. T. Gill to Secretary of State, Ottawa, "Conference of Independent African States," 28 April 1958, 3.

62. Touré's position taken from Roxanne Panchasi, "'No Hiroshima in Africa': The Algerian War and the Question of French Nuclear Tests in the Sahara," *History of the Present* 9, no. 1 (2019): 94–97.

63. NARA, RG.306, P249, box 10, f: Policy—French Atomic Tests [Folder1/2], Wilson Flake to secretary of state, 8 December 1959; FNSP, CM 7 1959, Couve de Murville to de Gaulle, 12 March 1960.

64. PRAAD, RG.17/2/802, Modibo Keita to Nkrumah, 7 July 1959.

65. Cartoon, *Evening News*, January 7, 1960.

66. "Prayer Protesting against French A-Test in the Sahara," *Ghana Times*, February 1, 1960.

67. Meredith Terretta, *Nation of Outlaws, State of Violence: Nationalism, Grassfields Tradition, and State Building in Cameroon* (Athens: Ohio University Press, 2013), 112.

68. Allman, "Nuclear," 90; Bill Sutherland and Matt Meyer, *Guns and Gandhi in Africa: Pan-African Insights on Nonviolence, Armed Struggle and Liberation* (Trenton, NJ: Africa World Press, 2000), 36–39.

69. "Anti-Atom Protest Demonstration Again," *Evening News*, September 1, 1960.

70. AMAE, DAL Généralités, 49QONT/72, f: Mesures de blocages des avions français a Ghana, Guiringaud to DAL, 8 February 1960,.

71. AMAE, DAL Généralités, 49QONT/72, "The Ghana Women's Anti-Atom Test Committee," 13 February 1960.

72. NAN, PX/D1, "Federal Nigeria 1960–62: A quarterly magazine first published in January 1958 by the Federal Information Service," 2 February 1960.

73. BNA, EG1/685, "Nigerian Ministers Visit to London: Talks with Macmillan and Mr. Lennox Boyd," 19 September 1959, "Note on Visit to Nigeria (February 13th–February 20th, 1960)," 21 March 1960; BNA, PREM 11/2694, secret minute, Macmillan, 30 October 1959 and "Note on Ghana Reactions," [October 1959].

74. PAAA, MfAA, A12703, "Stellungnahme zu den von der französischen Regierung angekündigten Atombombenversuchen in der Zeit von Mitt," 6 October 1960.

75. AMAE, DAL, Généralités, 49QONT/72, f: Mesures de blocages des avions français a Ghana, Guiringaud to DAL, "Note sur notre expérience nucléaire," 29 January 1960, Guiringaud to DAL, "Note sur notre expérience nucléaire," 25 January 1960.

76. AMAE, DAL, Généralités, 49QONT/72, Guiringaud to DAL, "Polémique sur notre experience nucléaire," 11 février 1960; "French Embassy Note Proved False," *Ghana Times*, February 11, 1960.

77. CHAN, Direction de la coopération technique et culturelle, 19810443/47, f: Historique de la DCT: Organization, Secrétaire d'etat aux relations avec les etats de la Communauté to l'envoyé exceptionnel et plénipotentiaire de la république française et de la Communauté à Abidjan, 11 October 1960; the pamphlet also ended up at the Belgian foreign affairs ministry, see ASPFAE, AA, 14563.

78. BNA, PREM11/2892, "The Visit of the Nigerian Prime Minister," 17 September 1959.

79. BNA, PREM11/2892, "Oral Answers," 10 November 1959, secretary of state for colonies to Sir J. Robertson, 31 March 1960; Osseo-Asare, *Atomic Junction*, 39.

80. BNA, DO35/9341, A.W. Snelling to J. Chadwick, 12 February 1960; BNA, PREM11/4242, FO to posts, 11 February 1960.

81. CHAN, Fonds de la présidence de la République de Charles de Gaulle, 5AG(1)/661, f: Janvier du 21 Decembre 1959, memcon, "Conference Occidentale a Quatre: Tete-a-tete du General de Gaule avec M. Macmillan, au Palais de l'Elysee le 21 Decembre 1959," 21 December 1959, 7–8.

82. NARA, RG.306, P249, box 10, f: Policy—French Atomic Tests [Folder 1/2], "Nigerians Protest French Atomic Tests in the Sahara," 21 July 1959, Allen to posts, "Infoguide: French Nuclear Test," 19 August 1959, Tom Graves to Glen Smith, "Making it Safe to Stop Nuclear Testing Part I II III," 14 October 1959, "Infoguide: French Nuclear Testing," 11 February 1960.

83. BNA, EG1/685, "Note on Visit to Nigeria (February 13th–February 20th, 1960)," 21 March 1960, Ottawa to CRO, 31 March 1960.

84. ANS, FM117 Renseignment sur la premiere Bombe Atomique, f: Premier Bombe Atomique, "concernant les retombées radioactives dans les Etats de la Communauté," 22 March 1960.

85. The committee consisted of J. R. Clackson, director of Meteorological Services, Nigeria; O. D. Macnamara, senior radiology specialist, Nigeria; B. E. C. Agu, physicist at the University College Ibadan; and J. A. T. Watson; see BNA, EG1/685, N. Levin to Roger Makins, 23 March 1960, 1, "Note on Visit to Nigeria (February 13th–February 20th, 1960)," 21 March 1960, 1.

86. BNA, DO35/9424, A. W. Snelling to Hunt, "Fake Independence," 2 March 1960.

87. The support for Ghana is remarkable, since historians point to the French referendum in 1958, not African activism, as a crucial factor in the dissolving of the British empire; see Frank Heinlein, British Government Policy and Decolonisation, 1945–63: Scrutinising the Official Mind (New York: Routledge, 2002), 299; Hyam, Britain's Declining Empire, 265; Darwin, The Empire Project, 649–52; Sue Onslow, "Resistance to the 'Winds of Change': The Emergence of the 'Unholy Alliance' between Southern Rhodesia, Portugal and South Africa, 1964–5," in The Wind of Change: Harold Macmillan and British Decolonization, ed. Sarah Stockwell and Larry J. Butler (London: Palgrave Macmillan, 2013), 215–34.

88. BNA, DO177/19, minute, N. Pritchard, 13 December 1960; BNA, FO953/2031, "Information Policy for Africa," 30 June 1961.

89. Tom Stacey, "They Call Him 'Sell-Out Mac': A Man under Torture Knows His Own People Hate Him in British Africa," Star, September 29, 1960.

90. AMAE, DAL, Ghana 1960–1965, 50QO/72, Guiringaud to Ministre des affaires Etrangères, "Information politique," 14 May 1960, 4, "Commonwealth Today," 2.

91. BNA, INF12/597, J.T. Hughes to Arnold Harrison, 27 January 1953; BNA, INF12/978, "Information activities undertaken by the Colonial Office in the African territories," [1958].

92. AMAE, DAL, Ghana 1960–1965, 50QO/34, Guiringaud to Ministre des Affaires Etrangères, "Information politique," 14 May 1960, 2; AMAE, DAL, Ghana 1960–1965, 50QO/72, "Histoire de l'Afrique racontée aux Ghanéens," 22 February 1960.

93. AMAE, DAL, Généralités, 49QONT/72, f: Mesures de blocages des avions français a Ghana, Guiringaud to DAL, "M. Nkrumah, la bombe et nos amis," 23 February 1960; Guiringaud to Couve de Murville, 14 February 1960, Documents Diplomatiques Français (hereafter DDF), 1960, Tome 1, 175.

94. "A French Bomb—Not Only for France?," Manchester Guardian, 10 July 1959.

95. NARA, RG.306, P249, box 10, f: Policy—French Atomic Tests [Folder 1/2], Donald Dumont to StateDept, "Position of UPS on French Atomic Explosion," 24 February 1960, "Reaction in Guinea to French Atomic Test," 20 February 1960; NARA, RG.306, P249, box 10, f: Policy—French Atomic Tests [Folder 1/2], Ambassade de France Service de Presse et d'Information, "France's First Atomic Explosion," 13 February 1960.

96. NASA, BTS1/169/7, "Sudan: Hostility to Nuclear Tests," 24 August 1959.

97. ANS, FM121, "Ministre de L'information et de la sécurité," [April 1959], "Service fédéral de l'information et de la Radiodiffusion Rapport d'activités," [1959]; ANS, VP131, Mamadou Dia to de Gaulle, 22 April 1959, "Note relative aux questions évoquées par M. Le Président Mamadou Dia dans sa lettre à M. Le Président de la Communauté," [1959].

98. Irwin M. Wall, *France, the United States, and the Algerian War* (Berkeley: University of California Press, 2001), 212.

99. Radoslav A. Yordanov, *The Soviet Union and the Horn of Africa during the Cold War: Between Ideology and Pragmatism* (Cambridge, MA: Harvard University Press, 2017), 16.

100. NARA, RG.306, P249, box 10, f: Policy—French Atomic Tests [Folder1/2], Howard W. Potter to StateDept, "Factors Causing Withdrawal of Sanctions Imposed in Protest against French Saharan Bomb Tests," 28 April 1960, Howard W. Potter to StateDept, "Ghana Reinforces Economic Sanctions against France in Protest against Saharan Bomb Tests," 14 April 1960.

101. KNADS, MAC/CON/196/1, "Conference on Positive Action for Peace and Security in Africa to be held in Accra, April 7th–9th," April 1961.

102. Sutherland and Meyer, *Guns and Gandhi*, 41–42; Allman, "Nuclear Imperialism," 97.

103. KNADS, MAC/CON/184/3, "Resolutions to All African Peoples Conference. Rev. Michael Scott—South West Africa," [1958].

104. MSRC, Dabu Gizenga Papers, box 128-6, f: 108 Conference, Kwame Nkrumah, "Conference on Positive Action and Security in Africa, Accra, 7th to 10th April, 1960. Opening Session," 7 April 1960; Allman, "Nuclear Imperialism," 93–96; Sutherland and Meyer, *Guns and Gandhi*, 41.

105. NARA, RG.306, P249, box 10, f: Policy—French Atomic Tests [Folder 1/2], Dorros to secretary of state, "House of Representatives Passes Strong Motion Regarding Future Sahara Bomb Tests," 7 April 1960.

106. NASA, BEV, box 12, f: Ghana, T. Hewitson to Secretary of State for External Affairs, "Pan-African Conference, Accra—April 1960," 21 April 1960; "M. N'Krumah a ajouté que l'exemple de la Belgique constitue un encouragement pour tous les peuples africains," see ASPFAE, AD, AFRI(127), f: 172, Walravens, "Entretien avec M. N'Krumah, Premier Ministre," February 1960.

107. KNADS, MAC/CON/181/4, "Resolution of the Steering Committee of the All-African People's Conference, AAPC Steering Committee, 15–16–17 April 1959," [April 1959].

108. Colin Legum, "The Belgian Congo (II) Towards Independence," *Africa South*, September 1960, 85; Patrice Lumumba, *Le Congo: Terre d'avenir, est-il menacé?* (Brussels: Office de Publicité, 1961), 19, 15; De Witte, *De Moord Op Lumumba*, 334; Georges Nzongola-Ntalaja, *Patrice Lumumba* (Athens: Ohio University Press, 2014), 1–10.

109. BNA, FCO141/6735, Howard W. Potter to StateDept, "Factors Causing Withdrawal of Sanctions Imposed in Protest Against French Saharan Bomb Tests," 28

April 1960, "Conference on Positive Action for Peace and Security in Africa to be held in Accra April 7th–9th," [April 1960]; NARA, RG.306, P249, box 10, f: Policy—French Atomic Tests [Folder 1/2], Washburn to African posts, "Infoguide: Emergency Conference For Peace and Security in Africa," 1 April 1960.

110. Osseo-Asare, *Atomic Junction*, 48.

111. Reem Abou-El-Fadl, "Building Egypt's Afro-Asian Hub: Infrastructures of Solidarity and the 1957 Cairo Conference," *Journal of World History* 30, no. 1 (2019): 157–92.

5. The Congo Crisis as the Litmus Test for Psychological Modernization, 1960–1961

1. AEB, Archief Gaston Eyskens, 6074, Eyskens, "A cet instant," [June 1960], Baudouin, "L'independence du Congo, [June 1960]," 1, 5, "De rede van premier Lumumba," 1 July 1960.

2. Lise Namikas, *Battleground Africa: Cold War in the Congo, 1960–1965* (Stanford, CA: Stanford University Press, 2013), 62–69.

3. AEB, Archief Gaston Eyskens, 6081, P. Meyers to Eyskens, 4 August 1960, Kabinet van de Eerste Minister, "Betreft: instructies gegeven aan alle parketten van België," 29 July 1960, 2.

4. David Van Reybrouck, *Congo: Een Geschiedenis* (Amsterdam: De Bezige Bij, 2010), 276; Namikas, *Battleground Africa*, 2013, 62–71.

5. Jean Allman, "Nuclear Imperialism and the Pan-African Struggle for Peace and Freedom: Ghana, 1959–1962," *Souls* 10, no. 2 (2008): 97; Brenda Gayle Plummer, *In Search of Power: African Americans in the Era of Decolonization, 1956–1974* (Cambridge: Cambridge University Press, 2012), 74; Ama Biney, *The Political and Social Thought of Kwame Nkrumah* (London: Palgrave Macmillan, 2011), 112, 152; Scott Thompson, *Ghana's Foreign Policy, 1957–1966: Diplomacy, Ideology, and the New State* (Princeton, NJ: Princeton University Press, 1969), 160; David Rooney, *Kwame Nkrumah: Vision and Tragedy* (Accra: Sub-Saharan Publishers, 2007), 284.

6. Sergey Mazov, *A Distant Front in the Cold War: The USSR in West Africa and the Congo, 1956–1964* (Stanford, CA: Stanford University Press, 2010), 2.

7. GPL, BAA/RLAA/370, A. K. Barden to Nkrumah, "Special Mission to East and Central Africa," 28 November 1960; Odd Arne Westad, *The Global Cold War: Third World Interventions and the Making of Our Times* (Cambridge: Cambridge University Press, 2005), 398; Paul Nugent, *Africa Since Independence: A Comparative History* (New York: Palgrave Macmillan, 2004), 83; Scopas S. Poggo, "General Ibrahim Abboud's Military Administration in the Sudan, 1958–1964: Implementation of the Programs of Islamization and Arabization in the Southern Sudan," *Northeast African Studies* 9, no. 1 (2002): 72.

8. Nicholas J. Cull, *The Cold War and the United States Information Agency: American Propaganda and Public Diplomacy, 1945–1989* (Cambridge: Cambridge University Press, 2009), 180.

9. DDEL, U.S. President's Committee on Information Activities Abroad (Sprague Committee) Records, 1959–61, box 27, f: Minutes (2), minutes, "Abbott: U.S. Information Agency: Notes for Sprague Committee Presentation—Monday Afternoon," 14 March 1960; Kissinger quoted in Ryan Irwin, *Gordian Knot: Apartheid and the Unmaking of the Liberal World Order* (Oxford: Oxford University Press, 2012), 172.

10. Quote taken from memcon, "President's Trip to Europe," August 31, 1959, *FRUS 1958–1960*, vol. 7, part 2, *Western Europe*, 735; Satterthwaite stated this in public and behind closed doors, see NARA, RG.306, UD-WW285, FRC 2, f: Conferences, Satterthwaite, "U.S. Objectives in Africa: Statement by Mr. Satterthwaite at Tangier Conference," 1960, 4; NARA, RG.469, P36, box 11, f: Africa Advisory Conference, "Views Expressed by the African Advisory Group Regarding the Report of the Study Group on U.S. Aid to Africa," 17 May 1960.

11. DDEL, US President's Committee on Information Activities Abroad: Records 1960–61, box 26, f: Report of the PCIAA, "Report of the President's Committee on Information Activities Abroad," 1960, 10.

12. DDEL, US President's Committee on Information Activities Abroad (Sprague Committee), box 23, f: PCIAA #31 (1), "Africa South of the Sahara," 1960, 16; Stephen G. Rabe, "Eisenhower Revisionism: The Scholarly Debate," in *America in the World: The Historiography of American Foreign Relations since 1941*, ed. Michael J. Hogan (Cambridge: Cambridge University Press, 1995), 306; DDEL, AWF, Ann Whitman Diary Series, box 11, f: [ACW] Diary December 1960, "Diary Memorandum for Records –December 26, 1960."

13. DDEL, US President's Committee on Information Activities Abroad: Records 1960–61, box 9, f: Africa # 31 (1), "Africa South of the Sahara," 1960.

14. AMAE, DAL, Généralités 1960–1965 AFR, 49QNT/90, f: Entretiens franco-americains juin 1959–aout 1962, Plans & Operations Militaires, "Reprise des Conversations Tripartites sur L'Afrique: Menaces et Zones Sensibles," 6 April 1960; BNA, FO371/137966, Chancery to African Department FO, 23 April 1959; BNA, CAB134/1558, "Colonial Policy Committee," 10 April 1959; NARA, RG.59, A1-3107, box 1, f: Communism in Africa, "President de Gaulle's Visit Position Papers: Soviet Penetration in Africa April 22–26, 1960," [April 1960], James Frederick Green to Satterthwaite, "Your Appointment with the French Minister," 8 December 1959.

15. NATO Archives, CM(59)32-e, "Communist Penetration in Africa," 20 March 1959, 1–5, NATO Archives, CM(61)112, "Communist Penetration in Africa," 23 November 1961; NATO Archives, CM(61)43-e, Evelyn Shuckburgh, "Communist Penetration in Africa," 23 April 1960, 6.

16. AMAE, DAL, Congo Belge 1960–65, 44QONT/49, f: CB-V-1-17 Assistance technique et culturel jan-déc 1960, M. Thibaut to DAL, 10 October 1960; Lise Namikas, "Battleground Africa: The Cold War and the Congo Crisis, 1960–1965" (PhD diss., University of Southern California, 2002), 73; Vincent Genin, "La Politique Étrangère de La France Face à La Crise Congolaise (1960–1961)," *Journal of Belgian History* 43, no. 1 (2013): 95.

17. Georges Nzongola-Ntalaja, *The Congo: From Leopold to Kabila: A People's History*, Second Impression ed. (London: Zed Books, 2002), 96; Colin Legum, "The Belgian Congo (II) Towards Independence," *Africa South*, September 1960, 81; PRAAD, BAA/RLAA/964, "The Last Message of Patrice Lumumba," 29 March 1961.

18. The Belgian government was also surprised, as the official investigation revealed, Luc De Vos, Emmanuel Gerard, Philippe Raxhon, and Jules Gérard-Libois *Lumumba: De Complotten? De Moord* (Leuven: Davidsfonds, 2004), 31; before independence there was little interest in Congo, see Catherine Hoskyns, "Sources for a Study of the Congo since Independence," *Journal of Modern African Studies* 1, no. 3 (1963): 373.

19. ASPFAE, AA, INFO(26), "The Belgian Congo Today," vol. I, no. 1, January 1952, 32.

20. BNA, BW154/1, Information Office Leopoldville to FO, 16 August 1960; NARA, RG.306, P86, box 2, telegram, USIS Leopoldville to Sec. of State, 10 April 1961; NARA, RG.306, UD-WW273, FRC 51, f: IAA Assessment Reports, USIS-Leopoldville to Washington, "Country Assessment Report," 13 February 1961; BNA, FO1110/1299, Elizabeth Wyndham to F. R. H. Hugh Murray, 31 October 1960, F. R. H. Murray to E. Wyndham British Embassy Leopoldville, 11 November 1960.

21. Genin, "La politique étrangère," 89; NARA, RG.59, CDF1960-63, 611.70/2-860-611.70/2-1362, "Exchange of Views on Africa," 15 April 1960, 5; ASPFAE, AA, AEII3211, Jean van den Bosch to Victor Larock, "Entretien avec le Président Nasser," 12 April 1958, 1.

22. BNA, CO1027/252, consulate general to information executive department, 25 November 1959; BNA, BW90/59, "C. W. de Kiewiet President University of Rochester: Education in the Congo, in the New York Herald Tribune," 8 January 1961; US headlines emphasized the chaos, see Kevin Dunn, *Imagining the Congo: The International Relations of Identity* (London: Palgrave Macmillan, 2003), 87–91.

23. NARA, RG.59, CDF1955-59, 611.55921/9-1257-611.565/11-2957, Amembassy Brussels, "United States Policy Toward the Belgian Congo," 10 December 1959, 3; Jef Van Bilsen, *Un plan de trente ans pour l'émancipation politique de l'Afrique Belge* (Kortrijk: Vooruitgang, 1956); General Andrew Goodpaster wrote to Herter, "The Congo crisis points up one of the world's most urgent needs: The absence of trained and educated people to take over leadership and administration of the new African nations," quoted in Tom Shachtman, *Airlift to America: How Barack Obama, Sr., John F. Kennedy, Tom Mboya, and 800 East African Students Changed Their World and Ours* (New York: St. Martin's Press, 2009), 151.

24. Harold Macmillan, *Pointing the Way, 1959–1961* (London: Macmillan, 1972), 430.

25. AEB, Archief Gaston Eyskens, 6081, Pholien to Eyskens, 30 July 1960.

26. AGRB, I528 Harold d'Aspremont Lynden, box 1–15, f: 7, P. Leroy, note pour monsieur le ministre, 16 March 1961; NARA, RG.59, CDF1960–1963, 561.913/8-560 to 570C.003/10-661, Amembassy Brussels to StateDept, "The Training of Africans in Belgium," 11 January 1963.

27. Special Collections Georgetown, Fitzhugh Green Papers, box 6, f: 23, Fitzhugh Green to USIA, 30 June 1960; the OCB also offered two hundred scholarships for technical and governmental administrators, see NARA, RG.306, P249, box 6, Dorothy Rigdon, "Draft of 15th Report to Congress," [1961]; NARA, RG.306, P249, box 8, f: Policy—OCB, Operation Committee Minutes, 23 March 1960, "Notes on OCB Meeting," 23 June 1960; AMAE, DAL, Congo Belge 1960–65, 44QONT/49, f: CB-V-1-17 Assistance technique et culturelle janv.-déc. 1960, Pierre Charpentier to Couve de Murville, "Object: Assistance Technique," 6 July 1960, Henri-Francis Mazoyer to DAL, "Object: Coopération technique aide culturelle au Congo belge," 7 April 1960.

28. NARA, RG.469, P206, box 1, f: Africa-General 7/60–12/60, memcon, StateDept, 11 July 1960; BNA, BW154/1, Information Office Leopoldville to FO, 16 August 1960.

29. PRAAD, SC/BAA/251, "Report on the 2nd all African People's Conference held in Tunis on 25th January, 1960," 25 January 1960; BAHDMNE, SR.255 S11/E10/P5/68842, f: Ajuda Ghana aos Movimentos 4, 21, A. K. Barden to Agostino Lunga, 9 September 1960; Congo-Leopoldville was also central to the French cultural diplomats after 1945, see AMAE, DAL Généralités 1944–1952, 49QO/96, Monod to Direction du Personnel, "Représentation française en Afrique Noire," 20 April 1945, 2.

30. Quoted in Thompson, *Ghana's Foreign Policy*, 124, 140; MSRC, Gizenga Papers, box 128-9, f: 209 The Congo, "Half of the Armed Force of Ghana Are Serving in the Congo," [1960]; quoted in ASPFAE, AD, Classement "B", 18.287/I, Nkrumah to Lefèvre, 22 December 1964.

31. ANS, FM 39, Edouard Terzian, "Rapport," 22 August 1960.

32. ASPFAE, AD, AFRI(134), f: 185. May–August 1961, "Progress Report No. 11 on United Nations Civilian Operations in the Congo during July-August 1961," August 1961.

33. "United Nations General Assembly Fifteenth Session Official Records, 869th Plenary Meeting, Friday 23 September 1960 at 10.30 a.m., UN Documents," accessed September 22, 2021, https://undocs.org/en/A/PV.869.

34. Quoted in Alistair Horne, *Macmillan: The Official Biography* (Basingstoke, UK: Pan Macmillan, 2008), 278.

35. CHAN, Fonds de la présidence de la République de Charles de Gaulle, 5AG1/722, Eisenhower to de Gaulle, 17 November 1959, de Gaulle to Eisenhower, 9 August 1960, Eisenhower to de Gaulle, 30 August 1960; FNSP, 2DE29, f: Lettres et notes de Michel Debré au général de Gaulle Dossier III (janvier–juillet 1960), Debré to de Gaulle, "Note sur les relations franco-américaines," 18 April 1960. De Gaulle reworked his old idea of a "three-power directorate," see memcon, "President Eisenhower's meeting with Foreign Minister Lunds and Monsieur Spaak," September 3, 1959, *FRUS 1958–1960*, vol. 7, part 1, *Western European Integration and Security*, Canada, 483–84.

36. Ana Mónica Fonseca and Daniel Marcos, "Cold War Constraints: France, West Germany and Portuguese Decolonization," *Portuguese Studies* 29, no. 2 (2013): 212.

37. M. Couve de Murville to A. Berard, February 4, 1960, *DDF*, 1960, Tome 1, 133.

38. Namikas, for instance, characterizes Eisenhower's speech as lifeless, see Namikas, "Battleground Africa" (PhD diss.), 109; NARA, RG.469, P206, box 1, f: Africa—General 7/60–12/60, "President Eisenhower Addresses U.N. General Assembly," 22 September 1960.

39. NARA, RG.469, P36, box 11, f: FY 1962 Africa Guidelines, memorandum, James Simsarian, 30 September 1960, Riddleberger to MSP, "FY 1962 Proposals for the United Nations Program in Africa," 11 October 1960; NARA, RG. 469, P206, box 1, f: Africa—General 7/60–12/60, secretariat note ICA, "President Eisenhower's Address to the UN General Assembly: Program for Africa Stressed," 20 October 1960.

40. NARA, RG.469, P206, box 1, airgram, Herter to Posts, "Aid to Education in Africa through the UN System of Organizations," 22 November 1960.

41. "Eisenhower, Dwight D. to Eric A. Johnston, 16 February 1960. In The Papers of Dwight David Eisenhower, ed. L. Galambos and D. van Ee, doc. 1444. World Wide Web facsimile by The Dwight D. Eisenhower Memorial Commission of the print edition; Baltimore, MD: The Johns Hopkins University Press, 1996," accessed April 1, 2014, http://www.eisenhowermemorial.org/presidential-papers/second-term/documents/1444.cfm; NARA, RG.306, P249, box 14, f: Policy US Tour for Africans—November and December 1960, StateDept, "Tour of the United States November 1960," [1960]; NARA, RG.306, P249, box 4, f: Policy-UN [Folder 3/3], USUN Edward Stansbury to IOP James J. Halsema, "Budget Proposal for USIA/UN," 23 November 1960.

42. DDEL, US President's Committee on Information Activities Abroad: Records 1960–61, box 26, f: Printed Committee Report, "Conclusion and Recommendations of the President's Committee on Information Activities Abroad," December 1960; "UN

Digital Library: A/PV.947, Declaration on the Granting of Independence to Colonial Countries and Peoples: Resolution," accessed September 22, 2021, https://digitallibrary .un.org/record/662085; Ebere Nwaubani, *The United States and Decolonization in West Africa, 1950–1960* (Rochester, NY: University of Rochester Press, 2001), 44.

43. "United Nations General Assembly Fifteenth Session Official Records, 869th Plenary Meeting, Friday 23 September 1960 at 10.30 a.m., UN Documents," accessed September 22, 2021, https://undocs.org/en/A/PV.869.

44. "United Nations General Assembly Fifteenth Session Official Records, 896th Plenary Meeting, Monday 10 October 1960 at 10.30 a.m., UN Documents," accessed September 22, 2021, https://undocs.org/en/A/PV.896; Julião Soares Sousa, "Amílcar Cabral, the PAIGC and the Relations with China at the Time of the Sino-Soviet Split and of Anti-Colonialism: Discourses and Praxis," *International History Review* 42, no. 6 (2020): 1275.

45. "United Nations General Assembly Fifteenth Sessions Official Records, 901st Plenary Meeting, Wednesday 12 October 1960 at 10.30 a.m.," https://undocs.org/en/A /PV.901.

46. "United Nations General Assembly Fifteenth Sessions Official Records, 879th Plenary Meeting, Friday 30 September 1960 at 10.30 a.m., UN Documents," accessed September 22, 2021, https://undocs.org/en/A/PV.879.

47. MSRC, Nkrumah Papers, box 128-6, f: Kwame Nkrumah Speeches—Fifteenth Session of the General Assembly of the UN, "Address by Osagyefo Dr. Kwame Nkrumah President of the Republic of Ghana to the Fifteenth Session of the General Assembly of the United Nations," 23 September 1960, 3; BNA, FO371/146697, restricted report, Ian Scott, 3 September 1960.

48. Nzongola-Ntalaja, *The Congo*, 108–10.

49. "United Nations General Assembly Fifteenth Session Official Records, 896th Plenary Meeting, Monday 10 October 1960 at 10.30 a.m., UN Documents," accessed September 22, 2021, https://undocs.org/en/A/PV.896.

50. "United Nations General Assembly Fifteenth Sessions Official Records, 879th Plenary Meeting, Friday 30 September 1960 at 10.30 a.m., UN Documents," accessed September 22, 2021, https://undocs.org/en/A/PV.879.

51. "United Nations General Assembly Fifteenth Sessions Official Records, 912th Plenary Meeting, Tuesday 8 November 1960 at 3 p.m., UN Documents," accessed September 22, 2021, https://undocs.org/en/A/PV.912; Thomas R. Kanza, *Conflict in the Congo: The Rise and Fall of Lumumba* (Harmondsworth: Penguin, 1972), 335.

52. "United Nations General Assembly Fifteenth Sessions Official Records, 880th Plenary Meeting, Friday 30 September 1960 at 3 p.m., UN Documents," accessed September 22, 2021, https://undocs.org/en/A/PV.880.

53. "United Nations General Assembly Fifteenth Session Official Records, 892nd Plenary Meeting, Friday 7 October 1960 at 10.30 a.m., UN Documents," accessed September 22, 2021, https://undocs.org/en/A/PV.892; "United Nations General Assembly Fifteenth Session Official Records, 897th Plenary Meeting, Monday 10 October 1960 at 10.30 a.m., UN Documents," accessed September 22, 2021, https://undocs.org/en/A /PV.897.

54. Sergei Khrushchev, ed., *Memoirs of Nikita Khrushchev*, vol. 3, *Statesman, 1953–1964* (University Park: Penn State University Press, 2013), 263.

55. Elizabeth Schmidt, *Foreign Intervention in Africa: From the Cold War to the War on Terror* (Cambridge: Cambridge University Press, 2013), 61; NARA, RG.306, P43, box 1, f: Belgian Congo Leopoldville, "Tour of the Congo," 14 June 1960.

56. Filipe Ribeiro de Meneses, *Salazar: A Political Biography* (New York: Enigma Books, 2010), 458.

57. The Foreign Office was eager to exploit the opportunities in the area of education and information; see BNA, BW154/1, Information Office Leopoldville to FO, 16 August 1960.

58. BNA, DO198/2, Embassy Leopoldville to Accra, "Congo/Ghana and Technical Assistance," 15 August 1960; BNA, FCO141/6227, "Government Propaganda," 4 August 1960; Alan James, *Britain and the Congo Crisis, 1960–1963* (New York: St. Martin's Press, 1996), 10.

59. BNA, DO198/2, embassy Leopoldville to Accra, "Congo/Ghana and Technical Assistance," 15 August 1960; BNA, FO1110/1299, Elizabeth Wyndham to Ralph Murray, 25 November 1960.

60. BNA, BW154/1, appendix B, J. D. B. Fowells, "Notes on the Congo—particularly Leopoldville," 6 September 1960, J. D. B. Fowells, "Report on Visit to the Congo by Mr. J. D. B. Fowells," 6 September 1960; some have seen the business and financial interests of the European powers as crucial in understanding the Congo crisis, see David N. Gibbs, *The Political Economy of Third World Intervention: Mines, Money and U.S. Policy in the Congo Crisis* (Chicago: University of Chicago Press, 1991); Alanna O'Malley, *The Diplomacy of Decolonisation: America, Britain and the United Nations During the Congo Crisis 1960–64* (Manchester: Manchester University Press, 2018); John Kent, "The US and Decolonization in Central Africa, 1957–64," in *The Wind of Change: Harold Macmillan and British Decolonization* (London: Palgrave Macmillan, 2013), 195–214.

61. AMAE, DAL, Congo Belge 1960–65, 44QONT/49, f: CB-V-1-17 Assistance technique et culturelle Janv.–déc. 1960, DGACT, "Assistance Technique de la France au Congo Ex-Belge," 21 October 1960, "Questions culturelles et techniques," 27 June 1960, Le Directeur General des Affaires Culturelles et Techniques, Le Ministre des Affaires Etrangère to l'ambassadeur de France à Leopoldville, "Mission de M. Gros," 16 December 1960.

62. NARA, RG.306, P249, box 11, memcon, "US-UK Talks on Africa," 17–18 November 1960; BNA, BW154/1, appendix, J. D. B. Fowells, "Notes on the Congo—particularly Leopoldville," J.D.B. Fowells, "Report on Visit to the Congo by Mr. J. D. B. Fowells," 6 September 1960.

63. BNA, FO1110/1299, Elizabeth Wyndham to Ralph Murray, 25 November 1960; MSRC, Gizenga Papers, box 128-9, f: 209 The Congo, "Half of the Armed Force of Ghana are serving in the Congo," [1960]; Thompson, *Ghana's Foreign Policy*, 133.

64. Biney talks about an "ideological comrade," see Biney, *The Political and Social Thought of Kwame Nkrumah*, 82; Emmanuel Gerard and Bruce Kuklick, *Death in the Congo: Murdering Patrice Lumumba* (Boston: Harvard University Press, 2015), 58; Patrice Lumumba, *Le Congo: Terre d'avenir, est-il menancé?* (Brussels: Office de Publicité, 1961), 151; MSRC, Nkrumah Papers, box 154-20, f:10, Andrew Djin to Nkrumah, 13 September 1960.

65. ANS, FM 39, Mamadou Dia to Philibert Tsiranana, 8 February 1961; Ferik Ibrahim Abboud to Mamadou Dia, [February 1961], Tubman to Mamadou Dia, 14 February 1961,

telegram, 7 February 1961, André Guillabert to Président du Conseil des Ministres du Gouvernement, 6 February 1961, "membres Africains . . . d'utiliser cette tribune internationale comme un instrument de propaganda et de demagogie en vérité," see "Le discourse de M. Ousmane Soce Diop devant le conseil de securite," s.d.; ANS, VP149, f: Tunésie, Senghor to Habib Bourguiba, 26 July 1964; "United Nations General Assembly Fifteenth Sessions Official Records, 940th Plenary Thursday, 8 December 1960 at 10.30 a.m., UN Documents," accessed September 22, 2021, https://undocs.org/en/A/PV.940.

66. Jean-Pierre Bat, *Le syndrome Foccart: La politique française en Afrique, de 1959 à nos jours* (Paris: Éditions Gallimard, 2012), 11–55; Frédéric Turpin, *Jacques Foccart: Dans l'ombre du Pouvoir* (Paris: CNRS Editions, 2015).

67. AEB, Archief Gaston Eyskens, 6066, van Overstraeten to Eyskens, 29 March 1960.

68. ASPFAE, AD, AF/I/1/1959 juillet–octobre, "Expose de Mr. Huybrechts ancien Conseil fédéral à Dakar," 15 octobre [1959].

69. BNA, FO371/137966, "Summary Record of the First Meeting at Ambassadorial Level Held on April 16," 27 April 1959, 2; Marry Montgomery's narrative uses this quotation to claim that Murphy agreed with Joxe even though the record implies disagreement, see Mary Montgomery, "The Eyes of the World Were Watching: Ghana, Great Britain, and the United States, 1957–1966" (PhD. diss., College Park, University of Maryland, 2004) 113.

70. NARA, RG.306, UD-WW 285, FRC 1, f: Briefing Paper, Nixon, "The Emergence of Africa: Report to the President by Vice President Nixon on His Trip to Africa: February 28–March 21, 1957," [March 1957], 1–2.

71. DDEL, Papers as President 1953–1961, NSC Series, box 11, f: 410th Meeting of NSC June 18, 1959, "Political Implications of Afro-Asian Military takeovers (State Department Presentation)," 27 May 1959.

72. David F. Schmitz, *The United States and Right-Wing Dictatorships, 1965–1989* (Cambridge: Cambridge University Press, 2006), 17; David F. Schmitz, *Thank God They're on Our Side: The United States and Right-Wing Dictatorships, 1921–1965* (Chapel Hill: University of North Carolina Press, 1999), 178–235; Bradley Simpson, *Economists with Guns: Authoritarian Development and U.S.-Indonesian Relations, 1960–1968* (Stanford, CA: Stanford University Press, 2008), 35; Richard Reid, *A History of Modern Africa: 1800 to the Present* (Oxford: Willey-Blackwell, 2008), 299; Mairi Stewart MacDonald, "The Challenge of Guinean Independence, 1958–1971" (PhD. Diss., University of Toronto, 2009), 113; Westad, *The Global Cold War*, 122.

73. Quotes taken from memdisc of the 410th Meeting of the National Security Council, 18 June 1959, 2, 3, Papers as President 1953–1961, NSC Series, box 11, f: 410th Meeting of NSC June 18, 1959, DDEL. Historians have used this document to show Eisenhower's approval for authoritarianism; Macdonald misattributes one of Joxe's quotations to Murphy; Schmitz states that the report is approved by the NSC, even though the NSC actually approves the production of follow-up studies, see MacDonald, "The Challenge of Guinean Independence, 1958–1971," 113; Schmitz, *Thank God They're on Our Side*, 17.

74. NARA, RG.306, UD-WW 285, FRC 1, f: Briefing Paper, Nixon, "The Emergence of Africa: Report to the President by Vice President Nixon on His Trip to Africa: February 28–March 21, 1957," [March 1957], 1–2.

75. DDEL, Papers as President 1953–1961, NSC Series, box 11, f: 410th Meeting of NSC June 18, 1959, memdisc of the 410th Meeting of the National Security Council, 18 June 1959, 4.

76. Matthew Connelly, *Fatal Misconception: The Struggle to Control World Population* (Cambridge, MA: Belknap Press, 2010), 186; DDEL, US President's Committee on Information Activities Abroad: Records 1960–61, box 9, f: Africa # 31 (1), "Africa South of the Sahara," 1960.

77. DDEL, US President's Committee on Information Activities Abroad: Records 1960–61, box 20, f: PCIAA #10(1), "The President's Committee on Information Activities Abroad: The Collateral Effects of Training Foreign Military Personnel," 16 May 1960, 2; NARA, RG. 59, CDF1955–59, 611.70/10-158–611.7194/12-457, Amembassy Addis Ababa to StateDept, "Role of Military in Less Developed Countries," 30 September 1959, Amembassy Tripoli to StateDept, "Role of Military in Less Developed Countries," 1 October 1959.

78. DDEL, US President's Committee on Information Activities Abroad: Records 1960–61, box 20, f: PCIAA #10(1), "The President's Committee on Information Activities Abroad: The Collateral Effects of Training Foreign Military Personnel," 16 May 1960, 2.

79. NATO Archives, CM(61)43-e, "Communist Penetration in Africa," 23 April 1960, 2.

80. "Interview with Andrew J. Goodpaster, Jr. on April 10, 1982 for Dwight D. Eisenhower Library," 33–35, in the Columbia University Oral History Research Office, New York.

81. Van Hemelrijck's adviser was named Georges Dumont, see NARA, RG. 59 CDF1955–59, 655.563/6 1256–655A.00/5-2959, Stanley M. Cleveland to StateDept, "Congo Minister's Chief Adviser Comments on Belgian Congo Policy," 29 May 1959.

82. NANTH, Archief Ambassade Congo-Kinshasa, 2.05.265, Nederlandse ambassade in Congo, 1950–1974, inventarisnummer 146, E. Boreel to Joseph Luns, 16 April 1960.

83. NARA, RG.59, CDF1960-63, 611.70/2-860–611.70/2-1362, Amembassy Brussels to StateDept, "Conversation with King Baudouin on African and Other Questions," 27 June 1960; Baudouin's private remarks three days before independence give more weight to the thesis that the Belgian government did not believe Lumumba was a Communist, see Anne-Sophie Gijs, "Une ascension politique teintée de rouge. Autorités, sûreté de l'état et grandes sociétés face au 'danger Lumumba' avant l'indépendance du Congo (1956–1960)," *Journal of Belgian History* 42, no. 1 (2012): 57.

84. Gijs, "Une Ascension Politique," 57; AEB, Archief Gaston Eyskens, 6081, Consulat général de Belgique a Brazza to Eyskens, 27 July 1960.

85. AMAE, DAL, Généralités, 49QONT/65, f: CB-V-7 Nationalisme, panafricanisme, Hervé Alphand to Maurice Couve de Murville, "a.s. Le Congo et l'opinion américaine," 29 July 1960; quoted in AEB, Archief Gaston Eyskens, 6073, Pierre Wigny, "Société de développement," 31 October 1960.

86. BAHDMNE, SR.66 Congo 1959–1973, pt. 2, Leopoldville to Lisbon, 20 August 1960.

87. BNA, FO371/146646, Ian Scott to FO, 10 October 1960; BNA, FO371/146650, H. F. T. Smith, "The Congo," 28 September 1960.

88. Dwight D. Eisenhower, *Waging Peace: 1956–1961* (London: Heinemann, 1965), 573.

89. LOC, Harriman Papers, box 517, f: Tito Josip Broz, "A summary of the conversation between President Tito and former governor W. Averell Harriman," 2 October 1960; US Embassy in the UK to the Department of State, September 13, 1960, *FRUS 1958–1960*, vol. 14, *Africa*, 486.

90. NARA, RG.306, P242, box 1, f: Africa 1961, USIS-Leopoldville to USIS, "Country Plan," 30 May 1961.

91. Timberlake on 26 September 1960, quoted in Ebere Nwaubani, "Eisenhower, Nkrumah and the Congo Crisis," *Journal of Contemporary History* 36, no. 4 (2001): 619.

92. William O. Brown, "The Outlook for the White Man in Africa, Particularly as Settler," *African Studies Review* 3, no. 3 (1960): 1.

93. BNA, FO371/146646, Z. R. Hoyer to secretary of state, 29 September 1960.

94. Editorial note, *FRUS 1958–1960*, vol. 14, *Africa*, 495.

95. Editorial note, *FRUS 1958–1960*, vol. 14, Africa, 274; Genin, "La politique étrangère," 102–103.

96. Memdisc at the 452d Meeting of the National Security Council, July 21, 1960, *FRUS 1958–1960*, vol. 14, *Africa*, 338–339; Larry Devlin, *Chief of Station, Congo* (New York: Public Affairs Press, 2007), 62–63.

97. MSRC, Nkrumah Papers, box 154-4, f: 10 Congo, Alexander to Nkrumah, "The Congo Mission of Mr. Barden and Capt. Hassan to Stanleyville," 11 April 1961.

98. For those rumors, see MSRC, Nkrumah Papers, box 154-4, f:10, letter, Djin to Nkrumah, 15 September 1960; Thompson employs the Cold War lens, see Thompson, *Ghana's Foreign Policy*, 140.

99. Ellis launched the term; see Stephen Ellis, "Writing Histories of Contemporary Africa," *Journal of African History* 43, no. 1 (2002): 19.

100. PRAAD, BAA/RLAA/964, "The Last Message of Patrice Lumumba," 29 March 1961, "Workers World: A Fighter to the End: Lumumba's Last Letter," 14 April 1961.

101. PRAAD, BAA/RLAA/964, ministry of foreign affairs to embassy Ghana in Somalia, "Mr. Alfred Maurice Mpolo," 31 August 1961.

102. "Why My Father Was Killed," *Voice of Africa*, July 1961, vol. 1, no. 7, 4–5.

103. GPL, BAA/RLAA/425, Sugiarti Siswadi, "Remember the Lesson of Lumumba's Life and Death," February 1962.

104. "J'estime que le moment est venu de faire toute la lumière et je ne peux rester plus longtemps sous le coup de cette accusation devant l'opinion africaine et l'opinion mondiale," see PRAAD, SC/BAA/307, Tshombe to Nkrumah, 31 January 1964; Raoul Peck's film has been particularly influential in maintaining the image of Lumumba as a hero, see Raoul Peck, *Lumumba* (Zeitgeist Video, 2000).

105. NARA, RG.306, A1-1029, box 4, f: RN-17-61, Office of Research and Analysis, "The Lumumba Symbol in Africa," 13 July 1961.

106. Nwaubani, "Eisenhower, Nkrumah and the Congo Crisis," 614.

107. PRAAD, SC/BAA/484, Notes on Government Policy, secret and personal notes, 25 March 1961, 2.

108. MSRC, Nkrumah Papers, box 154–45, f: Printed Material—Meeting of the Steering Committee at Dar es Salaam Jan. 26–30, 1961, "Meeting of the Steering Committee at Dar es Salam (Tanganyika) From 26 to 30th January 1961," 1961.

109. NA-A, Antonin Novotny, Guinea 1, "Zpréva s. Klindery pracovníka ČTK, o situaci v Guineji a Mali," 25 January 1961; Alessandro Iandolo, *Arrested Development: The Soviet Union in Ghana, Guinea, and Mali, 1955–1968* (Ithaca, NY: Cornell University Press, 2022), 151; Mazov, *A Distant Front*, 117.

110. BNA, FO953/2029, memcon, "United States–United Kingdom Information Working Group Meeting: The Congo as an Information Problem," April 1961, memcon, "United States–United Kingdom Information Working Group Meeting: United Kingdom Cultural and Education Effort in Africa," April 1961; BNA, DO 191/32, Minute, Mr. Morton, 2 December 1960.

111. BNA, FO953/2027, memcon, "US-UK Information Working Group Meeting," April 1961; Hyam, *Britain's Declining Empire*, 263–65.

112. CHAN, Ministère de la Coopération, Direction de la coopération technique et culturelle, 19810443/47 Histoire de la DCT, f: Historique de la DCT Organisation, memcon, "Compte-rendu de la reunion tenue au Quai d'Orsay le mardi 17 janvier 1961 de 17 h 30 à 19 h 15," 20 January 1961.

113. AMAE, DAL Généralités 1960–65, 49QONT/94, f: Chine, Confidential, "Anglo-French Talks on Information: Outline Record and Conclusions—the Foreign Office," 5 July 1960, 1–2.

114. The French estimated 6.6 million francs for the BBC, 5.1 million for the British Council, and the same amount again for the FO, CRO, and CO; see CHAN, Ministère de la Coopération, Direction de la coopération technique et culturelle, 19810443/47 Histoire de la DCT, f: Historique de la DCT Organisation, "Note sur les moyens d'information demandés par le Secrétariat d'Etat aux Relations avec les Etats de la Communauté," [1960].

115. António Tomás, *Amílcar Cabral: The Life of a Reluctant Nationalist* (London: Hurst, 2021), 85, 98; Amílcar Cabral, *Unity and Struggle: Speeches and Writings*, trans. Michael Wolfers (New York: Monthly Review Press, 1979), 17.

116. De Meneses, *Salazar*, 451; BAHDMNE, SR.255, S11/E10/P5/68842, f: Ajuda Ghana aos Movimentos, Embassy of Portugal, "The Strange Behaviour of the Leopoldville Government Allowing the Training of Terrorists in Her Territory," 10 September 1962; Lazlo Passemiers, "Safeguarding White Minority Power: The South African Government and the Secession of Katanga, 1960–1963," *South African Historical Journal* 68, no. 1 (2016): 2.

117. ASPFAE, AD, AFRI(135), f: 186, Dépêche d'information politique (61) 80, "Object: Communiqué du gouvernement à propos des officiers Belges au Katanga," 18 September 1961, "Livre Blanc du gouvernement Katangais sur l'agression de L'O.N.U. a Elisabethville," [1961], 16.

118. Kanza, *Conflict*, 146; KADOC, box 20, Archief Van Bilsen, Van Bilsen to Tshombe, 20 July 1960.

119. Ryan Irwin, "Sovereignty in the Congo Crisis," in *Decolonization and the Cold War: Negotiating Independence*, ed. Leslie James and Elisabeth Leake (London: Bloomsbury Academic, 2015), 206; AEB, Archief Gaston Eyskens, 6081, E. De Jonghe, Nota voor de Heer Eerste-Minister, 30 July 1960; De Witte, *Crisis in Kongo*, 315.

120. AEB, Archief Gaston Eyskens, 6079, Eyskens to Tshombe, 13 March 1961, Tshombe to Eyskens, 13 March 1961, Eyskens, 13 March 1961; ASPFAE, AD, AFRI(135), f:187, Text de résolution, 21 March 1961; ASPFAE, AA, 14320, "Note concernant le

problèmes financiers pour l'exercice 1961: De Inbel et Inforcongo," 10 October 1961; AGRB, 405 Inbel, no. 2, "Inbel Rapport 1963," 1963, 3.

121. Ludo De Witte, *Moord in Burundi: België En de Liquidatie van Premier Louis Rwagasore* (Antwerp: Epo, 2021), 15, 197.

122. NASA, BKL, box 8, f: Racial Policies in SA, De sekretaris van buitenlandse sake, "Duitse belangsteling in Afrika-aangeleetnhede: Belgies Kongo," 13 January 1960; NASA, BTS22/1/112, vol. 1, S.A. High Commissioner, Salisbury to Secretary of foreign Affairs, 3 August 1961; NASA, BKL, box 8, f: Racial Policies in SA, De sekretaris van buitenlandse sake, "Duitse belangsteling in Afrika-aangeleetnhede: Belgies Kongo," 13 January 1960.

123. Lazlo Passemiers, *Decolonization and Regional Geopolitics. South Africa and the "Congo Crisis,"* 1960–1965 (London: Routledge, 2019), 59–71.

124. AGRB, I591 Wigny, box 1–7, f: 2, Pierre Wigny, "Mémoires du Congo," s.d., 44; ASPFAE, AD, AFRI(135), Circulaire d'information P(61)56, "Vues de Sir Roy Welensky sur les événements du Katanga," 15 September 1961, 4–5.

125. Mazov, *A Distant Front*, 172–75; NARA, RG. 59, box 51, A1-1587-M, f: Congo Working Committee 1961–2, "Information System in the Congo," 2 March 1961, 1, Edwin M. J. Kretzmann to C. Vaughan Ferguson, "The Psychological Void in Africa," 15 February 1961.

126. NARA, RG.59, A1-1587-M, box 51, f: Congo Working Committee 1961–2, "Working Committee on the Congo," 8 February 1961, Roger Tubby to the Under Secretary for Economic Affairs, "Information Needs in Africa," 30 March 1961.

127. NARA, RG.59, box 51, A1-1587-M, f: Congo Working Committee 1961–2, Vaughan Ferguson and Edwin M. J. Kretzmann, "Information Program for the Congo," 15 February 1961, 2, "Contingency Planning for the Congo," [1961]; Natalia Telepneva, "Cold War on the Cheap: Soviet and Czechoslovak Intelligence in the Congo, 1960–3," in *Warsaw Pact Intervention in the Third World: Aid and Influence in the Cold War*, ed. Philip Muehlenbeck and Natalia Telepneva (London: I.B. Tauris, 2018), 133.

128. MIT Archives, MC440, Ithiel de Sola Pool Papers, f: Westpoint meeting 4/18/63, "A Review of Behavioral Sciences Research in Support of Air Force Programs in Counter-Insurgency and Limited Warfare by James L. Monroe," 18 April 1963; NARA, RG.59, A1-1587-M, box 51, f: Congo Working Committee 1961–2, "Information System in the Congo," 2 March 1961, 1.

129. NARA, RG.59, A1-1587-M, box 51, f: Congo Information Sub-Committee 1961–2, Roger Tubby to the Under Secretary for Economic Affairs, "Information Needs in Africa," 30 March 1961, confidential note, [1961], "Information System in the Congo," 2 March 1961, 1, memo, 13 September 1960.

130. NARA, RG.59, A1-1587-M, box 51, f: Congo Information Sub-Committee 1961, Donald M. Davies, "Congo Information Program," 6 March 1961.

131. See, for instance, Schmidt, *Foreign Intervention*, 68–69; Westad, *The Global Cold War*, 140–41.

132. Quoted in Irwin, "Sovereignty," 212.

133. Thompson, *Ghana's Foreign Policy*, 222, 305–306; NARA, RG.59, A1-1587-M, box 51, f: Congo Information Sub-Committee 1961, "Information System in the Congo," 2 March 1961, 3.

134. LOC, Harriman Papers, box 526, f; London, incoming telegram, 27 February 1961.

135. BNA, FCO141/6735, letter, T. Neil Permanent Secretary Office of the Chief Secretary, 18 April 1961; Milton Obote in Uganda remained a staunch supporter of Nkrumah's regime, see Opoku Agyeman, *Nkrumah's Ghana and East Africa: Pan-Africanism and African Interstate Relations* (Teaneck, NJ: Fairleigh Dickinson University Press, 1992), 96.

136. British business interests can only be understood as part of an ideology, unlike what some historians argue, see Gibbs, *The Political Economy of Third World Intervention*, 1–10; O'Malley, *The Diplomacy of Decolonisation*, 1–10; Kent, "The US and Decolonization," 1–15.

137. Stephen R. Weissman, *American Foreign Policy in the Congo, 1960–1964* (Ithaca, NY: Cornell University Press, 1974), 77; Mazov, *A Distant Front*, 98; Madeleine G. Kalb, *The Congo Cables: The Cold War in Africa, from Eisenhower to Kennedy* (New York: Macmillan, 1982), 374; Michael G. Schatzberg, *Mobutu or Chaos? The United States and Zaire, 1960–1990* (Lanham, MD: University Press of America, 1991), 14; Catherine Hoskyns, *The Congo since Independence, January 1960—December 1961* (Oxford: Oxford University Press, 1965); Namikas, *Battleground Africa*, 2013, 1–21.

138. Bambi Ceuppens, *Congo made in Flanders?: Koloniale Vlaamse visies op "blank" en "zwart" in Belgisch Congo* (Gent: Academia Press, 2003); Jonathan E. Helmreich, *United States Relations with Belgium and the Congo, 1940–1960* (Newark: University of Delaware Press, 1998), 1–10.

139. Idesbald Goddeeris and Sindani E. Kiangu, "Congomania in Academia: Recent Historical Research on the Belgian Colonial Past," *Low Countries Historical Review* 126, no. 4 (2011): 71; Guy Vantemsche, "The Historiography of Belgian Colonialism," in *Europe and the World in European Historiography*, ed. Csaba Lévai (Pisa: Pisa University Press, 2006), 89–119.

140. The "trouble spot" quotation is taken from Mazov, *A Distant Front*, 78; Götz Bechtolsheimer, "Breakfast with Mobutu: Congo, the United States and the Cold War, 1964–1981" (PhD diss., London School of Economics, 2012), 228; historical actors are still presented as characters from Joseph Conrad's *Heart of Darkness*, Gerard and Kuklick, *Death in the Congo*, 214.

6. Managing the Effects of Modernization, 1961–1963

1. NARA, RG.59, Records of Dean Rusk, Miscellaneous Subject Files, 1961–1968, box 65, f: Kennedy-Khrushchev Talks, memcon, "Vienna Meeting Between the President and Chairman Khrushchev, 12:45 p.m., 1–2, 3 p.m.," 3 June 1961, 4–5.

2. Colleen Bell, "Hybrid Warfare and Its Metaphors," *Humanity: An International Journal of Human Rights, Humanitarianism, and Development* 3, no. 2 (2012): 231; Nils Gilman, *Mandarins of the Future: Modernization Theory in Cold War America* (Baltimore: Johns Hopkins University Press, 2004), 197.

3. Paul Nugent, *Africa Since Independence: A Comparative History* (New York: Palgrave Macmillan, 2004), 139; Gilman, *Mandarins*, 197; David French, *The British Way in Counter-Insurgency, 1945–1967* (Oxford: Oxford University Press, 2012), 248.

4. BNA, FO371/161222, "Address by H.E. El Ferik Ibrahim Abboud President of the Supreme Council of the Armed Forces of the Republic of the Sudan at the Conference of the Non-Aligned Countries Held at Belgrade," September 1961, 11, "Address Delivered by

His Imperial Majesty Haile Selassie I to the Conference of Non-Aligned States Held at Belgrade," September 1961, 11.

5. Mark Atwood Lawrence, "The Rise and Fall of Nonalignment," in *The Cold War in the Third World*, ed. Robert J. McMahon (Oxford: Oxford University Press, 2013), 139–55; G. H Jansen, *Nonalignment and the Afro-Asian States* (New York: Praeger, 1966); Robert A. Mortimer, *The Third World Coalition in International Politics* (New York: Westview Press, 1980); Rinna Kullaa, *Non-Alignment and Its Origins in Cold War Europe Yugoslavia, Finland and the Soviet Challenge* (London: I.B. Tauris, 2012); Jason Parker, "Ideology, Race and Nonalignment in US Cold War Foreign Relations: Or, How the Cold War Racialized Neutralism without Neutralizing Race," in *Challenging US Foreign Policy: America and the World in the Long Twentieth Century*, ed. Bevan Sewell and Scott Lucas (London: Palgrave Macmillan, 2011), 75–98; Jürgen Dinkel, *The Non-Aligned Movement: Genesis, Organization and Politics (1927–1992)* (Leiden: Brill, 2018); Janick Marina Schaufelbuehl, Sandra Bott, Jussi Hanhimäki, and Marco Wyss, "Non-Alignment, the Third Force, or Fence-Sitting: Independent Pathways in the Cold War," *International History Review* 37, no. 5 (2015): 901–11; Peter Ruggenthaler and Aryo Makko, "Introduction," in *The Soviet Union and Cold War Neutrality and Nonalignment in Europe*, ed. Mark Kramer, Aryo Makko, and Peter Ruggenthaler (Lanham, MD: Rowman & Littlefield, 2021), 1–12.

6. "He has not wished to give clear authority to any one," JFKL, Papers of President Kennedy, NSF, box 405, f: Memos to the President: 6/6, "Current Organization of the White House and NSC for Dealing with International Matters," 22 June 1961, 2. On realist versus racial understanding, see Parker, "Ideology, Race and Nonalignment in US Cold War Foreign Relations," 77; Vijay Prashad, *The Darker Nations: A People's History of the Third World* (New York: New Press, 2007), 95–104; Kullaa, *Non-Alignment and Its Origins in Cold War Europe*, 1–20; Robert B. Rakove, "Two Roads to Belgrade: The United States, Great Britain, and the First Nonaligned Conference," *Cold War History* 14, no. 3 (2014): 337–57.

7. Gabriel Kolko, *Confronting the Third World: United States Foreign Policy, 1945–1980* (New York: Pantheon Books, 1988), 111–16, 191–205; Thomas G. Paterson, ed., *Kennedy's Quest for Victory: American Foreign Policy, 1961–1963* (Oxford: Oxford University Press, 1989); Thomas J. Noer, "The New Frontier and African Neutralism: Kennedy, Nkrumah, and the Volta River Project," *Diplomatic History* 8, no. 1 (1984): 61–80; Ibezim Chukwumerije, "The New Frontier and Africa, 1961–1963" (PhD diss., State University of New York at Stony Brook, 1976); Odd Arne Westad, *The Global Cold War: Third World Interventions and the Making of Our Times* (Cambridge: Cambridge University Press, 2005), 1–5; Ryan Irwin, *Gordian Knot: Apartheid and the Unmaking of the Liberal World Order* (Oxford: Oxford University Press, 2012), 64–65; Robert Dallek, *An Unfinished Life: John F. Kennedy, 1917–1963* (New York: Little Brown, 2003); Larry Grubbs, *Secular Missionaries: Americans and African Development in the 1960s* (Amherst: University of Massachusetts Press, 2009), 1–18; Philip E. Muehlenbeck, *Betting on the Africans: John F. Kennedy's Courting of African Nationalist Leaders* (Oxford: Oxford University Press, 2012); Stephen G. Rabe, *John F. Kennedy: World Leader* (Washington DC: Potomac Books, 2010).

8. Frank Heinlein, *British Government Policy and Decolonisation, 1945–63: Scrutinising the Official Mind* (New York: Routledge, 2002), 106; Ronald Hyam, *Britain's Declining Empire: The Road to Decolonisation, 1918–1968* (Cambridge: Cambridge University Press, 2007), 301–3; Alistair Horne, *Macmillan: The Official Biography* (Basingstoke: Pan Macmillan,

2008), 174–211; John Darwin, *The Empire Project: The Rise and Fall of the British World-System, 1830–1970* (Cambridge: Cambridge University Press, 2009); Sarah Stockwell and Larry J. Butler, "Introduction," in *The Wind of Change: Harold Macmillan and British Decolonization*, ed. Sarah Stockwell and Larry J. Butler (London: Palgrave Macmillan, 2013), 1–19; Robin Winks, William Roger Louis, and Alaine Low, eds., *The Oxford History of the British Empire*, vol. V, *Historiography* (Oxford: Oxford University Press, 1999); Marine Lefèvre, *Le soutien américain à la francophonie: Enjeux africains 1960–1970* (Paris: Presses de la Fondation Nationale des Sciences Politiques, 2010); François-Xavier Verschave, *La Françafrique: Le plus long scandale de la République* (Paris: Stock, 1998); François-Xavier Verschave, *De la Françafrique à la Mafiafrique* (Brussels: Éditions Tribord, 2004); Maurice Vaïsse, *La grandeur: Politique étrangère du Général de Gaulle, 1958–1969* (Paris: Fayard, 1998), 284; Frédéric Turpin, *De Gaulle, Pompidou et l'Afrique (1958–1974): Décoloniser et coopérer* (Paris: Les Indes savantes, 2010); Pierre-Michel Durand, *L'Afrique et les relations franco-américaines des années soixante: Aux origines de l'obsession américaine* (Paris: Editions L'Harmattan, 2007); Migani, "De Gaulle and Sub-Saharan Africa," 251–52; Jean-Pierre Bat, *Le syndrome Foccart: La politique française en Afrique, de 1959 à nos jours* (Paris: Éditions Gallimard, 2012); Yves Gounin and Jean-Christophe Rufin, *La France en Afrique le combat des anciens et des modernes* (Brussels: De Boeck, 2009); Ludo De Witte, *Huurlingen, Geheimagenten En Diplomaten* (Antwerp: Van Halewyck Uitgeverij, 2015).

9. Examples in Erik Linstrum, "Making Minds Modern: Experiments with Psychology in the British Empire" (PhD diss., Harvard University, 2012), 281; Kenneth D. Kaunda, *A Humanist in Africa: Letters to Colin M. Morris* (London: Longmans, 1967), 48–57.

10. PRAAD, RG.17/2/800, D. B. Sam, "The Concept of African Personality," 21 February 1962.

11. Lawrence, "The Rise and Fall of Nonalignment," 144.

12. Jeffrey James Byrne, "Our Own Special Brand of Socialism: Algeria and the Contest of Modernities in the 1960s," *Diplomatic History* 33, no. 3 (2009): 440; BNA, FO371/161222, "Address by H.E. El Ferik Ibrahim Abboud," [January 1961], 2, transcript, Nkrumah, 2 September 1961, 1–11.

13. Sergei Khrushchev, ed., *Memoirs of Nikita Khrushchev*, vol. 3, *Statesman, 1953–1964* (University Park: Penn State University Press, 2013), 542; Sergey Mazov, *A Distant Front in the Cold War: The USSR in West Africa and the Congo, 1956–1964* (Stanford, CA: Stanford University Press, 2010), 203.

14. JFK, Pre-presidential Papers, Task Force on Africa, box 1073, f: Task Force Reports, "Report to the Honorable John F. Kennedy by The Task Force on Africa," 31 December 1960, 8–10.

15. Bentley Historical Library, University of Michigan, Ann Arbor, Michigan, G. Mennen Williams Papers, box 16-N, f: Trips Africa March 1961, Eugene A. Raymond to Williams, [1961]; Ted Sorensen, *Kennedy* (New York: William S. Konecky Association, 1999), 646; Thomas Noer, *Soapy: A Biography of G. Mennen Williams* (Ann Arbor: University of Michigan Press, 2006), 226.

16. BNA, FO953/2050, "The Foreign Office General Instructions: Duties of Information Officers," [January 1961], 2, memcon, R. A. Burrows, "Official Committee on Overseas Information Services Third Meeting," 4 May 1961; BNA, DO35/9424, A. W. Snelling to Hunt, 23 March 1960.

17. BAHDMNE, GNP/RNP/0222/07701, "Conferência dos Países 'Neutralistas' em Belgrado," September 1961, memorandum sur l'Angola, 7 November 1961; in spite of historians who claim that modernization was never seriously questioned, Nick Cullather, "Damming Afghanistan: Modernization in a Buffer State," *Journal of American History* 89, no. 2 (2002): 537.

18. Alessandro Iandolo, "De-Stalinizing Growth: Decolonization and the Development of Development Economics in the Soviet Union," in *The Development Century: A Global History*, Global and International History, ed. Erez Manela and Stephen J. Macekura (Cambridge: Cambridge University Press, 2018), 208–9.

19. Cooper points out that modernization theorists were not merely driven by a hubristic attempt at making every problem technically legible, but he does not explain the origins of this tension, see James C. Scott, *Seeing Like a State: How Certain Schemes to Improve the Human Condition Have Failed* (New Haven: Yale University Press, 1999), 343; Frederick Cooper, *Colonialism in Question: Theory, Knowledge, History* (San Francisco: University of California Press, 2005), 141; Joseph Morgan Hodge, *Triumph of the Expert: Agrarian Doctrines of Development and the Legacies of British Colonialism* (Athens: Ohio University Press, 2007), 254.

20. David Ekbladh, *The Great American Mission: Modernization and the Construction of an American World Order* (Princeton, NJ: Princeton University Press, 2009), 158.

21. Margaret Mead, *Cultural Patterns and Technical Change: A Manual Prepared by the World Federation for Mental Health* (New York: New American Library, 1955), 270–73.

22. LSE Library Archives and Special Collections, Richards/14/12, Audrey Richards, "Concept of the Lazy African," 22 February 1961; British World Federation for Mental Health agreed with Lévi-Strauss, see Linstrum, "Making Minds Modern," 285, 302; John Strachey, *The End of Empire* (London: Gollancz, 1959), 242–45; David Richards, "Postcolonial Anthropology in the French-Speaking World," in *Postcolonial Thought in the French-Speaking World*, ed. Charles Forsdick and David Murphy (Liverpool: Liverpool University Press, 2009), 174–79.

23. Max F. Millikan and Walt W. Rostow, *A Proposal: Key to an Effective Foreign Policy* (New York: Harper, 1957), 142; Gilman, *Mandarins*, 194–195; Walt W. Rostow and Richard Hatch, *An American Policy in Asia* (New York: John Wiley/Technological Press of MIT, 1955), 50. Walt W. Rostow, *Eisenhower, Kennedy, and Foreign Aid* (Austin: University of Texas Press, 1985), 43; for an analysis of the intellectual debates on modernization, see Hodge, *Triumph of the Expert*, 207–53; Ekbladh, *The Great American Mission*, 173; Rostow, *Eisenhower*, 44

24. ASPFAE, AD, I5.608, Spaak to de Staercke, 30 June 1961; NATO Archives, CM(61)119, "The Belgrade Conference," [1961]; circulaire, Couve de Murville to représentants diplomatiques de France à l'étranger, 9 September 1961, DDF, 1961, Tome 1, 374–376; AMAE, DAO, Généralités, 124QO/412, Arnaud to affaires étrangères, 3 September 1961; Robert B. Rakove, *Kennedy, Johnson, and the Nonaligned World* (Cambridge: Cambridge University Press, 2012), 63.

25. JFKL, NSF, box 439, f: Non-Aligned Conferences 1961–1963 Cairo-Belgrade [White House Memoranda], "Pros and Cons of Message from President Kennedy," [1961]; BNA, FO1110/1421, IRD to information office Belgrade, 16 August 1961; NARA, RG.59, A1-1587-M, box 50, f: Belgrade Conference 1961, Foy Kohler to Charles Hulick, 23 August 1961, Federal Republic of Germany to Washington DC, 26 August 1961.

26. AEB, 6069, Eyskens, K. Van Cauwelaert to Eyskens, 31 December 1959; BNA, FO371/154740, "Meeting of Her Majesty's Representatives in West and Equatorial Africa," 16–19 May 1961; BNA, FO1110/1447, McMullen, "United Kingdom Information Office, Kenya," [1961].

27. BNA, FO371/154738, Ralph Murray to FO, 3 May 1961; BNA, BW143/1, "Report on the Prospects of British Council Development in the Countries of French-Speaking West Africa," 12 May 1963, 1, 13; BNA, FO1110/1447, McMullen, "United Kingdom Information Office, Kenya," s.d.; MSRC, Gizenga Papers, box 128-21, f: Pan Africanism, "'Pan-Africanism,' Prepared for British Information Services by the Central Office of Information," 1965.

28. BNA, FO953/2031, "Information Policy for Africa," 30 June 1961; BNA, BW143/1, "Confidential Report on the Prospects of British Council Developments in the Countries of French-Speaking West Africa," 12 May 1963, 13; BNA, FO371/154738, J. H. A. Watson to Roger, 27 April 1961, Roger Stevens to FO, 13 April 1961, BNA, FO953/2050, "Anglo-French Information Talks: Notes for Meeting," 19 December 1961; BNA, FO953/2029, "United States–United Kingdom Information Working Group Meeting: UK Brief: Other Western Efforts," April 1961.

29. AMAE, DAM, Généralités, 1089INVA/239 Coopération 1961–1975, Débuts politiques de la coopération (1961–1963), "Conference des chefs de mission: Synthèse des rapports des chefs de mission," January 1961, 1–7.

30. The decisive influence of the UAM on France is often ignored. Turpin argues the UAM was a "succès pour la France," see Turpin, *De Gaulle*, 151–154.

31. Charles de Gaulle, *Discours et messages*, vol. III (Paris: Plon, 1970), 329–30.

32. Jacques Foccart, *Dans les bottes du général: Journal de l'Élysée—III, 1969–1971* (Paris: Fayard, 1999), 525, 530; Durand, *L'Afrique et les relations franco-américaines*, 443–45; Lefèvre, *Le soutien américain*, 12.

33. ASPFAE, AD, AFRI(135), f: 186, memorandum, Louis Scheyven, 26 September 1961.

34. ASPFAE, AD, AFRI(135), f: 186, M. Taymans, "Coup d'œil sur la Guinée. Entretien avec l'Archevêque expulsé de Conakry," 1 September 1961.

35. ASPFAE, AD, AFRI (134), f: 185. Mai-Août 1961, Belgian Embassy in Addis, note pour monsieur le Secrétaire general, 27 May 1961

36. AHU, CX0079, Informaço N 67/62, 31 December 1962, Informaço N 139/63, 7 November 1963.

37. JFKL, Sorensen Papers, Subject Files 1961–1964, box 34, f: Foreign Policy Africa, transcript, "New Approaches to African Policy," s.d.

38. John F. Kennedy, "A Democrat Looks at Foreign Policy," *Foreign Affairs* 36, no. 1 (October 1959): 44, 48.

39. "John F. Kennedy, "Inaugural Address," 20 January 1961, *The American Presidency Project*, ed. Gerhard Peters and John T. Woolley, accessed 5 March 2019, http://www.presidency.ucsb.edu/ws/?pid=8032.

40. Walt W. Rostow, "Countering Guerrilla Attack," in *Modern Guerrilla Warfare: Fighting Communist Guerrilla Movements, 1941–1961*, ed. Franklin Mark Osanka (New York: Free Press of Glencoe, 1962), 465–66.

41. Rakove, *Kennedy, Johnson, and the Nonaligned World*, xxi.

42. Quotes taken from an interview with Joseph Alsop, who in the past had worked for the British Information Service, see Stewart Alsop, "Kennedy's Grand Strategy," *Saturday Evening Post*, March 31, 1962.

43. MIT Archives, MC 440, Ithiel de Sola Pool Papers, f: Westpoint meeting 4/18/63, "A Review of Behavioral Sciences Research In Support of Air Force Programs in Counter-Insurgency and Limited Warfare by James L. Monroe," 18 April 1963; JFKL, Papers of President Kennedy, NSF, box 338, Maxwell Taylor, "Counterinsurgency Doctrine," 13 August 1962, 30; NARA, RG.306, P296, f: C.I. Agency Doctrine and Organization, box 8, "Guidance for USIA Programs and Operations," [1963]; NARA, RG.306, P296, box 11, f: Edward R. Murrow—Speech July 31, 1963, "Problems of Development and Internal Defense Seventh Session: The Role of USIA in Modernization and Internal Defense by the Honorable Edward R. Murrow," 31 July 1963, 19, 4, 13–14.

44. Walt W. Rostow, *The Stages of Economic Growth: A Non-Communist Manifesto* (Cambridge: Cambridge University Press, 1960), 27; Ithiel de Sola Pool, "Information Goals," *Foreign Service Journal*, July 1963, 23–25.

45. NARA, RG.306, P296, box 2, f: C.I. West Africa, Edward V. Roberts to Frederic O. Bundy, "Internal Security Assessment of Africa," 1 March 1963, "Prospects in Brazzaville," 17 May 1965; NARA, RG.306, P296, box 11, f: C.I. Field Visits, "Liberia—USIA Program Summary," [1962]; NARA, RG.306, P296, box 5, f: C.I. Somali Republic, airgram, Amembassy Mogadiscio to StateDept, "Internal Security—Somali Republic," 14 December 1963; NARA, RG.306, P296, box 9, f: CI—Civil Action [Folder 1/2], Thomas C. Sorensen to Rowan, "Re-examining Counterinsurgency Policy and Programs," 22 June 1964.

46. This image of Kennedy refutes widely accepted claims in the historiography: Nicholas J. Cull, *The Cold War and the United States Information Agency: American Propaganda and Public Diplomacy, 1945–1989* (Cambridge: Cambridge University Press, 2009), 191; Rakove, *Kennedy, Johnson, and the Nonaligned World*, xxiv, 259.

47. Kennedy, "A Democrat Looks at Foreign Policy," 48; JFKL, Papers of John F. Kennedy, Pre-presidential Papers, Senate Files, box 784, f: Algeria Speech, "Remarks of Senator John F. Kennedy in the Senate," 2 July 1957; JFKL, Theodore Sorensen Papers, Subject Files 1961–1964, box 34, f: Foreign Policy Africa, "New Approaches to African Policy," s.d.; John F. Kennedy, *The Strategy of Peace*, ed. Allan Nevins (New York: Popular Library, 1960), 162; DDEL, Jackson, C. D.: Papers, 1931–1967, box 31, f: Baker Edgar, C. D. Jackson to Edgar R. Baker, 4 January 1961; DDEL, AWF, NSC Series, box 12, f: 432nd Meeting of NSC, "Memdisc of the 432nd Meeting of the National Security Council," 14 January 1960; NARA, RG.306, A1-1072, box 9, f: African Program, Historical Background 1970, Peter Koffsky, "The United States Information Program in Africa, 1945–1970: A History & Interpretation," 2-1.

48. Daniel Lerner, *The Passing of Traditional Society: Modernizing the Middle East* (New York: Free Press, 1958), 50, vii.

49. JFKL, Pre-presidential Papers, Task Force on Africa, box 1073, f: Task Force, "Report to the Honorable John F. Kennedy by the Task Force on Africa," 31 December 1960, 8–10.

50. Grubbs, *Secular Missionaries*, 77; JFKL, NSF, box 303, f: policy planning "Neutralism: Suggested United States Policy towards the Uncommitted Nations 5/29/61, Policy Planning Council," 29 May 1961.

51. JFKL, Pre-presidential Papers, Task Force on Africa, box 1073, f: Task Force Reports, "Report to the Honorable John F. Kennedy by the Task Force on Africa," 31 December 1960.

52. A. Susan Williams, *Who Killed Hammarskjold?: The UN, the Cold War and White Supremacy in Africa* (London: Hurst, 2011), 3.

53. Quoted in Gu Guan-Fu, "Soviet Aid to the Third World: An Analysis of Its Strategy," *Soviet Studies* 35, no. 1 (1983): 71.

54. Iandolo raises these examples but does not see this as part of a global shift from psychological to socioeconomic modernization, Iandolo, "De-Stalinizing Growth," 212; Natalia Telepneva, "Mediators of Liberation: Eastern-Bloc Officials, Mozambican Diplomacy and the Origins of Soviet Support for Frelimo, 1958–1965," *Journal of Southern African Studies* 43, no. 1 (2017): 81.

55. Karen Brutents, *Tridtsat' Let Na Staroi Ploshchadi* (Moscow: Mezhdunarodnye otnosheniia, 1998), 197; David C. Engerman, "Learning from the East: Soviet Experts and India in the Era of Competitive Coexistence," *Comparative Studies of South Asia, Africa and the Middle East* 33, no. 2 (2013): 232.

56. BNA, FO953/2076, "African Mental Attitudes," [1961]; AMAE, DAL, Généralités, 49QONT/69, f: AFR-III-1 Documentation générale sur la zone géographique, "Contribution à une définition du comportement psychologique africain en face de l'information et de l'action culturelle étrangères," [1960–61].

57. NAZ, Shelf 20, box 182D, Northern Rhodesia Miscellaneous Reports, 1950–1969, "The Human Factor in Rural Development in the Federation: The Impact of Historical Events on the African Peoples of Southern Rhodesia," 12 February 1962.

58. Rostow, *The Stages of Economic Growth*, 120–21; Gilman, *Mandarins*, 194.

59. NARA, RG.306, A1-1072, box 194, f: English Language Teaching 1962, "Know Your Agency—English Teaching," 1962.

60. NARA, Washburn, Abbott: Papers, 1938–2003, box 104, f: USIA (8), "They Wanted Freedom: Life Stories and Legends of West Africans, Americans and others who served their Peoples," [1964].

61. "Former une sorte de 'clientèle' du poste," see AMAE, DAL, Nord Est Afrique 1960–1965, 35QO/8, Jean Desparmet, "Mission d'étude des moyens d'information français en Afrique centrale et orientale," 6 May 1964, 33; AMAE, DAL, Ghana 1960–1965, 50QO/72, Guiringaud to DAL, "Information Politique," 14 May 1960, 2, Stephane Golmann, "Report de mission effectue par Monsieur Stephane Golmann pour le compte de La Direction rançais Des Affaires Culturelles et Techniques du Ministre des Affaires Etrangeres du Ministre des Affaires Etrangeres rançaises au Ghana," 31 December 1960, 8.

62. BNA, BW93/7, brief, "Heads of Mission Conference," [1963]; GULSC, Barbara Ward Papers, box 6, f: 34 Naval War College Papers: Problems of Communism, "African Journal October 10th—December 7th 1963," 10 October 1963; NARA, RG.306, A1-1072, box 9, f: African Program, Historical Background 1970, Peter Koffsky, "The United States Information Program in Africa, 1945–1970: A History & Interpretation," 2-1.

63. Agyeman and Thompson note that the Cairo conference signaled the end of Nkrumah's pan-African ambitions, see Opoku Agyeman, *Nkrumah's Ghana and East Africa: Pan-Africanism and African Interstate Relations* (Teaneck, NJ: Fairleigh Dickinson University Press, 1992), 83; Scott Thompson, *Ghana's Foreign Policy, 1957–1966: Diplomacy, Ideology, and the New State* (Princeton, NJ: Princeton University Press, 1969), 242.

64. Kwame Nkrumah, *Neo-Colonialism, The Last Stage of Imperialism* (London: Panaf Books, 1965), 239; PRAAD, RG.17/2/538, "Questions by Pravda Correspondent," [1963] 8; Kwame Nkrumah, *Axioms of Kwame Nkrumah* (London: Nelson, 1967), 6.

65. Priya Lal, *African Socialism in Postcolonial Tanzania: Between the Village and the World* (Cambridge: Cambridge University Press, 2015), 61; Thompson, *Ghana's Foreign Policy*, 307.

66. British Library, London (hereafter BL), EAP121-5-5-18, "UNIP: Accra Office, Ghana (Confidential Report)," 1963.

67. Kwame Nkrumah, "The Diplomat in Africa," *Voice of Africa*, vol. 4, no. 7/8, July–August 1964, 4–5; PRAAD, RG.17/2/247, E. K. Okoh to Nkrumah, "Re-Organisation of Ministry of Information and Broadcasting," 23 October 1962; MSRC, Gizenga Papers, box 128-16, f. 368, African Affairs Secretariat, "Conference of Ghana Envoys Volume I: Notes of Conference of Ghana Envoys in Africa, Held at Accra 7th—23rd October, 1961," 1960, 1, 37; GPL, BAA/RLAA/370, BAA, "Ghana's Role in Emergent Africa," 25 July 1960.

68. PRAAD, SC/BAA/244, note, 25 March 1961; "Two African leaders speak . . . ," *Voice of Africa*, vol. 1, no. 1, January 1961; "Ghana Trains Africans," *Voice of Africa*, vol. 4, no. 7/8, July–August 1964.

69. Ministry of Information, *Patterns of Progress in Ethiopia: Education* (Addis Ababa: Commercial Printing Press, 1967), 3–4.

70. Stephen Ellis, "Writing Histories of Contemporary Africa," *Journal of African History* 43, no. 1 (2002): 19; PRAAD, RG.17/2/48, Terry Bishop, "The Ghanaians: Master-scene script written by Terry Bishop for the Ghana Film Industry Corporation," [1963].

71. PRAAD, RG.17/2/256, E. K. Okoh to Dr. Conor Cruise O'Brien, 1 November 1963.

72. "A Warning," *Voice of Africa*, vol. 2, no. 1, January 1962; "Speech Delivered by Osagyefo the President at Conference at Cairo on Sunday, 19th July 1964," *Voice of Africa*, vol. 4, no. 7/8, July–August 1964; "Dangers of NATO War Bases in Africa," *Voice of Africa*, vol. 2, no. 10/11/12, October–December 1962, 20–21; GPL, BAA/RLAA/424, Barden to Magnus George, "Anti-Neo-Colonialist Demonstration," 12 August 1962.

73. GPL, BAA/RLAA/424, Magnus George, "Anti-Neo-Colonialist Demonstration: Meeting," 13 August 1962, Barden to Magnus George, "Anti-Neo-Colonialist Demonstration," 12 August 1962; Thompson, *Ghana's Foreign Policy*, 279; David Rooney, *Kwame Nkrumah: Vision and Tragedy* (Accra: Sub-Saharan Publishers, 2007), 308–10.

74. MSRC, Gizenga Papers, box 128-9, f. Foreign Relations—Ghana Foreign Affairs vol. 2 no. 2, "Ghana Foreign Affairs, A Monthly Bulletin of the Ministry of Foreign Affairs," July 1963.

75. Something that was not always appreciated by historians who have singled out Brezhnev's visit to illustrate the degree of Soviet penetration, MSRC, Gizenga Papers, box 128-16, f. 212 Ghana Foreign Affairs, "Ghana Foreign Affairs, vol. 1, no. 2," March 1961; Thompson, *Ghana's Foreign Policy*, 159, 166–67; Rooney, *Kwame Nkrumah*, 223.

76. PRAAD, SC/BAA/366, "Draft Portion of a Speech on Neutrality and Non-Alignment," [1961].

77. Thompson, *Ghana's Foreign Policy*, 223.

78. Nkrumah, *Neo-Colonialism*, 239–40.

79. Anna Locher and Christian Nuenlist, "NATO Strategies toward de Gaulle's France, 1958–1966: Learning to Cope," in *Globalizing de Gaulle: International Perspectives on French Foreign Policies, 1958–1969*, ed. Christian Nuenlist, Anna Locher, and Martin Garret (Lanham, MD: Lexington Books, 2010), 87–88. Kwame Nkrumah, *Africa Must Unite* (London: PanAf Books, 1963), 174–179; Jeffrey S. Ahlman, "Road to Ghana: Nkrumah, Southern Africa and the Eclipse of a Decolonizing Africa," *Kronos* 37, no. 1 (2011): 33–34; Nkrumah, *Neo-Colonialism*, 239–40.

80. AMAE, DAL, Ghana 1960–1965, 50QO/52, J. E. Bossman to Couve de Murville, "Telex Message from Osagyefo Dr. Kwame Nkrumah, President of the Republic of Ghana Addressed to His Excellency General Charles de Gaulle, President of the Republic of France," 2 June 1965.

81. PRAAD, RG.17/2/62, "Points for Discussion with the Ghana Press Corps," [1962]; PRAAD, RG.17/2/683, M. F. Dei-Anang, "Research of Psychological Operations," 1 November 1961; Thompson, *Ghana's Foreign Policy*, 183; Nkrumah, *Neo-Colonialism*, 239, 249.

82. MSRC, Nkrumah Papers, box 154-20, f. 12, Nkrumah to Nyerere, 8 December 1961.

83. PRAAD, RG.17/2/538, Nkrumah to Jomo Kenyatta, [1962–1966], 3.

84. Thompson, *Ghana's Foreign Policy*, 10–11, 308–16; Kate Skinner, "A Different Kind of Union: An Assassination, Diplomatic Recognition, and Competing Visions of African Unity in Ghana-Togo Relations, 1956–1963," in *Visions of African Unity: New Perspectives on the History of Pan-Africanism and African Unification Projects*, ed. Matteo Grilli and Frank Gerits (London: Palgrave Macmillan, 2020), 23–48.

85. JFKL, NSF, box 99, f. Ghana General, 1/62–3/62, "Ghanaian Subversion in Africa," 12 February 1962; NARA, RG.306 USIA Research Reports 1960–1999, P142, box 16, f. R-155-63, "The Ghanaian Propaganda Campaign against the U.S.: Motives and Implications," 12 August 1963, 18–19; NARA, RG.306, UD-WW92, FRC 1, USIS-Accra to USIA, "Country Plan for Ghana," 24 June 1960.

86. AMAE, DAL, Ghana, 50QO/15, f. Politique Intérieure, M. C. Renner to Minister of Foreign Affairs, "Marriage de M. Nkrumah," 2 January 1958; the British wanted to exploit the goodwill that Ghanaian independence had created, see BNA, INF12/863, R. H. K Marett, "Report on visit to East Africa by R. H. K," March/November 1960, 12; the ICA offered the best example of the US approach to Ghana when it described Nkrumah's Pan-African conference as a first step toward African economic cooperation and development, NARA, RG.469, P36, box 11, f. Africa Advisory Conference, memcon, "International Cooperation Administration: Advisory Conference on Africa May 17–27, 1960: Pan-Africanism," 27 May 1960, 2; BNA, CAB134/1357, A. W. Snelling, "Ghana: The Lurch to the Left," 1 December 1960; BNA, FO1110/1692, CRO, "The Influence of Ghana in East Africa," 27 September 1963; AMAE, DAL, Ghana 1953–1965, 50QO/37, de Guiringaud to DAL, "Le Nouveau Messie," 3 February 1960.

87. Nick Cullather, *The Hungry World: America's Cold War Battle Against Poverty in Asia* (Boston: Harvard University Press, 2010), 42; Frank Notestein, "The Economics of Population and Food Supplies: Economic Problem of Population Change," in *Proceedings of the Eighth International Conference of Agricultural Economists* (Oxford: Oxford University Press, 1953), 20.

88. NARA, RG.306, UD-WW285, FRC 2, f. ICA, Edward V. Roberts to George V. Allen, "Notes for Your Remarks at ICA Conference on Tropical Africa," 16 May 1960, 2–3; the Sprague Committee also wrote about the "psychological potentialities of foreign aid programs," see DDEL, US President's Committee on Information Activities Abroad (Sprague Committee) Records, 1959–61, box 26, f: Printed Committee Report, "Conclusions and Recommendations of the President's Committee on Information Activities Abroad," December 1960, 13; Rostow, *The Stages of Economic Growth*, 2.

89. DDEL, Pre-presidential Papers, Transition files, Task Force Reports, 1960, box 1074, f: Task Force Report, Rostow to Kennedy, "The Strategy of Foreign Aid 1961," 22 December 1960; in Pearce's estimation, Rostow referred to psychological effects only to convince Congress, see Kimber Charles Pearce, *Rostow, Kennedy, and the Rhetoric of Foreign Aid* (East Lansing: Michigan State University Press, 2001), 80, 93.

90. Memorandum from the President's Deputy Special Assistant for National Security Affairs (Rostow) to President Kennedy, February 2, 1961, *FRUS 1961–1963*, vol. 9, *Foreign Economic Policy*, 208.

91. Eugene Black, "The Diplomacy of Economic Aid," *Challenge* 9, no. 3 (1960): 40; Eugene Black, *The Diplomacy of Economic Development* (Boston: Harvard University Press, 1960); NARA, RG.306, P296, box 8, f: C.I. Agency Doctrine and Organization, Henry Ramsey, "Is the Service Ready for the Sixties: The Modernization Process and Insurgency," [1962]; MIT Archives, MC 440, Ithiel de Sola Pool Papers, box 96, f: US Congress, report, "Economic, Social and Political Change in the Underdeveloped Countries and Its Implications for United States Policy," 30 March 1960.

92. "Mr. Hammerskjold in Ghana," *Ghana Today*, January 20, 1960, vol. 3, no. 24, 6; Radoslav A. Yordanov, *The Soviet Union and the Horn of Africa during the Cold War: Between Ideology and Pragmatism* (Cambridge, MA: Harvard University Press, 2017), 23; Mazov, *A Distant Front in the Cold War*, 188.

93. Mazov, *A Distant Front in the Cold War*, 221, 224, 242.

94. KADOC, Archief Van Bilsen, box 24, f:6.6.2., CRISP Paper, "Belgique et Tiers-Monde," 22 December 1961, 5; KADOC, Archief Van Bilsen,, box 20, f: 6.4.1./1, Lode Bostoen, "De Belgisch kolonisatie mislukt?," 1960; Jacques Brassinne, "L'assistance technique belge au Congo juillet 1960–juin 1968," *Chronique de Politique Étrangère* 21, no. 3/4 (1968): 336–42.

95. Brassinne, "L'assistance technique belge," 366; Erik Kennes and Miles Larmer, *The Katangese Gendarmes and War in Central Africa: Fighting Their Way Home* (Bloomington: Indiana University Press, 2016), 1; ASPFAE, AD, AFRI(135), "Communiqué du gouvernement à propos des officiers Belges au Katanga," 18 September 1961, G. Cassiers to Spaak, Vice-Président du Conseil et Minstre des Affaires Etrangères, "Objet: Réactions à l'action de force des Nations-Unies au Katanga," 22 September 1961.

96. ASPFAE, AD, AFRI (135), G. Cassiers to Spaak, "Objet: Réactions à l'action de force des Nations-Unies au Katanga," 22 September 1961; Migani, "De Gaulle and Sub-Saharan Africa," 263. De Gaulle quoted in Guia Migani, *La France et l'Afrique Sub-Saharienne, 1957–1963* (Brussels: Peter Lang, 2008), 157.

97. CHAN, Ministère de la Coopération, Direction de la coopération technique et culturelle, 19810443/47, f: Historique de la DCT, "Le Ghana et le Panafricanisme," 16 September 1960, note pour M. le Directeur de la Coopération Culturelle et Technique, "Premiers éléments d'une étude relative aux programmes d'action culturelles des états

africains et malgache d'expression française," 16 March 1961; AMAE, DAL, Généralités, 49QONT/69, f: AFR-III-1 Documentation générale sur la zone géographique, "Contribution à une définition du comportement psychologique africain en face de l'information et de l'action culturelle étrangères," [1960–61].

98. "Bénéfice moral," see AMAE, DAM, Généralités, 1089INVA/239 Coopération 1961–1975, f: Débuts politiques de la coopération (1961–1963), "Conference des chefs de mission: Synthèse des rapports des chefs de mission," January 1961, 1–7.

99. LOC, W. Averell Harriman papers, 1869–2001, box 430, f: Africa General 1960–1966, "ICA Survey Team Mission to the Entente States Ivory Coast, voltaic Republic, Niger, Dahomey, September 12–October 5, 1960," October 1960.

100. BNA, INF12/882, Miss Fell to James Hadfield, "Theme of Aid to Developing Territories," 14 September 1960; BNA, INF12/863, R. H. K. Marett, "Report on Visit to East Africa by R. H. K.," March/November 1960, 11–12.

101. BNA, CO1027/406, "Ministerial Committee on Overseas Information Services Publicity for Aid to the Underdeveloped Countries," [1961]; BNA, DO35/8808, M. J. Moynihan, "Colombo Plan Publicity," [1960], 1; BNA, FO1110/1522, "United States–United Kingdom Information Working Group Meeting: Information Treatment of Internal Communist Bloc Developments," April 1961.

102. BNA, FO1110/1522, "United States–United Kingdom Information Working Group Meeting: Information Treatment of Internal Communist Bloc Developments," April 1961; BNA, FO 953/2029, "United States–United Kingdom Information Working Group Meeting: Sino-Soviet Activities in Africa," April 1961.

103. *Britain's Contribution to Economic Development Overseas* (London: Central Office of Information, 1960); BNA, INF12/882, Miss Fell to Mr. Hadfield, 14 September 1960.

104. BNA, INF12/882, "Publicity for U.K. Aid to Underdeveloped Countries," [1962]; BNA, FO953/2084, brief, "Background Note on Aid Publicity," [1962], "Report on the United States–United Kingdom Information Working Group which met in Washington, June 4–6," 7 June 1962.

105. FNSP, 2DE66, f: Conversations Franco-Américains, note d'information, 22 March 1961; Bat, *Le syndrome Foccart*, 87.

106. NARA, RG.59, CDF 1960–1963, 545J.603/6-1062–551J.61/10-361, Stephen Gurney Gebelt to StateDept, "Ghanaian Students to Study in Soviet Bloc," 12 December 1960; Julius Sago, "The Western Concept of Foreign Aid," *Spark*, January 12, 1963, 2.

107. Quoted in Daniel Speich, "'The Kenyan Style of 'African Socialism': Developmental Knowledge Claims and the Explanatory Limits of the Cold War," *Diplomatic History* 33, no. 3 (2009): 451.

108. Julius Nyerere, *Ujamaa: Essays on Socialism* (Oxford: Oxford University Press, 1968), 44–46.

109. *All-African People's Conference: Speeches by the Prime Minister of Ghana at the Opening and Closing Sessions on December 8th and 13th, 1958* (Accra: Community Centre, 1958), 2.

110. NARA, RG.306, P157, box 1, f: Agency Position Papers—Peace Corps—1961, John Pauker, Edgar D. Brooke to Sorensen, Bundy, "USIA Support of the Peace Corps," 14 June 1962; Elizabeth Cobbs Hoffman, *All You Need Is Love: The Peace Corps and the Spirit of the 1960s* (Cambridge, MA: Harvard University Press, 2000), 258; Stanley Meisler, *When the World Calls: The Inside Story of the Peace Corps and Its First Fifty Years* (Boston: Beacon Press, 2011), 1–30.

111. "Volontaires du Progrès," see Pierre-Michel Durand, "Le Peace Corps en Afrique française dans les années 1960," *Guerres Mondiales et Conflits Contemporains* 217, no. 1 (2005): 91–104; BNA, CO859/1448, memorandum, A. B. Horn, 5 July 1961.

112. UCL, FE016 Archives du cabinet de Maurice Brasseur, f:7 (LI à LX), "Causerie gehouden door de heer Minister Brasseur voor de C.V.P.-Jongeren," 11 December 1962, 6; UCL, FE 016 Archives du cabinet de Maurice Brasseur, f: 6, Belgian Information Center Nr. 67, "Belgian trade minister Brasseur announces technical assistance programs," [October 1962].

113. KADOC, Archief Jef van Bilsen, box 25, f: 6/10.2, "Ministre du Commerce extérieur et de l'assistance technique, par Monsieur Raymond Scheyven," 4 March 1963, 19.

114. AMAE, DA, États-Unis, 91QO/529bis, note, "U.S. Peace Crops, The Spark," 15 December 1962, 6; NARA, RG.490, A1-27, box 1, f: Ghana, l'Ambassade de France au Ghana to Couve de Murville, "Peace Corps et Volontaires du Progrès," 30 April 1963, "Monthly Country Report—Ghana," 14 June 1963; Hoffman does not explain how Nkrumah could be enthusiastic while simultaneously denouncing the Peace Corps, see Hoffman, *All You Need Is Love*, 155.

115. GULSC, John Brown Papers, f: Cultural Affairs Officer 52/1/457, box 52a, "The Cultural Attaché: His Formation, Function, and Future—(Some Observations on the Conduct of Intellectual Exchanges)," s.d., 5–6; Brown's views were part of a wider academic debate, see Quincy Wright, ed., *The World Community* (Chicago: University of Chicago Press, 1948).

116. "The Secret Plot Discovered," *Voice of Africa*, vol. 1, no. 10, October 1961; "The Secret War of the CIA: The Killer at Your Door," *Spark*, March 15, 1963; "The Concept of Partnership," *Voice of Africa*, vol. 1, no. 1, January 1961; P. A. V. Ansah, "Kwame Nkrumah and the Mass Media," in *The Life and Work of Kwame Nkrumah: Papers of a Symposium Organized by the Institute of African Studies, University of Ghana, Legon*, ed. Kwame Arhin (Trenton, NJ: Africa World Press, 1993), 89; NARA, RG.59, CDF54J.603/9-1062 to 551J.61/10-361, "Somali-Ghanaian Relations Reach New Low in an Exchange of Leaflets," 21 February 1962; GPL, BAA/RLAA/943, "Circulation of 'Spark,'" 8 February 1963; PRAAD, RG.17/2/796, E.N. Hanson to Barden, "Attitude of Some Government Officials towards 'The Spark,'" 3 April 1963.

117. GPL, BAA/RLAA/943, Barden to regional commissioner Ashanti Region, January 1963; Kofi Batsa, *The Spark: From Kwame Nkrumah to Hilla Limann* (London: Rex Collings, 1985), 14–15.

118. GPL, BAA/RLAA/941, H. K. Mould, Research Officer to the Executive Secretary, 27 May 1963, memorandum, 15 May 1963; "Ebony: An Instrument of Imperialism," *Spark*, November, 22, 1963.

119. PRAAD, RG.17/2/683, William Gardner Smith, "Revolutionary Journalism," [1964], 2.

120. NARA, RG.59, CDF1960–1963, 551.42/3-3060-511.45R3/1-1860, Accra to StateDept, 4 December 1962.

121. NARA, RG.306, P249, box 10, f: Press in Africa [Folder 1/2], Carl T. Rowan, "An Analysis of the Press in Africa," 24 March 1961; BNA, DO 195/34, A. W. Snelling, "Note of Discussion with Mr. Boateng, the Ghana Minister of Information," [1961]; BNA, DO195/36, minutes, McMullen, 17 October 1962; AMAE, DAL, Ghana 1960–1965,

50QO/34, Guiringaud to Direction des Archives, "Diffusion de la presse Ghanéenne," 24 February 1960, Guiringaud to DAL, "Action d'information," 28 October 1960.

122. NARA, RG.306, P249, box 10, f: Press in Africa [Folder 1/2], Accra to USIA, "RE USIA CA-852, October 4; USITO circular telegram 177, November 15," 20 November 1957; BNA, FO953/2029, memcon, "Anglo-French Talks on Information Expanded Record," April 1961.

123. JFKL, Papers of President Kennedy, NSF, box 100, f: Ghana-General 11/62–12/62, Accra to State Department, 4 December 1962; Rakove, *Kennedy, Johnson, and the Nonaligned World*, 177.

124. JFKL, Papers of President Kennedy, NSF, box 388, f: Volta River Project 9/61–11/61, Donald Dumont to G. Mennen Williams, "Critique of Ambassador Russell's Recommendations, Conclusion of the Volta River Project Agreements," 29 September 1961; Mazov, *A Distant Front in the Cold War*, 198.

125. MSRC, Gizenga Papers, box 128-10, f: 232 the USA, U.S. News & World Report, "Taking U.S. Aid—And Red Ideas: Question Now: More Dollars for Ghana?," 6 November 1961, 61; Montgomery, "The Eyes of the World Were Watching: Ghana, Great Britain, and the United States, 1957–1966," 168; JFKL, NSF, box 388, f: Volta River Project 9/61–11/61, memorandum, George Ball, 16 December 1961.

126. JFKL, Papers of President Kennedy, NSF, box 100, f: Ghana-General 2/1/63–2/10/63, William Brubeck to Carl Kaysen, "Criteria for Evaluation Future Ghanaian Activities," 1 February 1963; The State Department agreed: NARA, RG.59, A1-3112J, box 1, f: US-UK talks 1962, Position paper on Ghana, William C. Trimble, 19 November 1962.

127. JFKL, Papers of President Kennedy, NSF, box 100, f: Ghana, General 1/21/63–1/31/63, telegram, Mahoney to secretary of state, 31 January 1963.

128. MSCR, Gizenga Papers, box 128-10, f: 232 the USA, "Hearing before the Subcommittee to investigate the Administration of the Internal Security Act and other Internal Security Laws of the Committee on the Judiciary United States Senate, Eighty-Seventh Congress, Second Session, Testimony of K. A. Busia," 3 December 1962, "Senator Says Ghana is Cuba of Africa: Washington Denies It Is First African Satellite," 15 July 1963, "Sen. Dodd's View of Ghana: Red," 16 September 1963.

129. JFKL, Papers of President Kennedy, NSF, box 100, f: Ghana, General 1/1/63–1/20/63, Accra to secretary of state, 19 January 1963.

130. DDEL, Jackson C. D Papers, 1931–1967, box 63, f: Jackson Committee (2), C. D. Jackson to Abbott Washburn, 2 February 1953; Millikan and Rostow, *A Proposal*, 83; JFKL, Pre-presidential Papers, Task Force on Africa, box 1073, f: Task Force Reports, "Report to the Honorable John F. Kennedy by the Task Force on Africa," 31 December 1960; John F. Kennedy, "Special Message to the Congress on Foreign Aid," 22 March 1961, *The American Presidency Project*, ed. Gerhard Peters and John T. Woolley, accessed 5 March 2019, http://www.presidency.ucsb.edu/ws/?pid=8545.

131. DDEL, Washburn Papers, box 12, f: Educational Development 1959–60 (1), James Halsema to Washburn, "Role of USA in Overseas Education," 15 December 1960; DDEL, Papers as President, 1953–1961, NSC Series, box 12, f: 432nd Meeting of NSC, memdisc of the 432nd Meeting of the National Security Council, 14 January 1960; NARA, RG.306, A1-1072, box 9, f: African Program, Historical Background 1970, Peter

Koffsky, "The United States Information Program in Africa, 1945–1970: A History & Interpretation," 2-1; Philip Coombs, *The Fourth Dimension of Foreign Policy, Educational and Cultural Affairs* (New York: Harper and Row, 1964), 13, 28.

132. Quote taken from DDEL, Washburn Papers, box 12, f: Educational Development 1959–60 (1), George V. Allen to Abbott Washburn, "A Program for the Development of Education in the Emerging Countries," 30 March 1961.

133. DDEL, Washburn Papers, box 12, f: Educational Development 1959–60 (7), Washburn to Nielsen, 22 March 1961.

134. NARA, RG.306, P249, box 14, f: Policy—Education in Africa, Press Release No. 3674, "Statement by Ambassador Adlai E. Stevenson United States, Representative in Committee One on Africa," 23 March 1961.

135. KADOC, Archief Van Bilsen, box 20, f: 6.4.1./1, Van Bilsen to Lumumba, 8 July 1960.

136. KADOC, Archief Van Bilsen, box 24, f: 6.6.2., CRISP Paper, "Belgique et Tiers-Monde," 22 December 1961, 6.

137. BNA, FO924/1471, Hughes to Hall Lagos, 21 January 1963; AMAE, DAM, Généralités, 1089INVA/239, f: Débuts politiques de la coopération (1961–1963), "Conference des chefs de mission: Synthèse des rapports des chefs de mission," January 1961, 1–7; BNA, FO953/2029, memcon, "United States–United Kingdom Information Working Group Meeting April 1961: United Kingdom Cultural and Educational Effort in Africa," April 1961; BNA, BW93/7, "The British Council in Ghana 1944–1963," [1963]; Timothy Nartey, "Big Talks in Accra," *Daily Graphic*, February 26, 1963; BNA, BW143/1, A. Elwyn Owen, "Report on the Prospects of British Council Development in the Countries of French-Speaking West Africa," 12 May 1963, 1–8; NARA, RG.306, A1-1066, Historical Collection, box 194, f: English Language Teaching, 1963, Lucius Battle to Rostow, "English Language Teaching as an Important Tool of Foreign Policy," 11 April 1963, "USIA Policy, Specific Goals and Characteristics of Its English Teaching Program," 19 July 1962, 1–2.

138. Rachel Applebaum, "The Rise of Russian in the Cold War: How Three Worlds Made a World Language," *Kritika* 21, no. 2 (2020): 364.

139. *Ghana's Foreign Policy*, 160; GPL, BAA/RLAA/423, T. K. Impraim to Barden, "Scholarship Schemes for Kwame Nkrumah Institute," 5 October 1961.

140. GPL, BAA/RLAA/423, memorandum, [14 September 1961], "Development of the Kwame Nkrumah Institute, Winneba, as the Institute of Political Science," [1961], A. L. Adu to Barden, 3 February 1962, Barden to A. L. Adu, "Development of the Kwame Nkrumah Institute Winneba, as the Institute of Political Science," 1 February 1962, Barden, "Development of the Kwame Nkrumah Institute, Winneba, as the Institute of Political Science," [1961].

141. NARA, RG.59, CDF1960–1963, 54J.603/9-1062 to 551J.61/10-361, "Somali-Ghanaian Relations Reach New Low in an Exchange of Leaflets," 21 February 1962; GPL, BAA/RLAA/423, "Jackson Kaithula of Kenya," 18 March 1963; PRAAD, SC/ BAA/507, D. Busumtwi-Sam to permanent secretary ministry of education Nairobi, "Kenya Students in Ghana," 1 October 1964, "Kwame Nkrumah Ideological Institute Director's Report for the Year 1963/64," November 1964; BNA, FO1110/1679, J. C. Edmonds, "The Possibility of Turning to Our Advantage the Manifestations of Dissatisfaction by African Students in Bloc Countries," 8 March 1963; NARA, RG.306, UD-WW200,

FRC 175, Department of State Bureau of African Affairs, "Staff Paper: Prepared for Presentation to the Special Group (CI) at its Meeting on January 18, 1966," 12 January 1966, 9.

142. AMAE, DAM, Généralités, 1089INVA/239 Coopération 1961–1975, f: débuts politiques de la coopération (1961–1963), Ministère de la Coopération, "Note sur le centre culturel de Fort-Lamy," 8 November 1962; AF, Afrique Pays M à Z 1958–1963, f: Nigeria-Ibadan, David Weckselmann to Couve de Murville, "Report d'année universitaire," 1 June 1960; BNA, BW154/1, BC Chad to BC, September 1962.

143. "L'information est une technique, mais c'est surtout une attitude mentale," AMAE, DAL, Nord Est Afrique 1960–1965, 35QO/8, Jean Desparmet, "Mission d'étude des moyens d'information français en Afrique centrale et orientale," 6 May 1964, 15.

144. MSRC, Gizenga Papers, box 154-44, f: 29 fifty, G. K. Osei, "Fifty Unknown Facts about the African. With Complete Proof," s.d.; MSRC, Gizenga Papers, box 128-16, f: 368, confidential publication, African Affairs Secretariat, "Conference of Ghana Envoys Volume I: Notes of Conference of Ghana Envoys in Africa, Held at Accra 7th–23rd October, 1961," 1961, 3–4; Kwame Nkrumah, "Ghana Cultural History," *Voice of Africa*, vol. 2, no. 10/11/12, October–December 1962, 3–5, 11.

145. JFKL, Papers of President Kennedy, NSF, box 100, f: Ghana General Subject 1/1/63–1/20/63, memorandum for Mr. McGeorge Bundy, 18 January 1963; NARA, RG.59, CDF1960–63, 511.703/6-161-511.70E3/6-161, StateDept/USIA to Amembassy Bamako, 24 May 1961; Mazov, *A Distant Front in the Cold War*, 217.

146. BAHDMNE, SR.66 Congo 1959–1973 Pt. 1, letter, Senhor Director do Gabinette dos Negócios Políticos Ministério do Ultramar, 30 December 1961.

7. The Struggle to Defeat Racial Modernity in South Africa and Rhodesia, 1963–1966

1. NASA, BKL, box 7, f: Development in South Africa, Parliamentary Backgrounder V, "South Africa and the Outside World," 18 May 1964, 1–4.

2. LOC, Papers of Averell Harriman, box 543, f: Trips & Missions 1964-2, William Harbin to Mr. Axelrod, "Governor Harriman's Trip," 18 March 1964; LOC, Papers of Averell Harriman, box 543, f: Trips & Missions 1964-3, Nkrumah, "Aide Memoire," 21 March 1964, 5; Ryan Irwin, *Gordian Knot: Apartheid and the Unmaking of the Liberal World Order* (Oxford: Oxford University Press, 2012), 91.

3. Eric P. Louw, *The Rise, Fall, and Legacy of Apartheid* (Westport, CT: Praeger, 2004), vii–xi; Jamie Miller, *An African Volk: The Apartheid Regime and Its Search for Survival* (Oxford: Oxford University Press, 2016), 29–32.

4. Ali Mazrui, *Towards a Pax Africana: A Study of Ideology and Ambition* (Chicago: University of Chicago Press, 1967); Ian R. Phimister, *An Economic and Social History of Zimbabwe, 1890–1948: Capital Accumulation and Class Struggle* (London: Longman, 1988), 1–10; Terence O. Ranger, *Revolt in Southern Rhodesia, 1896–7: A Study in African Resistance* (London: Heinemann, 1967), 1–10.

5. Miller, *An African Volk*, 1–10; Andrew Cohen, *The Politics and Economics of Decolonization in Africa: The Failed Experiment of the Central African Federation* (London: I.B. Tauris, 2017); Carl Peter Watts, *Rhodesia's Unilateral Declaration of Independence: An International History* (London: Palgrave Macmillan, 2012); Rob Skinner, *The Foundations of Anti-Apartheid:*

Liberal Humanitarians and Transnational Activists in Britain and the United States, c. 1919–64 (London: Palgrave Macmillan, 2010); J. R. T. Wood, *So Far and No Further! Rhodesia's Bid for Independence during the Retreat from Empire 1959–1965* (Bloomington, IN: Traford Publishing, 2005).

6. Adom Getachew, *Worldmaking after Empire: The Rise and Fall of Self-Determination* (Princeton, NJ: Princeton University Press, 2019), 176–81; Priya Lal, *African Socialism in Postcolonial Tanzania: Between the Village and the World* (Cambridge: Cambridge University Press, 2015), 6; Poppy Cullen, *Kenya and Britain after Independence: Beyond Neo-Colonialism*, Cambridge Imperial and Post-Colonial Studies Series (London: Palgrave Macmillan, 2017), 114; Stephen Chan, *Kaunda and Southern Africa* (London: British Academic Press, 1992), 106.

7. Walter Mignolo, "Delinking: The Rhetoric of Modernity, the Logic of Coloniality and the Grammar of de-Coloniality," *Cultural Studies* 21, no. 2/3 (2007): 449–514.

8. ASPFAE, AD, AFRI(135), Circulaire d'information P (61) 56, "Vues de Sir Roy Welensky sur les événements du Katanga," 15 September 1961, 4–5.

9. Quoted in Susan Williams, *Who Killed Hammarskjold?: The UN, the Cold War and White Supremacy in Africa* (London: Hurst, 2011), 51.

10. Miles Larmer, "Nation-Making at the Border: Zambian Diplomacy in the Democratic Republic of Congo," *Comparative Studies in Society and History* 61, no. 1 (2019): 152.

11. David Gordon, *Invisible Agents: Spirits in a Central African History* (Athens: Ohio University Press, 2012), 176–77; Emma Hunter, *Political Thought and the Public Sphere in Tanzania: Freedom, Democracy and Citizenship in the Era of Decolonization* (Cambridge: Cambridge University Press, 2015), 6–7.

12. Frederick Cooper, *Africa since 1940: The Past of the Present* (Cambridge: Cambridge University Press, 2002), 127; Kenneth Kaunda, "The Future of Democracy in Africa," *Transition*, no. 15 (1964): 37–39; Gary Wilder, *Freedom Time: Negritude, Decolonization, and the Future of the World* (Durham, NC: Duke University Press Books, 2015), 214.

13. NAZ, Shelf 20, box 170, Zambia Broadcasting Corporation, 1950–1972, "The Report of the Inquiry into the Information and Broadcasting Services, Zambia," 1968.

14. Caroline Elkins and Susan Pedersen, "Settler Colonialism: A Concept and Its Uses," in *Settler Colonialism in the Twentieth Century: Projects, Practices, Legacies*, ed. Caroline Elkins and Susan Pedersen (New York: Taylor & Francis, 2005), 3–4; see Frantz Fanon, *The Wretched of the Earth*, trans. Constance Farrington (New York: Grove Press, 2004 [1963]), xiiv.

15. Louw, *The Rise, Fall, and Legacy of Apartheid*, 64.

16. MSRC, Nkrumah Papers, box 154-20, f: 12, Nkrumah to Nyerere, 8 December 1961; Louw, *The Rise, Fall, and Legacy of Apartheid*, 46; Miller, *An African Volk*, 8; Ron Nixon, *Selling Apartheid: South Africa's Global Propaganda War* (London: Pluto Press, 2016), 35–36.

17. NASA, BTS1/106/3, vol. 2, W. C Naude, "Jamming of Propaganda Broadcasts," 22 July 1960; Irwin, *Gordian Knot*, 44, 65.

18. ACA-UFS, PV4, f: 37.2 Speeches, "Press Statement by Mr. Eric Louw, Minister of Foreign Affairs," 27 December 1963.

19. ACA-UFS, PV 188, f: 48, "Fundamentals in the Southern African Situation, Address by Wentzel C. Du Plessis to the American Academy of Political and Social Science," 18 April 1960.

20. ACA-UFS, PV188, f: 48, Wentzel C. du Plessis, "White Man's Africa: Reflections on Colonialism and on Mr. Macmillan's speech 'The Wind of Change,'" February 1960, 2.

21. Quoted in ACA-UFS, PV 188, f: 44, du Plessis, "Egalitarisme," [1963]; NASA, BKL, box 7, "Parliamentary Backgrounder V," 18 May 1964, 6.

22. ACA-UFS, PV 188, f: 48, "Notas oor ons inligtingsdiens en sy optrede in Kanada Vir bespreking met Mnr. Meiring," 10 September 1965.

23. Jan Christian Smuts, *Holism and Evolution* (New York: Macmillan, 1926).

24. Ronald Hyam and Peter Henshaw, *The Lion and the Springbok: Britain and South Africa since the Boer War* (Cambridge: Cambridge University Press, 2003), 307, 314–20.

25. JFKL, Papers of President Kennedy, NSF, box 2, f: General, 6/60-1/61, State Department, "The White Redoubt," 28 June 1962.

26. National Policy Paper—South Africa Part one—U.S. Policy, January 18, 1965, *FRUS 1964–1968*, vol. 24, *Africa*, 1010.

27. NASA, BTS 1/33/8/3, vol. 7, Mennen-Williams, "The Future of Europeans in Africa," 28 June 1962; quoted in Thomas Borstelmann, *The Cold War and the Color Line: American Race Relations in the Global Arena* (Cambridge, MA: Harvard University Press, 2003), 190; according to Irwin, Williams's emphasis on South Africa's obligations under international law subtly reframed the Apartheid debate in June 1962, Irwin, *Gordian Knot*, 93.

28. William O. Brown, "The Outlook for the White Man in Africa, Particularly as Settler," *African Studies Review* 3, no. 3 (1960): 1–11.

29. Fanon, *The Wretched of the Earth*, 16.

30. Aimé Césaire, *Discours sur le colonialisme* (Paris: Éditions Présence Africaine, 1955), 6.

31. Mangesh Kulkarni, "The Ambiguous Fate of a Pied-Noir: Albert Camus and Colonialism," *Economic and Political Weekly* 32, no. 26 (1997): 1528–30; Cedric Watts, *Conrad's "Heart of Darkness": A Critical and Contextual Discussion* (Amsterdam: Brill, 2012), 113.

32. W. E. B. Dubois, *Darkwater: Voices from within the Veil* (New York: Harcourt Brace and Howe, 1920), 31.

33. Skinner, *The Foundations of Anti-Apartheid*, 2; BNA, FCO141/6983, Governor, "Ghana's Boycott of South Africa," 10 August 1960.

34. ACA-UFS, PV188, f: 48, "Die Blanke se Manifes (White Man's Manifesto)," s.d., 1; NASA, BKL 7, "En Kritiseer Dan," 27 April 1963.

35. NASA BTS 22/2/20, vol. 2, Persoonlik en Vertroulik, 4 March 1960.

36. LBJ, NSF, box 4, f: NSAM 295—US Policy toward South Africa, Secret, "Status Report on NSAM No. 295 of April 24, 1964—South Africa: Key Factors in Current Relations with South Africa," 24 April 1964, 6.

37. LOC, Harriman Papers, box 509, f: South Africa 1963–1966, G. Mennen Williams, "Proposed Approach to South Africa," 24 January 1964, G. Mennen Williams, "Proposed Strategy for Dealing with Southern African Issues," 12 October 1963.

38. LOC, Harriman Papers, box 509, f: South Africa 1963–1966, G. Mennen Williams, "Strategy for Dealing with Current Southern African Issues," 10 October 1963, 6.

39. LOC, Harriman Papers, box 509, f: South Africa 1963–1966, Averell Harriman, "Educational Assistance to Southern African Students," 4 November 1963, Alan W. Ford to J. Wayne Fredericks, "Southern Africa Education Proposals," 30 October 1963.

40. NARA, RG.306, UD-WW92, Augus J. Tresidder, "Country plan for republic of South Africa," 7 December 1963.

41. NAS, BTS22/1/33/5, memcon, the Secretary of Foreign Affairs, "Talk with General Eisenhower," 11 November 1966.

42. NAS, BTS1/20/8, W. D. van Schalwyck, "Mr. Macmillan's Visit to Africa," 17 March 1960.

43. John W. Young, "The Wilson Government and the Debate over Arms to South Africa in 1964," *Contemporary British History* 12, no. 3 (1998): 62–86; Alistair Horne, *Macmillan: The Official Biography* (Basingstoke, UK: Pan Macmillan, 2008), 195–96.

44. BNA, BW107/26, memorandum, 11 July 1963, memorandum, 25 May 1962.

45. AMAE, 32QO/47, Note Pour la Direction des relations culturelles, "Plan culturel pour l'Afrique du Sud 1956," 27 November 1956.

46. NASA, BTS109/5, vol. 3, A.B.F. Burger to Ministry of Foreign Affairs, "Mnr. Spaak se Intervensie," 22 July 1964; Jef Van Bilsen, *Kongo 1945–1965: Het Einde van Een Kolonie* (Leuven: Davidsfonds, 1993), 65.

47. NASA, BTS 14/11, "Portuguese Embassy's Request for Information about Non-European Political Organisations in South Africa and the Infiltration of Communism in South Africa and Elsewhere in Africa," s.d.

48. NAZ, MFA1/1/511/129, "Report of the Foreign Ministers of Liberia, Madagascar, Sierra Leone and Tunisia on Apartheid and Racial Discrimination in the Republic of South Africa," 19 November 1966.

49. Cohen, *The Politics and Economics of Decolonization*, 38; Richard Coggins, "Wilson and Rhodesia: UDI and British Policy Towards Africa," *Contemporary British History* 20, no. 3 (2006): 363–64.

50. PRAAD, RG.17/2/683, Kojo Botsio to High Commissioner, 6 July 1963, "Rhodesia: An African View—By Kwame Nrkumah," [1963], 2; PRAAD, RG.17/2/683, "Africa Neo-Colonialism and the Masses," [1961].

51. NA-A, KSČ-ÚV-02/1, "Pozadaveck Afrikého lidového svazu Zimbabwe (ZAPU) o speciální pomoc," 14 October 1965.

52. NAZ, MFA 1/1/498/36, memorandum, I. C. Mumpansha, ZL/02/65, 23 August 1965, 3.

53. BL, EAP121-2-7-1-77, "Report of Delegates to Katanga," 13 June 1963; BL, EAP121-2-7-1-77, Mainza, 28 March 1963; NAZ, MFA 1/1/501, "Annual Report for the Year 1965 London," January 1966, 10, 3; Larmer, "Nation-Making at the Border," 152, 157.

54. NAZ, MFA1/1/508/105, memorandum, R. B. Banda, 10 November 1967.

55. NAZ, MFA1/1/498/36, memorandum, I. C. Mumpansha, ZL/02/65, 23 August, 1965, 1.

56. NAZ, MFA1/1/502/59, Report no. Ac.1—For the Period 1st to 15th January 1966, 15 January 1966; MAC/KEN/91/6, L.O. Kibinge, "Subjects to Be Discussed with the President," 3 January 1966, "Rhodesia: Lagos Conference of Commonwealth Prime Ministers," January 1966.

57. Rosalynde Ainslie, Basil Davidson, and Conor O'Brien, *The Unholy Alliance: Salazar, Verwoerd, Welensky* (London: Columbia Printers, 1962).

58. Kenneth Kaunda, *Humanism in Zambia and a Guide to Its Implementation* (Lusaka: Government Printer, 1970), 32.

59. Hunter, *Political Thought*, 231.

60. ACA-UFS, PV188, f: 48, Wentzel C. Du Plessis, "White Man's Africa: Reflections on Colonialism and on Mr. Macmillan's speech 'The Wind of Change,'" February 1960.

61. Saul Dubow, "Smuts, the United Nations and the Rhetoric of Race and Rights," *Journal of Contemporary History* 43, no. 1 (2008): 60.

62. NAZ, Shelf 20, box 170, Zambia Broadcasting Corporation, 1950–1972, confidential, "The Report of the Inquiry into the Information and Broadcasting Services, Zambia," 1968.

63. NARA, RG.59, CDF611.45C/3-862–611.45N/9-1961, box 1250, f: 611.45C/3-862, incoming telegram, Emmerson, 8 March 1962.

64. LOC, W. Averell Harriman papers, 1869–2001, box 430, f: Africa General 1960–1966, Planning Group Members, Henry Owen, "The White Redoubt Revisited," 12 March 1965, 2–4, confidential, "Summary of Policy Recommendations on East and Central Africa by Chiefs of Mission," [November 1965], G. Mennen Williams to Under Secretary, "Meeting the Chinese Challenge," 8 June 1965.

65. BNA, DO183/578, K. J. Nelae, "Mr. Watson, Sir Arthur Snelling," 21 September 1965; BNA, DO183/578, "Rhodesia: The British Attitude in the Post U.D.I. Situation," March 1965.

66. BNA, DO183/578, top secret minutes, J. N. Allan, 24 May 1965.

67. Quote taken from BNA, DO183/578, Note, N. D. Watson, 16 September 1965; BNA, DO183/578, Johnston to Watson, 10 September 1965.

68. NAZ, MFA1/1/498/36, "Full Text of Prime Minister's Statement on Rhodesia to House of Commons on Monday," 1 November 1965.

69. ASPFAE, AD, AFRI(135), Jacques Houard to Spaak, 27 October 1961.

70. KADOC, Archief Van Bilsen, box 20, f: 6.4.1./1, Van Bilsen to Tshombe, 20 July 1960.

71. Filipe Ribeiro de Meneses, *Salazar: A Political Biography* (New York: Enigma Books, 2010), 533; Filipe Ribeiro de Meneses and Robert McNamara, *The White Redoubt, the Great Powers and the Struggle for Southern Africa, 1960–1980* (London: Palgrave Macmillan, 2018), 45; Ian Smith, *The Great Betrayal: The Memoirs of Ian Douglas Smith* (London: John Blake Publishing, 1997), 127.

72. KNADS, MAC/OAU/214, "Analysis News Cables," 17 November 1965.

73. Borstelmann, *The Cold War*, 195; BNA, DO207/220, "Independence L.P. Disk Issued by the Ministry of Information, Salisbury," s.d., 1.

74. NAZ, MFA1/1/500/52, "Question of Southern Rhodesia Report of the Council of Foreign Ministers of the Organization of African Unity by the Foreign Ministers of Algeria and Zambia," February 1967, 3; for Algeria's internationalization strategy, see Matthew Connelly, *A Diplomatic Revolution: Algeria's Fight for Independence and the Origins of the Post-Cold War Era* (Oxford: Oxford University Press, 2003), 3–16.

75. BNA, DO183/578, FO to NY, 12 October 1965.

76. KNADS, KA/11/2, Neto to Kenyatta, 6 December 1965; NAZ, MFA1/1/500/52, H. S. Meebelo, "Report on the Accra (OAU) Conference of October 1965," 5 November 1965; NAZ, MFA1/1/498/36, "Press Statement by the Office of the Zimbabwe African Peoples' Union of Southern Rhodesia Cairo U.A.R.," 17 June 1965, 2; KNADS, MAC/OAU/214, "Analysis News Cables," 17 November 1965.

77. NAZ, MFA 1/1/501, C.C. Chimpampata, Report No. Lon. 4 for the Period 11th November–24th November 1965.

78. KNADS, MAC/OAU/214, "Analysis News Cables," 17 November 1965; NAZ, MFA 1/1/507/98, memorandum, V. J. Mwaanga, 18 March 1966.

79. NAZ, MFA 1/1/500/52, H. S. Meebelo, "Report on the Sixth Ordinary Session of the Council of Ministers Held in Addis Ababa, 28th February–6th March, 1966," March 1966, 3.

80. BNA, DO206/8, Annex B, "Page One Comment of the 'Zambia Mail' of 10th June 1966," 10 June 1966.

81. NAZ, MFA 1/1/502/59, Matiya Ngalande, "Report on Visit to Guinea and Mali," 23 February 1966.

82. Brown, "The Outlook for the White," 4.

83. BNA, DO206/8, "Zambia's Stand on Rhodesia," 25 June 1966.

84. Kwame Nkrumah, *Rhodesia File* (London: PanAf Books, 1976), 136; quoted in African Union Archives, Addis Ababa (hereafter AUA), CM/165/Add.1, "Report of the Foreign Ministers of Algeria, Senegal and Zambia on the Southern Rhodesian Question," September 1967.

85. NAZ, MFA1/1/500/52, "Record of a Discussion Held between the Minister of Foreign Affairs and the Sudanese Envoy, Ambassador Hashim," 15 January 1966.

86. NAZ, MFA1/1/498/36, memorandum, I. C. Mumpansha, ZL/02/65, 23 August, 1965, 3.

87. NAZ, MFA1/1/515, "U.K. May Recognise Smith Regime in Rhodesia," 18 August 1966; LOC, Harriman Papers, box 448, memorandum for the files, 2 December 1964; Andy DeRoche, "Non-Alignment on the Racial Frontier: Zambia and the USA, 1964–68," *Cold War History* 7, no. 2 (2007): 237.

88. BNA, DO206/8, outward telegram, 12 June 1966.

89. NAZ, MFA1/1/500/47, "Message to H.E. Dr. Kenneth Kaunda, M.P. President of Zambia, form the Hon. I. D. Smith, M.P. Prime Minister of Rhodesia," 3 December 1965.

90. NAZ, MFA1/1/502/59, Report Ac. 4 for the Period 17th February 1966, Ghana Government protest against America's authorization of the rebels of Rhodesia's opening of the Information Centers in Washington, 17 February 1966.

91. Eddie Michel, "Those Bothersome Rho-Dents: Lyndon B. Johnson and the Rhodesian Information Office," *Safundi* 19, no. 2 (2018): 227–45; NAZ, MFA1/1/502/59, Report Ac. 4 for the Period 17th February 1966, Ghana Government Protest against America's Authorization of the Rebels of Rhodesia's Opening of the Information Centers in Washington, 17 February 1966; BNA, DO207/220, Salisbury to Commonwealth Office, 10 December 1966.

92. BNA, DO207/220, "No Hide-Out," s.d.

93. NAZ, MFA1/1/153/148, "Rhodesian Publication: Activities of the Zambian Broadcasting Corporation," 4 April 1966.

94. BNA, PREM11/5040, "Visit of Mr. Ian Smith to London," 1964.

95. LBJ, NSF, Files of Edward K. Hamilton, box 3, f: Rhodesia, RWK (Komer), note, 6 December 1965, Memorandum for the President, Komer, 6 December 1965.

96. NAZ, MFA1/1/501, Report No. Lon. 5 for the period 24th November—15th December 1965.

97. NAZ, MFA1/1/498/36, "Broadcast by the Prime Minister the Rt. Hon Harold Wilson, O.B.E. M.P. on BBC Television at 21.05 hours B.S.T. on Tuesday," 12 October 1965.

98. BNA, DO183/578, minutes, J. N. Allan, 24 May 1965.

99. Harold Wilson, *The War on World Poverty: An Appeal to the Conscience of Mankind* (London: Gollancz, 1953), 14.

100. NAZ, MFA1/1/499/45, "Communist Policy and Tactics," 1965–1966.

101. NAZ, MFA1/1/497/32, "Statement of the Czechoslovak News Agency," [1965]; NA-A, Antonin Novotny, Jihoafrická Republika 1, "Platy a odměňování Afričanù," 6 December 1962.

102. Philip Muehlenbeck, *Czechoslovakia in Africa, 1945–1968* (London: Palgrave Macmillan, 2015), 111.

8. The Collapse of Anticolonial Modernization, 1963–1966

1. NAZ, MFA1/1/500/52, H. S. Meebelo, "Report on the Accra (OAU) Conference of October 1965," 5 November 1965, 5–6.

2. Africa Information Service, *Return to the Source: Selected Speeches of Amilcar Cabral, Edited by Africa Information Service* (New York: Monthly Review Press, 1973), 44.

3. Jeffrey James Byrne, *Mecca of Revolution: Algeria, Decolonization, and the Third World Order* (Oxford: Oxford University Press, 2016), 167.

4. Steven Jensen, *The Making of International Human Rights: The 1960s, Decolonization and the Reconstruction of Global Values* (Cambridge: Cambridge University Press, 2016), 227; Tehila Sasson, "Milking the Third World? Humanitarianism, Capitalism, and the Moral Economy of the Nestlé Boycott," *American Historical Review* 121, no. 4 (2016): 1196–1224; Oona A. Hathaway and Scott J. Shapiro, *The Internationalists: How a Radical Plan to Outlaw War Remade the World* (New York: Simon & Schuster, 2017); Byrne, *Mecca*, 286; Klaas van Walraven, *Dreams of Power: The Role of the Organization of African Unity in the Politics of Africa 1963–1993* (Aldershot, UK: Ashgate Publishing, 1999), 387; Frederick Cooper, *Citizenship between Empire and Nation: Remaking France and French Africa, 1945–1960* (Princeton, NJ: Princeton University Press, 2014), 440; Adom Getachew, *Worldmaking after Empire: The Rise and Fall of Self-Determination* (Princeton, NJ: Princeton University Press, 2019), 138; Chris Vaughan, "The Politics of Regionalism and Federation in East Africa, 1958–1964," *Historical Journal* 62, no. 2 (2019): 519.

5. Vaughn Davis Bornet, "Reappraising the Presidency of Lyndon B. Johnson," *Presidential Studies Quarterly* 20, no. 3 (1990): 601; Robert Dallek, *An Unfinished Life: John F. Kennedy, 1917–1963* (New York: Little, Brown, 2003); H. W. Brands, *The Wages of Globalism: Lyndon Johnson and the Limits of American Power* (Oxford: Oxford University Press, 1995); Francis Gavin and Mark Atwood Lawrence, eds., *Beyond the Cold War: Lyndon Johnson and the New Global Challenges of the 1960s* (Oxford: Oxford University Press, 2014); Nick Cullather, *The Hungry World: America's Cold War Battle Against Poverty in Asia* (Cambridge, MA: Harvard University Press, 2010); Mitchell B. Lerner, *A Companion to Lyndon B. Johnson* (New York: John Wiley & Sons, 2012); Terrence Lyons, "Keeping Africa off the Agenda," in *Lyndon Johnson Confronts the World: American Foreign Policy, 1963–1968*, ed. Warren Cohen (Cambridge: Cambridge University Press, 1994), 245–78; Thomas Borstelmann, *The Cold War and the Color Line: American Race Relations in the Global Arena* (Cambridge, MA: Harvard University Press, 2003), 172–221; Robert B. Rakove, *Kennedy, Johnson, and the Nonaligned World* (Cambridge: Cambridge University Press, 2012), 249; Mitch Lerner, "Climbing off the Back Burner: Lyndon Johnson's Soft Power Approach to Africa," *Diplomacy & Statecraft* 22, no. 4 (2011): 578–607; Penny Von Eschen, *Satchmo*

Blows Up the World: Jazz Ambassadors Play the Cold War (Cambridge, MA: Harvard University Press, 2006), 151; Roger E. Kanet, "The Superpower Quest for Empire: The Cold War and Soviet Support for 'Wars of National Liberation,'" *Cold War History* 6, no. 3 (2006): 331–52.

6. Marine Lefèvre, *Le soutien américain à la francophonie: Enjeux africains 1960–1970* (Paris: Presses de la Fondation Nationale des Sciences Politiques, 2010), 1–10; Mylène Théliol, *Léopold Sédar Senghor: De La négritude à la francophonie*, vol. 21, Grandes Personnalités (Paris: 50MINUTES.fr, 2015), 1–10; François-Xavier Verschave, *La Françafrique: Le plus long scandale de la République* (Paris: Stock, 1998), 1–5; François-Xavier Verschave, *De la Françafrique à la Mafiafrique* (Brussels: Éditions Tribord, 2004), 1–7; Jean-Pierre Bat, *La fabrique des barbouzes: Histoire des réseaux Foccart en Afrique* (Paris: Nouveau Monde éditions, 2015), 1–15; Philip Murphy, *The Empire's New Clothes: The Myth of the Commonwealth* (London: Hurst, 2018), xii; Timothy M. Shaw, "The Commonwealth(s) and Global Governance," *Global Governance* 10 (2004): 499–516; Shaw; Preston Arens, "'To Tidy Minds It May Appear Illogical': How the Commonwealth Evolved from an 'Imperial Club' to an International Organisation" (PhD diss., University of Waterloo, 2020).

7. NAZ, box 174A, Zambia Information Service, "A Humanist Handbook," 21 January 1982.

8. Jaramogi Oginga Odinga, *Not Yet Uhuru: Autobiography* (London: Heinemann International, 1968), 255.

9. Philip Muehlenbeck, *Czechoslovakia in Africa, 1945–1968* (London: Palgrave Macmillan, 2015), 43; PAAA, MfAA, A 14177, "Aktenvermerk: über eine Aussprache mit Herrn Odinga, Vizepräsident der KANU," 19 October 1960.

10. LOC, Papers of Averell Harriman, box 543, f: Trips & Missions 1964–3, "Aide Memoire," 21 March 1964.

11. Lyndon Baines Johnson Library, Austin, Texas (hereafter LBJL), Papers of LBJ President, 1963–69, NSF, Country File, box 77, f: Africa-General, vol. 5 [2 of 3], Sherman Kent, "Another Round of Instability in West-Africa," 17 February 1962, 1–3.

12. LBJL, Papers of LBJ President, 1963–69, NSF, Subject File, box 15, f: Food for Peace, For release to Sunday A.M. Papers, "The White House: Statement by the President upon Signing H.R. 14929—Food for Freedom Bill," 12 November 1966, 1; Vladislav M. Zubok, *A Failed Empire: The Soviet Union in the Cold War from Stalin to Gorbachev* (Chapel Hill: University of North Carolina Press, 2008), 247; Austin Jersild, *The Sino-Soviet Alliance: An International History* (Chapel Hill: University of North Carolina Press, 2014), 17.

13. Kenneth Kaunda, *Humanism in Zambia and a Guide to Its Implementation* (Lusaka: Government Printer, 1970), 9; Julius Nyerere, *Ujamaa: Essays on Socialism* (Oxford: Oxford University Press, 1968), 4.

14. Sean Delehanty, "From Modernization to Villagization: The World Bank and Ujamaa," *Diplomatic History* 44, no. 2 (2020): 289–314.

15. Julius Nyerere, "A United States of Africa," *Journal of Modern African Studies* 1, no. 1 (1963): 1, 6.

16. Julius Nyerere, "Education for Self-Reliance," in *Freedom and Socialism* (Oxford: Oxford University Press, 1968), 30.

17. Kwame Nkrumah, *Rhodesia File* (London: PanAf Books, 1976), 36.

18. NAZ, Shelf 20, box 172, Zambia Information Service, "Zambia and Non-Alignment," s.d.; NAZ, box 174 A, Zambia Information Service, "A Humanist Handbook: How to Understand and Practice Humanism," 21 January 1982.

19. KNADS, MAC/ZAM/126/1, Kenneth Kaunda, "ANC Northern Rhodesia, Congress circular, vol. III, no. 3," January 1957.

20. KNADS, AHC/8/135, "Kenya News Agency Handout, No. 296: Assistant Minister on African Socialism," 6 May 1965.

21. Immanuel Wallerstein, *Africa: The Politics of Unity: An Analysis of a Contemporary Social Movement* (New York: Random House, 1967), 237, 126.

22. Nyerere, "A United States of Africa," 4; Nyerere, *Ujamaa*, 76.

23. Grilli, *Nkrumaism and African Nationalism: Ghana's Pan-African Foreign Policy in the Age of Decolonization* (New York: Palgrave MacMillan, 2018), 275; Scott Thompson, *Ghana's Foreign Policy, 1957–1966: Diplomacy, Ideology, and the New State* (Princeton, NJ: Princeton University Press, 1969), 331; Julius Nyerere, "Freedom and Unity," *Transition*, no. 14 (1964): 40–45.

24. KNADS, MAC/KEN/77/1, Murumbi to Kenyatta, 12 August 1963.

25. Vaughan, "The Politics of Regionalism," 520.

26. NAZ, MFA1/1/506/88, Kenneth Kaunda to Robert C. Good, 18 June 1968.

27. Odinga, *Not Yet Uhuru*, 273.

28. Priya Lal, "African Socialism and the Limits of Global Familyhood: Tanzania and the New International Economic Order in Sub-Saharan Africa," *Humanity* 6, no. 1 (2015): 18; PRAAD, RG.17/2/683, "Conference in Cairo of the Organisation of African Unity Speech by Julius K. Nyerere," 20 July 1964.

29. Historical Archives of the European Commission, Brussels BAC-4-1969, Annexe 1, "Memorandum from the East African Common Services Authority to the President of the European Economic Community," 1969.

30. MSRC, Kwame Nkrumah Papers, box 154-20, f: 12, Nkrumah to Nyerere, 8 December 1961.

31. PRAAD, RG.17/2/1047, "Union Government Is Essential to Economic Independence and Higher Living Standards [1963]," 2, "Appendix I, East African Common Services Organisation."

32. Kwame Nkrumah, *Africa Must Unite* (London: Heinemann, 1963), 110.

33. PRAAD, RG.17/2/1047, "Union Government Is Essential to Economic Independence and Higher Living Standards [1963]," 2, "Appendix I, East African Common Services Organisation."

34. Simon Toner, "'The Life and Death of Our Republic': Modernization, Agricultural Development and the Peasantry in the Mekong Delta in the Long 1970s," in *Decolonization and the Cold War: Negotiating Independence*, ed. Leslie James and Elisabeth Leake (London: Bloomsbury Academic, 2015), 43–62; Nils Gilman, *Mandarins of the Future: Modernization Theory in Cold War America* (Baltimore: Johns Hopkins University Press, 2004), 203.

35. Gunnar Myrdal, *Economic Theory and Underdeveloped Regions* (London: Gerald Duckworth, 1957); François Perroux, "Economic Space: Theory and Applications," *Quarterly Journal of Economics* 64 (1950): 89–104.

36. Ali Mazrui, "Tanzaphilia," *Transition* 31 (1967): 20–26.

37. LBJL, Papers of LBJ President, 1963–69, NSF, Name File, box 7, f: Rostow memos [1 of 2], Walt W. Rostow, "The United States and the Changing World: Problems and Opportunities Arising From the Diffusion of Power," 8 May 1968, 1.

38. Lyndon Baines Johnson, *The Vantage Point: Perspectives of the Presidency, 1963–1969* (New York: Holt, Rinehart and Winston, 1971), 348; Memorandum from Edward Hamilton of the National Security Council Staff to the President's Special Assistant (Rostow), September 8, 1967, *FRUS 1964–1968*, vol. 24, *Africa*, 380–381.

39. James Bickerton and Alain G. Gagnon, "Regions," in *Comparative Politics*, ed. Daniele Caramani (Oxford: Oxford University Press, 2017), 260–73.

40. Johnson, *The Vantage Point*, 348.

41. Walt W. Rostow, *The United States in the World Arena: An Essay in Recent History* (New York: Harper & Brothers Publishers, 1960), 438.

42. LBJL, Walt W. Rostow Oral History I (21 March 1969).

43. LBJL, Dean Rusk Oral History Interview III (2 January 1970); Mark Mazower, *Governing the World: The History of an Idea, 1815 to the Present* (New York: Penguin Books, 2013), 242; LOC, Papers of Averell Harriman, box 543, f: Trips & Missions 1964–3, "Aide Memoire," 21 March 1964.

44. Robin Edmonds, *Soviet Foreign Policy: The Brezhnev Years* (Oxford: Oxford University Press, 1983), 52; Sergey Mazov, *A Distant Front in the Cold War: The USSR in West Africa and the Congo, 1956–1964* (Stanford, CA: Stanford University Press, 2010), 105; Alessandro Iandolo, "De-Stalinizing Growth: Decolonization and the Development of Development Economics in the Soviet Union," in *The Development Century: A Global History*, Global and International History, ed. Erez Manela and Stephen J. Macekura (Cambridge: Cambridge University Press, 2018), 216; Alessandro Iandolo, *Arrested Development: The Soviet Union in Ghana, Guinea, and Mali, 1955–1968* (Ithaca, NY: Cornell University Press, 2022), 152; Raúl Prebisch, *El desarrollo económico de la América Latina y algunos de sus principales problemas* (Santiago: CEPAL, 1948).

45. David W. McIntyre, *Colonies into Commonwealth* (London: Blandford Press, 1966), 338–39; David W. McIntyre, *The Commonwealth of Nations: Origins and Impact, 1869–1971* (Minneapolis: University of Minnesota Press, 1977), 449–50; David W. McIntyre, *The Significance of the Commonwealth, 1965–90* (London: Palgrave MacMillan, 1991), vii, 4; Stephen Chan, *The Commonwealth in World Politics: A Study of International Action, 1965–1985* (London: Lester Crook Academic Publishing, 1988), 15; Arens, "'To Tidy Minds It May Appear Illogical,'" 13.

46. BNA, CAB 21/5573, A. B. Cohen to Mboya, 3 August 1962, "Official Overseas Co-Ordinating Committee Commonwealth Advisory Group for East Africa Note by Department of Technical Co-operation," 10 August 1962.

47. AMAE, DAL Généralités 1960–65, 49QONT/94, f: Chine, telegram, 3 October 1964.

48. PRAAD, RG. 17/2/1079, "Discours prononcé le 5 juin 1965 par le sec," 5 June 1965, 13.

49. NAZ, MFA1/1/502/59, Matiya Ngalande, "Report on Visit to Guinea and Mali," 23 February 1966

50. NAZ, MFA1/1/502/59, Report no. Ac.1—for the Period 1st to 15th January 1966, "What Befalls on OCAM States," 15 January 1966.

51. PRAAD, RG.17/2/1047, Untitled memorandum, [1964].

52. AUA, CM/212(Part 1), "Report of the Administrative Secretary-General of the OAU: A Review of the Years 1963–1968," September 1968; KNADS, KA/11/2, "Inter-African Co-operation," s.d.; ZNA, MFA 1/1/499/40, "CM/78, Note on the Proposed Pan-African News Agency," [1964]; NARA, RG 59, SNF1967–1969, box 2389, "OAU Affairs: Secretariat Appoints New Information Officer," 7 February 1968.

53. KNADS, MAC/GHA/12/2, "Press Conference by H.E. Mr. D. Busumtwi-Sam, Ghana High Commissioner in Kenya to State Ghana's Position with Regard to the Threatened Boycott of Accra Summit Conference and to Correct Press Misrepresentation of the Issue," 2 June 1965, 1–3; Grilli, Nkrumaism, 275.

54. PRAAD, RG.17/2/1079, "Discours prononcé le 5 juin 1965 par le sec," 5 June 1965, 13; BAHDMNE, SR.177, Ministerio do Ultramar, "Assunto Conferência da Organizaçaão da Unidade Africana, realizada no Cairo em julho de 1964, a Conferencia Pan-Africana do Cairo," 26 August 1964.

55. "Lyndon B. Johnson: "Annual Message to the Congress on the State of the Union," January 12, 1966, The American Presidency Project, ed. Gerhard Peters and John T. Woolley, accessed 5 March 2019, http://www.presidency.ucsb.edu/ws/?pid=28015; the PR argument in Lyons, "Keeping Africa off the Agenda," 261.

56. LBJL, Papers of LBJ President, 1963–69, NSF, Files of Walt Rostow, box 76 [2 of 2], f: Africa, General, Volume 4 3/66–5/66 [2 of 2], The White House, "Remarks of the President at the White House Reception Celebrating the Third Anniversary of the Organization of African Union," 1966

57. LBJL, Papers of LBJ President, 1963–69, NSF, Country Files, Africa, box 76 [2 of 2] f: Africa, General, volume 4 3/66–5/66 [2 of 2], Bill Moyers to Johnson, 26 May 1966.

58. LOC, Papers of Averell Harriman, box 430, f: Africa General 1960–1966, Henry Owen, "The Congo and Africa," 12 March 1965, 6; Piero Gleijeses, Conflicting Missions: Havana, Washington, and Africa, 1959–1976 (Chapel Hill: University of North Carolina Press, 2002), 66.

59. PRAAD, RG.17/2/683, telegram, Ghana embassy, Léopoldville, 1964; PRAAD, RG.17/2/56, "A Re-appraisal of the Congo Policy of Ghana by M.F. Dei-Anang," [1964].

60. ASPFAE, AD, Classement B, 18.287/I, Spaak to Gbenye, 3 August 1964, Gbenye to Spaak, 16 July 1964, Note, Davignon, 22 August 1964.

61. LOC, Papers of Averell Harriman, box 509, f: Spaak Paul-Henri, memcon, Harriman, Spaak, Davignon, 8 November 1964; LOC, Harriman Papers, box 448, f: Congo, 1961–1962 (2), Henri J. Tasca to Governor Harriman, "Talks with Certain NATO Ambassadors," 11 August 1964, memorandum for McGeorge Bundy, "The Congo," 11 August 1964; LBJL, Papers of LBJ President, 1963–69, NSF, Name File, box 7, f: Rostow memos [1 of 2], W. W. Rostow, "The United States and the Changing World: Problems and Opportunities Arising from the Diffusion of Power," 8 May 1968, 11.

62. LOC, Papers of Averell Harriman, box 543, f: Memcons and Background, incoming telegram, Léopoldville, 31 March 1964; Kris Quanten, Operatie Rode Draak: De Bevrijding van 1800 Blanken Door Belgische Para's in Congo in 1964 (Antwerp: Manteau, 2014), 176–77.

63. ASPFAE, AD, Classement B, 18.287/I, Nkrumah to Lefèvre, "Situation in the Congo," 22 December 1964.

64. ASPFAE, AD, Classement B, 18.287/I, Rusk "East African Attitudes Towards Congo," 18 January 1965; LOC, Papers of Averell Harriman, box 430, f: Africa General

1960–1966, Henry Owen, "The Congo and Africa," 12 March 1965, "Summary of Policy Recommendations on East and Central Africa by Chiefs of Mission," [April 1965], 2.

65. LBJL, Papers of George W. Ball, box 1, f: Congo [B], Tshombe to LBJ, 19 October 1966, "Call by Tshombe's Emissaries at Department," 28 December 1966.

66. Sönke Kunkel, "Contesting Globalization: The United Nations Conference on Trade and Development and the Transnationalization of Sovereignty," in *International Organizations and Development, 1945–1990*, ed. Marc Frey, Sönke Kunkel, and Corinna Unger (London: Palgrave Macmillan, 2014), 245.

67. Jens Steffek, *Embedded Liberalism and Its Critics: Justifying Global Governance in the American Century* (London: Palgrave Macmillan, 2006), 86, 68.

68. Guy Vanthemsche, *Congo: De impact van de kolonie op België* (Tielt: Lannoo, 2007), 219; UCL, FE016 Archives du cabinet de Maurice Brasseur, Farde 12 (CI à CX), "La Tribune Economique: Le Plan Brasseur, Vers l'Avenir," 25 November 1963, "Verklaring van de afvaardiging van België," 7 November 1963, "Vraaggesprek met de Heer Maurice Brasseur, Minister van buitenlandse handel en technische bijstand," 8 November 1963; KADOC, Archief Van Bilsen, box 24, f: 665, "Organisation for Economic Co-operation and Development Preliminary Report about the question of establishing a Development Centre," 16 February 1962, 2; Jef Van Bilsen, *Kongo 1945–1965: Het Einde van Een Kolonie* (Leuven: Davidsfonds, 1993), 197; Steffek, *Embedded Liberalism and Its Critics*, 87.

69. Jacques Brassinne, "La coopération belgo-zaïroise 1960–1985," *Courrier hebdomadaire du CRISP* 34–35, no. 1099–1100 (1985): 14; Quanten, *Operatie Rode Draak*, 158.

70. KADOC, Archief Van Bilsen, box 24, f: 6.10./3, "Communication téléphonique de M. Brasseur," 2 August 1963; Godfried Kwanten, "Jef Van Bilsen En de Overgang van Een Koloniaal Naar Een Ontwikkelingsbeleid," in *Congo in België: Koloniale Cultuur in de Metropool*, ed. Bambi Ceuppens, Vincent Viaene, and David Van Reybrouck (Leuven: Universitaire Pers Leuven, 2009), 295.

71. Quoted in Odd Arne Westad, *The Global Cold War: Third World Interventions and the Making of Our Times* (Cambridge: Cambridge University Press, 2005), 205.

72. Migani sees the Jeanneney report as an example of the successful French management of decolonization but does not explain why the report was written after the cooperation structure had already been created; see Guia Migani, "De Gaulle and Sub-Saharan Africa: From Decolonization to French Development Policy, 1958–1963," in *Globalizing de Gaulle: International Perspectives on French Foreign Policies, 1958–1969*, ed. Christian Nuenlist, Anna Locher, and Martin Garret (Lanham: Lexington Books, 2010), 264.

73. Quoted in Wallerstein, *Africa*, 132.

74. KNADS, MAC/KEN/90/4, F. M. Kasina, "Report of Mr. Murumbi's Visit to Paris," 5 April 1965, 3.

75. PRAAD, RG. 17/2/1047, "Union Government Is Essential to Economic Independence and Higher Living Standards [1963]," "Appendix III, Association with European Economic Community."

76. BNA, CAB21/5573, A. B. Cohen to Mboya, 3 August 1962, "Official Oversea Coordinating Committee Commonwealth Advisory Group for East Africa Note by Department of Technical Co-operation," 10 August 1962.

77. BNA, FO953/2201, FO, "Advice on Television," January 1964.

78. PRAAD, RG.17/2/56, Nkrumah, "The Commonwealth in Action," [1962].

79. It was not voted on in June 1960; DDEL, Educational Development 1961 (1), box 12, Washburn Papers, "Johnson Bill for Overseas Education," 2 June 1960, Jerome Plapinger to Washburn, September 21, 1960; LBJ, Files of S. Douglass Cater, box 40, f: Cater Douglass Material on the Task Force on Educational Television, memorandum for the USIA Director, 26 November 1966.

80. Lyndon B. Johnson, "Special Message to the Congress on Education: The Fifth Freedom," February 5, 1968, *American Presidency Project*, ed. Gerhard Peters and John T. Woolley, accessed 5 March 2019, http://www.presidency.ucsb.edu/ws/?pid=29182.

81. LBJL, Papers of LBJ President, 1963–69, Administrative History, USIA vol. II, box 2, f: Vol. II Documentary supplement 1 of 2, McGeorge, Bundy, "Document 1–6 Presidential Delegation of Authority to USIA for Overall Coordination of Psychological Activities in Vietnam, 1965," 9 April 1965; LBJL, Walt W. Rostow Oral History Interview I (21 March 1969); LBJL, Papers of LBJ President, 1963–69, Administrative History, USIA vol. I, box 1, f: Vol. I: Administrative History [1 of 2], Murray G. Lawson, "Chapter 5 (Africa): Sections A & B," s.d.; Memorandum from the Under Secretary of the Treasury (Barr), the Under Secretary of State (Katzenbach), and the Administrator of the Agency for International Development (Gaud) to President Johnson, "African Development Bank," August 14, 1967, *FRUS 1964–1968*, vol. 24, *Africa*, 376–377; Memorandum from Acting Secretary of State Katzenbach to President Johnson, "Action Program to Carry Out the Recommendations of the Korry Report on African Development Policies and Programs," December 17, 1966, *FRUS, 1964–1968*, vol. 24, *Africa*, 364–365; Philip E. English and Harris M. Mule, *The African Development Bank* (Boulder, CO: Lynne Rienner Publishers, 1996).

82. LBJL, Papers of LBJ President, 1963–69, NSF, files of Walt Rostow, box 15, f: [Non-Vietnam: July-September 1966] [1 of 2], Rostow, "A Qualitative Concept of African Aid," 10 August 1966.

83. LBJL, Papers of LBJ President, 1963–69, NSF, Country File, box 77, f: Africa-General, vol. 5 [2 of 3], Nicholas Katzenbach, "Status Report on Major Action Programs Stemming from the Korry Report on African Development Policies and Programs," 18 April 1967.

84. LOC, Papers of Averell Harriman, box 543, f: Trips & Missions 1964-3, "Aide Memoire," 21 March 1964, 7.

85. Ethan R. Sanders, "Conceiving the Tanganyika-Zanzibar Union in the Midst of the Cold War: Internal and International Factors," *African Review: A Journal of African Politics, Development and International Affairs* 41, no. 1 (2014): 36.

86. LBJL, Papers of LBJ President, 1963–69, NSF, Hamilton, box 1, f: Aid Policy, G. Mennen-Williams to David E. Bell, "Shift of Small African Aid Programs to Regional Basis," 17 December 1965; Thomas Noer, *Soapy: A Biography of G. Mennen Williams* (Ann Arbor: University of Michigan Press, 2006), 293.

87. LBJL, Papers of George Ball, box 1, f: AID [12/16/63–10/7/65], Telcon, Dungan, Ball, 16 December 1963.

88. LBJL, Papers of LBJ President, 1963–69, NSF, Subject File, box 15, f: Food Aid Policy [2 of 2], Jerome F. Fried, "A Multilateral Approach to the World Food Problem: Dimensions of the Food Problem," 4 June 1966, 1, 11.

89. LBJL, Papers of LBJ President, 1963–69, NSF, box 15, f: Food for Peace, "The White House: Statement by the President upon Signing H.R. 14929—Food for Freedom Bill," 12 November 1966, 1.

90. Iandolo, "De-Stalinizing Growth," 216; Guy Laron, "Stepping Back from the Third World: Soviet Policy toward the United Arab Republic, 1965–1967," *Journal of Cold War Studies* 12, no. 4 (2010): 103.

91. BNA, DO195/200, "Visit of Mr. Chou En-Lai," 22 January 1964, 1–3; Gregg A. Brazinsky, *Winning the Third World: Sino-American Rivalry during the Cold War* (Chapel Hill: University of North Carolina Press, 2017), 207.

92. BNA, DO195/200, Summary of the Accra Despatch No. 3 of 1964, "Chou En-Lai's Visit to Ghana," [1964].

93. AMAE, DAL Généralités 1960–65, 49QONT/94, f: Chine, Consul Général de France à Hongkong to DAO, "Action de la Chine en Afrique," 27 August 1960, 2–3, telegram, 3 October 1964.

94. ASPFAE, AD, AF-1-33, Congo-Chine, "Rapport relations diplomatiques des pays africains avec Pékin et Taöeh," s.d.; BAHDMNE, SR.22, Circular UL 35, 1 April 1965.

95. NARA, RG. 59, Lot Files, 70D215, 72D41, 74D342, box 2, f: Sino-African States (General) 1964, David Green to David Dean, "Our Response to Chinese Communist Efforts in Africa," 21 August 1964.

96. Quoted in Paul Nugent, *Africa Since Independence: A Comparative History* (New York: Palgrave Macmillan, 2004), 260; June Milne, ed., *Kwame Nkrumah: The Conakry Years, His Life and Letters* (Bedford: Panaf Books, 1990), 16; "Letter, Cabral to Nkrumah, 13 April 1963," accessed September 9, 2021, http://casacomum.org/cc/visualizador?pasta=04621.115.019.

97. Branwen Gruffydd Jones, "Race, Culture and Liberation: African Anticolonial Thought and Practice in the Time of Decolonisation," *International History Review* 42, no. 6 (2020): 1252; António Tomás, *Amílcar Cabral: The Life of a Reluctant Nationalist* (London: Hurst, 2021), 83.

98. Kwame Nkrumah, *Handbook of Revolutionary Warfare: A Guide to the Armed Phase of the African Revolution* (London: Panaf Books, 1968), 16.

99. Africa Information Service, *Return to the Source*, 59.

100. Nugent, *Africa*, 266; Amilcar Cabral, "Sur le rôle de la culture dans la lutte pour l'independance: Réunion d'experts sur les notions de race, identité et dignité-UNESCO, Paris, 3–7 Juillet 1972," accessed September 9, 2021, http://casacomum.org/cc/visualizador?pasta=04602.125.

101. Patrick Chabal, *Amilcar Cabral: Revolutionary Leadership and People's War* (Cambridge: Cambridge University Press, 1983), 169.

102. BAHDMNE, SR.035 1957–1968, Pt.2, "Actividades do P.A.I.G.C.—Partido africano da independenceia da guine et cabo Verde," 29 September 1964.

103. BAHDMNE, SR.035 1957–1968, Pt.2, "Informacao, No. 1028, A propaganda do P.A.I.G.C. E Rossi Bilidades de A contrariar, 9-9-64 e 19-9-64," 19 September 1964.

104. Rodrigues, "'For a Better Guinea,'" 121–23.

105. AMAE, DAL, Guinee Portugaise 1953–1966, 52QO/4, f: Politique intérieure mouvements de libération nationalisme OUA, Guinee Portugasie 1960–1965, Victor Revelli to Monsieur de Beauverger, "a.s. propagande nationaliste," 6 December 1962, telegram, G. Barioulet, 19 July 1961, M. Philippe Koenig to Maurice Couve de Murville, "Guinée Portugaise," 26 May 1964, H. F. Mazoyer to Couve de Murville, "Visite à Sofia du Sec Gene de Parti," 7 September 1965.

106. Robert A. Mortimer, "From Federalism to Francophonia: Senghor's African Policy," *African Studies Review* 15, no. 2 (1972): 296; ASPFAE, AD, 14320, Inbel to Maurice Brasseur, 4 December 1964.

107. Westad, *The Global Cold War*, 398; Heonik Kwon, *The Other Cold War* (New York: Columbia University Press, 2010), 1–10; Frederic Pearson, Robert Baumann, and Gordon Bardos, "Arms Transfers: Effects on African Interstate Wars and Interventions," *Conflict Quarterly* 9, no. 4 (1999): 36–62; Paul Thomas Chamberlin, *The Cold War's Killing Fields: Rethinking the Long Peace* (New York: Harper Collins, 2018), 1–24.

108. NARA, RG.469, P36, box 9, f: Africa Dillon Meeting, James L. Saccio to Joseph C. Satterthwaite, "ICA Paper on U.S. Assistance to Tropical Africa for Mr. Dillon," 25 March 1960, 8.

109. Dwight D. Eisenhower, "Address before the 15th General Assembly of the United Nations, New York City," September 22, 1960, *The American Presidency Project*, ed. Gerhard Peters and John T. Woolley, accessed 5 March 2019, https://www.presidency.ucsb.edu/documents/address-before-the-15th-general-assembly-the-united-nations-new-york-city.

110. LBJL, Papers of LBJ President, 1963–69, NSF, Files of Edward K. Hamilton, box 1, f: Arms Control in Africa, "A New String in our African Bow," 12 September 1966; Westad, *The Global Cold War*, 398.

111. LBJL, Papers of LBJ President, 1963–69, NSF, Files of Edward K. Hamilton, box 1, f: Arms Control in Africa, Ed Hamilton, "More on Arms Control in Africa," 15 September 1966.

112. LBJL, Papers of LBJ President, 1963–69, NSF, Files of Edward K. Hamilton, box 1, f: Arms Control in Africa, Thurston, "Soviet Attitude Arms Race in the Horn of Africa," 9 September 1966.

113. National Archives of Ethiopia, Addis Ababa, f: 1.2.51.03, Soviet Union to Haile Selassie, [1964].

114. MSRC, Gizenga Papers, box 128–10, f: The USSR, "Shipments to Ghana Stir Suspicion, the Christian Science," 15 May 1961; PRAAD, RG.17/2/683, "Angola," [1964]; the documents thus confirm a suspicion harboured by historians: Thompson, *Ghana's Foreign Policy*, 224; PRAAD, RG.17/2/536, "UAR using Somalia as Springboard in East Africa," s.d.

115. LBJL, Papers of LBJ President, 1963–69, NSF, Files of Edward K. Hamilton, box 1, f: Arms Control in Africa, incoming telegram, 11 September 1966.

116. KNADS, AHC/1/22, H. A. Cross for commissioner of policy, 17 June 1966.

117. KNADS, AHC/1/22, "Joint Memorandum submitted by the minister for information and broadcasting," 5 January 1966.

118. KNADS, AHC/1/22, "Minutes of a Meeting held on Tuesday, 13th September 1966, to discuss certain aspects of propaganda," 14 September 1966.

119. KNADS, AHC/1/22, P. J. Gachathi, "Somali Propaganda Broadcasts," 18 June 1966.

120. LOC, Papers of Averell Harriman, box 545, f: 23–29 May, African Chiefs of Mission (2), "African Attitudes toward the U.S.," [1965].

121. Patrick O'Cohrs, "Towards a New Deal for the World?: Lyndon Johnson's Aspirations to Renew the Twentieth Century's Pax Americana," in *Beyond the Cold War:*

Lyndon Johnson and the New Global Challenges of the 1960s, ed. Francis Gavin and Mark Atwood Lawrence (Oxford: Oxford University Press, 2014), 45–71.

Conclusion

1. BNA, INF 12/863, R. H. K Marett, "Report on visit to East Africa by R. H. K," March/November 1960, 7.

2. Odd Arne Westad, *The Cold War: A World History* (New York: Basic Books, 2017), 8.

3. Jeffrey James Byrne, "Our Own Special Brand of Socialism: Algeria and the Contest of Modernities in the 1960s," *Diplomatic History* 33, no. 3 (2009): 427.

4. Emmanuel Chukwudi Eze, "The Color of Reason: The Idea of 'Race' in Kant's Anthropology," in *Postcolonial African Philosophy: A Critical Reader*, ed. Emmanuel Chukwudi Eze (Oxford: Blackwell Publishers, 1997), 118.

5. Westad, *The Cold War*, 16.

6. Westad, *The Cold War*, 628.

7. Quote taken from Odd Arne Westad, *The Global Cold War: Third World Interventions and the Making of Our Times* (Cambridge: Cambridge University Press, 2005), 398; Gregg A. Brazinsky, *Winning the Third World: Sino-American Rivalry during the Cold War* (Chapel Hill: University of North Carolina Press, 2017), 354.

8. Dane Kennedy, *Decolonization: A Very Short Introduction* (Oxford: Oxford University Press, 2016), 5.

9. LBJL, Papers of LBJ President, 1963–69, NSF, name file, box 7, f: Rostow memos [1 of 2], "The United States and the Changing World," 1.

10. Michael Collins, "Decolonisation and the 'Federal Moment,'" *Diplomacy & Statecraft* 24, no. 1 (2013): 21–40.

11. Jeffrey James Byrne, *Mecca of Revolution: Algeria, Decolonization, and the Third World Order* (Oxford: Oxford University Press, 2016), 294; Lorenz M. Lüthi, *Cold Wars: Asia, the Middle East, Europe* (Cambridge: Cambridge University Press, 2020), 3; Jason Parker, *Hearts, Minds, Voices: US Cold War Public Diplomacy and the Formation of the Third World* (Oxford: Oxford University Press, 2016), 175; Kenneth Osgood, "Words and Deeds: Race, Colonialism, and Eisenhower's Propaganda War in the Third World," in *The Eisenhower Administration, the Third World, and the Globalization of the Cold War*, ed. Kathryn C. Statler and Andrew L. Johns (Lanham, MD: Rowman & Littlefield, 2006), 9; Sergey Mazov, *A Distant Front in the Cold War: The USSR in West Africa and the Congo, 1956–1964* (Stanford, CA: Stanford University Press, 2010), 256.

12. Mohammad-Mahmoud Ould Mohamedou, "The Rise and Fall of Pan-Arabism," in *Routledge Handbook of South-South Relations*, ed. Elena Fiddian-Qasmiyeh and Patricia Daley (New York: Routledge, 2020), 168–78.

13. Jeremy A. Yellen, *The Greater East Asia Co-Prosperity Sphere: When Total Empire Met Total War* (Ithaca, NY: Cornell University Press, 2019), 1–24; Sara Castro-Klarén, "Framing Pan-Americanism: Simón Bolívar's Findings," *New Centennial Review* 3, no. 1 (2003): 25–53.

14. Benjamin J. Thorpe, "Eurafrica: A Pan-European Vehicle for Central European Colonialism (1923–1939)," *European Review* 26, no. 3 (2018): 503–13; Sven Beckert, "American Danger: United States Empire, Eurafrica, and the Territorialization of Industrial Capitalism, 1870–1950," *American Historical Review* 122, no. 4 (2017): 1137–70; An-

tonio Moreno Juste, "The European Economic Community and the End of the Franco Regime: the September 1975 Crisis," *Cahiers de la Méditerranée*, no. 90 (2015): 25–45.

15. Jean-Robert Lalancette, "Conflict, Cooperation, and the Creation of the Postcolonial African Regional Order, 1957–1963" (PhD diss., Cambridge University, 2020), 10; counter to Byrne, *Mecca*, 286–98.

16. François Roc, *Dictionnaire de la Révolution haïtienne, 1789–1804: Dictionnaire des événements, des emblèmes et devises, des institutions et actes, des lieux et des personnages* (Montréal: Éditions Guildives, 2006), 35.

17. Byrne, "Our Own Special Brand," 427–28.

18. Fareed Zakaria, *Post-American World and the Rise of the Rest* (London: Penguin Books, 2009); Niall Ferguson, *Civilization: The West and the Rest* (London: Allen Lane, 2011).

BIBLIOGRAPHY OF
PRIMARY SOURCES

Archives and Libraries

Belgium

Archives de l'état en Belgique, Leuven (AEB)
Archives de service public fédéral affaires étrangères, Brussels (ASPFAE)
Archives générales du Royaume de Belgique, Brussels (AGRB)
Archives of the North Atlantic Treaty Organization, Evere (NATO Archives)
Historical Archives of the European Commission, Brussels (HAEC)
Katholiek archief- en documentatiecentrum, Leuven (KADOC)
Université catholique de Louvain, Louvain-la-Neuve (UCL)

Canada

Library and Archives Canada, Ottawa (LAC)

Czech Republic

Národní archiv, Prague (NA-A)

Ethiopia

African Union Archives, Addis Ababa (AUA)
National Archives of Ethiopia, Addis Ababa (NAE)

France

Archives d'Alliance Française, Paris (AF)
Archives de ministère des affaires étrangères, La Courneuve (AMAE)
Centre des archives d'outre-mer, Aix-en-Provence (CAOM)
Centre historique des archives nationales, Cedex, Paris (CHAN)
Fondation nationale des sciences politiques, Paris (FNSP)

Germany

Politisches Archiv des Auswärtigen Amts, Berlin (PAAA)

Ghana

George Padmore Library, Accra (GPL)
Public Records Archives and Administration Department, Accra (PRAAD)

Italy

Historical Archives of the European Union, Florence (HAEU)

Kenya

Kenya National Archives and Documentation Services, Nairobi (KNADS)

Nigeria

National Archives of Nigeria, Ibadan (NAN)

Portugal

Arquivo Histórico Ultramarino, Lisbon (AHU)
Biblioteca e Arquivo Histórico Diplomático Ministério dos Negócios Estrangeiros,
    Lisbon (BAHDMNE)
Hemeroteca Municipal de Lisboa, Lisbon (HML)

Senegal

Archives nationales du Sénégal, Dakar (ANS)

South Africa

Archives for Contemporary Affairs—University of the Free State, Bloemfontein
    (ACA-UFS)
National Archives of South Africa, Pretoria (NASA)

The Netherlands

International Institute of Social History, Amsterdam (IISH)
Nationaal Archief van Nederland, The Hague (NANTH)

United Kingdom

British Broadcasting Corporation Written Archives Centre, Caversham (BBCWAC)
British Library, London (BL)
The British National Archives, Kew (BNA)
London School of Economics Library Archives and Special Collections, London
    (LSEASC)

United States

Bentley Historical Library, University of Michigan, Ann Arbor, Michigan (BHL)
Columbia University Oral History Research Office, New York (CUOHRO)
Dwight D. Eisenhower Library, Abilene, Kansas (DDEL)
Georgetown University Library Special Collections Research Center, Washington,
    DC (GULSC)
Harry S. Truman Library Presidential Library and Museum, Independence,
    Missouri (TL)
John F. Kennedy Library, Boston, Massachusetts (JFKL)
Library of Congress, Washington, DC (LOC)
Lyndon Baines Johnson Library, Austin, Texas (LBJL)
Massachusetts Institute of Technology Archives, Cambridge, Massachusetts (MIT
    Archives)
Moorland-Spingarn Research Centre, Howard University, Washington, DC (MSRC)
National Archives and Records Administration, College Park, Maryland (NARA)

Zambia

National Archives of Zambia, Lusaka (NAZ)

Newspapers and Periodicals

Commonweal
Daily Graphic
Een Blik op Kongo
Evening New
Ghana Times
Ghana Today
Le Peuple
Liberation
London Review of Books
New York Times
New York Times Magazine
Revue générale belge
Saturday Evening Post
The Ghanaian Times
The Guardian
The Manchester Guardian
The Observer
The Reporter
The Star
The Times Saturday
Voice of Africa

Online Resources

"BlackPast." Accessed August 10, 2020. https://www.blackpast.org/
"CasaComun. Desenvolvido por Fundação Mário Soares." Accessed September 9, 2021. http://casacomum.org/cc/arquivos
"CVCE.eu." Accessed August 23, 2021. https://www.cvce.eu
"Frontline Diplomacy: The Foreign Affairs Oral History Collection of the Association for Diplomatic Studies and Training." Accessed November 4, 2021. https://www.loc.gov/ collections/foreign-affairs-oral-history/about-this-collection/
"The American Presidency Project." Accessed March 5, 2019. https://www.presidency.ucsb.edu/
"The Papers of Dwight David Eisenhower, ed. L. Galambos and D. van Ee, by The Dwight D. Eisenhower Memorial Commission of the print edition; Baltimore: The Johns Hopkins University Press, 1996." Accessed April 1, 2014. http://www.eisenhowermemorial.org
"United Nations Digital Library." Accessed September 22, 2021. https://digitallibrary.un.org/?ln=en
"United Nations Documents." Accessed September 22, 2021. https://undocs.org/
"Wilson Center, Digital Archive." Accessed March 30, 2020. https://digitalarchive.wilsoncenter.org/

Published Document Collections

France

Documents diplomatiques français (DDF)
  DDF, 1960, Tome 1
  DDF, 1961, Tome 1

United Kingdom

Goldsworthy, David, ed. The Conservative Government and the End of Empire
  1951–1957, *British Documents on the End of Empire (BDEE)*, vol. 3, part 1, no. 169
  (1994), 408–411

United States

Foreign Relations of the United States (FRUS) (Washington: Government Printing
  Office, for the Department of State)
  FRUS 1949, vol. 6, *The Near East, South Asia and Africa*
  FRUS 1951, vol. 5, *The Near East and Africa*
  FRUS 1952–1954, vol. 2, part 1, *National Security Affairs*
  FRUS 1952–1954, vol. 24, part 1, *China and Japan*
  FRUS 1955–1957, vol. 8, *South Asia*
  FRUS 1955–1957, vol. 9, *Foreign Economic Policy, Foreign Information Program*
  FRUS 1955–1957, vol. 10, *Foreign Aid and Economic Defense Policy*
  FRUS 1955–1957, vol. 18, *Africa*
  FRUS 1955–1957, vol. 21, *East Asian Security*
  FRUS 1955–1957, vol. 22, *Southeast Asia*
  FRUS 1955–1957, vol. 27, *Western Europe and Canada*
  FRUS 1958–1960, vol. 7, part 1, *Western European Integration and Security, Canada*
  FRUS 1958–1960, vol. 7, part 2, *Western Europe*
  FRUS 1958–1960, vol. 14, *Africa*
  FRUS 1958–1960, vol. 7, part 2, *Western Europe*
  FRUS 1961–1963, vol. 9, *Foreign Economic Policy*
  FRUS 1964–1968, vol. 24, *Africa*
Louis Galambos and Daun Van Ee, *The Papers of Dwight David Eisenhower* (Balti-
  more: John Hopkins University Press, 2001)
  Vol. 17
  Vol. 18

Interview

Interview with K. B. Asante by Frank Gerits on March 13, 2012, in Labadi, Accra, Ghana

INDEX

Page numbers in italics refer to figures and maps.